MW00532562

The Direction of War

The wars since 9/11, in both Iraq and Afghanistan, have generated frustration and an increasing sense of failure in the west. Much of the blame has been attributed to poor strategy. In both the United States and the United Kingdom, public enquiries and defence think tanks have detected a lack of consistent direction, of effective communication and of governmental coordination. In this important new book, Sir Hew Strachan, one of the world's leading military historians, reveals how these failures resulted from a fundamental misreading and misapplication of strategy itself. He argues that the wars since 2001 have not in reality been as 'new' as has been widely assumed and that we need to adopt a more historical approach to contemporary strategy in order to identify what is really changing in how we wage war. If war is to fulfil the aims of policy, then we need first to understand war.

Hew Strachan is Chichele Professor of the History of War at the University of Oxford and a Fellow of All Souls College. Between 2004 and 2012 he was the Director of the Oxford Programme on the Changing Character of War. He also serves on the Strategic Advisory Panel of the Chief of the Defence Staff, on the UK Defence Academy Advisory Board, and on the Council of the International Institute for Strategic Studies. *Foreign Policy* listed him as one of the most influential global thinkers for 2012 and he was knighted in the New Year's Honours for 2013. Professor Strachan's books include the first volume of his projected three-volume work *The First World War* (2001), which was awarded two American military history prizes and nominated for the Glenfiddich Scottish book of the year; *The First World War: a New Illustrated History* (2003), published to accompany a ten-part television series for Channel 4 and nominated for a British Book Award; and *Clausewitz's 'On War': a Biography* (2007). His recent edited volumes include *The Changing Character of War* (2011) and *How Fighting Ends* (2012).

THE DIRECTION OF WAR

Contemporary Strategy in Historical Perspective

Hew Strachan

CAMBRIDGE
UNIVERSITY PRESS

CAMBRIDGE
UNIVERSITY PRESS

University Printing House, Cambridge CB2 8BS, United Kingdom

Cambridge University Press is part of the University of Cambridge.

It furthers the University's mission by disseminating knowledge in the pursuit of education, learning, and research at the highest international levels of excellence.

www.cambridge.org
Information on this title: www.cambridge.org/9781107654235

First published 2013
4th printing 2014

Printing in the United Kingdom by TJ International Ltd. Padstow Cornwall

A catalogue record for this publication is available from the British Library

Library of Congress Cataloguing in Publication data
Strachan, Hew.
The direction of war : contemporary strategy in historical perspective / Hew Strachan.
    pages   cm
ISBN 978-1-107-04785-3 (hardback)
1. Strategy.   2. Military history, Modern – 21st century.   I. Title.
U162.S725   2013
355.4–dc23

                                                                2013026729

ISBN 978-1-107-04785-3 Hardback
ISBN 978-1-107-65423-5 Paperback

CONTENTS

ACKNOWLEDGEMENTS

This book is the product of the past decade. Externally, its departure points are a bit longer ago than that, beginning with the attacks of 9/11 and the invasions of Afghanistan and Iraq. Personally, they are marked by my appointment to the Chichele Professorship of the History of War at Oxford in 2001, which I took up in January 2002, and by the subsequent award to the university in 2003 of a large grant from the Leverhulme Trust to study the changing character of war.

In 2001 I had just completed the first volume of a planned three-volume account of the First World War and planned to use the next ten years to complete the next two. Initially, therefore, I was reluctant to head Oxford's bid to the Leverhulme Trust, but pressure from a number of quarters, and in particular from the Chairman of the Faculty of Modern History, Christopher Haigh, and from the Head of the Department of Politics and International Relations, Mark Philp, persuaded me that I should. The resulting inter-disciplinary programme, incorporating not only history and politics but also philosophy and law, was in part a product of circumstance: no single Oxford department had enough concentrated expertise in war to mount a credible bid. In part, however, it was good luck: the combination of disciplines produced a wonderfully creative discussion and one entirely appropriate to the complexity and diversity of the subject. I owe an enormous debt not only to the Leverhulme Trust for its five-year funding of the Changing Character of War Programme (from 2004 to 2009) but also to my colleagues in it, Guy Goodwin-Gill, Sir Adam Roberts, David Rodin and Henry Shue. Since 2009, the programme has been supported by the Fell Fund, and at the time of writing its future has just been assured for a further five years (until 2017). The burden of its administration has fallen on four directors of studies, successively Audrey Kurth Cronin, Sibylle Scheipers, Andrea Baumann and Jan Lemnitzer, from all of whom I have learned a great deal – as I have from our research associates, Alia Brahimi, Alexandra Gheciu, Thomas Hippler, Sarah Percy, Uwe Steinhoff and Gil-li Vardi. Since 2008 I have relied above all on Rob Johnson, whose own expertise, both in central Asia and in military affairs, has given fresh impetus to activities in Oxford, and who took over the directorship of the programme from me in September 2012. Several of my research students will recognise in this book arguments which we have developed in supervisions, and I am no longer sure who thought of what first, but in particular I should single out Mike Finch, Gabriela Frei, T. X. Hammes, Walter Ladwig, Jacqueline Newmyer and Timo Noetzel.

From the first the Changing Character of War Programme sought engagement with practitioners, even if in 2004 we did not see how protracted and intense that experience or that opportunity would be. Major General Jonathan Bailey joined us when he retired from his last post in the Army as Director General Development and Doctrine, and for the ensuing seven years ran a seminar on 'campaigning and generalship', which brought both senior officers and their political and legal advisers to Oxford to discuss their experiences. My thinking has been immeasurably sharpened as a consequence, as it has been by the armed forces' increasing recognition of the value which a spell at Oxford can give serving personnel. The growing readiness over the past five years to create opportunities for those at war to have the space to think and to educate themselves may have been belated but it has now become impressive and mutually valuable. I only hope it is sustained, as the national interest demands it must be.

In 2009 the Chief of the Defence Staff, Air Chief Marshal Sir Jock (now Lord) Stirrup, involved a small group in a series of discussions about strategy, what it is, how it might be done and how it might be reinvigorated in Britain. From those discussions his Strategic Advisory Panel was formed. I owe a considerable debt, both to him and to his successor, General Sir David Richards. All the single service chiefs have invited me to speak on several occasions at their conferences, and I have been grateful to Admiral Sir Jonathon Band and Admiral Sir Mark Stanhope of the Royal Navy, General Sir Richard (now Lord) Dannatt and General Sir Peter Wall of the Army, and Air Chief Marshal Sir Glenn

Torpy and Air Chief Marshal Sir Stephen Dalton of the Royal Air Force. The opportunity to try out my ideas on hard-headed practitioners has also come in several other forms. When General Sir Mike (now Lord) Walker and General Sir Mike Jackson were successively Chiefs of the General Staff I was invited to take part in their Future Army Study Periods at Warminster, so acquiring a renewed awareness of operational practicalities. I had not had much exposure to the latter since the late 1970s, when I had participated in war games in the Alanbrooke Hall of the Army Staff College at Camberley. The latter tended to end with a big, if fortunately metaphorical, nuclear bang somewhere in north Germany; the former were more indeterminate in their outcomes, entirely conventional in their weaponry, and focused away from central and western Europe. Perhaps most significant of all, operations were shaped by brigades, not corps-level commands.

Camberley was where I began my engagement with real soldiers. In 1978 the intervention of the late Sir John Keegan brought me to the Royal Military Academy Sandhurst, and those whom I met then and who have continued to influence my thinking have included Christopher Donnelly, the late Richard Holmes and Keith Simpson MP. In 1988 I returned to lecture on the first Higher Command and Staff Course, then created for and run solely by the Army, an experience that was at once energising and enlightening: the Army was thinking. HCSC is now a joint offering and is run at the Defence Academy at Shrivenham, but I have lectured to it almost without a break since my first initiation and have benefited enormously from interaction with the best brains of the services. The opportunities to lecture on the Advanced Command and Staff Course and at the Royal College of Defence Studies have given similar engagement, and become increasingly important as the level and depth of front-line experience have risen. The creation of the Joint Doctrine and Concepts Centre, now the Defence Concepts and Doctrine Centre, at Shrivenham has renewed my involvement with the development of military doctrine begun by Major General Christopher Elliott when he held the Army post subsequently taken up by Jonathan Bailey and appointed me his academic adviser. Successive Directors of DCDC, Rear Admiral Chris Parry, Lieutenant General Sir Paul Newton, Air Vice Marshal Paul Colley and Major General Andrew Sharpe, have all fed ideas to me and also made me think in return. Others from the British armed services to whom I am indebted (at least some of them through the institutional links mentioned above), many of whom I count as friends, include: Commander Simon Atkinson, Brigadier Tim Bevis, Lieutenant General Sir Adrian Bradshaw, Lieutenant General Sir James Bucknall, Air Chief Marshal Sir Brian Burridge, Lieutenant General Nick Carter, Major General James Cowan, Major General Tim Cross, Lieutenant General Andrew Graham, Brigadier Charles Grant, Field Marshal Lord Guthrie, Group Captain Mike Hart, General Sir Nick Houghton, Field Marshal Lord Inge, Brigadier Richard Iron, Lieutenant General Sir Alistair Irwin, Vice Admiral Philip Jones, Lieutenant General Sir Graeme Lamb, Rear Admiral Tom Karsten, Lieutenant General Sir John Kiszely, General Sir John McColl, Major General Andrew Mackay, Air Vice Marshal Iain McNicoll, Lieutenant General Simon Mayall, Major General Mungo Melvin, Lieutenant General Jacko Page, General Sir Nick Parker, Lieutenant General Jonathon Riley, Major General Sir Sebastian Roberts, Lieutenant General Sir Bill Rollo, Major General Andy Salmon, Major General Jonathan Shaw, General Sir Richard Shirreff, Captain Emile Simpson, General Sir Rupert Smith, Captain Georges Strachan-Heyes, Air Commodore Edward Stringer, Group Captain Johnny Stringer, Rear Admiral Bob Tarrant, Brigadier Ian Thomas and Admiral Lord West. I know there are many others to whom I am indebted, and I hope they will forgive my unconscious omission of their names.

I have lectured and conducted seminars at least twice a year over the past decade in Norway, principally at the Royal Norwegian Air Force Academy in Trondheim but also at the Staff College in Oslo, and I am grateful to Tom Christiansen, Karl Erik Haug, Lieutenant Colonel Harald Høiback, Ole Jørgen Maaø, Janne Haaland Matlary, Nils Naastad and Colonel John Andreas Olsen. In France, where strategic thought remains wonderfully fertile, I have benefited from interactions at the École Militaire in Paris and from conferences at the École de Saint-Cyr Coëtquidan, and have learnt much from the late Hervé Coutau-Bégarie, Didier Danet, Général Vincent Desportes, Etienne de Durand, Colonel Benoît Durieux, Colonel Michel Goya, Laurent Henninger, Bastien Irondelle, and especially Christian Malis. In Italy my debt is to another Frenchman, Pascal Vennesson (who is now based in Singapore), as well as to Elizabetta Brighi (who is now based in London) and to Nicola Labanca. In Germany, I must thank Michael Epkenhans, Bernd Greiner, Andreas Herberg-Rothe, Herfried Münkler and Dierk Walter.

Outside Europe, thanks to invitations from Audrey Kurth Cronin and John Maurer, I have been able to lecture at regular intervals at the US National War College in Washington, DC and at the US Naval War

College in Newport, Rhode Island, and so have been exposed to American service thinking. I have also spoken at Harvard (thanks to Stephen Rosen), at Tufts (thanks to Leila Fawaz) and to the Triangle Institute for Security Studies (TISS) in North Carolina. My gratitude is also due to Stephen Biddle, Eliot Cohen, Peter Feaver, Bruce Hoffman, Frank Hoffman, Isabel Hull, David Kilcullen (even if he is really an Australian), Richard Kohn, Brian McAllister Linn, Major General H. R. McMaster, Carter Malkasian, Daniel Marston, General James Mattis, Williamson Murray, John Nagl, Admiral Gary Roughead and Todd Greentree. In Australia, the Australian Defence Force Academy of the University of New South Wales, the Land Warfare Studies Centre of the Australian Army and the Australian Strategic Policy Institute have all given me platforms, and I have incurred debts to Major General Peter Abigail, Brigadier Adam Findlay, Rear Admiral James Goldrick, Jeffrey Grey, Raspal Khosa, Lieutenant Colonel Malcolm McGregor, Lieutenant Colonel Mark O'Neill and Hugh White. In New Zealand, where, through the generosity of the Garfield Weston Foundation, I enjoyed the Kippenberger visiting professorship at the Centre for Strategic Studies at Victoria University Wellington in 2009, I have to thank Robert Ayson, Peter Cozens, Glyn Harper, Gerald Hensley, Emmet McElhattan, Ian McGibbon, John Mackinnon, the late Denis McLean, and Robert Patman. Finally, the focus for much of my thinking has been in Afghanistan. I have managed to return twice to a country whose beauty, frustrations and peoples first bewitched me in happier times in 1971, and I owe much to the wisdom, good sense and experience of Daniele Riggio. Those trips were organised by NATO, but most of my other travel, as well as the attendant complications of my commitments, has been handled with wonderful efficiency and aplomb by Rosemary Mills. It is as a concession to her and to my wife's long-suffering patience that I have now finally acquired a mobile telephone – but secure in the assurance that we have no signal at home, amid the hills of the Scottish Borders.

In Britain, the three London think tanks which focus on security issues, the International Institute for Strategic Studies, the Royal Institute for International Affairs (Chatham House) and the Royal United Services Institute, have all involved me in their conferences, seminars and lectures. Much that is contained in this book found its first shape in their publications. My debts are to Dana Allin, Brigadier Ben Barry and Jeffrey Mazo of IISS; to Paul Cornish, formerly of Chatham House and now of Exeter University; and to Malcolm Chalmers, Michael Clarke, Rear Admiral

Richard Cobbold, Michael Codner, Terry McNamee and Elizabeth Quintana of RUSI. Others from whom I have learnt when discussing the issues raised in what follows have included James Arbuthnot MP, Tarak Barkawi, Antony Beevor, Mats Berdal, David Betz, Desmond Bowen, Lindy Cameron, Bruno Colson, Tam Dalyell, Vincent Devine, James de Waal, Theo Farrell, Nik Gowing, Gary Hart, Sir Max Hastings, Simon Hornblower, Bernard Jenkin MP, Anthony King, Baroness Neville-Jones, Richard Norton-Taylor, Patricia Owens, Hugh Powell, the late Sir Michael Quinlan, Cheyney Ryan, the Marquess of Salisbury, Paul Schulte and Emma Sky.

Needless to say, many of those named above disagree with some of what follows, but our discussions have deepened my understanding and have made me realise how frequently the character of war has changed over the past decade. It has been a privilege to have been in a position where I could observe that process, could study its consequences and could test my thoughts with those who – unlike me – have had to put ideas into practice.

A couple of years ago, one of my former research students, Jacqueline Newmyer, returned to Oxford and asked how I was getting on with the writing of the second and third volumes of my history of the First World War. It is a question to which I have grown accustomed over the past ten years. My response was to say that I had become so caught up in the analysis of current conflict and the public policy aspects associated with it that progress had been slow. I went on to remark that, as the holder of a distinguished chair dedicated to the study of war, with friends and even close family putting their lives at risk in dangerous places, I felt I was under some sort of moral obligation to address more immediate problems rather than pursue my own preference to study the past. I promptly added that of course that sounded ridiculously pompous; Jackie replied that it sounded not pompous but patriotic.

Jackie Newmyer is an American. No British academic could justify what he or she does in terms of patriotism without losing caste or credibility. However, I suspect that my family will tend to agree with Jackie: having had no family holiday since 2004, they, and especially my wife, have lived through too much separation and too little recreation. If there is a form of service in these pages, it may go some way to compensate for the opportunity costs that they represent. On 7 June 2012 the Chief of the General Staff introduced his Land Warfare conference at RUSI by talking about the plans for the future Army, Army 2020 or Future Force

2020 as they have been variously dubbed. He generously attributed to me an input that was undoubtedly greater in the telling than it was in actuality. He said that I gave the Army 'tough love'. I hope he is right: the academic profession has little to give the profession of arms if it does not tell it as it sees it, even at the risk of sometimes getting things wrong. The British Army – great institution though it is – can still hold on to fixed ideas for too long and without thinking through their real meaning or implication. Believing something to be other than it is has repercussions in war which do not just produce exchanges of fire in learned journals. People get killed and wounded, and as importantly they kill and wound others. The consequences are too fraught for any other type of love to be acceptable.

This book is derived from pieces already published elsewhere, but all the chapters have been revised, in some cases extensively, in order to update them, to remove duplication and to add fresh matter.

Chapter 1 was delivered as a lecture at a conference organised by the Norwegian Institute for Defence Studies and was first published as 'War and strategy', in *On new wars* (Oslo: Norwegian Institute for Defence Studies, 2007), pp. 13–27, edited by John Andreas Olsen.

Chapter 2 was delivered as (my somewhat belated) inaugural lecture in the University of Oxford in December 2003. It was published as 'The lost meaning of strategy', *Survival*, 47, no. 3 (2005), pp. 33–54, and was reprinted in Thomas G. Mahnken and Joseph A. Maiolo (eds.), *Strategic studies: a reader* (Routledge, 2008).

Chapter 3 was first published as 'A Clausewitz for every season', in *American Interest*, July–August 2007.

Chapter 4 was delivered as a paper at a conference on European and American ways of warfare, at the Robert Schuman Centre for Advanced Study of the European University Institute in Florence in June 2006, and was published as 'Making strategy: civil–military relations after Iraq', *Survival*, 48 (Autumn 2006), pp. 59–82.

Chapter 5 was a delivered as a paper at the Global Security Conference of the International Institute for Strategic Studies in Geneva, and was then developed as the Annual History Lecture at the University of Hull, both in 2007. It was published as 'Strategy and the limitation of war', *Survival*, 50 (February–March 2008), pp. 31–53, and reprinted in Patrick M. Cronin (ed.), *The impenetrable fog of war: reflections on modern warfare and strategic surprise* (Westport, CT: Praeger Security International, 2008), pp. 67–84.

Chapter 6 was first published as 'Les armées européennes ne peuvent-elles mener que des guerres limitées?', *Politique étrangère*, 2 (2011), pp. 305–17.

Chapter 7 began as a paper delivered to a conference on 'L'Européen et la guerre', held at the Écoles de Saint-Cyr Coëtquidan, on 24–25 November 2010, and is due to appear in a volume of the same name published by Economica in Paris and edited by Christian Malis.

Chapter 8 is derived from a talk given at the First Sea Lord's conference in 2006 and published as 'Maritime strategy: historical perspectives', *Journal of the Royal United Services Institute*, 152 (2007), pp. 29–33.

Chapter 9 is built round a lecture on Douhet delivered at the Royal Norwegian Air Force Academy in 2011 and published as 'Technology and strategy: thoughts on Douhet', in Øisten Espenes and Ole Jørgen Maaø (eds.), *Luftmaktstenkningens 'enfant terrible': Festkrift til Nils E. Naastad på 60-årsdagen* (Trondheim: Tapir Akademisk Forlag, 2012), pp. 187–96.

Chapter 10 was first delivered as the Kippenberger Lecture in Wellington on 5 August 2009 and published as 'War is war: current conflicts in historical perspective', in Geoffrey Till and Hew Strachan, *The Kippenberger Lectures 2008–2009*, Discussion Paper 08/10, Centre for Strategic Studies: New Zealand, Victoria University of Wellington. It also makes use of the annual lecture of the Oxford History Faculty in January 2009, and of a talk delivered at the Chief of the General Staff's Land Warfare Conference in June 2009 and published as 'One war but joint warfare', *Journal of the Royal United Services Institute*, 154, no. 4 (August 2009).

Chapter 11 was first published as 'Strategy or alibi? Obama, McChrystal and the operational level of war', *Survival*, 52, no. 5, (October–November 2010), pp. 157–82.

Chapter 12 was delivered as a lecture at the annual conference of the Australian Strategic Policy Institute in Canberra in August 2011, and was published as 'Strategy and contingency', *International Affairs*, 87, no. 6 (November 2011), pp. 1281–97.

Chapter 13 was delivered as a paper called 'Strategy in the twenty-first century' at the summation conference of the Changing Character of War Programme in March 2009, and was published under the same title in Hew Strachan and Sibylle Scheipers (eds.), *The changing character of war* (Oxford University Press, 2011), pp. 503–23.

INTRODUCTION

Many world events, however much they are dwelt on by the media, have no direct effects on us as individuals. Watching television, we see the lives of others thrown into chaos, while our own continue their even tenor. However, very occasionally something occurs which is both shocking in its own right and also personally destabilising. Of such (very rare) occasions, we recall where we were, what we were doing and how we heard the news. Those who were alive when the First World War broke out nearly always recalled the event not just in terms of its global significance but also in its personal context. City-dwellers were on the streets, in a café or buying the latest edition of a newspaper; peasants working in the fields were surprised when they heard the church bell ringing for no obvious reason.

In our own era, the attacks on the United States on 11 September 2001 provoke similar conflations of the massive with the microscopic: they too were one of those defining moments in world history which we understand not just in international terms but also in personal. Each of us tends to recall the circumstances in which we first saw the television images of the jets crashing into the Twin Towers of the World Trade Center. Unlike the beginning of the First World War, the events in New York – and to a lesser extent in Washington – had an immediate global audience. They were communicated with images in real time, not in words after a lapse of time. They reached an audience so stunned that at first it suspended belief, unsure whether it was watching fact or fiction. Those who were stopped in the street by the screens in television shop windows or who were alerted by their friends to turn on their radios were more than observers; they also became participants. It was precisely the attacks' capacity to acquire a global audience within minutes of their initiation that gave them their strategic effect. Each of us who recalls the circumstances in which we first heard and saw the news is to some extent an involuntary partner in terrorism.

I may be an exception to these generalisations. I am not claiming exemption from the lure and even voyeurism of genuinely shocking news: I still remember the circumstances in which as a fourteen-year-old I heard of President Kennedy's assassination on 22 November 1963. But on 11 September 2001, I had escaped my study at home, given that we had a house full of guests, for the relative tranquillity of my office in the History Department of Glasgow University. The vacation still had some weeks to run and the silence provided ideal conditions in which to work (on the First World War, as it happened). My wife knew better than to tell the Scottish press where I was when our telephone at home began to ring and I was asked to comment. So rather than look at the present and its implications for the future, my day was spent considering the past. By the time I returned home in the evening most of the world had known of the attacks for several hours and the images from the Twin Towers, seemingly filmed in slow motion, had been replayed many times over.

One of my pet refrains as a historian is that the end of the Cold War has had a far more profound long-term effect on the shape of international relations since 1945 than have the 9/11 attacks. In part that assertion, which may or may not be true, does no more than reflect my desire for context and my determination not to privilege the significance of the present just because it is bound up with our personal experience. This is particularly important when speaking to service personnel, who naturally see 'their' war as the embodiment of all war, or to politicians, who seem only to live in the present without anything more than a romanticised and self-serving sense of the past. But in the case of the 9/11 attacks, the effects have proved much more decisive for my own intellectual trajectory than I anticipated in 2001.

I am not an expert in terrorism, nor did the events of 9/11 prompt me to join the flood of academics who then decided to become one. For those who worked in strategic studies, left beached by the end of the Cold War and the seeming end of the threat of major conflict, terrorism became the new nuclear deterrence: a vehicle to secure research grants and to promote careers. I am a historian, albeit one who has taught contemporary war studies and who even as Professor of Modern History at the University of Glasgow had retained a more than passing interest in current conflict. However, in September 2001 I was due to leave Glasgow to become Professor of the History of War at Oxford. During my interview I had said that I was determined to develop military history at Oxford, rather than to build on what was already in place in strategic studies. Intellectually and increasingly the two disciplines, even if united by the study of war, have pulled in divergent directions, the first locating itself more firmly in what it has called 'total history', and the second moving away from history towards political science. In this respect the Oxford chair is an anomaly, a survivor from the study of history as it was practised and taught before the First World War. In 1909, when Spenser Wilkinson was appointed to be the first Professor of Military History (as it was then called), the Oxford Faculty of Modern History saw history as a discipline appropriate for those who planned careers in public life. Wilkinson interpreted his subject matter in terms which embraced what today would be called war studies as much as military history, and his colleagues in history, not least Sir Charles Firth, then the Regius Professor of Modern History and no mean military historian himself, expected him to do so.

Wilkinson spent the First World War consumed by frustration: few in government turned to his strategic expertise, despite his public role before the war and despite *Punch*, the once famous but now defunct London weekly, calling him 'the British Clausewitz' as the war neared its close in 1918. When the Second World War broke out in 1939, the Oxford chair had just become vacant and the decision to fill it was postponed for the duration of hostilities. So, while Britain fought, the university was home neither to strategic thought nor to public commentary on the war's conduct. With Sir Michael Howard's return to Oxford in 1968, and his election first to the Professorship of the History of War in 1977 and then to the Regius Professorship of Modern History in 1980, the university resumed both functions. As well as being a historian, Michael Howard promoted strategic studies and he pronounced on public policy. The growth in demand for an academic input in both areas was stoked by the Cold War. Indeed so dominant was the threat of nuclear weapons and so potentially catastrophic the consequences of their use that they shaped debate in ways that now – in hindsight – can seem disproportionate, even if that could hardly have been evident at the time. The result was that by the early 1960s, once the contours of nuclear deterrence had been put in place, the debate on strategy had assumed a static and repetitious quality. It was also relatively untouched by actual war, since those wars which were being waged were deemed to be less significant than the major war which might eventuate. For Britain in particular the wars of counter-insurgency were shaped by the end of empire, not by the beginning of something new. And the fact that Britain remained aloof from the Vietnam War meant that the conflict which marked the United States, and in which Michael Howard's successor as Chichele Professor, Robert O'Neill, served as an officer of the Australian army, had less impact on the British debate than it might otherwise have done.

So, when I arrived in Oxford in January 2002, I did so at a point when – although I had not yet realised it – the position of the Professor of the History of War was going to be put in a context whose only previous parallel was that enjoyed – or suffered – by Spenser Wilkinson in the First World War. What were intended to be short, sharp conflicts which delivered on their policy objectives, as the Falklands War in 1982 or the first Gulf War in 1990–1 had done, became protracted and messy. Over the ensuing decade Britain's armed forces were to find themselves exposed to more sustained overseas conflict than the Strategic Defence Review of 1997–8 had anticipated, and than they themselves had experienced for several generations. As a result the wars in which Britain has been engaged since 2003 have shaped my time in the professorship. My ambition to develop the study of military history, and my personal commitment to the history of the First World War, have frequently had to play second fiddle to the wars in Iraq and Afghanistan, to the impact of those wars on the British armed forces and on their relationship to British society, and to understandings of strategy. None of these were issues in which I was not engaged or interested before 2002, but they had been secondary concerns, fitted in when I had a moment. The terms of my Oxford appointment required me to teach modern strategic studies as well as military history. They also required an engagement with public policy, as the Ministry of Defence is represented on the board of electors.

The theme which holds this book together is strategy, what we understand by it, and how that understanding has changed. It rests on the presumption that strategy is useful, and even necessary, if states are to exercise military power. Since 9/11 I have written more than twenty articles shaped by current conflicts, even if they have been refracted through the prism of history, and thirteen of them provide the basis for this book. All have been revised and some considerably so. At least a third of the total content has not been published before and, when allowance is made for matter first published in French, about half should be new to an English readership.

The book opens with a scene-setting chapter, which considers developments in war since the beginning of the millennium. The real departure point, both chronologically in terms of my own thinking and in publishing terms, is Chapter 2, which appears here under the title I used when I delivered it as my inaugural lecture in Oxford, but was called 'The lost meaning of strategy' when it was printed in *Survival*. It uses a historical approach to the evolution of the word 'strategy' and the ideas which underpin it to argue that we have so stretched our understanding of the term that it is in danger of losing its usefulness. In particular, we have conflated it with policy. The chapter sees the manifestations of this ambiguity in the decisions and – above all – in the rhetoric of George W. Bush and Tony Blair in 2002–3. However, the causes of the confusion are deeper and lie in the legacy of the Second World War.

The thinking which underpins this chapter, and the approach of the whole book to understanding war, has been profoundly shaped by Carl von Clausewitz's *On war*. There ought not to be much new there and yet in the 1990s many criticised Clausewitz, who served in the Napoleonic Wars and died in 1831, for being focused solely on certain forms of war which now belonged in the past. Chapter 3 makes the case for valuing Clausewitz when we think about strategy today. His critics have rested their interpretations on a selective and Anglophone reading of the text of *On war*, divorced from the context of Clausewitz's other writings and insufficiently mindful of his determination to use history to develop a trans-historical understanding of the phenomenon of war.

One modern misreading of Clausewitz, evident in particular in Samuel Huntington's *The soldier and the state*, published in 1957, is that *On war* stresses the need for the constitutional subordination of the general to the politician and hence to civilian control. This effort to apply a norm developed in the context of the United States's constitution to the circumstances of nineteenth-century Prussia is more than historically illiterate. It is also pregnant with consequences for the making of strategy today. It simplifies the need for much more complex and iterative institutional arrangements in order to enable the integration of professional military opinion with political direction. The Huntingtonian norm, whose antiquity rests on a deliberately selective reading of history, certainly has very slender foundations in the United Kingdom. It draws its inspiration from a 'Whig' view of history and the perceived legacy of the 1688 'glorious revolution' in Britain – to which the United States became heir. The more firmly founded it has become, the more difficult has been the challenge of coherent strategy-making. This is the theme of Chapter 4, which explores its consequences for the wars in Iraq and Afghanistan.

A central theme in the rest of the book, and especially of Chapters 5 and 6, is the need for a conceptual vocabulary which better captures the limited ways in which western powers want to use military force. Chapter 5 argues that the long shadow of the Second World War, reinforced by the subsequent threat of an all-out nuclear exchange during the Cold War, divorced our ideas about war from their practice. Theory has rested disproportionately on the concept of total war and has denigrated efforts to come to grips with post-1945 realities, in which wars have been more limited. One reason (of many) for this development is that politicians, who in practice exercise strategic responsibility, have been persuaded by neo-Clausewitzians that war really is the continuation of policy by other means. This is to elevate theory over actuality. Of course, ideally war and policy must relate to each other, but they are – as Clausewitz recognised – very different in their natures, to the point at times of being antithetical. The Clausewitzian norm has at times led politicians to see even armed conflict itself as little more than a form of enhanced diplomatic signalling, separated from its destructive effects. That tendency has produced confusion since the 9/11 attacks. While continuing to want to wage war in limited ways, national leaders have applied to it slogans which suggest the opposite. First 'the global war on terror' and then 'the long war' have not helped address the need to sort out ground truth from verbal inflation. Chapter 6 continues the examination of these themes by considering the historical antecedents of limited war theory provided by Clausewitz and the British naval historian, Julian Corbett (1854–1922). The progressive abandonment of conscription, either formally through legislation or informally through a more self-selecting form of call-up, has unfitted western armies for major war. All war ought by definition to be necessary, in that it should be seen as a last resort, only exercised when all other options have failed. However, we have further confused our thinking about when war is required, and whether it is a major war or not, by adopting as a generic title, 'wars of choice'. This suggests that we are fighting wars which are neither necessary nor – by implication – worth the candle of being 'major'.

Limited war is also a sub-theme of Chapter 7, and again Clausewitz and Corbett are among its exemplars. But the personality on whom the chapter principally focuses is Basil Liddell Hart, the British strategic thinker who between the two world wars rejected Clausewitz with so much vehemence and so little insight, while at the same time embracing Corbett without acknowledgement. However, the target is not Liddell Hart himself, but more the current enthusiasm within political science for 'strategic culture'. Although strategic culture uses history to shape its understanding of strategic practice, it is insufficiently attentive to change and contingency, while at the same time being in danger of not fully acknowledging the true source of the continuities which underpin its propositions: that is, geography more than culture.

Chapter 8 tackles the geographical point head on. The populations of two states with traditional maritime strengths, the United Kingdom and the United States, have become remarkably complacent about their reliance on the sea, in terms both of their security narrowly defined and of their economic needs. However, 'sea blindness' is not simply to be blamed on the usual suspects, a triumvirate of press, people and politicians. It is also self-generated, with navies themselves too often addressing maritime strategy in terms that are platitudinous or which duck the big issues, including the strategic function of the sea-borne nuclear deterrent.

Navies, like air forces, define themselves in terms of their equipment. Their people achieve strategic effect by serving their weapons and the platforms on which those weapons are mounted. Chapter 9 argues that both services have therefore been more disposed to interpret technological innovations – the steamship or the fixed-wing aircraft – as such massive and revolutionary effects that they can be called strategic. Here they contrast with armies, which have tended to see technology as changing tactics, but less often strategy, where they have more often found continuity. In the second half of the twentieth century nuclear weapons have provided the clearest example of a new weapons system seeming to revolutionise strategy. Their effect was so discontinuous as to lead strategic thought to distance itself from one of its core disciplines – if not *the* core discipline of classical strategy – that of history.

Chapters 10 and 11 address the consequences of the current tendency to elevate counter-insurgency to the status of a 'strategy', rather than seeing it in more restricted and operational terms. The first of the two argues that all war has certain generic qualities, and that an adaptable understanding of war may not be helped by attempts to disaggregate it into separate categories. It uses the tension for the pre-1914 British empire between the experience of colonial warfare and the theory of European warfare to illustrate the point. Before 2003 most western armies drew a sharp distinction between 'conventional' war and counter-insurgency; today they are less certain and many of their leaders and thinkers are seeking a synthesis.

Chapter 11 moves on to the displacement effect of elevating an operational method, and specifically of counter-insurgency, to the level of strategy. Its departure point is the strategy which President Obama sought to impose on Afghanistan in 2009–10. Its lack of clarity and the push-back from the military, who wanted a fully resourced counter-insurgency campaign, culminated in the president's decision to dismiss General Stanley McChrystal in 2010. At the time the tendency of the press was to place this episode in the context of the classical theory on civil–military relations as discussed in Chapter 4, and so to see McChrystal as violating the norms laid down by Huntington in 1957. Chapter 11 argues that in practice counter-insurgency requires generals to be 'political' if it is to be effective, and so the problem is less that of military subordination to political control and more the imperative to develop policies which convert into effective strategy and contain the operational framework set by the professional military.

The last two chapters point towards the future. Chapter 12 addresses the failure of strategy to be an effective predictive tool, and so meets the criticism that its application robs the politician of the flexibility which he or she needs when confronting a crisis. It makes the case for the primacy of contingency in strategic thought. Grand strategy as articulated in national defence policies aspires to meet requirements twenty or thirty years out, despite its uncertainty as to what will happen between now and then. Traditional definitions of strategy, with their focus on the operational level of war, have been more focused on the present and the immediate future, particularly in wartime. They have used planning to mediate between the present and the future – and often are informed by the past in the choices they exercise. Plans need constant adaptation, particularly in a resistant and hostile environment like war, and they are therefore acutely susceptible to continuous adaptation. The strategist has to acknowledge this while not losing contact with his overall intent. So, just as events can determine policy, so they can also affect strategy. Chapter 13 accordingly considers the likely changes as well as continuities in the mid-term future. It makes its peace with those anxious to replace strategic studies with security studies by considering the challenges for the former raised by the imminent dangers to human security. Climate change, the exhaustion of fossil fuels, the possibility of pandemics and so on could – but don't have to – cause armed conflict. The chapter's tone may be too panglossian for some; and I have my own doubts about the argument. While it accepts that the competition for resources could cause war, as it did even in the twentieth century as well as in the more distant past, it sees the potential to limit war geographically. Resource wars are more likely to be regional, and therefore have the potential to be stripped of the ideological and global vocabulary of the first decade of the twenty-first century.

This book is rooted in the experiences of the west since the beginning of the new century (and the new millennium). Its geographical focus is the Atlantic, although not exclusively so: its attention is on the United States, the United Kingdom and western Europe – the old world not the new. Not only does it neglect Asia and the rise of China, it also ignores Africa and Latin America. But while acknowledging these limitations, it uses history to try to escape them. Its approach to events that are current or lie in the very recent past is informed by a historical awareness that reaches further back. While it resists using history to 'tell you so', it does employ it to give context. Its aim is not to deny change, but to identify what is really changing as opposed to what only seems to be changing.

1 WAR AND STRATEGY AT THE BEGINNING OF THE TWENTY-FIRST CENTURY

Over the past decade the armed forces of the western world, and particularly those of the United States and the United Kingdom, have been involved in waging a war for major objectives – or so at least the rhetoric of that war's principal advocates, George Bush and Tony Blair, had us believe. It is a war to establish the values of the free world – democracy, religious toleration and liberalism – across the rest of the globe. In his speech on 11 September 2006, delivered to mark the fifth anniversary of the attacks in 2001, President Bush, showing a prescience denied to the rest of us, declared that it is 'the decisive ideological struggle of the twenty-first century. It is a struggle for civilisation.' This war may have its principal focus in the Middle East and Central Asia, but it is also being waged within Europe, with the supporting evidence provided by the bomb attacks in Madrid on 11 March 2004 and in London on 7 July 2005.

Bush and Blair called this war 'the global war on terror'. In February 2006 US Central Command, based at Tampa in Florida but with responsibilities which span the Middle East and south-west Asia, recognised the conceptual difficulties posed by the 'global war on terror' and rebranded it the 'long war'. Both titles treated the conflicts in Iraq and Afghanistan as subordinate elements of the grand design. Moreover, the design was so grand that it was one on to which other conflicts could be grafted, even when the United States was not a direct participant. The prime minister of Australia, John Howard, used his country's peace-keeping commitments in East Timor in 1999, and his wider concerns about Indonesia more generally, not least after the Bali bomb attack of 12 October 2002, to sign up to the war on terror (with some reason). In

2006, Israel presented its actions against the Hizbollah in Lebanon as part of the same greater struggle (with rather less).

'The global war on terror' was a statement of policy; it was not a statement of strategy. By 2006 the coalition forces in both Iraq and Afghanistan found themselves overcommitted and confronting the possibility of defeat. One of the reasons that they were in this situation was that they lacked a strategy. The fact that so many parties to debates on war are ready to use the word strategy seems to suggest they also understand what strategy is. But they don't. At the beginning of the nineteenth century Clausewitz defined strategy as the use of the battle for the purposes of the war. For him, and just about everybody else in Europe until 1918, strategy was the art of the commander. Today strategy is too often employed simply as a synonym for policy. Bush and Blair said they had strategies when they did not. They had policies, idealised visions of a post-war order, but these were policies which were not linked to regional realities or military capabilities. The circumstances prevailing in Iraq were different from those in Afghanistan, and they in turn were unlike those on the borders of Israel and in Indonesia. What gave each of these conflicts homogeneity was less their underlying natures than the 'war on terror' itself, a phrase which created the very unity of effects which waging that war in the first place sought to deny.

The 'global war on terror' was astrategic (if such a word exists). Its declared objective was to eliminate a means of fighting, not to achieve a political goal. It lacked a clear geographical focus: specific wars in particular parts of the world were subsumed in an overarching but amorphous and ill-defined bigger war. Traditionally strategy has been shaped above all by considerations of space and time. The 'global war on terror' was unclear about the space in which it was set, or, rather, it was clear, but the notion that it embraced the whole world was not particularly helpful. It created a field of operations too big even for the world's only superpower. The United States adopted a strategy where it could not use battle for the purposes of the war. The scale and reach of even its military power could not be sensibly and successfully applied within such a framework.

Washington's definition of time was equally destructive of a coherent approach to strategy, as the alternative title of the 'long war' indicated. How long is 'long'? The adjective 'long' is a relative term whose only counterpoint is 'short', and the definition of what wars are long and what short lies in the eye of the beholder. We only see the First World War as long because we are told that those who went to war, partly conditioned by the sweeping Prussian victories of 1866 and 1870, expected to be home by Christmas. However, that was not a general staff planning assumption in 1914: before the First World War most senior officers were well aware that if a major war broke out, it was likely to be longer than what had gone before. Helmuth von Moltke the elder, the chief of the Prussian general staff in 1866 and 1870, expected it to be another Seven Years War or even a Thirty Years War.[1] In fact he was being too pessimistic. As the First World War was finished in just over four years, it could actually be argued that it was in fact a 'short war' after all. Not only was it much shorter than either the Thirty Years War or the Seven Years War, it has also proved to be shorter than many wars which have followed it, including the Second World War and the wars in Iraq and Afghanistan.

And there is a further major block to the formation of a coherent strategy. At least all those wars had clearly defined enemies; neither the 'global war on terror' nor the 'long war' did. Wars are defined by the hostility which underpins them: the participants need to know who the enemy is, not least in order to be able to construct a strategy with which to direct the war. The enemy in the 'global war on terror' ranged from evil individuals, notably Osama bin Laden and Saddam Hussein, to entire ethnic and religious groups. It is revealing that 'defining the enemy' is now a growth area in strategic studies.

Strategy is a profoundly pragmatic business: it is about doing things, about applying means to ends. It is an attempt to make concrete a set of objectives through the application of military force to a particular case. Even when the Bush administration seemed to be applying strategy it was not. The 'surge' in Iraq in 2007 found its overall direction simply from the resolve to increase the number of troops in the theatre of war. Nothing was being done to produce a viable political solution towards which their efforts could be directed, a point made by General David Petraeus on 8 March 2007, in his first major statement to the press after his arrival in Iraq: 'military action is necessary ... but it is not sufficient', he said.[2] He worked hard to ensure his military efforts coincided with the so-called Sunni awakening in al-Anbar province, the moment when Iraqis themselves sought to curb the violence. In other words strategy lies at the interface between operational capabilities and political objectives: it is the glue which binds each to the other and gives both sense. But it is even more than that: it is based on a recognition of the nature of war itself.

Strategy has to deal in the first instance not with policy, but with the nature of war. To be sure, strategy should serve the ends of policy, but it cannot do that if it is not based on a clear-eyed appreciation of war. War is distinct from policy. Over the past thirty years western military thought has been hoodwinked by the selective citation of one phrase from Carl von Clausewitz's own introduction to his unfinished text, *On war*, that 'war is nothing but the continuation of policy with other means'.[3] That is a statement about how governments might use war; it is not a statement about the nature of war, as a reading of what Clausewitz goes on to say makes clear. *On war* is a book, as its title self-evidently indicates, about war, not about policy. In their translation, Michael Howard and Peter Paret have privileged that opening chapter over the rest of the text, and so elevated the nostrum concerning war's relationship to policy over many other – often competing and sometimes contradictory – ideas advanced by Clausewitz. Much of the rest of the text, and especially book VIII, says different things about the relationship between war and policy, and about the nature of war.[4]

There is of course a problem in translating the German noun *Politik* into English, since it can be rendered both as politics and as policy. Politics are inherently adversarial, and in this respect at least are like war. Policy has a more unilateral thrust. Its application is not necessarily impeded by the machinations of adversaries. The problems which governments tackle with policies may be the product of economic and social change or of acts of God, rather than of human design. They may adapt and refine those policies in the light of circumstances and as they implement them. (In this respect of course war shapes policy, not the other way round.) But a policy, at least in its idealised form, remains a statement of one government's intent.

War on the other hand is bilateral and even (as in the case of the Iraq and Afghan wars) multilateral. Governments have policies which lead them into wars, but once they are engaged in conflict those policies are shaped by the actions of the adversary. War is therefore no longer the unilateral application of policy but the product of reciprocal exchanges between diverging policies. Moreover, that interaction itself creates an independent dynamic, which is both incremental and unpredictable. The wars which have fulfilled the policy objectives of one side, such as the wars of German unification in 1866 and 1870, have been few – and mostly also very short. More often wars themselves have shaped the policies of the belligerents, so that the governments' policies at the outset of a war have not proved consistent over its course. The actual outcomes of the war, even if still desirable from the point of view of at least one of the belligerents, are likely to have been very different from the objectives entertained at its outset. The Second World War is a case in point, the wars in Iraq and Afghanistan even more so. As one Iraqi exile, Sami Ramadani, wrote in 2007, Bush and Blair 'allegedly launched the war at first to save the world from Saddam's WMD, then to establish democracy, then to fight al-Qaida's terrorism, and now to prevent civil war and Iranian or Syrian intervention'.[5] There could be no more graphic illustration of war's reciprocal effect on policy.

Strategy therefore has to rest on an understanding of war and war's nature because it will shape policy. That is why both Bush and Blair have lacked a strategy, because neither understood the nature of war. Both were hoodwinked by the dominant narratives used to explain the recent wars of the west, wars which put them in the framework of 1866 and 1870, not of 1914–18 or of 1939–45. From the Falklands War of 1982, through the first Gulf War of 1990–1, to the Kosovo campaign of 1999, their countries waged wars that were short and sharp, and incurred minimal casualties for their armed forces. They – and not only they, but also their electorates – came to believe that war was indeed a reliable and malleable instrument of policy.

In the first decade of the twenty-first century strategy collapsed as a tool for the shaping and understanding of war. It no longer had coherence as an intellectual concept. It was also homeless: it forfeited the institutional framework, which provided the basis for the national use of armed force. In 2002–3 the Bush administration sidelined the Joint Chiefs of Staff and ignored the National Security Council; in London, the British government left those with real and strong concerns about the management of the post-conflict phase of the invasion of Iraq without a forum in which to express their anxieties. Neither Bush nor Blair promoted a style of government which exploited existing institutions; both favoured informal networks, which sidestepped established procedures. If that was the will of the leader, it was probably impossible to counter it. However, the fact that in both the United States and Britain strategy not only had little intellectual purchase but also lacked a governmental body responsible for its creation had much older and deeper roots than the naivety of George W. Bush and Tony Blair.

Until 1918, as the references to Clausewitz have already suggested, strategy rested on a fairly widespread and common set of assumptions, at least within armies and within Europe. Clausewitz's definition, that it was the use of the battle for the purposes of the war, was much narrower than anything current today. For him, but also for most of those who waged war in the nineteenth century, strategy was the province of generals, not of politicians, and it concerned the conduct of war within a particular theatre of war: it was therefore much closer to what today's NATO armies would call the operational level of war. But in 1918, that definition of strategy could not account for the outcome of the First World War. The operational concepts of classical strategy could not wholly explain even the military outcome of the fighting: the German armies on the western front had not been defeated by military manoeuvres, such as envelopment or breakthrough. In a broader context, strategy as it had been defined by Clausewitz and his peers (if such there were) did not allow for the economic blockade of the Central Powers, or for the argument that Germany had been 'stabbed in the back' because starvation at home had led to revolution and the abdication of the Kaiser.

Clausewitz had said nothing about sea power, and one challenge that classical strategy had to confront in 1918 therefore was that posed by maritime strategy, particularly if the allied victory in the First World War was indeed brought about by sea power, as thinkers like Basil Liddell Hart argued in the inter-war period. Although the application of British sea power in the era of *Pax Britannica* had pointed the way to the importance of maritime strategy, then as now there was a tendency to see it as belonging in a separate compartment from strategy itself. This was an issue for the United States as much as for Britain, even more cut off from mainland Europe and equally reliant on its navy rather than its army for its principal defence.

In 1911 Julian Corbett, the first really important strategic thinker produced by Britain, who had read Clausewitz, argued that naval strategy was not a thing by itself. His lectures to the Royal Naval War College distinguished between what he called minor strategy and major strategy. The latter

> in its broadest sense has to deal with the whole resources of the nation for war. It is a branch of statesmanship. It regards the Army and Navy as parts of the one force, to be handled together; they are instruments of war. But it also has to keep in view constantly the politico-diplomatic position of the country (on which depends the effective action of the instrument), and its commercial and financial position (by which the energy for working the instrument is maintained).[6]

Corbett's 'major strategy' prefigured what Britain would call 'grand strategy' and the United States 'national strategy'. Although Corbett himself fleetingly used the phrase 'grand strategy', its real introduction to British military thought dates from the aftermath of the First World War and its use by J. F. C. Fuller in 1923. Fuller added a further dimension to Corbett's notion of major strategy. He stated that 'our peace strategy must formulate our war strategy, by which I mean that there cannot be two forms of strategy, one for peace and one for war'.[7] Strategy was now to be applied in peacetime, since how a nation fought a war would in large part be the product of the preparations, planning and procurement it had done in peacetime. Grand strategy was what Britain and its allies put into effect in the Second World War. It was the application of national policy in the war, and it involved the coordination of allies and of efforts in different theatres of war.

After 1945, therefore, strategy and policy had become conflated in people's minds, and this conflation remained entirely appropriate in the Cold War. As Fuller had demanded, strategy was now applied in peace as well as in war; it focused on the threat to use force, in the shape of nuclear deterrence, in order to prevent war rather than to wage it. Moreover, if there were to be war, it would be an existential war, a war for national survival, like the two world wars but even more so. These were the circumstances in which the conflation of strategy and policy made most sense. If a nation is fighting for its existence, its national policy is to wage war: all that it does in the political realm is bent to that end. As Clausewitz observed in book VIII of *On war*, 'As policy becomes more ambitious and vigorous, so will war, and this may reach the point where war attains its absolute form.'[8] In other words, in major wars policy sets goals which are more fully consonant with war's true nature, with the unfettered violence that is at its core, than is the case in wars for lesser objectives. Since 1990, the United States and Britain have fought wars that have not been wars for national survival, and so the paths of policy and strategy, which were convergent in the two world wars and in the Cold War, have become divergent. After 9/11, Bush and Blair tried to overcome this divergence by using the rhetoric of 'total war', or rather of the 'global war on terror'. But in doing so, they failed to understand the nature of the war on which they had embarked, which seemed far from 'total' to the societies which they sought to mobilise. A policy for national mobilisation for war did not make sense either to neutral opinion or even to their own electorates, not least when the efforts of both administrations continued to give priority to a whole raft of issues which would have been of second-order importance if either country were really engaged in what it saw as a major war. The true nature of the war on which their countries were embarked required the intellectual recognition that the two elements, strategy and policy, were both separate in their needs and possibly divergent in their directions. The object was of course to bring them into harmony, but that is not easy: they are different in their natures and pursue different sorts of outcomes. Generals seek outstanding victories on the battlefield, but even when they achieve them they still don't necessarily win the war: Napoleon learned that, and the United States has relearnt it.

We live with the intellectual legacy of the Cold War more than we recognise. Then deterrence and dissuasion were the essence of strategy: this was where reciprocity was played out, but it was a field of activity devoid of actual fighting. The wars which actually occurred were defined, in the jargon of the 1960s, as 'limited wars' or 'low intensity conflicts': in other words they were not assimilated into mainstream thinking about war, but were treated as exceptions to the rule. The latter was identified more with the war in Europe in 1944–5, but in an increasingly idealised and remote form. 'Major war', confined to a theoretical existence through war games and exercises, promoted the notion that battle was fought 'symmetrically', between forces that emulated each other and had comparable capabilities. The pursuit of balance was vital to mutually assured destruction, the foundation stone on which deterrence came to rest. But deterrence said nothing much about what generals did in wartime. Notions of victory seemed irrelevant at best and often obscene, since victory in European warfare would not, it seemed, be secured without the use of nuclear weapons and that would involve catastrophic destruction. Soldiers lost control of strategy, and so the discipline which defined and validated the art of the commander, the business of general staffs and the processes of war planning, was no longer theirs.

The discovery of operational thought, first by the army of the United States and then by the armies of NATO, was a way out of this dilemma. Required in the 1980s to think about conventional warfare, partly because of the body blow inflicted on the army of the United States by the defeat in Vietnam and partly because of the need to find useable alternatives to an all-out nuclear exchange within Europe, armies found themselves tackling war, not policy: they had to embrace war's reciprocal nature. However, in doing so, they still accepted the superstructure of the Cold War and the final arbitration of nuclear deterrence, and so continued to allow strategy to be a synonym for policy. When generals now thought about war, they called it 'operational art', although at one level it was no more than a reiteration of classical strategy. Its obvious product, 'manoeuvre warfare', drew a reasonably straight line from Napoleon at Marengo or Jena to Norman Schwarzkopf in the first Gulf War.

Two major deficiencies have, however, increasingly dogged the dominance of operational thought in military doctrine. The first has been its tendency since the end of the Cold War to ignore the true nature of war, its reciprocity, its unpredictability and its friction. In the 1991 Gulf War none of these played as significant role as in most wars in the past: the tenets of manoeuvre war, the product of the thinking of the 1980s, were implemented with overwhelming success in short order, and so became enshrined, not as the last hurrah for Cold War military thought, but as the benchmark for the future. The victory spawned a succession of ideas, among them the 'revolution in military affairs', 'network-centric warfare' and 'transformation', all of which focused on the unilateral application of military superiority. It is worth recalling that NATO's thinking on manoeuvre war had been developed against the background of presumed inferiority in the face of a Soviet invasion of northern Germany: its core idea was to use the counter-stroke within a defensive context and as a substitute for the conventional strength of the Soviet Union. Its successor concepts assumed the use of military force in an offensive mode, based on overwhelming and apparently unanswerable military superiority.

Increasingly too operational thought was developed in a policy-free environment. This did not matter in the 1980s as the political framework was implicit within the Cold War. With the end of the Cold War, NATO armies lacked scenarios into which their operational capabilities fitted. For an army like Britain's this was not a new experience. In the nineteenth century its imperial responsibilities had put a premium on flexibility and adaptability. For other armies, used to thinking about possible wars predominantly against their neighbours, the lack of an obvious threat within Europe created intellectual uncertainty. The presentation of 'manoeuvre war' as a one-size-fits-all model covered over the fact that in the past flexibility did not necessarily have much to do with the operational level of war. Concepts like tempo and 'manoeuvrism' did not worry the heroes of Victorian 'small wars' like Garnet Wolseley. Success was predicated on an awareness of the vagaries of the climate, on its impact on medical requirements and transport needs, and on the economic infrastructure and social conditions of the region. Effective commanders had to be anthropologically and politically aware if they were to understand the dynamics of war in different regions of the globe. The 'operational level of war' tried to ignore this problem by treating the 'battlespace' as something to be shaped by common military doctrines and their attendant technologies. The only anthropological revelations contained in 'the revolution in military affairs', 'effects-based war' and 'transformation' were those which concerned their authors.

Thanks to Colin Powell and his intellectual legacy, American military thought at the dawn of the new millennium had become quite explicit about its separation from the context of policy. Powell was the military adviser to Caspar Weinberger, the Secretary of Defense, who in 1984 articulated the so-called 'Weinberger doctrine'. In 1992, as Chairman of the Joint Chiefs of Staff, Powell himself set out the 'Powell doctrine'. Smarting from the effects of the Vietnam War on the US army, Powell said that US forces should be used to achieve clear political objectives, which should be determined in advance, and that they should be deployed with overwhelming military force to achieve a quick victory: their 'exit strategy' should be clear. Powell thought he was being Clausewitzian; he was trying to integrate strategy and policy by setting clearly defined and separate spheres of responsibility for each. What he had failed to do was to recognise Clausewitz's distinction between norms and practices, between the ideal and the real. Strategy and policy are indeed distinct in theory, but strategy in practice rests on a dialogue with policy. Confronted in 1992 with Powell's logic, which effectively blocked the deployment of American troops in Bosnia, the Secretary of State, Madeleine Albright, memorably asked, 'What's the point of having this superb military that you're always talking about if we can't use it?'[9]

The Powell doctrine collapsed when it confronted the practice of war in the first decade of the twenty-first century. The Bush administration was determined to use its armed forces, even when the chiefs of those armed forces advised against it or urged their employment in ways other than those favoured by the administration. Today Powell might say that the results of not using overwhelming force and not having a clear 'exit strategy' are evident for all to see. But in advocating a clear demarcation between strategy and policy, he prevented the engagement of one with the other, and his legacy survives in principles to which many in the United States army still adhere. The fact that General David Petraeus's call on 8 March 2007 for a political solution in Iraq was still seen as sufficiently exceptional to be newsworthy makes the point. The generals' normal currency, the operational level of war, had been kept in a separate box from policy, and there was a collective failure to appreciate the effect of war itself on the evolution and even transformation of policy, despite the fact that the war in Iraq provided vivid evidence of exactly that. What the Iraq War also showed, and a point that Powell also failed to address, presumably as a consequence of his belief in American military superiority, was the fact that it would be the enemy – more than the American government – that would be trying to prevent the United States army from achieving quick victory. Classical strategy, and Clausewitz in particular, recognised that the relationship between strategy and policy was central, even if contested. Powell and his heirs worked hard to resolve that contest by divorcing policy from operational thought. Prussian generals did much the same in 1870–1: Helmuth von Moltke the elder argued that the politician should fall silent when the war broke out. Bismarck would not accept Moltke's argument, but the latter's case had more legs than it deserved partly because Moltke was perceived to have delivered an overwhelming victory which did provide the political outcome which Bismarck sought.

In the twenty-first century American generals, however much they may sound like Prussian generals in some of their nostrums, have not been so lucky. In Afghanistan in 2002 Bush and Rumsfeld asked the United States armed forces to fight a war totally different in design and nature from that for which they had prepared. The Joint Chiefs of Staff, equipped with one set of operational concepts, found themselves at odds with a Secretary of Defense who thought he could shape the conflict in Afghanistan to suit another. In Iraq the problem was overcome by the simple decision not to coordinate policy and the operational level of war. Once into Iraq, Ambassador Paul Bremer said that his job was policy and General Ricardo Sanchez's was the war, and that each should stick to his own sphere. So he should not have been surprised when he, not unreasonably, asked Sanchez for details of his tactical plans, and Sanchez responded, 'Stop right there, sir. I am not going to give you the details of our tactical plan.'[10]

Strategy, however, lay exactly where the two spheres intersected. By 2003 it had lost its identity: part of it had been subsumed by policy and part of it had been subsumed by operational thought. Because neither the politicians nor the soldiers had a clear grasp of what strategy was, they could neither put the pieces back together again nor develop a clear grasp of the nature of the wars in which they were engaged. Moreover, without a clear grasp of strategy, they could not see what had really changed in war as opposed to what merely seemed to have changed. By confusing strategy with policy, and by calling what were in reality political effects strategic effects, governments denied themselves the intellectual tool to manage war for political purposes, and so allowed themselves to project their daily political concerns back into strategy.

Terrorism is the most obvious case in point. Terrorism was not invented on 9/11. It is a means to wage war not an objective of war: this is why the 'global war on terror' was so strategically illiterate. But what was new was the exaggeration of its effects through the media and in turn through the reactions of political leaders. Strategy, because it is in dialogue with policy, was affected accordingly. Its ability to put terrorism in context and in perspective was undermined. The novelty of terrorism after 2001 lay not in its own actions but in the responses of the governments trying to oppose it, which paradoxically themselves accorded it the very effects that they sought to deny it.

Terrorism is not the only facet of contemporary conflict that is not new. Non-state actors, many of them in the business of war for personal profit, were features of medieval and early modern warfare: indeed the effort by seventeenth-century European states to establish a monopoly on the use of armed force was in part a direct response to the suffering and destitution, the rape and pillage, wrought by competing freebooters, mercenaries and private military companies. Moreover, outside Europe many of those native populations which resisted colonialism in the nineteenth century did so not as representatives of states or to further political objectives, but to defend their religious beliefs, their ways of life or their control of resources: their motivations were existential rather than utilitarian. The methods that they used against their European opponents were (in today's jargon) asymmetric. Knowing that, if they directly confronted an organised and disciplined military force, they would lose, they reacted pragmatically and avoided battle. Their strengths in war rested on their local knowledge and their links to the population, and their methods were those of guerrilla warfare and even terrorism.

The identification of 'asymmetric warfare' as a fresh phenomenon after 9/11 revealed how naïve western strategic thought had become. As any decent commander knows, even when two armies with comparable organisations and similar weapons systems confront each other, they will not fight 'symmetrically'. Instead they seek to exploit each other's weaknesses, often looking for the line of least expectation to maximise their own relative advantage. Even the application of overwhelming military force by one side against another is 'asymmetric'. 'Symmetrical warfare' was a product of the Cold War, of the absence of war: it is what armies do in their peacetime imaginations, when they compare a putative enemy's capability with their own and then convert their conclusions into demands for fresh equipment in the defence budget. The popular belief that 'asymmetric war' is new is therefore a reflection of the way in which peacetime norms have shaped the understanding of strategy.

Nor are many of today's wars being fought for reasons that look very new. The impending security concerns of the twenty-first century, climate change, the growth of urban shanty towns, the spread of global epidemics, immigration, competition for resources, have yet to have much impact on strategy in practice. They provide the framework for modelling in defence departments, building scenarios for the future, but their consequences are not yet with us – and it could be argued that with good management they never will be, at least as causes for war. Today's wars are being fought for very traditional reasons – for religious faith, political ideology, nationalism and ethnic identity. Moreover they are being waged in parts of the world where armed conflict and political instability have been endemic for decades, including in Iraq, Israel and Afghanistan, as well as in far too much of Africa. Historical illiteracy is a besetting sin of western governments anxious to deploy forces in regions where memories are somewhat longer. Old conflicts have been given fresh energy by the rationalisations for war embraced in the west. Regional wars have been subsumed within the 'global war on terror' and so gained greater significance. Humanitarian intervention, however laudable its motivation, has frequently done less to end the sufferings of a subject people than to make them the concern of the wider international community.

In other words the big change in war has been the overt readiness of the west to use it as an instrument of policy. The chronological caesura was less 2001, more 1990, less 9/11 and more the end of the Cold War.

Since then deterrence has lost its salience in both the United States and the west. The former has not used the concepts of the Cold War to manage its relationship with Iran; the United Kingdom, debating the future of the Trident missile system, has made no effort to incorporate deterrence thinking into the wider context of national strategy or of its defence capabilities. Before 1990 strategic studies flourished on the back of the idea that their purpose was to avoid war; since 1990 we have not woken up to the consequences of using war. If war is an instrument of policy, strategy is the tool that enables us to understand it and gives us our best chance of managing and directing it.

Part of the solution to our present dilemmas is conceptual. Reading the bits of Clausewitz that we glossed over in the Cold War would not be a bad beginning. On war's opening definition of war is not that it is a political instrument but that 'it is an act of force to compel our enemy to do our will':[11] in other words, it is the clash of two competing wills. An unopposed invasion of Iraq would not have resulted in war. An attacker needs to be resisted for fighting to occur: as Clausewitz made clear in book VI of On war, which accounts for a quarter of the whole, war therefore begins with defence. As a result the directions which war takes are unpredictable, because its nature is defined by the competition between two opposing elements, with each side doing its best to prevent the other achieving its objectives. Those objectives will themselves be adapted in the light of the war's conduct and course. The more protracted the conflict, the more other factors – both those extraneous to the war itself and those intrinsic to it (including chance and what Clausewitz called 'friction' and the 'fog of war') – will shape it.

There is plenty in Clausewitz that can continue to inform our current concerns, but On war will rarely, if ever, be read by statesmen or politicians: not even Bismarck, as far as we are aware, did so. The bigger and more difficult challenge is the need for institutional change, not intellectual awareness. Governments at war need and use different agencies from those they use in peace. Those NATO states contributing forces to ISAF in Afghanistan do not see themselves as at war: the domestic impacts of their military actions overseas are limited. That observation is possibly applicable even in the United States and certainly in the United Kingdom. As a result no state has sufficiently adapted its defence agencies from their Cold War focus on acquiring capabilities to the current priority which is the business of making strategy. Waging war requires institutions which can address problems that lie along the civil–military interface, and can do so on the basis of equality rather than of military subordination to civilian control. Politicians need to listen to soldiers, to what can be done in practice as opposed to what the politicians might like to be done in theory, and to do that states need institutions within which soldiers feel ready to be realistic about the military issues – and about the nature of war.

In 2006 public pronouncements in both the United States and the United Kingdom made clear the absence of institutions which enabled this to happen – or their failure to deliver where, as in the United States, they already existed. In the United States service discontents were in the main confined to the anger of retired senior officers. In Britain, both the Chief of the General Staff in October 2006 and the First Sea Lord in February 2007 briefed journalists on issues that belonged squarely at the interface between civil and military leadership, and where their views appeared to differ from those of the government. Their statements, and the press's reaction to them, suggested that Britain lacked the machinery for the proper articulation of their concerns. This had not always been the case. In 1902, in the era of classical strategy, Britain created the Committee of Imperial Defence to bring service chiefs and political leaders around the same table. In 1916 David Lloyd George established a war cabinet for the same purpose, and, unlike the Committee of Imperial Defence, it possessed executive as well as advisory powers. This was a mechanism adopted as recently as 1982 by Margaret Thatcher for the Falklands War. The essential features of such bodies were: comparable representation from both sides of the military and political divide; regular, even daily, meetings in time of war, so that strategy remained rooted and responsive to the situation on the ground; and equality in the weight given to military and political viewpoints. In 2003 Britain did not even possess the institutional basis from which to begin. The Nott–Lewin reforms of 1982 had given the Chief of the Defence Staff his own staff, and so emancipated him from reliance on the single service staffs. They made him the government's principal strategic adviser. But no sooner had this structure been put in place than it was effectively dismantled by Michael Heseltine, who was Secretary of State for Defence between 1983 and 1986. He elevated the management of budgets over the direction of strategy. Throughout the first decade of the twenty-first century the Ministry of Defence struggled to assert itself as a strategic headquarters, ironically while also failing to be effective as a department of account. When David Cameron became prime minister in 2010, his government asked Lord Levene to report on the ministry's structures for the acquisition of equipment and the management of costs, but not those for the production of strategy.

If wars are to be waged in the twenty-first century, those waging them will need a firm grasp of strategy. Strategy will not flourish if the armed services are silent on the issue, or feel themselves to be constrained by norms in relation to the proper and 'politically correct' conduct of civil–military relations. Just as politicians will never read *On war*, and so – by extension – will fail fully to understand war's true nature, so it is beholden on service personnel to embrace a sense of strategy that is at once both classical and unfettered by recent notions regarding the subordination of the military to political control. The first step in this process is a clear articulation of what strategy is; the second is its application in the machinery of state.

2 THE MEANING OF STRATEGY: HISTORICAL PERSPECTIVES

On 19 November 2003, President George W. Bush delivered a major speech on international relations at the Royal United Services Institute in Whitehall, London. Security was intense: many Britons were unhappy that the privileges of a state visit were being accorded an American president who had gone to war in Iraq when the justification for doing so in international law was at best unclear. The event was therefore controversial; however, the speech was less so. Indeed, most British commentators welcomed it as a clear statement of United States foreign policy, and probably George Bush's most coherent comments on the subject to date. 'We will help the Iraqi people establish a peaceful and democratic country in the heart of the Middle East. And by doing so, we will defend our people from danger,' he declared. He then went on: 'The forward strategy of freedom must also apply to the Arab–Israeli conflict.'[1]

This last sentence is puzzling. Strategy is a military means; freedom in this context is a political or even moral condition. Strategy can be used to achieve freedom, but can freedom be a strategy in itself? A fortnight after Bush's speech, on 2 December 2003, the British Foreign and Commonwealth Office published its first White Paper on foreign policy since the Callaghan government of 1976–9. Its focus was on terrorism and security; it was concerned with illegal immigration, drugs, crime, disease, poverty and the environment; and it included – according to the Foreign Office's website – 'the UK's strategy for policy, public service delivery and organisational priorities'. The punctuation created ambiguity (were public service delivery and organisational priorities subjects of the paper or objects of the strategy?), but the central phrase was the first one. It suggested that the Foreign Office now developed strategy to set policy, rather than policy to set strategy. The title of the White Paper was *UK international priorities: a strategy for the Foreign and Commonwealth Office*.[2] Introducing it in Parliament, the Foreign Secretary, Jack Straw, explained that 'The FCO strategy analyses the ways in which we expect the world to change in the years ahead.' There was no mention of diplomacy or foreign policy, the traditional domains of foreign ministries. Moreover, the timing of the White Paper's publication created wry, if cynical, comment. It managed – just – to put the horse before the cart: the Ministry of Defence's White Paper, *Delivering security in a changing world*, appeared a week later.[3] Those who wondered whether that too would establish a strategy for policy, as opposed to a policy for strategy, might point to the degree to which the Ministry of Defence had already come to set the foreign policy agenda. The key statement on British policy after the attacks of 9/11 was neither *UK international priorities: a strategy for the FCO* nor *Delivering security in a changing world*, but the so-called *New chapter* to the Ministry of Defence's *Strategic defence review* published over a year previously, in July 2002.[4]

The confusion in Bush's speech and in the Foreign Office's White Paper embodies the existential crisis which strategy confronts. The word strategy has acquired a universality which has robbed it of meaning, and left it only with banalities. Governments have strategies to tackle the problems of education, public health, pensions and inner-city housing. Advertising companies have strategies to sell cosmetics or clothes. Strategic studies flourish more verdantly in schools of business studies than in departments of international relations. Airport bookstalls carry serried ranks of paperbacks reworking *The art of war* by Sun Tzu. Gerald Michaelson is a leader in this field: his titles are self-explanatory – *Sun Tzu: the art of war for managers – 50 strategic rules* (2001) and *Sun Tzu strategies for marketing: 12 essential principles for winning the war for customers* (2003). But strategic studies are not business studies, nor is strategy – despite the beliefs of George Bush and Jack Straw to the contrary – a synonym for policy.

Clausewitz defined strategy as 'the use of the engagement for the purpose of the war'.[5] He did not define policy. Clausewitz's focus was on the nation and the state, not on party politics. Too much, therefore, can be made of the ambiguity created by the fact that the German word,

Politik, means policy and politics: this may matter less for our understanding of *On war* than for our interpretations of later commentators. Clausewitz was at least clear that conceptually *Politik* was not the same as strategy, even if the two were interwoven. When he concluded that war had its own grammar but not its own logic, he implied that strategy was part of that grammar. By contrast policy provided the logic of war, and therefore enjoyed an overarching and determining position which strategy did not. Clausewitz's definition of strategy was therefore much narrower than that of contemporary usage. He too would have been perplexed by George Bush's 'strategy of freedom' and the Foreign Office's 'strategy for policy'.

The word 'strategy' may have its roots in ancient Greek but that language preferred concrete nouns to abstract ones. Στράτηγος meant general, but what the commander practised was more likely to be expressed by a verb. Moreover, for the Greeks, as for the medieval knights, what was done on the battlefield or in a siege was the conduct of war, and more a matter of what today would be called tactics.[6] The general's plans and his execution of manoeuvres in the lead-up to battle had no clear name until the late eighteenth century. The idea of strategy was a product of the growth of standing, professional armies on the one hand and of the Enlightenment on the other. In 1766 a French lieutenant colonel, Paul Gideon Joly de Maizeroy, wrote: 'in an enlightened and learned age in which so many men's eyes are employed in discovering the numerous abuses which prevail in every department of science and art, that of war has had its observers like the rest'.[7] That book, *Cours de tactique, théoretique, pratique et historique*, as the title reveals, was about tactics, but more than ten years later Joly de Maizeroy published his *Théorie de la guerre* (1777), in which he identified a second level to the art of war, a level which he called strategy, and which he saw as 'sublime' and depending on reason rather than rules: 'Making war is a matter of reflection, combination of ideas, foresight, reasoning in depth and use of available means ... In order to formulate plans, strategy studies the relationship between time, positions, means and different interests, and takes every factor into account ... which is the province of dialectics, that is to say, of reasoning, which is the highest faculty of the mind.'[8]

The Napoleonic Wars confirmed the distinction between tactics and strategy, between what happened on the battlefield and what happened off it. The introduction of conscription meant that field armies tripled in size within two decades. Their coordination and supply made demands of a general that were clearly different from the business of firing a musket or thrusting with a sword. Napoleon himself did not use the word strategy until he was exiled to St Helena,[9] but those who wrote about what he had achieved certainly did – not only Clausewitz, but also Jomini, the most important military theorist of the nineteenth century, and the Austrian Archduke Charles. The last-named had proved one of Napoleon's most redoubtable opponents, fighting him to a standstill at Aspern-Essling in 1809. Charles was of the view that, 'Strategy is the science of war: it produces the overall plans, and it takes into its hands and decides on the general course of military enterprises; it is, in strict terms, the science of the commander-in-chief.'[10]

Jomini for his part saw the campaign of Marengo in 1800 as the defining moment of the new era, the moment that 'the system of modern strategy was fully developed'.[11] In his *Précis de l'art de la guerre* (1838), he split the art of war into six parts, of which – in rank order of importance – statesmanship was the first and strategy the second. The latter he defined as the art of properly directing masses upon the theatre of war, either for defence or for invasion,[12] and later in the same book he wrote: 'Strategy is the art of making war upon the map, and comprehends the whole theatre of operations.'[13]

Jomini's classification dominated land warfare in Europe until the First World War. His ideas were plagiarised by military theorists across the continent, and they provided the axioms inculcated in the military academies which proliferated from the turn of the eighteenth and nineteenth centuries. His emphasis on planning, cartography and lines of communication meant that his definition of strategy became the *raison d'être* and even justification of the general staffs which were similarly institutionalised during the course of the nineteenth century. By 1900 military men were broadly speaking agreed that strategy described the conduct of operations in a particular theatre of war. It involved encirclement, envelopment and manoeuvre. It was something done by generals.

This was 'traditional' strategy – based on universal principles, institutionalised, disseminated and at ease with itself. It acknowledged too that strategy did not embrace the entire phenomenon of war. Strategy was only one of three components which made up war – the central element sandwiched between national policy on the one hand and tactics on the other. Each was separate but all three had to be kept in harmony.

The problem that confronted traditional strategy lay not in its self-definition but in its boundaries with policy. Many generals came to believe, as Moltke the elder told Bismarck in the Franco-Prussian War, that once war was declared the statesman should fall silent until the general delivered the victory.[14] Friedrich von Bernhardi, writing in *On war of today* in 1912, said that, 'If war is resolved upon, the military object takes the place of the political purpose.' But Bernhardi should not be quoted selectively (as he so often was in Britain after the outbreak of the First World War). He fully recognised that the object could not be fixed from a purely military viewpoint, but had to take into account the reciprocal effects of military action on political affairs. The commander who demanded the right to set the object himself, without regard to the political purpose, had to be rebuffed. 'War is always a means only for attaining a purpose entirely outside its domain. War can, therefore, never itself lay down the purpose by fixing at will the military object.'[15]

Nor was this ambivalence about the dividing line between strategy and policy a symptom of Prussianism. A French general and one of the great military writers of his day, Jean Colin (whose works were translated into English under the supervision of Spenser Wilkinson, Oxford's first professor of military history), declared in 1911 that, 'once the war is decided on, it is absolutely necessary that a general should be left free to conduct it at his own discretion'.[16] Colin died on active service in 1917, the year in which another French general, Henri Mordacq, became the military aide of Georges Clemenceau, the prime minister who not only united France's efforts in the prosecution of the First World War but also established most clearly the Third Republic's political primacy over the nation's army commanders. In 1912 Mordacq wrote a more nuanced discussion than that of Colin on the relationship between policy and strategy in a democracy, one in which he stressed the need for the general to submit his plans for governmental approval to ensure that they conformed with the political objective. But he also reminded the government of its obligations: the civil power should indicate to the high command its political objective, and then it should let the soldiers get on with their job free of intervention. He quoted Moltke: 'strategy works uniquely in the direction indicated by policy, but at the same time it protects its complete independence to choose its means of action'.[17]

Strategy's propensity to replace policy was reflected at the institutional level. In the eighteenth and the early nineteenth century policy and strategy were united in one man – the king or the emperor, Frederick the Great or Napoleon. In the states of the early twentieth century they could not be, however much Kaiser Wilhelm II may have believed they were. During the First World War, the machineries for the integration of policy and strategy either did not exist, as in Germany or Austria-Hungary or Russia, or emerged in fits and starts, as in Britain and France. Even in March 1918, when the Entente allies appointed Ferdinand Foch their generalissimo, his principal task was the coordination of land warfare on the western front. He took charge of strategy traditionally defined. Less clear were the lines of responsibility between him and the allied heads of state.

When the war was over, some strategic thinkers, most notably Basil Liddell Hart, would argue that it had been won not by land operations on the western front, but by the application of sea power through the blockade. Traditional definitions of strategy, those developed between, say, 1770 and 1918 by thinkers whom we would now classify as the classical strategists, were limited by more than just their focus on operations. They also neglected war at sea. The military historian needs to confront an existential question: why is there strategy on the one hand and naval strategy on the other? Why is the use of the adjective 'naval' an indication that those who have written about the conduct of war at sea have not been incorporated into the mainstream histories of war?

'We are accustomed, partly for convenience and partly from lack of a scientific habit of thought, to speak of naval strategy and military strategy as though they were distinct branches of knowledge which had no common ground.'[18] So wrote Julian Corbett in his *Some principles of maritime strategy* (1911). Corbett went on to argue that both naval and military strategy were subsumed by the theory of war, that naval strategy was not a thing by itself. His thinking in this respect was directly shaped by his reading of Clausewitz. In other words he located himself not in some maritime backwater but in the mainstream of classical strategic thought. His theory of war was that 'in a fundamental sense [war] is a continuation of policy by other means'.[19] He went on: 'It gives us a conception of war as an exertion of violence to secure a political end which we desire to attain, and . . . from this broad and simple formula we are able to deduce at once that wars will vary according to the nature of the end and the intensity of our desire to attain it.'[20]

When Corbett addressed the officers at the Royal Naval War College before the First World War, he distinguished between what he called 'major strategy' and 'minor strategy'. Plans of operations, the selection of objectives and the direction of the forces assigned to the operation were now not strategy but minor strategy. Major strategy 'in its broadest sense has also to deal with the whole resources of the nation for war'.[21] Corbett had therefore begun to apply the word strategy to policy and to see the two as integrated in a way that Clausewitz had not. In this, more unites him to his near contemporary, Alfred Thayer Mahan, than divides him. Both then and since, commentators on the two founders of naval thinking have tended to polarise their views. Corbett argued that sea power was only significant when it affected events on land; Mahan was critical of amphibious operations. Corbett concerned himself with trade defence; Mahan was sceptical about cruiser war. Corbett doubted the importance of fleet action; Mahan was its greatest advocate. But Mahan, like Corbett, was working towards a theory of grand strategy. Like Corbett and Clausewitz, Mahan was rooted in the classical strategic tradition, in his case through Jomini. But Jomini's influence, although evident in what Mahan said about naval strategy narrowly defined, should not obscure the novelty and innovatory quality of what he said about sea power more broadly defined. For Mahan, strategic arguments were based on political economy. Maritime trade was vital to national prosperity, and naval superiority was essential to the protection of the nation's interests. That naval superiority in itself depended on the seafaring traditions of the population, the nation's culture and the state's political structure.[22] There was therefore a symbiotic link between sea power, liberal democracy and ideas of grand strategy. All three elements seemed to have been required to achieve synergy – a point made clear if we look at the third great titan of naval thought, Raoul Castex.

Castex wrote a five-volume treatise on strategy in the inter-war period. He was a French admiral, and France was a liberal democracy which had been sustained during the First World War through British credit and Atlantic trade. But France saw itself as a land power before it was a sea power. Castex began his five volumes by defining strategy in terms identical to those of the pre-1914 military writers: 'Strategy is nothing other than the general conduct of operations, the supreme art of chiefs of a certain rank and of the general staffs destined to serve as their auxiliaries.'[23] He had not changed this formulation, originally written in 1927, a decade later. His discussion of the relationship between politics and strategy, and their reciprocal effects, treated the two as entirely separate elements, and concluded with a chapter entitled

'Le moins mauvais compromis'.[24] The key factor determining Castex's reluctance to embrace grand strategy as Corbett and Mahan had done was that France had vulnerable land frontiers. Its army was more important than its navy.

Sea-girt states, like Britain and the United States, freed – unlike France – from the need to maintain large standing armies for the purposes of defence against invasion, could develop along political lines that favoured individualism and capitalism. The prosperity that that engendered then became the means to wage war itself – what Lloyd George, as Britain's Chancellor of the Exchequer in 1914, called the 'silver bullets'.[25] These links – between peacetime preparation and the conduct of war itself, and between economic capability and military applications – prompted J. F. C. Fuller to entitle a chapter of his book, *The reformation of war*, published in 1923, 'The meaning of grand strategy'. He regarded the division of strategy into naval, military and now aerial components as 'a direct violation of the principle of economy of forces as applied to a united army, navy and air force, and hence a weakening of the principle of the objective'. Moreover,

> our peace strategy must formulate our war strategy, by which I mean that there cannot be two forms of strategy, one for peace and one for war, without wastage – moral, physical and material when war breaks out. The first duty of the grand strategist is, therefore, to appreciate the commercial and financial position of his country; to discover what its resources and liabilities are. Secondly, he must understand the moral characteristics of his countrymen, their history, peculiarities, social customs and systems of government, for all these quantities and qualities form the pillars of the military arch which it is his duty to construct.[26]

Here, as in other respects, Fuller's ideas were aped and developed by Basil Liddell Hart. Pursuing also the trajectory set by Corbett, Liddell Hart believed that Britain's strategy should be shaped not according to patterns of continental land war but in a specifically British context, conditioned by politics, geography and economics. He therefore distinguished between 'pure strategy' and 'grand strategy'. Pure strategy was still the art of the general. But the role of grand strategy was 'to coordinate and direct all the resources of the nation towards the attainment of the political object of the war – the goal defined by national policy'.[27]

Liddell Hart cast a long shadow forward, influencing both the allies' conduct in the Second World War and their subsequent interpretation of it. The political leaders of Britain, the United States and the Soviet Union coordinated their plans: they practised grand strategy, refusing to treat the theatres of war in isolation and settling the relationship of one theatre to another. The coping stone to the British official history of the Second World War was the six volumes of the deliberately titled 'grand strategy' series, two of them written by holders of the Chichele chair in military history at Oxford, Norman Gibbs and Michael Howard. Although Howard's was the fourth volume in chronological sequence, it was the last but one to appear, and was published sixteen years after the first. However, Howard found that the series editor, J. R. M. Butler, had attempted no more helpful statement than to say of grand strategy that 'it is concerned both with purely military strategy and with politics'.[28] Howard therefore began his volume with a definition of grand strategy: 'Grand strategy in the first half of the twentieth century consisted basically in the mobilisation and deployment of national resources of wealth, manpower and industrial capacity, together with the enlistment of those of allied and, when feasible, of neutral powers, for the purpose of achieving the goals of national policy in wartime.'[29]

What had now happened – at least in Britain and also in the United States – was the conflation of strategy and policy. When Liddell Hart had himself defined grand strategy, he had admitted that it was 'practically synonymous with the policy which governs the conduct of war' and 'serves to bring out the sense of "policy in execution"'.[30] Edward Mead Earle in the introduction to *Makers of modern strategy*, published in 1943, in the middle of the Second World War, defined strategy 'as an inherent element of statecraft at all times', and contended that grand strategy so integrated the policies and armaments of a nation that it could render the resort to war unnecessary.[31]

This conflation of strategy and policy has created particular problems for strategic theory shaped in the Anglo-American tradition since 1945, and particularly since the 1970s. Earle was the dominant text up to and including that decade, which was distinguished in 1976 by the publication of the English translation of Clausewitz's *On war* by Michael Howard and Peter Paret. Howard and Paret's edition gave Clausewitz a readership far larger than he had ever enjoyed before. Those readers, responding to Earle's injunction that strategy was an activity to be pursued in peace as well as in war, not least because the advent of nuclear weapons apparently gave them no choice, focused their attentions on chapter 1 of book 1 of *On war*, the only book which Howard and Paret deemed to be fully finished and the one which they argued contained the most developed discussion of the relationship between war and policy. However, they tended to interpret Clausewitz's understanding of policy and politics according to their own liberal lights, and not according to his. Policy was seen as controlling, guiding and even limiting war. The integration of strategy and policy was therefore a 'good thing' in a liberal and rationalist sense. But in Clausewitz's own day politics had the opposite effect – they removed the restraints on war. The French Revolution transformed the power of the state, and so transformed France's capacity to wage war. This is most evident not in book 1 but in book VIII of *On war*. 'As policy becomes more ambitious and vigorous, so will war, and this may reach the point where war attains its absolute form.'[32] In this passage Clausewitz seems clear in his own mind that the Napoleonic Wars had rendered real something that in book 1 of *On war* he would treat as ideal: the notion of absolute war.

Moreover, the link between war and revolution suggests another reversal in the standard Anglo-Saxon interpretation of Clausewitz. War itself could effect political change – the nation was constituted and defined through struggle. Clausewitz, for all that he sought to rationalise war's purpose and to systematise its conduct, was interested in war above all as a phenomenon. War could be existential, not instrumental, its waging a social and moral catharsis. War could itself create a political identity.[33] Clausewitz was a German nationalist, who hated France and who often expressed himself in accents that link him to the so-called German *Sonderweg* and even to the Nazis. With Prussia defeated at Jena in 1806 and humiliated thereafter, war had become for Clausewitz not an instrument of policy but policy in its highest form. Prussia had to wage war to define itself: its readiness to sustain the struggle was an end in itself.[34]

Revolutionaries like Giuseppe Mazzini in the nineteenth century or Franz Fanon in the twentieth expressed themselves in comparable terms.[35] So too did many Germans in the inter-war period, convinced by the defeat of 1918 that the army had been 'stabbed in the back'. Clausewitz the German nationalist was at times closer in his thinking to Erich Ludendorff, the First Quartermaster General of 1916–18, than we care to acknowledge or than Ludendorff himself did. In *Der totale Krieg*, published in 1935, Ludendorff wrote, 'Politics, at least during the

[First World] War, ought to have fostered the vital strength of the nation, and to have served the purpose of shaping the national life.' It was – and is – fashionable to see Ludendorff as deranged by 1935, if not before, but his prediction of the next war, that it 'will demand of the nation to place its mental, moral, physical, and material forces in the service of the war', was not so inaccurate. Ludendorff was writing about what his English translators called totalitarian war, a conflict which would require the mobilisation of the entire population for its prosecution. 'War being the highest test of a nation for the preservation of its existence, a totalitarian policy must, for that very reason, elaborate in peace-time plans for the necessary preparations required for the vital struggle of the nation in war, and fortify the foundations for such a vital struggle so strongly that they could not be moved in the heat of war, neither be broken or entirely destroyed through any measures taken by the enemy.'[36]

As Carl Schmitt put it after the Second World War, only a people which can fight without consideration of limits is a political people. The idea that politics could expand the way in which war was conducted was not just one entertained by fascists or Germans. Total war was a democratic idea. Clemenceau's government of 1917–18 had invoked the rhetoric of the French Revolution to summon the nation and Churchill spoke of total war in Britain in 1940–2. Definitions of strategy therefore broadened because of the ambiguity between the categories of war and of politics which world war generated. In the immediate aftermath of 1945 the powers assumed, as Clausewitz had tended to do in 1815, that the future pattern of war would pursue a trajectory derived from the immediate past. Total war would become the norm.

The advent of nuclear weapons confirmed and consolidated those trends. If used, they would ensure that war was total – at least in its destructive effects. To obviate this, theories of deterrence were developed and employed, which themselves conflated strategy and foreign policy. Deterrence itself then became the cornerstone of a new discipline, strategic studies, but strategic studies were concerned not so much with what armies did in war as with how nations used the threat of war in peace. By 1960 Thomas Schelling defined strategy as concerned not with the efficient application of force but with the exploitation of potential force.[37] Strategy itself therefore helped erode the distinction between war and peace, a trend confirmed by the high levels of military expenditure in the Cold War, and by the tendency to engage in proxy wars and guerrilla conflicts below the nuclear threshold.

The meaning of strategy had now changed. Conventional strategy was a strategy of action; it prepared for war and then implemented those preparations. Nuclear strategy was a strategy of dissuasion; it prevented war. Conventional strategy was built up through historical precedent. Nuclear strategy had no real precedents, beyond the dropping of the two atomic bombs on Japan. And so it focused on finding a new methodology, building scenarios and borrowing from mathematics and probability theory. Indeed methodology itself seemed on occasion to be the *raison d'être* of strategic thought. Nuclear strategy abandoned the focus on victory. It was, in the opinion of one French commentator, 'astrategic'.[38] Another Frenchman, General André Beaufre, demonstrated in his *Introduction to strategy*, first published in 1963, the impasse which strategy had reached. War, he declared, was total, and therefore strategy must be total. That meant that it should be political, economic, diplomatic and military. Military strategy was therefore one arm of strategy.[39] But what then was political strategy? Beaufre did not confront his own oxymoron.[40] Strategy without any adjective was for him both political and military, and therefore was about outcomes, not means.

None of this was too problematic for the navies of the Cold War. Naval strategists had seen strategy as operative in peace as well as war. Fleets and bases, even more than armies and fortifications, had to be prepared before a war broke out, and their shape and distribution moulded the strategy to be followed once hostilities began.[41] Those patterns provided their own forms of security in peace as well as in war: for example, they underpinned the notion of *Pax Britannica*. But for the classical strategists of land war the notion of strategy in peace was inherently illogical. This had begun to change in the period before the First World War, when the attention given to war plans and peacetime military preparations led to arguments that these activities could properly be considered part of strategy. But the presumption was not that the end was the application of strategy in peacetime but its better use when war came. For the armies the end remained combat. For the navies the end might turn out not to be war at all.

Armies and their generals lost their way in the Cold War. The discipline of strategy, which defined and validated the art of the commander, the business of general staffs and the processes of war planning, was no longer theirs – or at least not in the United States or in Great Britain. Beaufre wrote in *An introduction to strategy*, 'The word strategy may be used often enough, but the science and art of strategy have become museum pieces along with Frederick the Great's snuff-box and Napoleon's hat.' Strategy, he concluded, 'cannot be a single defined doctrine; it is a method of thought'.[42] Edward Luttwak, writing towards the end of the Cold War, in 1987, defined strategy as 'the conduct and consequences of human relations in the context of actual or possible armed conflict'.[43]

Strategy was appropriated by politicians and diplomats, by academics and think-tank pundits, and it became increasingly distant from the use of the engagement for the purposes of the war. The latter activity was given new titles. Barry Posen, in *The sources of military doctrine* (1984), distinguished between grand strategy and military doctrine. The former was 'a political-military, means–ends chain, a state's theory about how it can best "cause" security for itself'. The latter was a sub-component of grand strategy and concerned the means used by the military.[44] In the 1980s the American and British militaries responded to this crisis by inventing a new level of war – sited between grand strategy and tactics. Calling it the operational level of war, they even invented a spurious genealogy for it. If it had roots, they were Russian. Aleksandr A. Svechin, writing in 1927, placed operational art between tactics and strategy, and defined strategy as 'the art of combining preparations for war and the grouping of operations for achieving the goal set by the war for the armed forces'.[45] However, it proved more convenient for most commentators to locate the evolution of the operational level of war in Germany – perhaps because Germany was now an ally and perhaps because there was an Anglo-American conspiracy to laud Germany's military achievements in the two world wars despite its defeat in both.[46]

Most German generals before 1914 divided war into tactics and strategy, just like generals of every other state. The tasks and problems, which Schlieffen set the German general staff while its chief between 1891 and 1905, were called 'Taktisch-strategischen Aufgaben', or tactical-strategic, not operational, problems. The First World War showed the generals of Germany, like those of every other state, that the conduct of war was not just a matter of strategy in an operational sense, but also involved political, social and economic dimensions. However, the veterans of the supreme command, the *Oberste Heeresleitung*, did not respond to this realisation as the British did: grand strategy figured neither as a phrase nor as a concept in the immediate aftermath of the armistice. Ludendorff entitled his reflections on the war *Kriegführung und Politik*, 'The conduct of war and policy', published in 1922. The title was significant on two counts.

First, the waging of war was kept separate from policy, although yoked to it. In 1916–18, the German supreme command under Hindenburg and Ludendorff had established de facto roles in areas of public life that were neither operational nor strictly military, even if they did indeed have implications for the conduct of the war. Ludendorff's conclusions from this experience were threefold. The first was to stress that operational matters, strategy as it was traditionally understood, were the business of professional soldiers: in many ways this was a reiteration of pre-war demands, and it was reflected in a number of works by former staff officers. The second was to blame the civil administration for not supporting the military as Ludendorff felt it should have done. The third conclusion was that government needed to develop mechanisms to enable it to resolve the tensions between the conduct of war and policy. For some that pointed to the creation of joint civil and military bodies, as in the Entente powers; for others it was an argument for the restoration of the monarchy; for Ludendorff it was a case for embodying the direction of policy and *Kriegführung* in a single leader, a *Führer*.[47]

The second point evident in Ludendorff's book was how little it said about strategy. Ludendorff had been contemptuous of strategy in 1917–18, and had as a result fought offensives in the west in the first half of 1918 that had succeeded tactically but had failed to deliver strategic outcomes. In 1922, he did no more than repeat the lapidary definition of the elder Moltke, that strategy was a system of expedients. A truism, it conveyed little. German military thought in the inter-war period followed suit. Strategy dropped out of currency. In 1936–9, three massive volumes on the military sciences were published in four parts, the first appearing with an imprimatur from the minister of war, Werner von Blomberg. They had no separate entry for strategy, which was subsumed under *Kriegskunst* or the art of war. What was said about strategy was new only in so far as it stressed that it was no longer simply a matter for the army, but now had to combine all three services. In other respects it remained what it had been before the First World War, a matter of operational direction: 'Thus strategy embraces the entire area of the military conduct of war in its major combinations, especially the manoeuvres (operations) and battles of armies and army components to achieve mutual effects and ultimately the military war aim.' The hierarchy of policy, strategy and tactics also remained intact: 'So strategy makes available to tactics the means for victory and at the same time sets the task, just as it itself derives both from policy.'[48]

The relationship between war and policy was treated under a separate heading, 'Politik und Kriegführung', and the latter word itself was now taken to mean not just the conduct of war in an operational sense but the combination of political and military factors by the supreme powers.[49] The domain of the army specifically was increasingly described not as strategy but in related terms, as *Militärische* or *Operative Kriegführung*. The achievements of the Wehrmacht in 1939–41 conformed to the expectations generated by these guidelines. They were the consequence of applied tactics more than of any over-arching theory, and they confirmed – or so it seemed – that strategy was indeed a system of expedients. The German army which invaded France in 1940 was doing little more than following its own nose.[50] But after the event its victory was bestowed with the title *Blitzkrieg* and became enshrined in doctrine. Germany lost the Second World War in part for precisely that reason, that it made operational thought do duty for strategy, while tactical and operational successes were never given the shape which strategy could have bestowed.

This pedigree to the operational level of war, which is the focus for doctrine in so many western armies, raises some interesting points. The first is an easy and largely true observation, that the so-called operational level of war is in general terms little different from what generals in 1914 called strategy. The second is that, like those generals, armed forces today are attracted to it because it allows them to appropriate what they see as the acme of their professional competence, separate from the trammels and constraints of political and policy-making direction. However, there is a crucial difference. In 1914, the boundary between strategy and policy, even if contested, was recognised to be an important one, and the relationship was therefore addressed. Generals, not least in Britain in both world wars, were less circumscribed in their capacity to intervene in policy when policy might affect strategy. Today, the operational level of war occupies a politics-free zone. In the 1990s it spoke in a self-regarding vocabulary about manoeuvre, and increasingly 'manoeuvrism', that was almost metaphysical and whose inwardness made sense only to those initiated in its meanings. What follows, thirdly, is that the operational level of war is a covert way of reintroducing the split between policy and strategy. Yet, of course the operational level of war determines how armed forces plan and prepare in peacetime, and therefore shapes the sort of war they can fight. The American, British and (to an extent now largely forgotten) German armies developed their enthusiasm for the operational level of war in the 1980s, for application in a corps-level battle to be fought against an invading Soviet army in northern Europe. The successes of the 1991 Gulf War created the illusion that it was an approach of universal application. It was now applied in situations, such as peace support operations, in which the profile of politics was much greater than would have been the case in a high intensity major war. One consequence for the United States army was the disjunction between the kind of war for which it prepared in 2003 and the war in which its government actually asked it to engage. Thinking about the operational level of war can diverge from the direction of foreign policy.

In 2003 strategy should of course have filled the gap. But it did not, because strategy had not recovered from losing its way in the Cold War. In the 1990s nuclear weapons and nuclear deterrence were deprived of their salience. The strategic vocabulary of the Cold War – mutual vulnerability, bipolar balance, stability, arms control – was no longer relevant. However, nobody wanted to revert to the vocabulary of traditional strategy. Strategic studies had been replaced by security studies. At times they have come to embrace almost everything that affects a nation's foreign and even domestic policy. They require knowledge of regional studies – of culture, religion, diet and language in a possible area of operations; they demand familiarity with geography, the environment and economics; they concern themselves with oil supplies, water stocks and commodities; they embrace international law, the laws of war and applied ethics. In short, by being inclusive they end up by being nothing. The conclusion might be that strategy is dead, that it was a creature of its times, that it carried specific connotations for a couple of centuries, but that the world has now moved on, and has concluded that the concept is no longer useful.

That would be a historically illiterate response. Classical strategy was a discipline rooted in history, based, in other words, on reality not on abstraction. Strategy after 1945 may have been materialist, in the sense that it responded to technological innovation more than it had in the past, and it may have used game theory and probability more than experience and principle. But that was not true of any major strategist writing before 1945. Such men used history for utilitarian and didactic purposes, some, like Liddell Hart, in quite shameful ways.

Even Clausewitz was more selective in his study of military history than he cared to admit. But he, like Jomini, or like Mahan or Corbett, wrote history. They all believed that strategy involved principles that had some enduring relevance. They mostly accepted that those principles were not rules to be slavishly followed, but they did believe that principles could give insight. Two obvious conclusions follow. First, history is necessary to put their theories in context. We have, for instance, to approach Clausewitz's discussion of the relationship between war and policy recognising that he was a product of Napoleonic Europe and not of the nuclear age. Second, a grasp of strategy traditionally defined is required if we are to appreciate the classical texts on the subject.

Strategy, however, is not just a matter for historians. It concerns us all. Strategy is about war and its conduct, and if we abandon it we surrender the tool that helps us to define war, to shape it and to understand it. In the 1990s Martin van Creveld, John Keegan and Mary Kaldor, among others, argued that war traditionally defined, that is war between states conducted by armed forces, was obsolescent.[51] The fact that we do not possess a clear understanding of what strategy is, just as we are unsure how to define a war, deepens our predicament; it does not resolve it. Van Creveld, Keegan and Kaldor pointed to a fundamental but under-appreciated truth, that war is an existential phenomenon before it is a political or possibly even a social one.[52] The western powers have unwittingly colluded in a process in which war is once again to be understood in its primitive state. War has been wrenched from its political context. In Hobbesian terms, the state's legitimacy rests in part on its ability to protect its citizens through its monopoly of violence, but the state's right to resort to war in fulfilment of its obligations has been reduced. One reason is that international law has arrogated the decision to go to war, except in cases of national self-defence, to the United Nations. Even states involved in a de facto war do not declare war, so as to avoid breaches of international law. Paradoxically, therefore, international law has deregulated war. The notion that waging war is no longer something that states do is particularly prevalent in America and Europe for three further reasons. First, enemies tend to be portrayed either as non-state actors, or, when they are not, as failed states (the description applied to Afghanistan) or rogue states (that deemed appropriate in the case of Iraq). Either way their political standing is compromised. Secondly, the armies of the United States, Britain and France are professional bodies, drawn from a narrow sector of the society on whose behalf they are fighting: such armies have become the role models in contemporary defence. But they do not represent their nations except in symbolic terms. The same could be said of the private military companies, bodies without a formal national identity but on which even states with competent armed forces rely. Thirdly, and the logical consequence of all the preceding points, European states (thanks to 9/11 this applies less to the United States) have come to identify war with peace-keeping and peace enforcement. However, they are not the same. Peace support operations make problematic the traditional principles of war, developed for inter-state conflict. The objects of peace-keeping are frequently not clear, and the operations themselves are under-resourced and driven by short-term goals. On the ground command is divided, rather than united, and forces are dispersed, not concentrated; as a result the operations themselves are in the main indecisive.

Wars persist and even multiply, but the state's involvement and interest in it are reduced. The issues raised by war too often seem to be ones not of their conduct and utility but of their limitation. The overwhelming impression is that they are initiated by non-state actors, that they are fought by civilians and that their principal victims are not soldiers but non-combatants. The reality is of course somewhat different. States do still use war to further their national self-interest. The European members of NATO did so in Kosovo and the United States did so in Iraq. The infrequency of intervention, despite the atrocities and humanitarian disasters in sub-Saharan Africa, provides counter-factual evidence to support the point. Without perceived self-interest, the western powers are reluctant to use military force.

The state therefore has an interest in re-appropriating the control and direction of war. That is the purpose of strategy. Strategy is designed to make war useable by the state, so that it can, if need be, use force to fulfil its political objectives. One of the reasons that we are unsure what war is is that we are unsure about what strategy is or is not. It is not policy; it is not politics; it is not diplomacy. It exists in relation to all three, but it does not replace them. Widening definitions of strategy may have helped in the Cold War, but that was – ironically – an epoch of comparative peace. We now live in an era when there is a greater readiness to go to war. Today's wars are not like the two world wars, whose scale sparked notions of grand strategy. The big ideas helped tackle big problems. But the wars that now confront the world are robbed of scale and definition. Threats are made bigger and less manageable by the use of vocabulary that is imprecise. The 'war on terror' is a case in point. In its understandable shock, the United States maximised the problem, both in terms of the original attack (which could have been treated as a crime, not a war) and in terms of the responses required to deal with the subsequent threat. The United States failed to relate means to aims (in a military sense) and to objectives (in a political sense). It abandoned strategy. It used words like prevention and pre-emption, concepts derived from strategy, but without context. They became not principles of military action but guidelines for foreign policy.

Britain's position is also instructive. Its assertion of the right to pre-emptive action was not first set out in *UK international priorities: strategy for the Foreign and Commonwealth Office* but in the Ministry of Defence's *New chapter* to the *Strategic defence review* in 2002. The Ministry of Defence, not the Foreign Office, was therefore articulating the policy which would guide Britain's decision to use force. One of the reasons why strategy fell into a black hole in Britain in 2002 was that the government department most obviously charged with its formulation expanded its brief into foreign policy, and that in turn was a consequence of widening definitions of war. Britain did not have an identifiable governmental agency responsible for strategy (despite the Foreign Office's apparent but perverse claim that that is its task). When the Falklands War broke out in 1982, Mrs Thatcher, as prime minister, had to improvise a war cabinet, a body that brought together the country's senior political and military heads: it left no legacy, any more than did its prototype, the Committee of Imperial Defence, an advisory committee of the full cabinet set up in 1902.

The point is not that generals should go back to what they were doing at the beginning of the twentieth century, but that politicians should recognise what it is the generals still do in the twenty-first century – and do best. If strategy had an institutional home in the United States or in the United Kingdom in 2001, it was located in the armed services. And yet in the planning of both the wars undertaken by the United States after the 9/11 attacks, those in Afghanistan and Iraq, professional service opinion, from the Chairman of the Joint Chiefs of Staff downwards, often seemed marginal at best and derided at worst. The attacks found the Secretary for Defense, Donald Rumsfeld, already at odds with his generals over the 'transformation' of the armed forces. His reactions exposed the mismatch between his aspirations and their expectations. In the words of Bob

Woodward: 'Eighteen days after September 11, they were developing a response, an action, but not a strategy.' The military 'had geared itself to attack fixed targets', while the politicians were talking about doing a 'guerrilla war'. The consequence would be regime change, but the president then flipped back, saying 'our military is meant to fight and win war', and denying that US troops could be peace-keepers.[53]

Broadly similar failings emerged in the planning for Iraq. Clearly the US armed forces displayed their competence at the operational level of war. They were also able to recognise the manpower needs of post-conflict Iraq and the requirement to cooperate with non-governmental organisations. Theoretically they could see the campaign in strategic terms, with a planning cycle that embraced four phases – deterrence and engagement; seizing the initiative; decisive operations; and post-conflict operations. But strategy was driven out by the wishful thinking of their political masters, convinced that the United States would be welcomed as liberators, and determined that war and peace were opposites, not a continuum. This cast of mind prevented consideration of the war's true costs or the implications of occupation, and the United States found itself without a forum in which the armed forces could either give voice to their view of the principles at stake or be heard if they did.[54]

President Bush's speech of November 2003 made clear that he had a policy. Indeed he has courted criticism because he was so clear and trenchant on precisely that point. But that is not strategy. The challenge for the United States – and for the United Kingdom – was, and is, the link between the policy of its administration and the operational designs of its military agents. In the ideal model of civil–military relations, the democratic head of state sets out his or her policy, and armed forces coordinate the means to enable its achievement. The reality is that this process – a process called strategy – is iterative, a dialogue where ends also reflect means, and where the result – also called strategy – is a compromise between the ends of policy and the military means available to implement it. The state, and particularly the United States, remains the most powerful agency for the use of force in the world today. Lesser organisations use terror out of comparative weakness, not out of strength. The conflation of words like 'war' and 'terror', and of 'strategy' and 'policy', adds to their leverage because it contributes to the incoherence of the response. Awesome military power requires concepts for the application of force that are robust because they are precise.

3 THE CASE FOR CLAUSEWITZ: READING *ON WAR* TODAY

In 1975 Colin Powell entered the National War College in Washington. Once there, Colonel Powell (as he was then), a veteran of two tours in Vietnam, read Carl von Clausewitz's *On war* for the first time. He was bowled over. *On war* was, Powell recalled, 'like a beam of light from the past, still illuminating present-day military quandaries'.[1] What particularly impressed him was Clausewitz's view that the military itself formed only 'one leg in a triad', the other two elements of which were the government and the people. All three had to be engaged for war to be sustainable; in the Vietnam War America's had not been.

Powell may have been right about the Vietnam War, but not about Clausewitz. Powell had misread the final section of the opening chapter of *On war*, that which describes war as 'a strange trinity'. Its three elements are not the people, the army and the government, but passion, chance and reason. Clausewitz went on to associate each of these three elements more particularly with the feelings of the people, the exercise of military command and the political direction of the government. But in doing so he moved from the 'trinity' itself to its application. The people, the army and the government are elements of the state, not of war. The distinction is crucial not only to the relevance of *On war* today but also to what follows in this book. Clausewitz informs much of its content; he does so because he emphatically sought to understand war in terms as broad as possible, and to be as little bounded by the circumstances of his own time as his not inconsiderable intellectual powers enabled.[2]

Powell was not the only American soldier to misinterpret Clausewitz's 'trinity'. In 1982 Colonel Harry Summers wrote one of the most influential explanations for the United States's failure in Vietnam. Called *On strategy*, it too used Clausewitz to say that war consisted of the people, the army and the government. Summers saw the Vietnam War as an inter-state struggle in which the enemy was North Vietnam, but in which the US army had allowed itself to be distracted by the Vietcong operating in the south and so been sucked into a peripheral conflict, shaped by guerrilla warfare and pacification. Summers had used Clausewitz to explain how the United States had failed strategically, but he also rejected counter-insurgency warfare and encouraged the American army in its determination to refocus on conventional combat.[3] In 1991, with Powell as Chairman of the US Joint Chiefs of Staff, and Summers providing press commentary on the conduct of the Gulf War (having retired from a post at the US Army War College), the state-centric interpretation of Clausewitz's 'trinity' was installed in high places. Sir Michael Howard, the joint-translator of the third English-language edition of *On war*, whose fluency ensured that it was now read in all American war colleges, was then professor of military and naval history at Yale. Asked by the *New York Times* to name his man of the year for 1991, he chose the long-dead Prussian general.[4]

Almost immediately others began to take a somewhat different view, seeing in this moment of triumph the seeds of Clausewitz's downfall. 'The Persian Gulf War was perhaps the last Clausewitzian war ever to be fought,' wrote one commentator, Delbert Thiessen, in 1996.[5] Thiessen's opinion was shaped less by the political framework of war and more by its technological drivers. The impact of emerging technologies on warfare, popularised as a shift from 'brute force to brain force' by Alvin and Heidi Toffler,[6] was packaged in US military circles as the 'revolution in military affairs' or RMA. One of the RMA's leading advocates, Admiral William Owens, became vice-chairman of the US Joint Chiefs of Staff in 1994 and contributed a chapter on 'The emerging US system of systems' to *Dominant battlespace knowledge*, a book produced for the US National Defense University in 1995. In 2000, after he had retired, he wrote *Lifting the fog of war*. The title was a reference to Clausewitz, and designed to point to the impending irrelevance of at least one of *On war*'s major themes. In the 'information age' the armed forces of the United States would develop 'systems of systems', or even 'the' system of systems, which would enable them to establish 'full spectrum dominance' and so use precision and agility to win their wars in short order. This reading of future warfare associated Clausewitz with the past, with war in the industrial age. Having quoted Clausewitz's image of war ('war is the realm of uncertainty; three quarters of the factors on which action is based are wrapped in a fog of greater or lesser uncertainty'), Owens conjured up a very different vision of the future – one in which 'a military commander [had] been granted an omniscient view of the battlefield in real time, by day and night, in all weather conditions', or at least over 'as much of the battlefield and an enemy force to allow vital manuever and devastating firepower to deliver the coup de grace in a single blow'.[7]

The 'revolution in military affairs', if successfully implemented, promised technological change in war sufficient to undermine one aspect of Clausewitz's analysis of war: indeed it would change war's very nature, devaluing or making redundant the factors which Clausewitz had seen as continuous in war – courage, uncertainty, fear, chance and friction. Nonetheless, Owens's vision of the future did not alter the aspects which had concerned Powell and Summers, which were political and social rather than technological. Here the challenge to Clausewitz's status came from a different direction.

After the end of the Cold War, with wars allegedly being waged to an increasing extent by non-state actors, such as guerrillas, terrorists and warlords, who in turn funded their efforts by crime and drug-trafficking, neither Powell's nor Summers's definitions were of much help. And as they became less helpful, so too, it seemed, did Clausewitz. Their take on the 'trinity' tied On war indissolubly to the inter-state wars of Clausewitz's own lifetime. If the so-called Westphalian order, the era between 1648 and 1990 when (again allegedly) nation states enjoyed the monopoly on armed force and used armies to wage war in pursuit of policy objectives, waned, so too would the applicability of Clausewitz's insights. This was the thesis which sustained Martin van Creveld's *The transformation of war*, published in 1991. By identifying Clausewitz's understanding of war with the people, the army and the government, what he called 'the Clausewitzian universe', van Creveld was able to invent and therefore reject something called 'trinitarian war'. The timing of the publication of van Creveld's book proved ill judged: the United States and its allies had just fought an inter-state war against Iraq, and won it in short order, a point which Michael Howard himself was not slow to make. However, as the 1990s progressed, so the themes which van Creveld had stressed gained greater purchase. Their impact in the United States was limited.

In October 1993 a US force, operating with the United Nations in Mogadishu in support of humanitarian objectives, captured two Somali warlords. On almost every count the United States's intervention in Somalia was a success, but the raid into Mogadishu, in which a Black Hawk helicopter came down and eighteen Americans were killed, over-shadowed the numbers of Somali lives that had been saved through the intervention itself. 'Black Hawk Down' resonated with Vietnam not with the first Gulf War. In 1994 Bill Clinton issued Presidential Directive 25 which stated that the United States should not expand its involvement in peace operations. It became an axiom of US defence policy that the American army did not 'do' nation-building; it fought proper inter-state wars with clear-cut objectives. That, after all, was what Colin Powell's own doctrine, promulgated when its author was Chairman of the Joint Chiefs of Staff in 1992, had also said.[8]

In Europe the opposite view took hold. After the end of the Cold War, peace operations and nation-building were the new forms of war-fare. The arguments advanced by Martin van Creveld coalesced around the notion of 'new wars'. An outlier here was John Keegan, whose *A history of warfare*, published in 1993, began with a robust denial of what had become for many Clausewitz's central premise: 'war', Keegan said, 'is not the continuation of politics by other means'. Keegan had lectured at the Royal Military Academy Sandhurst for twenty years, and was at the time the defence correspondent of the *Daily Telegraph*. He was centrally placed to influence strategic debate in Britain, but that was not the purpose of his assertion. He did not go on to think about how, if he were right (and in some respects he was), war might become useful by being made to serve the ends of policy: how, in other words, strategy was to be given effect. His purpose was rather to stress that the conduct of war was culturally determined, and to argue that the sort of war which Clausewitz was describing belonged to a short period of history, essentially the nineteenth and twentieth centuries, and to a limited part of the globe; in particular it left out of account what Keegan said Clausewitz had called 'savage' wars. Clausewitz believed that backward cultures (the Tatars were his preferred example, although he called them 'half-civilised', not 'savage') could produce great war-riors, but not commanders of genius or the strategies which required moral courage to be linked to an educated mind. Keegan had over-simplified an admittedly complex text: Clausewitz had not said, as Keegan claimed he had, that the so-called 'western way of warfare' was 'war itself: a continuation of politics, which he saw as intellectual and ideological, by means of combat, which he took to be face to face, which he took for granted'.[9]

The book that has had greater impact on students of international relations than those of either Martin van Creveld or John Keegan was the one that aimed directly to advance the 'new wars' thesis, Mary Kaldor's *New and old wars*, first published in 1999 but revised and reissued twice since then. For Kaldor, as for Martin van Creveld, new wars were 'irregular', conflicts in which the participants used guerrilla tactics and aimed to avoid battle rather than to seek it. New wars were waged by warlords for profit not for policy; their leaders derived their income from sustaining and continuing armed conflict, not by terminating it once it had reached its political objectives. By contrast, old wars were what Clausewitz had addressed. Unlike Keegan, Kaldor accurately described Clausewitz as defining war, not as a political instrument, but as 'an act of violence intended to compel our opponent to fulfil our will'. But she then went on: 'this definition implied that "we" and "our" opponent were states, and the "will" of one state could be clearly defined'. Kaldor's approach to the trinity was as state-centric as was van Creveld's. She argued that 'old' war was composed of three levels – 'the level of state or the political leaders, the level of the army or the generals, and the level of the people'. She then went on to say that, 'roughly speaking, these three levels operate through reason, chance or strategy, and through emotion'. In other words what for Clausewitz was the primordial trinity became the secondary one: his interpretation had been reversed to put the components of the state in front of the attributes which make up war.[10]

None of these critics of Clausewitz had read the text of *On war* with sufficient care, or thought much about Clausewitz's use of language (which was of course German, not English). Clausewitz, like some other military theorists, most obviously the British major general, J. F. C. Fuller, had a penchant for thinking in threes (a point to which we shall return). But the significance of this triad is more than that; it is not in fact a 'triad' or three 'levels'; it is a trinity; it is three in one. The Christian connotations are self-evident, and could not be anything other than deliberate for an author whose family came from a long line of Lutheran pastors. Therefore, the first issue posed by the trinity in book I, chapter I of *On war* is not what its three constituent elements are but what its mystical unit is: what is the God in which the Father, Son and Holy Ghost are united? The answer, once the question is posed, ought to be self-evident. It is war itself, whose essential element (and Clausewitz says this quite explicitly in the opening paragraph of the section) is violence. The definition of war which begins the same chapter (and the whole book), and which Mary Kaldor quoted, makes this plain: 'war is an act of force to compel our adversary to do our will'. Even if war can change its character, like a chameleon (the analogy Clausewitz uses in the section on the 'trinity'), its nature must, according to this simple description, be unchanging.

What war is not, or at least not by nature, is a political instrument. To this extent Keegan was right: reason, and its extrapolation, the political objects of the government, is one subordinate element of the trinity, not the trinity itself. Clausewitz likened each of the three elements of the trinity to magnets, alternately attracting and rejecting each other, and so never forming a fixed relationship. 'A theory, which insisted on leaving one of them out of account, or on fixing an arbitrary relationship between them, would immediately fall into such contradiction with reality that through this alone it would forthwith necessarily be regarded as destroyed.'[11]

One theory had been used to form an arbitrary and fixed relationship between war and policy, and we are living with the consequences. When Powell went to the National War College, strategic thought had a vested interest in elevating Clausewitz's interest in the relationship between war and policy. This is what the epithet 'Clausewitzian' has come to mean. The great French thinker Raymond Aron, in his book on Clausewitz, published in 1976, simply called it the 'formula'.[12] The Cold War gave him little choice. The possession of nuclear weapons, and their incorporation into a system of international relations which pivoted on deterrence and the threat of mutually assured destruction, meant that war had to be avoided, not waged. War was to be subordinated to policy if mankind was to survive. Clausewitz's axiom, as stated in the heading to another section in the opening chapter of *On war*, that 'war is a mere continuation of policy by other means',[13] therefore placed Clausewitz on the side of the angels. He could be associated with notions of limited war, with the need to moderate and even avoid war. According to this interpretation, those like Basil Liddell Hart who had linked Clausewitz to Prussian militarism, to the mass army, to the brutality of battle and to wars of annihilation, had misjudged him.[14]

The 'liberal' Clausewitz was the construct of two of the most distinguished scholars of modern war, Michael Howard and Peter Paret,

whose readable translation of *On war* appeared in 1976. Their edition
became a bestseller in a way that the original German has never done.
Most students, particularly in the English-speaking world, when they refer
to *On war*, cite Howard and Paret, not Clausewitz himself. And in so
many ways we and Clausewitz have both benefited: the text has acquired a
fluency which early nineteenth-century German, with its predilection for
passive constructions, does not have. Its English version also possesses a
greater coherence than is immediately evident in the German.

Howard and Paret gave it consistency by their choice of English
words and, occasionally, by their glosses on the text itself. As a result
they do not always translate the same German word with the same
English word, instead preferring the English that is consonant with its
immediate context, or with their interpretation of the text.[15] A significant
exception is the German noun *Politik*, which they tend to translate as
'policy' rather than use the equally acceptable alternative of 'politics' (as
Keegan did). This is not just a matter of semantics. 'Policy' conveys an
impression of direction and clear intent; politics, like war, is an adversarial business, whose implementation, like war, is messy and confused.

On war seeks to understand war, and it does so through a
dialectical process, a balancing of propositions and counter-propositions,
of norms and reality, a method which became stronger the more
Clausewitz developed his grasp of military history. As a young man in
the 1790s, Clausewitz had focused his self-education on philosophy, an
exposure to the ideas of the Enlightenment which left him constantly
searching for an overarching theory of war. His mentor, Gerhard von
Scharnhorst, was anxious that he should counter his search for the ideal
with a dose of the real. Between 1806, when the Prussian state was
smashed by Napoleon at Jena, and 1815, when Napoleon was finally
defeated at Waterloo, Clausewitz's views on war were shaped predominantly by his own experience. The Napoleonic Wars were the most
protracted and violent conflict in Europe since the Thirty Years War,
and at the time he not unreasonably assumed that they would be the
pattern for the future: the description of their character takes up the bulk
of *On war*. But after his own active career was over, he was able to put that
experience in context. Between 1815 and his death in 1831 he devoted
himself not only to writing the great work of theory for which he is best
known today but to military history. Indeed in that time he wrote more
history than he did theory. In 1827, not least as a result of his need to take
account of other wars, and especially those of Frederick the Great, he

realised that policy (or politics) could provide the unifying element which would enable him to construct a single way of looking at war, even if over time war, like a chameleon, changed its character.

But *On war* presents us with two different ways of examining the relationship between war and policy. The first is that of book I, where policy permeates war and moderates it. This is the view favoured by Howard and Paret, and indeed Peter Paret in his masterly biography, *Clausewitz and the state*, reproduces the first chapter of book I as an appendix, as though this were Clausewitz's final and definitive statement on the subject. The intellectual justification for this is a note in which Clausewitz states that in the event of his death only book I, chapter I should be regarded as complete. Howard and Paret date this note to 1830, the year that Clausewitz was recalled to the active service which effectively marked the end of his intellectual life. The pre-eminent German Clausewitz scholar of modern times, Werner Hahlweg, believed that the note was written three years earlier, in 1827, and if he was right it belongs at the beginning, not at the end, of what we know to have been a very productive period for Clausewitz's thought.[16] In other words there is a good case for saying that book I, chapter I should not be alone in receiving canonical status, and that hard-pressed staff college students cannot just accept Peter Paret's view that the essence of Clausewitz's thought is conveyed in *On war*'s opening chapter, allowing the lazy to leave aside the rest of the text. A great deal else in *On war* can be regarded as the fruit of the 'late' Clausewitz. Much of it says different things about the relationship between war and policy, and about the nature of war.

In particular we have to look harder at book VIII, the last book in *On war*, which has an alternative view of policy's influence on war. Here Clausewitz provides a historical overview of war, culminating in the French Revolution and Napoleon. His conclusion is that social and political change has removed the constraints on eighteenth-century war-fare: that politics has made war more destructive, not less so. In the era of Frederick the Great policy stood outside war, acting as an alien element and rendering it a 'half-thing'. In the era of Napoleon policy was in harmony with war's nature, enabling it to reach its 'absolute' form. Howard and Paret, following the logic of book I, argue that 'absolute war' was for Clausewitz an ideal construct, a fiction designed to point up the contrast between war in theory and what happens in reality. But this is not what Clausewitz says in book VIII. 'We might doubt', he wrote, 'whether our notion of its absolute nature had any reality, if we had not seen real warfare make its appearance in this absolute completeness in our own times.'[17] Moreover, in their own writings on Clausewitz, Howard and Paret do something rather different with absolute war from the interpretation they favour in their translation. They align 'absolute war' with the twentieth-century idea of total war.[18] In so doing they give Clausewitz's ideas greater purchase in relation to the Second World War and the Cold War. Here 'absolute war' is foreshadowing the 'absolute weapon', which has turned a Clausewitzian concept into reality. In the short term Howard and Paret enhanced Clausewitz's claim to enduring relevance, but in the longer term they had undermined it. Clausewitz struggled to make his theory as timeless as possible, but by locating his interpretation of war so firmly in the 1970s Howard and Paret reduced the force of what he is actually saying for a post-Cold War generation.

Above all they rendered Clausewitz's idea of an entire or whole war (der ganze Krieg as opposed to war as ein Halbding or a half-thing) as total war.[19] For Clausewitz, an entire war was one where its own nature – an escalating tendency to greater extremes – was in harmony with the other forces which it brought into play, particularly policy. Napoleon's wars fulfilled his expectations of 'absoluteness' because the emperor himself pursued a policy which was in step with war's own nature, and so liberated it from the constraints imposed upon it from outside by eighteenth-century monarchs. Here, as much as anywhere, Clausewitz shows how policy stands outside war, and can be as frequently independent of it and at odds with it, as it is convergent with it. Indeed in the post-Cold War era, as opposed to the western experience of the earlier twentieth century, that has been the dominant experience of war, and has become the source of so much friction and inadequacy in the making of strategy.

Book VIII therefore matters not least because it highlights the reciprocal nature of the relationship between war and policy more than book I. War is not simply the continuation of policy or politics by other means. Of course in theory war should be used, as it frequently is used, as an instrument of policy. But in reality that is a statement about its causation more than its conduct, and about intent more than practice. Once war has broken out, two sides clash, and their policies conflict: that reciprocity generates its own dynamic, feeding on hatred, on chance and on the play of military probabilities. War has its own nature, and can have consequences very different from the policies that are meant to be guiding it.

In other words war itself shapes and changes policy. Clausewitz stresses the need for an offensive campaign to be speedy in its execution if it is to deliver on its objectives. He therefore sees time as the great asset enjoyed by the defender: by refusing battle and by trading space for time, the defender dissipates the initial advantages enjoyed by the attacker. The policies each follows will therefore be adapted in the light of the military situation. Indeed it was in book VI, that on the defence and the fullest, if in some respects the least polished, of *On war*, that Clausewitz first confronted the role of policy in war. The defender, who counter-attacks against an invader who has passed 'the culminating point of victory', will face a political choice that will arise out of the evolving military situation: will he turn his tactical success from defence of his own territory into a full-blown invasion of the attacker's?

Only rarely does war fulfil the ideal objectives of the side that initiates it. Policy in wartime therefore has to reflect the nature of war, and be embedded in it. The over-emphasis on book I of *On war* is still to be found in the United States today. The notion of war's subordination to policy is congruent with democratic norms of civil–military relations. It implies, as did both the Weinberger doctrine of 1984 (in whose formulation Powell is presumed to have played a leading role) and the Powell doctrine of 1992, that all that is required for success is the establishment of clear aims and the provision of overwhelming force to achieve those aims. As a theoretical requirement of policy, that is fair enough; as a statement about war's true nature it is demonstrably false.

Moreover, such a view carries an assumption that ultimately is profoundly un-Clausewitzian, that the army – once set in motion – should be left, unfettered by politicians, to deliver the policy objectives that those politicians have set it. The unreflective reiteration of a Clausewitzian norm has not only blocked our understanding of war's true nature, it has also provided a barrier to the re-engagement of politicians and soldiers with each other just when policy and war need to be brought back into step. In 2003 the operational virtuosity of the American army was not linked to policy by strategy: their separation was not only the fault of Donald Rumsfeld, it was also the baleful consequence of the Powell doctrine.

Clausewitz recognised the practical difficulties which the harmonisation of policy and war presents. Much was made by Howard and Paret of their restoration to the text of *On war* of the first edition's wording concerning the construction of cabinet government: 'If war is to be fully consonant with political objectives, and policy suited to the means available for war, then unless statesman and soldier are combined in one person, the only sound expedient is to make the commander-in-chief a member of the cabinet, so that the cabinet can share in the major aspects of his activities.'[20] Later editions had suggested that the commander-in-chief should be a member of the cabinet at all times, in peace as well as in war. What Howard and Paret were therefore apparently doing was rescuing Clausewitz from the imputation that he favoured generals who interfered in the domestic politics of their states. But for some the original phrasing, which Howard and Paret restored to their English edition, suggested that Clausewitz's model general was a political neuter. He was not. Clausewitz's own text gave the lie to that. The commander of an army, he said, needed to 'be familiar with the higher affairs of state' and to possess a 'keen insight into state policy in its higher relations'; in sum 'the general becomes at the same time the statesman'.[21] Of course in Clausewitz's day the commander-in-chief could well be both king and general, not purely a general, but that was precisely why his own experience also gave the lie to any suggestion that Clausewitz favoured either the separation of military power from political authority in time of war, or the formal subordination of the military authorities to the political. First of all, the cabinet which Clausewitz was talking about was not the sort of ministerial government familiar to a British readership. What he had in mind was the private office of the king, made up of his personal staff and advisers, and more like the French meaning of *cabinet*. Its strength was therefore contingent on the authority of the king. The cabinet of Clausewitz's king, Friedrich Wilhelm III of Prussia, had performed disastrously in the Jena campaign in 1806 because it itself lacked executive powers, and yet its very existence encouraged the king to consult rather than to lead.[22] Clausewitz therefore believed that the commander-in-chief should be in the cabinet so that the cabinet could share in his decisions concerning strategy. In other words the thrust here was not the need to subordinate the military to political control, but to ensure that policy did not ask of strategy things that it could not deliver.

Because Clausewitz saw war as a whole of which policy is but one part, it follows that the object in government is the harmonisation of those parts. Clausewitz talked of the absurdity of asking for a *'purely military judgment'*. He went on, 'It is an unreasonable procedure to consult professional soldiers on the plan of war, that they may give a *purely military* opinion, as is frequently done by cabinets.' But it followed that policy is required to be in step with military judgement: 'When people speak, as they often do, of the harmful influence of policy on the conduct of war, they really say something very different from what they intend. It is not this influence, but the policy itself, which should be found fault with. If the policy is right, that is, if it achieves its end, it can only affect the war favorably – in the sense of that policy. Where this influence deviates from the end, the cause is to be sought only in a mistaken policy.'[23]

Policy therefore needs to be rooted in a recognition of war's true nature. Most of *On war* is about the latter, not about the relationship between war and policy. The central dialectic of *On war* is not in fact that between war and policy, the discussion of which only develops from book VI and is largely confined to books I and VIII. The bulk of the work, that is to say books II to VII, is focused on the relationship between strategy and tactics, and their reciprocal effects. Most modern readers skip these chapters, convinced that they are no more than a description of late Napoleonic War, and bored (understandably) by advice on the conduct of river crossings and the defensive values of mountain ranges. But they are the bedrock from which Clausewitz's ideas about war's true nature, about its inherent 'friction', about the role of chance and probability, and about the function of military genius are derived.

Clausewitz never adequately defined *Politik*. He defined strategy and tactics early in his intellectual career, and those definitions are still present in *On war*. Strategy he saw as the use of engagement for the purposes of the war, tactics as the use of armed forces in the engagement. Tactics he thought a matter of routine, and his views on them were unremarkable. Strategy was what seemed to him to be new in war; it was where the art of the commander lay; and it was the central and unifying theme of the book. It is extraordinary that those who have denied the contemporary relevance of Clausewitz have not exploited this point more frequently. Clausewitz's book is about strategy, but what he meant by strategy is not what modern thinkers have come to mean by strategy. They have located strategy not in the art of the commander but in the links which tie war to policy. Clausewitz's redeeming feature in the eyes of modernists is that, although he did not give a name to this process, he recognised its necessity. When, in 1827, Clausewitz realised the explanatory power of the role of policy, he could go on to construct a 'trinitarian' view of war that was made up not of people, army and government, but of tactics, strategy and policy – a construction that could be further developed in another 'triad', that of means, aims and objectives.

In theory each of these levels is distinct, and the philosopher in Clausewitz was keen to maintain the difference. He did not, for example, use the words 'operations' or 'operational' to describe and even elide the interface between tactics and strategy, preferring much more amorphous words like *Unternehmungen* (or undertakings) and *Handeln* (business or affairs). Clausewitz the realist did of course appreciate that tactics, strategy and policy interact with each other in practice, but the theorist needed to use language, and the concepts which underpin language, with precision. He achieved precision through self-questioning, through a debate with himself which is sustained, not just through his principal theoretical work, but also through the military history he wrote at the same time and in which he could explore the applicability and accuracy of his arguments. This is why *On war* has more durability as a text than its recurrent condemnation would suggest. Clausewitz's own self-criticism, his belief that the dialectical method enhanced understanding, means that many of the best answers to Clausewitz's critics are to be found in *On war* itself.

Nowhere is this more true than in Clausewitz's realisation that war was not simply utilitarian and instrumental, but existential as well. The association of Clausewitz with 'old' wars does not allow for Clausewitz as an insurgent, a label that applies to him in two senses in the years between November 1807, when he returned to Prussia after his incarceration as a prisoner of war in France, and April 1814, when he was restored to the uniform of the Prussian army after serving in that of Russia. The argument that *On war* does not really address guerrilla and insurgency warfare was the third line of criticism directed at Clausewitz in the 1990s. It is also the least well founded.

Between 1807 and 1812 Clausewitz and his seniors, particularly August von Gneisenau, humiliated by Prussia's subservience to France, planned a war of national liberation similar to those being fought against Napoleon elsewhere in Europe, especially in Spain. They proposed to mobilise the population as a whole, using guerrilla warfare and even terrorism. So Clausewitz was an insurgent in terms of the methods he advocated. Prussia was weaker than France and needed military 'asymmetry' to achieve effect. Clausewitz's lectures on 'small war', delivered at the war academy in 1810 and 1811, give the lie to those who ignorantly maintain that he never addressed the themes of guerrilla war.[24] One of the reasons why 'small war' so interested him was that its effects lay athwart the relationship between strategy and tactics. Partisans or guerrillas might lack tactical effectiveness, in that the regular force would always beat them in open battle, but they could have effects at the strategic level by harassing lines of communication across the entire theatre of the war and by exploiting terrain, especially mountains and forests, which would not suit the tight and drilled formations of regular armies. He acknowledged that 'a war of the people' would be bloodier than any other, but he said that would not be their fault but the fault of those who had forced such a war on them.[25]

As this sort of language revealed, Clausewitz was also an insurgent in a political sense, and his focus was directed internally as much as externally. Frustrated by the complaisant attitude of the Prussian king, he and those who thought like him spoke less of service to the Prussian state, whose army they served in, and more of the German nation. He was in danger of being less a reformer and more a revolutionary. In February 1812, the king fell in with Napoleon's demand that Prussia provide a contingent for the imperial army which France was forming for the invasion of Russia, Prussia's former ally. Further subordination to France was more than Clausewitz could bear, and his response encapsulated his notion of the soldier as a political actor. He penned a series of three political declarations with potentially revolutionary implications, addressing the king not as sovereign but as representative of the nation – a nation, moreover, which he described as German not Prussian. The first manifesto (for such it was) concluded with a creed: 'I believe and confess that a people can value nothing more highly than the dignity and liberty of its existence; that it must defend these to the last drop of its blood; ... that a people courageously struggling for liberty is invincible; that even the destruction of liberty after a bloody and honorable struggle assures the people's rebirth.'[26]

Policy in other words could demand a fight to the end, even to apparent extinction. It was not necessarily a moderating influence on war. This was the Clausewitz cited by Hitler in *Mein Kampf*, if not by the deterrence theorists of the Cold War. It finds more muted reflection in *On war* itself, composed in the peaceful tranquillity of his study and not amidst the visceral emotions of war. However, book VI addresses the possibility that the new phenomenon of people's war within civilised

Europe might become more common as the nineteenth century progressed. The fact that he described *Vom Kriege* as a book on 'major war' therefore raises the intriguing question as to whether he planned a second book on 'small war'. In any event he was clear about the nature of such a war. Chapter 26 of book VI describes the actions of a politically aware, passionate people, fighting for national independence, and not ready to accept the outcome of battle: 'There will always be time enough to die; like a drowning man who will clutch instinctively at a straw, it is the natural law of the moral world that a nation that finds itself on the brink of the abyss will try to save itself by any means.'[27]

People's war, Clausewitz noted, was 'a consequence of the way in which in our day the elemental violence of war has burst its old artificial barriers'. As in his passage on the 'trinity', he recognised the tensions between reason and passion, and acknowledged that there was no inherent presumption in war's nature that the former would prevail over the latter. Indeed his own experience told him that it should not, or not inevitably so. In 1812 he had followed the logic of his own convictions, and left the Prussian army to serve that of Russia. The campaign that followed found him fighting against his own people. Although the Prussian contingent changed sides at the end of November 1812, Clausewitz was not restored to the Prussian army until after what the Germans called the 'war of liberation'. The refusal of men like Clausewitz to accept the clear political aims of the enemy or to accept the logic of overwhelming military force had resulted in a far swifter end to Bonapartist tyranny than he could have ever hoped in February 1812.

These historical correctives are not the reason why Clausewitz has retained or even regained his credibility in American military circles since 2001. However, the fact that he has can be attributed in large part to the increasing salience of insurgency and counter-insurgency in western military thought. In *On strategy*, Harry Summers had attacked the US army's use of counter-insurgency in the Vietnam War as a diversion from the war's centre of gravity, and through his interpretation of Clausewitz's trinity he had put the bulk of the blame on the government, not the army. In 1986 Major Andrew Krepinevich's book, *The army and Vietnam*, took the opposite line. It attacked the army's and hence Summers's view as to why it had lost in Vietnam. It wanted the army to examine its own failings, and it stressed the need to think rather harder about counter-insurgency. Initially the army did not welcome Krepinevich's interpretation, but as his arguments gained traction they caused soldiers to reject Summers. As a result they could also have turned against Clausewitz, and some did. In 2009, Stephen Melton, a retired officer teaching at the Army Command and General Staff College, saw Summers's influence as a symptom of the 'intellectual confusion attendant on our losing the Vietnam War'. His real ire, however, was directed at the army's too-ready assimilation of Clausewitz. He pointed out, reasonably and relevantly, that Clausewitz was a creature of his own times, the product of a monarchy determined to limit war. So for him, 'much of *On war* is a philosophical attempt to resolve the dialectical contradiction between the unlimited violence of battle and the very limited political objectives of monarchical war'. He took the army's operational doctrine of 2001 to task for its determination to make its planning processes heavily dependent on the need to analyse and identify what Clausewitz had called war's centre of gravity, whether 'physical or moral, military or non-military, single or multiple'. So he described Tommy Franks, the CENTCOM commander in the same year, as a Clausewitzian, 'who, from the first discussion of an invasion of Iraq in early December 2001, viewed the upcoming battle in terms of applying "the necessary lines of operation to attack or influence what Clausewitz has described more than a hundred years before as the enemy's 'centers of gravity'"'.[28] Melton's problem was not Clausewitz, but how some elements of the American army had elected to read *On war*. If he too had read Clausewitz more carefully, he might have realised that his solution to the challenges facing the United States – strategic defence and limited wars – was entirely compatible with another (albeit equally selective) reading of *On war*.

For Melton 'The populace ... is nearly absent from the Clausewitizian calculus.'[29] Others disagreed. John Nagl, the armour officer credited with a key role in the development of Field Manual 3–24, the army's counter-insurgency doctrine issued in December 2006, argued the opposite: Clausewitz, while focusing on conventional war, realised that 'the feelings, aspirations and energies of the people ... would play a dramatic role in modifying the nature of unconventional warfare'.[30] Nagl's patron was David Petraeus, who saw Clausewitz in very different terms from both Melton and Franks. For Petraeus the point of *On war* was not operations, but strategy, by which he meant not the narrower definition of strategy given by Clausewitz, but the link between war and policy

In 1987 Petraeus completed his doctoral thesis at Princeton on 'The American military and the lessons of Vietnam'. 'Maybe', Petraeus wrote to Major General Jack Galvin, 'we should marry Andy [Krepevinich]'s book and Harry Summers' *On Strategy* (which, as you know, criticizes our preoccupation with insurgency). The two together might have provided a solution [to the war in Vietnam].'[31] Because Summers was important to Petraeus's thesis, so was Clausewitz. Petraeus wrote in his conclusion: 'Though most military officers quote flawlessly Clausewitz' dictum that "war is the continuation of politics by other means", many do not appear to accept the full implications of his logic.'[32] Petraeus's thesis was an attack on the Weinberger doctrine (and prospectively on the Powell doctrine, whose promulgation was still five years away). By accepting Summers's recommendations, the army had come to believe – according to James Schlesinger, the Secretary of Defense, as quoted by Petraeus – that it 'must only fight popular, winnable wars'. These convictions had made the senior officers of the army into doves, separated from their political masters. Because America's generals would only countenance the employment of military forces in the sorts of operations for which the army was optimised, they effectively rendered them unusable. They failed to acknowledge, in Petraeus's words, 'that involvement in small wars is not only likely, it is upon us'. Petraeus argued that those who opposed American involvement in counter-insurgencies unless certain exacting conditions were met failed to realise the logic of Clausewitz's 'dictum that "war is the continuation of politics by other means"'.[33]

Petraeus's subsequent career is evidence of much more than the need to relate war to politics in counter-insurgency campaigns; it also shows by example the value of Clausewitz's endorsement of prior education and serious theoretical study before going to war. Amercia's readiness to go to war since 9/11, and its grudging and gradual acceptance of counter-insurgency doctrine, not least thanks to Petraeus's own efforts, have encouraged a more sophisticated engagement with Clausewitz. Over the subsequent decade another quotation from Clausewitz has begun to supplant that on the relationship between war and policy in military doctrine circles: 'the first, the supreme, the most far-reaching act of judgment that the statesman and commander have to make is to establish by that test the kind of war on which they are embarking; neither mistaking it for, nor trying to turn it into, something that is alien to its nature. This is the first of all strategic questions and the most comprehensive.'[34] Assessing the character of an individual war seems to be a task for the military professional – is it regular or irregular, high intensity or low intensity? But the answer has profound political implications. Less often cited or explained by soldiers who use this Clausewitzian dictum is the previous sentence, which explains what he meant by 'that test'. There Clausewitz made clear that, because wars should be thought of as acts of policy, not as something autonomous, they 'must vary with the nature of their motives and of the situations which give rise to them'.

The Clausewitz so readily condemned by the commentators of the 1990s was the Clausewitz fashionable in the 1970s. The fact that the rationality of the 'formula', of war's relationship to policy, has looked less clear cut since 9/11 does not invalidate it as an interpretative tool. The problem has arisen from its exclusivity. There is much more to *On war* than one hackneyed catchphrase, particularly when it is put in a straitjacket to serve the needs of current doctrine or of national policy. The tragedy for the armed forces of the United States and for their allies is that greater attention to rather more of the text would have provided the intellectual underpinnings for greater self-awareness and strategic sensitivity than has been evident over the past decade. The need is not to ditch *On war*, but to read more of it and to read it with greater care.

4 MAKING STRATEGY WORK: CIVIL–MILITARY RELATIONS IN BRITAIN AND THE UNITED STATES

The most damning criticism of the American conduct of the war in Iraq was that it lacked a strategy. 'All too often', Colin Gray wrote in 2005, 'there is a black hole where American strategy ought to reside.'[1] Of course there were other failings, but this was the most significant because from it many of the others flowed. Strategy implies that the government has a policy and that the strategy flows from the policy: it is an attempt to make concrete a set of objectives through the application of military force to a particular case. But the 'war on terror', embraced in September 2001, was profoundly astrategic. Directed not towards a political goal, but against a means of fighting, it set an agenda that lacked geographical precision. Its successor and reconfiguration, 'the long war', enunciated in February 2006, recognised the problem but did not solve it. 'The long war' is about shaping military means to political objectives, but conceptually it remains devoid of strategic insight and of political context. Strategy needs to recognise war's nature; this one uses a policy statement as a substitute for defining the war. The concept of length only acquires meaning when contrasted with brevity, as both long war and short war are relative terms. Moreover, the 'long war' deliberately minimised the wars that were then being waged, in Iraq and Afghanistan, by placing them in the context of something bigger but altogether more amorphous. Wars require enemies and it is not clear exactly who in this case they were.

Strategy's absence is not an exclusively American problem. The same point can be made about Britain. In 2003 British forces were committed to Iraq before the criteria for war proposed by British

campaign planners were fulfilled, and in particular in the certain knowledge that there was no structure for the post-conflict phase of occupation, despite that being a key element of any 'three-block' war. London
tended to excuse its own failings in this respect by saying that it had to
follow Washington, that Britain could not have a strategy for Iraq
because that was made in America (only it was not).

Policy, not strategy, was where the public debate about the
Iraq War focused before the invasion, and it remained there thereafter,
especially in Britain thanks to the David Kelly affair and Lord Butler's
subsequent report on the intelligence services.[2] This was understandable,
not least because the politicians' responses to these and other revelations
have been to shift their justifications for the war. In early 2003, George
Bush decided, using a logic which has escaped all informed observers,
that Saddam Hussein had to be removed to further the war on terrorism.
No link between Saddam Hussein, Iraq and al-Qaeda had been proved,
then or since. For Tony Blair, the threat was Iraq's weapons of mass
destruction. Today, both objectives look even more threadbare than they
did then: the invasion did not reveal any weapons of mass destruction
(let alone the 946 potential sites identified by American intelligence),[3]
and the ongoing conflict itself spawned terrorism. Nonetheless, these
changes have also obscured an underlying continuity. The 'neo-
conservative' agenda, that the establishment of democracy in
Iraq could create a new dynamic in the Middle East, proved more
resilient. It evolved before the 9/11 attacks in 2001, and it became the
rationalisation for war to which both Bush and Blair increasingly turned.
The suggestion of confusion created by their tergiversations masked an
underlying consistency of purpose.

The military instruments to which they entrusted their intentions
were, however, designed for somewhat different undertakings from
those to which the armed forces of America and Britain found themselves
committed. In the 1980s the United States army, rethinking its approach
to doctrine after Vietnam, rejected its lessons on counter-insurgency and
state-building, preferring to latch on to what it called the operational
level of war. It focused on 'manoeuvre', an idea which it contrasted with
attrition (despite the fact that the antithesis is a false one), as it planned to
defeat a Soviet invasion of north Germany with an armoured counter-
stroke. The USA's NATO allies, not least Britain, followed suit. The
operational level of war appeals to armies, as it puts primacy on their
professional skills. In the 1980s concepts like 'follow-on force attack'

and 'AirLand battle' could be developed as ways of fighting Soviet forces in depth without consideration of the political consequences, and despite the fact that such battles would be waged in densely populated and industrialised regions of Europe. For the British army the creation of the Ace Command Europe Rapid Reaction Corps (renamed the Allied Rapid Reaction Corps in 2002 and known by the acronym ARRC) became an end in itself as it ensured the primacy of the corps, and of Britain's case for exercising command at that level – the level at which the operational level of war was deemed to function.

Fortunately such a war was never fought in Europe, but it was conducted in the Gulf in 1990–1. The effect of easy victory was to confirm the wisdom of the approach. Cold War theories of major war were found to be practicable against foes other than the Soviet Union and in climes different from Europe. The operational level of war, and the primacy of manoeuvre within it, became a panacea for all wars. The trajectory followed by the US armed forces since 1991 – from the revolution in military affairs, through network-centric warfare and even on to the fad current in 2003, that of 'transformation' – was impelled by the same concentration on the operational level of war. The central issues revolve around the uses of new technologies as force-multipliers, both to offset manpower inferiority and to disperse the fog and friction of the battlefield. In other words 'manoeuvrism' and its derivatives attempted to deal simultaneously both with issues of national capability and with the inherent nature of war. The first is unilateral in its implications, the second bilateral (or even multilateral). War is a reciprocal activity, a point which many of the derivatives from the operational level of war tend to forget.

For all that it encompasses much that Clausewitz and many nineteenth-century commanders would have described as strategy, the operational level of war is not strategy in itself – any more than it is policy. The problem of strategy is located along the fault-line between policy and the operational level of war. The consequence of politicians pretending that policy is strategy and of soldiers focusing on operations has been to leave strategy without a home. America's weakness, Antulio Echevarria wrote in 2004, lies in how it 'relates its military performance to political purpose even when the performance is first-rate'.[4] In the planning for the invasion of Afghanistan Richard Cheney, the US vice-president, and Donald Rumsfeld, the Secretary of Defense, confronted the fact that the war their policy demanded that the United States fight was not the sort of war for which the armed forces had prepared. Bringing doctrine and policy into line was the task of strategy. That did not happen. On 26 April 2006, more than four years after the initiation of the war in Afghanistan, the Secretary of State, Condoleezza Rice, told reporters on her aeroplane on the way to Baghdad, where she was to join Donald Rumsfeld: 'We just want to make sure there are no seams between what we're doing politically and what we are doing militarily. Secretary Rumsfeld and I are going to be there because a lot of the work that has to be done is at that juncture between political and military.'[5]

In the aftermath of the 9/11 attacks, Rumsfeld's short-term answer was not to adapt policy to current operational capabilities but to demand that the armed forces conform to his vision of future operations. The same was true of his long-term intentions. They included the power to project force to distant theatres, to deny the United States's enemies sanctuary anywhere in the world, and to maintain unhindered access to space. The 2001 Quadrennial Defense Review, according to Rumsfeld in May 2002, aimed to sustain deterrence in four critical theatres, to defeat swiftly two aggressors at the same time, and to preserve the option for one massive counter-offensive designed to occupy a capital and replace a regime.[6] These goals did not lack ambition, but they were too abstract to be defined as policy: where were these wars to be fought, against whom, and – above all – for what purposes? The Quadrennial Defense Review was not strategy, as it saw war as a unilateral instrument of policy, not a reactive environment with its own 'non-linear' dynamic.[7] As Rumsfeld himself acknowledged, the approach was capability-based, not threat-based. He set about 'transforming' the armed forces by making them less reliant on heavy platforms inherited from the Cold War, expanding the special forces and using technology as a force-multiplier. Neither policy nor strategy, 'transformation' sought to develop another operationally derived concept to oust the old. It aroused animosity within the armed forces not least because a civilian minister was trespassing on an area of professional competence. The battle between the Secretary of Defense and his generals was over how the United States should fight, not what it was fighting for. The tragedy for the USA was that the services were right to be sceptical but did not challenge their political master at his weakest point. The core difficulty was that, although operational doctrine must be congruent with strategy, it is not strategy itself.

Thus Rumsfeld's response was to bypass the problem of strategy, not confront it. In 2001–2, he, and with him the President and the vice-president, marginalised the Chairman of the Joint Chiefs of Staff. Frustrated by the fact that the Pentagon did not have plans for the war they had decided to fight, they went ahead and fought it anyway. In other words the war in Afghanistan was waged without a strategy, which could only have been developed by means of a proper dialogue between the politicians and the armed forces. 'We have to say things in a general way because we don't know what we're going to do until we get there,' Rumsfeld acknowledged in the autumn of 2001.[8] The Americans were saved from the consequences of their own temerity because of the sudden and wholly unexpected collapse of Kabul, thanks to the military contribution of the Northern Alliance. The success fostered the belief (not for the first time in military history) that what had happened by accident represented the triumph of method, or could be made into method. The failure to deal with the original problem, that of al-Qaeda, was glossed over. Before Afghanistan, Rumsfeld had argued that 'If you're fighting a different kind of war, the war transforms the military.' In other words the war itself would effect the changes which he had been seeking. Accordingly, after the capture of Kabul, he claimed that the United States had created a new defence strategy for the twenty-first century, and others found it hard to gainsay him.[9] The initial and easy successes in the invasion of Iraq in 2003 seemed to confirm the wisdom of that approach. 'By a combination of creative strategies and advanced technologies', George W. Bush declared on 16 April 2003, 'we are redefining war on our terms.'[10] The president's hubris represented the triumph of the operational level of war, and the excellence of America in conducting it. The ongoing conflict shows the failure of strategy, and the inadequacy of operational art as a tool for decoding a war's reciprocal nature. Policy had set goals which the operational concepts of the US army could not deliver.

At one level the challenge was intellectual, but if it had only been that the United States and Britain would not have found themselves in the quagmire which confronted them by 2006. The best ideas and the clearest concepts can still be set aside by strong and determined personalities. That was exactly what happened in 2002–3. Plenty of informed and sensible planners on both sides of the Atlantic flagged their major worries about the need for post-conflict planning as part of an overall strategy for Iraq.[11] They were pushed aside – not only by the politicians, who failed to understand war's true nature, its own inherent dynamic, but also by soldiers, who remained fixated by the operational level of war. Here the arrogance and naivety of General Tommy Franks stood out. His belief that military victory defined in traditional and narrowly operational terms would deliver victory in a strategic and ultimately therefore political sense was Prussian in its simplification. Challenged in March 2002, when Operation Anaconda failed to prevent the escape of Osama bin Laden from eastern Afghanistan into Pakistan, he responded by defending the tactical performance: 'I thought the planning that was done was very good planning, and I think the result of the operation was outstanding.'[12] In reality the attack was as much a tactical disaster as it was a strategic one. If America had possessed sensible structures for the formation of strategy, Franks's posturing would not have mattered. He was not Chairman of the Joint Chiefs of Staff; he was Commander-in-Chief of the US Central Command (CENTCOM) in Tampa, Florida. Answerable directly to the president and to Rumsfeld, he was able to bypass the Chairman of the Joint Chiefs. He later argued that 'Operation Enduring Freedom in Afghanistan had been nitpicked by the Service Chiefs and the Joint Staff, and I did not intend to see a recurrence of such divisiveness in Iraq.'[13] In other words, the issues were institutional as well as intellectual. The problem was not just the issue of what strategy was, but where strategy was made. Franks's own memoirs both acknowledge the point and highlight the gap: 'While we at CENTCOM were executing the war plan, Washington should focus on "policy-level issues."'[14] He did not ask how and where the war plan and the policy were to be integrated.

These were not new problems for the United States or – for that matter – for the United Kingdom. The lack of coherence between political expectations of what military power might be asked to do and the military's understanding of its own capabilities dogged American government during the Vietnam War and into its aftermath.[15] As Deborah Avant has written, 'The US Army's doctrine in Vietnam', geared to the Cold War expectations of major European war, 'was not integrated with the nation's grand strategy'.[16] The problems were partially addressed by the Goldwater–Nichols act of 1986, which strengthened the Chairman of the Joint Chiefs of Staff at the expense of the individual service chiefs precisely so as to produce more coordinated strategic advice for the government. In Britain the 1982 reforms of John Nott, the Secretary of State for Defence, and Sir Terence Lewin, the Chief of the Defence Staff, gave the Chief his own staff and made him the government's principal strategic adviser. They led to the creation of the Permanent Joint Headquarters at Northwood in 1994–6, and culminated with the appointment of the Chief of Joint Operations in 1996. Both countries came out of the Cold War, therefore, with organisations seemingly better adapted to the delivery of effective strategy. In reality neither had.

In the United States, the new procedures were decisively shaped by Colin Powell. American forces, he believed, should only be used to achieve clear political objectives, and should be deployed with overwhelming force to achieve a quick victory. After Vietnam the army configured itself precisely so that it was fitted only for major war, not only through its doctrinal emphasis on the operational level of war but also through its organisation of reservists. Although Powell's pronouncements and personal influence provoked fears that the military was escaping the control of civilians, the long-term effects of the Powell doctrine went on to acquire somewhat different hues. Powell's position was entirely compatible with the notion of military subordination to political control: war would be used to achieve the objectives of policy. But the terms of its use also created a division between policy and war: the first would set the objective, the second would deliver it. This was close to the Prussian concept of victory enunciated by another apparent Clausewitzian, Helmuth von Moltke the elder, Chief of the General Staff in the German wars of unification (1864–71). He accepted entirely that policy should determine when to go to war and should settle the terms of the peace, but he rejected its role in war itself. Eliot Cohen provided a corrective in *Supreme command*, an influential book published in 2002. He argued for the benefits conferred on the conduct of war by statesmen who recognised that politics permeated war, and who were therefore ready to interfere with their field commanders and challenge the assumptions of military professionalism. He reasserted the hierarchical relationship between civilians and soldiers, although significantly his examples were all derived from wars in which the states concerned were fighting for their survival; they were major wars which did not readily fit with the lesser conflicts subsumed within the 'war on terror' or 'the long war'.

Powell's views have had a profound influence on American generals' beliefs with regard to civil–military relations and the use of force, but it was Cohen who reflected, and even shaped, the views of

American politicians in 2002–3. The disjunction helps in part to explain the outbursts of retired American generals in April 2006, as they attacked the Defense Secretary for his conduct of the war in Iraq. Clearly these soldiers were not apolitical; clearly too, however, they felt that their voices had not been heard in the production of strategy.[17] Personalities were important here, and so too were institutions. If the Defense Secretary does not like the advice he is receiving, and Rumsfeld rejected that of the army chief of staff, Eric Shinseki, in the run-up to the invasion of Iraq, the Goldwater–Nichols act gives him access to alternative counsels. Although the act beefed up the position of the Chairman of the Joint Chiefs of Staff, he is not formally in the command chain, and the act also created the powerful theatre commands, of which CENTCOM is one. Franks showed in 2003, as General Wesley Clark had also revealed when Supreme Allied Commander Europe in the Kosovo campaign in 1999, that the theatre commanders can cut the joint staff out of the loop by speaking directly to the Secretary of Defense and the president. Clark's alienation from the Joint Chiefs of Staff reinvigorated civilian supremacy, enabling the Bush administration in particular to divide and rule the military. The 2006 plans for a 'long war', which included 'reposturing' US forces in an arc running through the Middle East and Asia over an indefinite period, were set out not by the Joint Chiefs of Staff, nor for that matter by the State Department or by the Department of Defense, but by a staff officer from Central Command in Tampa, Florida. The challenge that strategy confronts is not just conceptual; it is also institutional.

Britain has had comparable problems. The Permanent Joint Headquarters is in Northwood, not in the Ministry of Defence in Whitehall. The relationship between its head, the Chief of Joint Operations, and the Chief of the Defence Staff was not clearly defined, at least not until the creation of the Joint Forces Command in April 2012. In 2003, there were two centres for strategy and no clear wiring diagrams to show how either linked to the Foreign and Commonwealth Office or the Department for International Development. Later glosses have stressed that the Permanent Joint Headquarters was the operational hub (a point reinforced by the fact that the Chief of Joint Operations was a three-star, not a four-star, appointment), and the Ministry of Defence the strategic headquarters. This distinction made sense before 2003, when British forces could find themselves engaged in several relatively minor theatres simultaneously, and when each could be seen as limited in its demands on resources and restricted in time. The position became confused when one major commitment – first Iraq and then Afghanistan – dominated all others in both respects, so rendering the division between operations and strategy less clear and instead demanding that they be coordinated more effectively. In 2012, the personnel of the Permanent Joint Headquarters became the responsibility of the Joint Forces Commander, while they were answerable for their operational output to the Chief of the Defence Staff.

In the Blair government, all three departments of state, the Ministry of Defence, the Foreign and Commonwealth Office, and the Department for International Development, were represented on the Committee on Defence and Overseas Policy, chaired by the prime minister, but the Chief of the Defence Staff only attended by invitation. In other words the professional head of the armed forces had no direct personal responsibility for the positions adopted by the government in relation to security matters. In July 2007, the Labour government formed a Ministerial Committee in National Security, International Relations and Development (NSID). In the view of one (admittedly controversial) British diplomat, 'it was not the easiest place for the discussion of sensitive issues'.[18] Chaired by the prime minister, its meetings under Gordon Brown were infrequent and its profile low.[19]

Neither point holds true for the National Security Council created by the coalition government when it took power in May 2010. David Cameron has been an energetic and enthusiastic chairman, and both the main body and its sub-committees have met with remorseless frequency. However, the question as to the coherence of its approach to strategy has persistently resurfaced. One accusation levelled at the sub-committee formed to conduct the Libya campaign in 2011 was that it became too focused on issues of operational and even tactical significance, to the detriment of strategy. When giving evidence to the Parliamentary Joint Committee on the National Security Strategy on 24 October 2011, Oliver Letwin, Minister of State in the Cabinet Office, was asked why the National Security Strategy's risk assessment register had not incorporated the United Kingdom's current commitment to Afghanistan, particularly given the possibility that the government's plan to withdraw British troops by 2014 might prove undeliverable. He replied that the risk register was only concerned with issues that were not yet actual problems. He said that the choice of the date for withdrawal had been the product of two considerations: the need not to leave too soon, in other words before the Afghan security forces were sufficiently strong to take over, and the need not to leave too late, when the British presence might become part of the problem. In his words, 'We balanced those out and came to the view that we had to set a date which was not very far out but on the other hand was far enough out so that it could be done in an orderly and proper fashion.' The implication was that the National Security Council's approach had been to take two possible dates and split the difference. He made no reference to the situation in Afghanistan itself, to the policy of the United States and its effect on British strategy, or to any British national security interests which Britain might be pursuing in the country.[20]

The committee structure has changed and evolved since 2003, but the position of the Chief of the Defence Staff has not. As with the earlier committees, the Chief of the Defence Staff attends the meetings of the National Security Council but is not formally a member. Since all these committees have been constitutionally subordinate to cabinet, there would be no challenge to political primacy if he were. Moreover, successive Chiefs of Defence Staff have discovered that the organisation of which they have nominally been the head possesses little of the capacity which Nott and Lewin gave it in 1982. When Field Marshal Sir Edwin (now Lord) Bramall became Chief of the Defence Staff in succession to Lewin he found an organisation in which 'the Defence Staff operated under the firm direction of the CDS, and the other chiefs were only brought in officially at a late stage to comment and amend if necessary'. He decided that 'the time was ripe to commission a series of staff studies to form the basis of a Chiefs-driven review of strategy'.[21] So for an all-too-brief couple of years Britain enjoyed both the instrument to develop strategy, a proper defence staff, and a body of senior officers with the appetite for it. It did not last. In the wake of the 1983 general election, Michael Heseltine was appointed Nott's successor as defence minister, and set out both to strengthen the powers of the minister through the appointment of a 2nd Permanent Under-Secretary and to create an office of management and budget at the heart of the process to decide the shape and size of the armed forces. His aim was to 'function-alise' the defence staff and to weaken the service departments. The defence staff became a joint civil–military body, chaired by both the Chief of the Defence Staff and the ministry's senior civil servant, the Permanent Under-Secretary. The arrangements worked well enough in the comparatively peaceful context of the later stages of the Cold War and its immediate aftermath. However, the long-term consequence of the joint body's creation was the professional emasculation of the chiefs of staff as a strategic advisory body and the elevation of financial management over military thought. Initially this trend was held in check by the balanced structures put in place by Bramall, not least because the Chiefs of Staff Committee 'remained firmly above the Defence Staff as the final arbiter of advice tendered to the CDS'.[22] However, the 1994–5 defence review effectively displaced the strategic planning function of the defence staff in favour of management processes by dismantling Bramall's arrangements and putting the senior civil servants in a commanding position. General Sir Charles (now Field Marshal Lord) Guthrie, Chief of the Defence Staff from 1997 to 2001, exercised an influence over Tony Blair, which relied on his personality and on the newness of the prime minister to office.[23] The new structure failed, as Bramall had anticipated it might,[24] when confronted with protracted and significant operations after 2003. 'The chiefs of staff', a former Foreign Secretary, Douglas Hurd, wrote on 18 May 2006, 'lack the public authority that they once exercised'.[25] With the defence staff reduced in numbers and capacity, such political leverage as the chiefs of staff possessed devolved to the proportionately larger single service staffs, which – particularly in the army's case – became more vocal. Bramall had seen the Chiefs of Staff Committee as the power base of the Chief of the Defence Staff. 'Without it, the CDS is little more than the head of a purely bureaucratic structure subject to political manipulation.'[26] Without it, the Chief of the Defence Staff also found himself robbed of the capacity to develop strategy.

Neither of those who followed Guthrie, Admiral Sir Michael (now Lord) Boyce and General Sir Mike (now Lord) Walker, was allowed to have much impact on Blair or the development of strategy. Gordon Brown's relationship with the service chiefs was distant. That of his successor, David Cameron, is not, in the sense that, like Blair, he is actively involved in defence and foreign policy, even if, unlike Blair, he has in the National Security Council a proper forum for its direction. But what Cameron does not seem to recognise is that professional judgement may run counter to political priorities, and that these clashes need to be confronted and debated, not denied. When in 2011 the First Sea Lord, Admiral Sir Mark Stanhope, gave it as his view that the fleet 'could not continue the Libya campaign without harming other naval operations', he was voicing exactly the professional opinion required of his office; his reward was to be summoned to see the prime minister, and the next day

No. 10 issued a statement saying that the First Sea Lord 'agreed that we can sustain this mission as long as we need to'. As David Cameron is reported to have told General Sir David Richards, the Chief of the Defence Staff since 2010, 'you do the fighting, I'll do the talking'.[27]

The gap which opened between the Ministry of Defence, fighting inter-departmental battles in Whitehall, and the operational direction of war in Iraq and Afghanistan, was one of the key deficits exposed in Britain's conduct of war after 2003. But it was not addressed in the report on the ministry commissioned from Lord Levene by the Cameron government in 2010, and delivered in 2011. If the Levene report considered strategy, it did so in the sense of the business school; if it employed the word 'strategy', it did so without precision or clarity, and certainly without an understanding of its place in military thought. The best that can be said is that the Chief of the Defence Staff managed to claw back some of his powers in the making of strategy, through the Chiefs of Staff Committee and through the appointment of a Deputy Chief of Defence Staff (Operations), but while the former sits below both the newly formed Defence Board and the Defence Staff in the ministerial hierarchy it will never have the influence or role in making strategy that it enjoyed in (say) the Second World War, and strategy itself will not drive the work of the ministry.

The arrangements in place by 2012 had put a massive burden on the shoulders of the Chief of the Defence Staff. He is the only uniformed officer on the Defence Board, and he also enjoys an increasingly defined role in the inter-departmental groups which function below ministerial level. In 2003 the most important of these, and the obvious hub in the making of strategy, was the Defence and Overseas Secretariat of the Cabinet Office. The proliferation of such groups in the latter years of the Labour government, and the ensuing confusion, with consequences for the lines of communication and of authority,[28] have at least been offset since 2010 by the coordinating and streamlining effects of the National Security Council's creation. However, the National Security Council still fails to address issues of central significance, including – extraordinarily – the reduction and restructuring of the British army in the process known as Army 2020, and instead prioritises the short-term and operational over the long-term and strategic. The role of Britain's National Security Adviser has been defined in terms that reflect less the potential implicit in the title and more the functions of coordination and facilitation. His secretariat is under-resourced, deprived of specifically military expertise and unable to shape the agendas of the principal government departments to fulfil the needs of an inter-departmental national security strategy. Where inter-departmental working has flourished, it has done so principally through improved bilateral relationships, especially between the Ministry of Defence and the Foreign and Commonwealth Office. Despite the recognition of the links between external and internal security through the conduct of counter-terrorism, much remains to be done in the integration of those two departments with the Home Office. The small numbers of service personnel and civil servants involved in defence policy at the centre have at least meant that personal links and the familiarity of shared experience act as lubricants, so minimising the consequences of institutional confusion. But that does not address the issue of strategy as process: strategy is a matter of implementation as well as of planning, and that happens on the ground as much as in the capital.

Even if America and Britain were clearer about strategy as a concept, they would still not be able to say definitively which governmental body makes strategy. This second question is, in the first instance, a matter of civil–military relations. The principal purpose of effective civil–military relations is national security: its output is strategy. Democracies tend to forget that. They have come to address civil–military relations not as a means to an end, not as a way of making the state more efficient in its use of military power, but as an end in itself. Instead the principal objective, to which others become secondary, has been the subordination of the armed forces to civil control.

The legacy of Britain's so-called 'glorious revolution' of 1688 has cast a long shadow in the English-speaking world. James II of England (and VII of Scotland) was ousted by a military coup, but thereafter – in the received wisdom – the British army has remained subordinate to parliamentary authority. The British practice was in reality different, with the boundaries between the soldier and the politician frequently confused, and with soldiers often ready to speak 'truth to power' without any sense of constitutional impropriety. The United States is an heir of the same constitutional legacy, but has gone much further in its determination that reality should reflect theory. The issue of civilian control of the military animated Samuel P. Huntington's *The soldier and the state: the theory and practice of civil–military relations*, published in 1957, despite the fact that the United States (which was the principal object of his concerns) has never experienced a military coup.

Specific criticisms of *The soldier and the state*, both historical and theoretical, have been voiced in the years since its appearance.[29] However, it
has continued to set the standard in the field, not least in affecting the self-
perceptions of the United States armed forces themselves. Huntington
wrote against the background of the Cold War. He and others were
concerned about the implications for liberal and democratic values of the
maintenance of large military establishments in peacetime. 'The tension
between the demands of military security and the values of American
liberalism can, in the long run,' he wrote, 'be relieved only by the
weakening of the security threat or the weakening of liberalism.'[30] His
solution was to stress the division of labour between the military and the
state, and so to define military professionalism in terms of political
subordination and apolitical behaviour. 'Politics is beyond the scope of
military competence, and the participation of military officers in politics
undermines their professionalism, curtailing their professional competence, dividing the profession against itself, and substituting extraneous
values for professional values. The military officer must remain neutral
politically.'[31]

     The effect of Huntington's pronouncements – and even more of
his continuing influence – was to elevate a norm over the reality. What
Huntington termed 'objective civilian control' assumed the subordination of the military to political direction. He deemed the British chiefs of
staff of the Second World War to be 'good military men' precisely
because 'they supported the government decisions with which they disagreed'.[32] In practice effective civil–military relations rely on a dialogue.
Policy is ill conceived if it asks the armed forces to do things which are not
consistent with their capabilities or with the true nature of war.
Clausewitz's perceptiveness on this very point is too often overlooked.
Clausewitz's own norm stresses that war is an instrument of policy and
therefore appears entirely congruent with Huntington's. In reality it is
not. For a start, as Eliot Cohen has pointed out, if politics permeate
military life at every level, civil–military relations can never be as uncom-
plicated as Huntington's norm suggests.[33] Clausewitz himself, it is worth
recalling, was a deeply politicised officer, to the extent that in 1812 he
abandoned the service of his own state, Prussia, for that of Russia,
because he could not accept his king's policies. His description of what
his own norm means in practice is much more subtle than the simple
repetition of the aphorism that war is a true political instrument suggests.
The discussion of 'war as an instrument of policy' in book VIII, chapter 6B

of *On war* includes some pointed observations on good policy. 'If the policy is right, that is, if it achieves its end, it can only affect the war favorably – in the sense of that policy. Where this policy deviates from the end, the cause is to be sought only in a mistaken policy.' In other words policy must recognise and be in harmony with war's true nature. 'It is only when policy promises itself a wrong effect from certain military means and measures, an effect opposed to their nature, that it can exercise a harmful effect on war by the course it prescribes.'[34]

Policy which sees war simply as an instrument but fails to understand the nature of the instrument is bad policy. Strategy is therefore the product of the dialogue between politicians and soldiers, and its essence is the harmonisation of the two elements, not the subordination of one to the other. This is much more evident in war than before it. 'The decision whether to use force is binary', Peter Feaver has written, 'while the decision how to use force is a continuum.'[35] The Weinberger and Powell doctrines set the conditions for going to war. Strategy at this point is a unilateral business, largely unaffected by the reactions of the putative enemy. They went on to assume that the war itself should not affect the objectives for which the war was being waged. But war is a reciprocal activity which itself shapes the war's outcomes. Strategy in war is a process. The issue now is not that of overall political direction, but of coherence between policy, military capabilities and the events on the ground. Civilian interference in war is not the evil that Powell portrayed, but nor is the assertion of clear military priorities: the true evil in war is the inability to hammer out how the two are to be reconciled.

Clausewitz's chapter went on to recommend that the commander-in-chief should be a member of the cabinet. Mature states between 1871 and 1945 recognised the force of this, creating bodies which united political heads and military chiefs and brought them together round the same table. Britain in 1902 established the Committee of Imperial Defence as an advisory body of the cabinet. Between then and the outbreak of the First World War the Committee of Imperial Defence acted as a forum within which ministers and professional service chiefs, chaired by the prime minister, could thrash out matters of national security in conditions of equality and open debate. Service members were permanent members of the committee, not 'in attendance'.[36] As Julian Corbett wrote in 1911, in the making of strategy 'conference is always necessary', and, he went on, 'for conference to succeed there must be a common vehicle of expression and a common plane of thought'.[37] Britain had the institutional framework within which strategic theory could confront what Corbett called 'the higher responsibilities of the imperial service' to produce strategy in practice.

In 1914, with the outbreak of the First World War, the functions of the Committee of Imperial Defence were usurped by the cabinet, precisely because the main, if not the sole, business of the state was now waging war. Even in major war, cabinet government was not the best instrument for formulating strategy: there were too many competing voices, too many ministers whose departments had no direct stake in the conduct of war, and too little representation for the views of the armed services themselves: crucially the First Sea Lord and the Chief of the Imperial General Staff were not members. In December 1916 the incoming prime minister, David Lloyd George, created a war cabinet, whose select membership was charged solely with the war, and whose meetings were attended by the service chiefs. Its meetings may not have been harmonious but they worked. The clashes between 'frocks' and 'brasshats', civilians and soldiers, produced a strategy that led to victory, and debate was therefore constructive, however fiery.

Churchill rejected the option of a war cabinet in the Second World War, despite the advice of its principal progenitor in the First, Maurice Hankey. But he treated the Chiefs of Staff Committee as a source of strategic advice, and it is with good reason that the statue in Whitehall of its chairman between 1942 and 1945, Alan Brooke, bears the words 'master of strategy' on its plinth. As Brooke's diaries make plain, the relationships between the prime minister and his chiefs of staff could be just as fraught as those between Lloyd George and his, but effective compromises were forged from these clashes. Brooke's frustrations did not lead the military to topple the prime minister but they did shape strategy. Importantly, the frictions of the Churchill government never became the stuff of public debate (at least at the time) in the way that those of Lloyd George's did. This may explain why the war cabinet model could be seen as dispensable. It has left no institutional legacy in Britain. Seen as at best an ad hoc creation, designed for wars which were discrete and major events, it rested on the presumption of 'total' war. True, the model was revived in Britain by Margaret Thatcher as recently as 1982, when its principal strategic adviser was the Chief of the Defence Staff, Sir Terence (later Lord) Lewin. Tony Blair did not really resuscitate the idea for any of his wars. In 2003 an 'ad hoc' war cabinet was created but it met infrequently and it seems to have had little practical effect. The prime minister realised that the full cabinet was not an appropriate body for the making of strategy, not least because two of its members, the Foreign Secretary Robin Cook and the Development Minister Clare Short, were deeply opposed to the war on which he had resolved to embark, but his solution was effectively to dispense with formal structures entirely, opting instead for so-called 'sofa government'. In the words of one victim of this approach, Sir Hilary Synnott, who took on the running of southern Iraq after the invasion, 'a small team within Number 10 Downing Street' gave 'broad policy direction but all too often based, it seemed, on inadequate study of the consequences'.[38]

So effective did the British hold on strategy appear during the Second World War that the United States came to believe that its own conduct of the war had been subverted by superior British institutions. The postponement of the second front in northern Europe until 1944, and America's contribution first in North Africa and then in Italy, were interpreted not as the products of common sense (which they were) but as the results of American political naivety when confronted by British adroitness. The result was the creation in the United States of the National Security Council in 1947. As with the Committee of Imperial Defence and then the war cabinet in Britain, here was the answer to the question as to where in America strategy was made. Unlike Britain's wartime institutions, the American arrangement still holds – or at least nominally so. Made up of the appropriate ministers, supported by intelligence chiefs and able to draw on service advice, the National Security Council exists to make strategy, to align policy with operational capabilities. But in the cases of Afghanistan and Iraq it did not. 'The normal planning procedures were marginalized', in the words of Seymour Hersh. 'Careful preliminary studies under the control of the National Security Council and the Joint Chiefs of Staff' were bypassed, in favour of what Hersh called '"under VFR direct" – that is, under visual flight rules, an air-traffic controllers' term for proceeding with minimal guidance'.[39] The clashes and the competition between the State Department and the Department of Defense, like those between the Joint Chiefs of Staff and CENTCOM, were not reconciled: strategy fell through the cracks.

The reasons for this go beyond the styles of government favoured by Bush and Blair (although they are undoubtedly important). Just as important was the change in the character of war. The war cabinet and the National Security Council were responses to what, at the time, was called 'total war', and what today's commentators increasingly call 'major war'. Huntington's norm rested on the same expectation, the fear that the Cold War might become hot. If war were to come, it would be a matter of national survival – or national extinction. It would require the mobilisation of all the resources of the state, and its conduct would be the principal function of government. The dilemma which *The soldier and the state* confronted was the need to have the capacity for such a war while living in conditions of peace.

Models of civil–military relations have been revised since the end of the Cold War (and this was what effected significant change in the character of war, not the attacks of 9/11 in 2001), but their drift has been to reassert norms, albeit in fresh ways. In 2003 Peter Feaver imposed 'agency theory' on what he called the 'civil–military problematique', the latter meaning that the military must be strong enough to do their job of protecting society without themselves being a danger to the civil liberties of society itself. He argued that before the 1990s the military in the United States accepted its subordination to political direction, aware of the punishment for not doing so after Harry S. Truman's dismissal of General Douglas MacArthur in 1951. In the 1990s – its attitudes shaped by the Weinberger and Powell doctrines – it became much more vocal, and much more effective, in setting the terms for its employment. Broadly speaking this behaviour, at least until the Kosovo War of 1999, resulted in a reluctance to use force, rather than the reverse. Changes since 1999 have largely been attributed to the change in president, George W. Bush not having to struggle to assert his credentials as commander-in-chief in the same way as did Bill Clinton – seen by one air force general as 'gay-loving, pot-smoking, draft-dodging, and womanizing'.[40] Feaver and, even more specifically, Eliot Cohen in *Supreme command* argued that civilians must trust their own judgements, that they must assert themselves over the military and that they have the right to be wrong.

What seemed sensible in 2002–3, when Feaver and Cohen published their books, looked less so by 2006. H. R. McMaster's book on the war in Vietnam, *Dereliction of duty*, published in 1997, acquired fresh relevance.[41] It had excoriated the Secretary of Defense between 1961 and 1968, Robert McNamara, and his 'whiz kids' for their distrust of the military, but it also criticised the Joint Chiefs of Staff for not stating what they believed with more force and clarity. Like McNamara, Rumsfeld became the fall guy for a war gone wrong, but as in Vietnam the Joint

Chiefs stand accused of collusion, at least by failing to state their position with more directness. Common to both conflicts is the issue of how to make strategy in the course of a war. Revisions to the Huntingtonian model of civil–military relations, as well as the Huntington model itself, need to do much more to take on board wars of different characters, even if that means paying less attention to the balance of domestic power within the United States.

There are at least three profound challenges for the inherited wisdom on civil–military relations in democratic states which the changes in the character of war since 1990 pose. First, and probably most importantly, the clear distinction between war and peace which prevailed in the era of so-called 'total war' has been eroded. Since 1990 America's and Britain's forces have been engaged in various forms of conflict, virtually without pause. Yet neither has been a state formally at war in the sense that both were in the two world wars. Most citizens have conducted their daily lives as though their countries have been at peace. They have been affected by these conflicts indirectly through the media but in most cases not directly – since the burdens of war have been borne by professional armed forces drawn from a small sector of society, and in some cases only by special forces.

Secondly, and relatedly, these have been conflicts which have been, in the current jargon, 'asymmetric' and increasingly 'hybrid'. Both are profoundly misleading descriptors since all war is potentially 'asymmetric', in that an intelligent opponent should try to maximise the enemy's vulnerability rather than play to their strength, and much in any war is made up of activity that is 'hybridised'. The very use of the term 'asymmetric' has reflected the weakness of war's conceptual vocabulary, happier as it is with major war than with small wars. Asymmetric war lacks either definition or clarity, embracing low intensity conflict, guerrilla war, terrorism, insurgency and even, at times, peace-keeping and peace-enforcement. Similarly it is unclear whether 'hybrid wars' are those which occupy some middle point in the spectrum between regular and irregular, or whether they are characterised by simultaneous activity on both ends of that spectrum. Asymmetry and hybridisation have become catch-alls applied to any war in which the two sides have not been made up of armies organised and equipped on similar lines. In this context, it is worth remembering that the opening phases of the war in Iraq were to that extent 'symmetrical', even if the balance of forces was not.

The effect of the declining incidence of major war on the exercise of command is profound – and the third relevant change in war's character. In the two world wars, corps commanders were responsible for bodies of, say, 30,000 men but could take decisions devoid of direct political consequences. This was the notion of the operational level of war which inspired the American and British armies when the Cold War ended and which fostered both the concept of manoeuvre war and institutions like the ARRC. The overarching structure of civil—military relations and the exercise of strategy were immaterial in such contexts. Even during the first half of the twentieth century there was a shift in the level at which the command of combined arms was exercised, from the corps down to the division, itself very often a reflection of defensive and even static intent rather than offensive and mobile war. Since 1990, that shift has progressed even lower, to the brigade, although paradoxically its justification has not been tactical defence, but flexibility and rapid deployment. At its most absurd the prevalence of operations of low intensity has given rise to the tautology of 'the strategic corporal'. Corporals do not shape strategy by intention, although they can by neglect and abuse – as the Abu Ghraib and Camp Breadbasket cases showed in the cases of the US and British armies respectively. What is true, and this is what Tommy Franks was reacting to, is that politicians wish to establish direct controls at lower levels of command and the improvement in real-time communications enables them to do so. As a result the Huntingtonian model of civil—military relations is increasingly proving to be profoundly at odds with the practice of war in the twenty-first century. It creates a clash between the theory and what happens in practice.

The theory says that the military is subordinate to political control. The professional soldier's traditional justification for being left to run the war untrammelled by politicians does not reject the idea that war is a political instrument. It just says that the politics can be left to one side until the victory is delivered. When the soldier says that, he implies not only that the politician should stay clear of his business, but also that policy is not part of the soldier's business. Each has his own sphere of responsibility: these were exactly the positions adopted by General Ricardo Sanchez and Ambassador Paul Bremer in Iraq in 2003–4. But the military, which wages war in 'rogue states' or 'failed states', and so builds new states, is shaping and even formulating policy as it fights. Politics have the potential to permeate all military action, but in conflicts like those waged in Iraq and Afghanistan war and policy are even more deeply intertwined.

The theory goes on to assume that, when the military is subordinate to political control, the control is itself exercised by the nation state. Since the Second World War, that has in general been true for the United States, but it has not been so for its allies. Between 1945 and 1990 this did not matter too much as the coalitions themselves had an institutional authority, which conferred continuity on civil–military relations and legitimacy on the use of force. Globally the United Nations has been the expression of this view; if the allies did not go to war in self-defence, they went to war under the authority of a UN resolution. Regionally, NATO fulfilled elements of the same function, at least until the end of the Cold War. The latter has confronted its most severe extra-European test in Afghanistan. Since 1990, however, practice has made both collective institutions increasingly peripheral. American actions are essentially unilateral, however much Washington may seek to validate them through 'coalitions of the willing'. When, in the aftermath of the 9/11 attacks, NATO invoked Article 5 of its charter, thus calling into play the principle of collective self-defence, the United States did not respond. Unsurprisingly, when the United States in turn looked to NATO to endorse its 'long war' strategy in 2006, at first it found little echo. Its own actions had played their part in robbing alliances of their robustness, with the result that the old organisations for the use and management of military force looked less suited to new political conditions. When NATO assumed responsibility for the mission in Afghanistan, many predicted that failure there would mean the collapse of the alliance. One of the more remarkable developments between 2006 and 2012 was that NATO looked more robust, rather than less so. In Afghanistan it was supported by a phalanx of associated powers and overcame its initial division of the country into a collection of regional fiefdoms operating under different rules of engagement. In Libya in 2011 it provided the headquarters to direct the campaign even with the United States taking a back seat. To be sure, Britain had 'gapped' too many NATO staff jobs, and not all powers – particularly Germany – responded to the demand for intervention, despite the sanction of a UN Security Council resolution. However, the effect of experiencing these deficiencies has been salutary and, it would seem, beneficial for the long-term health and development of the alliance.

The dominance of alliance warfare does not in itself change the norm of military subordination to political control. Indeed it should enhance it, as the commander of an alliance force is less free to plead his independence of national control on the grounds that he owes his greater loyalty to the coalition – an argument used in Britain's case by General Sir John Hackett as commander-in-chief of the British Army of the Rhine and of NATO's Northern Army Group in 1967 and by Lieutenant General Sir Michael Rose as UNPROFOR commander in Bosnia in 1994–5. An American general, Wesley Clark, was able to exploit a similar duality of allegiance when Supreme Allied Commander Europe in 1999. But the generals find themselves between a rock and a hard place. The notion of the national use of force outside the context of self-defence has lost legitimacy, particularly in Europe. The United States may see this reaction as a failure to recognise Hobbesian realities; Europeans see it as a response to the devastation of two world wars. Thus 'expeditionary war', waged at a distance for causes which do not seem immediately to impinge on the national interest, threatens the domestic political standing of the forces that implement that policy – or at least that is the forces' fear. This is where Huntington's norm of 'objective' political control clashes with his alternative model of 'subjective' control – the idea that armed forces acquire political legitimacy from their association and integration with society at large. In *The soldier and the state*, the professional soldier is separate from society; it is the more politicised conscript who reflects the society from which he is drawn and who therefore remains loyal to it. Undoubtedly, today's professional soldiers in America and Britain retain many of the characteristics which Huntington's notion of objective control ascribes to them: they take pride in doing their job well, and they can be put in harm's way by their governments with greater impunity than conscripts could be. However, they are not as untouched by links to wider society as the Huntingtonian norm suggests. Ultimately society is the source of their recruits, and its approbation and endorsement – not least through the media – validate what they do. In 2012 Britain's plan for military reform, Army 2020, specifically sought to align the army more closely with society; two decades previously, when attacked for its failure to integrate women, homosexuals and ethnic minority recruits, it had asserted its 'right to be different'.

Popular consent for the war in Iraq, uncertain in Britain from the outset, wavered in the United States in its later stages. The publics of both states were asked to endorse the professionalism and dedication of their armed forces while disapproving of the wars they were being told to wage. By and large they did so. In other words mass opinion is sufficiently sophisticated to distinguish between the soldier and his qualities on the one hand, and the cause for which he fights and perhaps dies on the other. But this tension is not necessarily sustainable in the long term, any more than it is desirable in the short term. Ultimately the bereaved families of those killed or wounded in combat seek the comfort that the cause in which they suffer is a good one. Nobody knows this better than the American army, which took two decades and more to slough off the legacy of Vietnam. For Britain, it has been a new phenomenon.

Caught in a potential cross-fire between their governments and their peoples, between 'objective' control and 'subjective' control, how do armed forces react? Their immediate response, which conforms to the requirements of objective control, is to ask the public to support the war, and so to suspend criticism of government policy until after the war is over. British opinion has tended to do this anyway. Support for the war in Iraq soared when British troops were first committed: it was unpatriotic to oppose a war for which soldiers were putting their lives at risk. But latent here was a threat to democracy, freedom of speech and the politics of accountability. The 'wars of choice', waged by the United States and Britain since 1990, cannot be treated as the existential wars of national survival fought between 1914 (or 1917) and 1918, and 1939 (or 1941) and 1945. Those who opposed the administrations of George Bush or Tony Blair also opposed at least some of their policies, potentially including the war in Iraq. The longer the war and the more elusive the decision, the greater was the difficulty for debate to disaggregate the issue of why the nation was at war from the manner in which it was fought. Differences over the war's conduct cannot be suspended in the name of bi-partisan politics, if it comes at the cost of legitimate criticism and – possibly – at the price of more effective strategy. Those armed forces which remain loyal to the norm of 'objective control' in an unpopular war put at risk the benefits of 'subjective control', the links – however thin they may at times seem to be for professional armies – which unite the forces to the people. The forces fear being tarred with the brush of a failed government policy.

Scandals like those perpetrated at Abu Ghraib and Camp Breadbasket therefore become of disproportionate importance to civil–military relations. They strain at the threads of subjective control. The armed forces' response in the early stages of the Iraq War was to ask for exceptions and revisions to the laws of armed conflict. In Britain in 2005 retired officers, including two former Chiefs of Defence Staff who had served under the Labour government, Lords Guthrie and Boyce, publicly voiced their disquiet concerning the laws of war and their application. War, they reminded the newspapers (not unreasonably), is a matter of life and death, where split-second decisions have to be made, and whose strains can promote behaviour not condoned by peacetime expectations. The need to vent such views showed exactly the nature of the problem: those digesting them over their breakfast tables did not feel themselves or their nations to be at war, while the services needed them to be aware that they were. The imperative to revalidate the services in the eyes of the British public became so strong that in April 2006 the Secretary of State for Defence, Dr John Reid, called for a revision of the Geneva convention.[42] The demands of 'subjective' civil–military relations required the machinery of 'objective' control to be invoked.

These are palliatives and not very good ones. The Geneva convention and its subsequent protocols are perfectly adequate for the purposes which Dr Reid wished to address. One cannot help feeling this was the action of a government concerned less with assuaging public discontent with the behaviour of the armed forces than with appeasing the worries of the armed forces' senior ranks. Moreover, the simultaneous court martial of a medical officer of the RAF who refused to serve in Iraq on the grounds that the war was illegal raised a distinction in law which the public found harder to sustain in morality. The officer was convicted of disobeying a legal order; his defence cited the principle, established at Nuremberg in the trials of German war criminals, that superior orders were not in themselves a defence in mitigation of a war crime. The legal argument rested on the disciplinary good order of the service; the moral argument raised the issue of the war's legitimacy in the eyes of the public. The first was being challenged, and potentially undermined, by the latter.[43]

More high profile was the effect of an interview given to Sarah Sands of the *Daily Mail* by General Sir Richard Dannatt on 10 October 2006. Dannatt, who had been in post as Chief of the General Staff for less than three months, was concerned that the army was 'running hot', and that the organisation for whose integrity and future capability he was responsible was in danger of being broken in a war in which he thought the British presence had become part of the problem. Dannatt was very conscious of the need for him to engage the media, partly because he feared that the unpopularity of the war in Iraq could adversely affect the army's own reputation, and partly because he recognised the need for the press to carry better informed comment.[44] The *Daily Mail* episode reflected badly both on the individuals involved and on the institutional framework within which they were operating. Dannatt's concerns for the army arose directly from his professional position, but they led him into seeming to trump the government's responsibility for the policy dimensions of strategy. He suggested in the interview that the British army would be out of Iraq by the end of 2007, a decision which the government had not reached, and a timetable which was out of kilter with American plans and with the intentions of British troops on the ground. In Washington, Britain's principal ally was about to increase – not reduce – its commitment to Iraq, and in Basra British commanders in theatre were trying to win the war in which they were engaged, albeit with inadequate resources. What was not so obvious at the time but was even more culpable than Dannatt's stance was the position of the British government. Britain was fighting a demanding campaign in the full glare of national attention but the prime minister, Tony Blair, had not been personally involved himself in Dannatt's appointment as chief and, even after the *Daily Mail* story broke, did not then meet him for another six weeks. The man who had agreed the Ministry of Defence's recommendation that Dannatt become Chief of the General Staff was Jonathan Powell, Blair's chief of staff, even if initially he had no memory of his having done so.

Jonathan Powell has since argued that generals want wars and politicians don't; in fact Dannatt's position was much closer to Colin Powell's when in 1992 he proved reluctant to use the United States army in Bosnia. Powell was also naïve in his assertion that what Dannatt was saying was in effect news to the government; it was not news to anybody who had his or her ear to the ground, and if those sorts of opinions had not reached the prime minister's office he clearly lacked an efficient machinery for the direction of strategy. What mattered was that they had been voiced by the head of the British army in a popular newspaper. But Powell was certainly right to say that 'the sort of surprise attack that Dannatt launched will make political leaders think twice if military action is proposed in future, certainly if the military engagement is likely to be sustained over a year or more. Our armed forces will no longer be deployed so regularly and will lose their cutting edge.'[45]

This is the tightrope which the chiefs of staff have to walk. Their services are trained for war, and respond positively to its challenges; they do not want to be consigned to a career set entirely by a training cycle. Indeed they need operational experience to make them effective – just as much as that same experience exhausts personnel and equipment, putting strains on service families and resulting in death and disablement for some personnel. An army which lacks a 'can do' mentality and feels it cannot use its capabilities to good effect is not of any value to the state which pays for it. Richard Dannatt was not opposed to sending the army to war, but he wanted it used in Afghanistan, not Iraq. It lacked the means to do both at once, and the former, not the latter, was the 'good' war.

Since 2006, the story of British civil–military relations has therefore developed a further twist. The army that went to Helmand in that year was not ready for what hit it; politicians may have addressed the possible effects with seeming insouciance, but the army itself looked too keen to give itself a new mission. It went to Afghanistan ill prepared – not just in force strengths and equipment levels, but also intellectually and culturally. As British soldiers found themselves in desperate fire-fights around 'safe houses', robbed of the power to manoeuvre and stirring up an opposition which, if present, had previously been latent, they blamed the politicians for their travails. However, by 2010 some began to question this narrative, pointing to the army's own optimism and to its determination to find a war to justify its existence – not least in terms of primacy in relation to the other two armed services. Sustained in a series of articles by Deborah Haynes and Tom Coghlan in *The Times*, it was a theme developed in 2011 by Frank Ledwidge, a naval reservist who had been deployed as a lawyer, and Sir Sherard Cowper-Coles, who served both as Britain's ambassador in Kabul between 2007 and 2009, and as the Foreign Secretary's special representative to Afghanistan and Pakistan between 2009 and 2010. Ledwidge accused senior officers of making a virtue of doing too much with too little, of taking pride in 'punching above your weight', and of using courage and improvisation to make good on poor planning.[46] For Cowper-Coles, the British army in 2008 was anxious to increase its numbers in Afghanistan in order to avoid losing them in the next defence review, which all the armed forces knew would follow the 2010 election, if not before. In his view the army was responsible for the expansion of the campaign and then complained when the personnel and equipment to fight it were not forthcoming.[47]

Since publishing his book his accusations have become wilder and less discreet, charging the army with deploying 'spurious' arguments and with submitting to ministers 'papers that were incurably optimistic'.[48] Senior officers have not been as vocal or as indiscreet in their reactions, although the three most senior, the Chief of the Defence Staff, General Sir David Richards, the Vice-Chief, General Sir Nick Houghton, and the Chief of the General Staff, General Sir Peter Wall, all used the opportunity provided by the requirement to give evidence to the House of Commons Defence Committee to blame others – both the Foreign and Commonwealth Office within the United Kingdom and the United States military.[49]

There are true and fair points on both sides of the argument. Cowper-Coles is right when he identifies the current generation of soldiers as shrewd political operators who have managed to manipulate politicians who are both in thrall to their professional expertise and naïve about war. He is justified in his criticism of what he has called 'supply-side strategy', in other words that strategy becomes defined in terms of its means not its ends. And he is also right to say that the army was looking for a success in a 'good' war to make up for its lack in what the public saw as a bad one.[50] But his solution is not right. He quotes Eliot Cohen on the politician's right to be wrong, failing to note that that approach, Huntington updated, was the principle applied to the invasion of Iraq and also produced bad strategy. The simplistic model of military subordination to civilian control is one of the principal sources of our problems. As Ledwidge rightly points out, the 'normal' theory of civil–military relations allows generals to get on with what they are good at.[51] It relieves them of responsibility for what fails, very often even at the operational and tactical level, because they are able to pass the buck to the strategic direction they have received – or the lack of it. We are in danger of constructing a false polarity: in arguing that the problems of Afghanistan have been the product of enthusiastic generals 'cracking on', we denigrate the very professionalism that we need our armed forces to possess. Professional qualities have political effects by definition, and not just in war or in the armed forces: the same points apply to teachers or doctors or police officers. If the political effect of professional quality is disproportionate, that is because we have politicians who fail to understand how to provide the policy context and because we do not possess the institutions within which the two perspectives, military and political, can be integrated to produce strategy.

A new model of civil–military relations is required, and it has to reflect the changing character of war. It has to take into account four factors. First, today's wars are de facto wars, not wars in a strictly legal sense. They include 'operations other than war'; they are not necessarily, or even normally, preceded by a declaration of war; and they are conflicts in which frequently the parties are not state actors. Secondly, the conflicts may be of low intensity (an unsatisfactory label, if better than asymmetric), but are often persistent, continuous and simultaneous: they can involve national military commitments against different enemies in different theatres at the same time. Thirdly, those who do the fighting are cut off from society in general; they are voluntarily enlisted; they represent a society almost totally lacking in direct military experience of its own. Fourthly, that society's image of war is mediated by the press, and not just, or not even, the printed word, but by television, the internet and mobile telephones.

Paradoxically, we are not totally without signposts here, even if we have tended to ignore them, at least in this context. Paradoxically too, those signposts are themselves just as much the outgrowth of the Cold War and the 1950s as was Huntington's *The soldier and the state*.

The Malayan campaign has become a model of successful counter-insurgency. It has probably improved with the telling and it is not as apposite a model for application in Iraq as some current American enthusiasts suggest. The British were the colonial authority, not the invader. They relied on the ethnic division between Malays and Chinese to divide and rule. And they used methods, like the forcible resettlement of the population, which would be unacceptable today. But the corner-stone of the whole structure was the integration of civil and military authorities, not the subordination of the military to political control. Government, army and police worked together at every level of command; political decisions were taken by those cognisant of the military and operational realities; and intelligence was fully coordinated with operations and with policy. At its apex, General Sir Gerald Templer, like many nineteenth-century colonial governors before him, combined civil and military power in one man – and that man was a soldier, not a civilian.[52]

Clearly the Templer model is not simply and straightforwardly transferable to the wars of today. Moreover, Templer was of course ultimately accountable to an elected and civilian government in London. But this model focuses on the implementation of strategy, not its planning, on the issue of 'how', rather than on 'why'. It also introduces a principle, which suggests that we have been hoodwinked by a non-existent threat into endorsing a model of military subordination which is now unhelpful, and even self-defeating. The fear of tanks rumbling down Whitehall or parked on the lawn of the White House is not real. In Britain, as in the United States, the practices of good democracy are too well embedded for the military to undermine constitutional government. Indeed, such concerns as are voiced over the future of constitutional government revolve less around 'the man on horseback' than around the arrogation of presidential power and of prime ministerial authority. The principle which we need to embrace is that of civil–military integration, founded on the notions of equality in counsel and of harmonisation of effects. There is no merit in the government trying to endorse a policy through the use of war in countries like Iraq or Afghanistan if it does not possess the military capability to give it effect.

The application of the principle in practice cannot proceed without personal goodwill. Obviously, strong personal relations between civilians and soldiers, such as those between Thatcher and Lewin in the Falklands War, or between George Bush senior and Colin Powell in the first Gulf War, help. But the key is institutional, so that there is a default mechanism when personal relations are less good (and when there are no Lincolns or Churchills to hand). Current conflicts demand a range of expertise which spans several ministries, not just those intimately involved with defence. Foreign policy and reconstruction, aid and policing have to be integrated both in the plan of campaign and in the generation of the forces to fight it. The United States has such a mechanism in the National Security Council, but its political leaders and its theatre commanders have of late been determined to bypass it. Colin Powell, by then the Secretary of State, allegedly told the president after the fall of Baghdad in 2003 that 'the national security decision-making process was broken'.[53] Condoleezza Rice was marginalised as National Security Advisor in the decision-making process as the United States prepared for war in Iraq. Her office lacked in-house expertise on Iraq, and its ability to intervene was 'diminished by a series of resignations and reassignments, some of them said to be the result of internal bickering'.[54] General James Jones, when he was appointed National Security Advisor by President Obama, described the office he inherited as 'understaffed, under-resourced and deeply dysfunctional'. It did not improve on his watch: his deputy, Tom Donilon, who had no overseas or military experience, had direct access to the president and used it to vent his frustration with Jones, eventually supplanting him in October 2010.[55] In March 2004 the report of the Center for Strategic and International Studies on defence reform 'beyond Goldwater–Nichols' highlighted the issue of inter-agency cooperation and called for a new office in the National Security Council.[56]

Britain has the historical precedent of the war cabinet, but that body left no institutional legacy in government. In Washington, the turf wars between departments can become more influential than the real war. In London, the British government has struggled to integrate the Foreign Office, the Ministry of Defence and the Department for Foreign and International Development. Only with the publication of the first National Security Strategy in 2008 did Britain make a coherent effort to coordinate strategic planning. That first attempt was long on global threats but short on the defence of national interests; it was, according to the US diplomatic traffic revealed by Wikileaks, 'greeted with a collective yawn'. It reflected 'the Brown approach to government – lots of detail, ensuring all possible policy factors are identified before decisions are reached, focused on improving government process over articulating broad new strategies'.[57] Its 2010 successor was much better in that it took national security as its focus, but it still said more about process than about strategy. It was, however, given – through the creation of the National Security Council – a body charged with its execution.

Strategy depends on more than inter-departmental planning; it also – as Malaya demonstrated – requires inter-departmental execution on the ground. The establishment of Provincial Reconstruction Teams in Afghanistan in 2003 was a first step in this direction. In late 2004 the United Kingdom created the Post-Conflict Reconstruction Unit, an inter-departmental agency shared by the Foreign and Commonwealth Office, the Ministry of Defence and the Department for International Development, but in reality inadequately supported by each of them. By 2007 it had a staff of only thirty-four and a budget of £6 million.[58] It was strengthened and reconfigured in that year as the Stabilisation Unit. Bureaucratic battles in Whitehall, and the mutual incomprehension generated by different methods and philosophies, have given way to increasingly effective cooperation on the ground. Compromise between departments can be a strength, not a weakness. Committees may bring institutional clashes and differences into open forum, but they also enable an astute bureaucracy to garner collective wisdom, to harmonise different capabilities and to take on board collective truths as opposed to individual perceptions. They are also more consonant with democratic notions of collective accountability.

The issue of accountability also affects the armed services themselves. In the United States in the early 1990s the power of the Joint Chiefs of Staff created concerns for the balance in civil–military relations. A decade later, they had been bypassed or silenced – not only by Rumsfeld but also by their nominal subordinates: in one of his less profane utterances, Franks, anxious to meet the planning requirements of his political masters without taking on board the Joint Chiefs' proper concerns about force numbers and logistics, called them 'meddlesome bureaucrats'.[59] One suggestion, made in March 2004, was that the Department of Defense should integrate, where appropriate, the military staffs of the Joint Chiefs of Staff with their civilian counterparts in the Office of the Secretary of Defense.[60] In Britain too, the Chief of the Defence Staff needs to rediscover his voice in the formulation of strategy. The Levene reforms may not have addressed the issue of strategy directly, but they have at least reactivated the Chiefs of Staff Committee, albeit placed under the Defence Board and so removed from any direct relationship with the prime minister or even with their ministerial superiors of the sort which they enjoyed in the past. The Chief of the Defence Staff himself, by sitting on the Defence Board and attending the National Security Council, has the opportunity to make his view known. The question is whether the government wants to listen. In the lead-up to the Iraq War Britain's ministers were content simply to follow the lead of the United States, taking American ability to make strategy for granted and not paying attention to the caveats of their own military advisers. As far as the public was concerned, the services were silenced. The lobbying of the single service chiefs before 1982 created the opportunity for their civilian masters to divide and so rule them, but at least ensured that defence debates received a wider hearing. Since then they have undergone a massive loss of status and authority. Strategy is now joint; the single services' role is to provide capabilities rather than to shape the application of those capabilities.

Accountability is also a civilian matter. One way in which the American military has been heard has been through Congress. The Joint Chiefs have the power to present to Congress, whose historic duty is to provide for the 'common defense', and which holds the purse strings and retains the power to declare war. But the division of powers between president and Congress has been eroded by the failure to declare war in the cases of Kosovo, Afghanistan and Iraq, and as a result Congress has been increasingly marginalised.[61] In the words of a recent report: 'Congress is engaged in too much of the wrong kind of oversight – too few national debates on major issues and far too much time and energy spent on relatively minor and parochial issues.'[62] Many would say much the same of the British House of Commons. The brief of the House of Commons Select Committee on Defence has been massively widened since the creation of the defence and external affairs sub-committee of the Expenditure Committee in 1971, but it still labours under limitations which defy norms of democratic governance. In 1979 the Minister of Defence refused to permit civil servants or serving personnel to give the committee evidence on the Polaris nuclear missile replacement. This decision was only partially offset in 1980–1, when civil servants appeared before what had now become the Defence Committee: their obfuscating evidence was marked by a refusal to give straight answers to direct questions.[63] Confronted in 2006 with the issue of the Trident replacement (or more immediately the submarines in which Trident is carried), the Defence Committee found little had changed: the Ministry of Defence refused to give evidence.[64] The committee cannot consider strategy in the round when its powers both to enquire and to generate proper debate are so constrained. Not only should civil servants be required to appear if needed, so should military chiefs; indeed, they should be asked to give evidence on an annual basis as a matter of course.

Such steps would begin to address the challenges confronted not only by Huntington's model of objective control but also by that of subjective control. If the media is such a powerful tool in the debates on the use of military force, the armed forces need to cease behaving like rabbits caught in the headlights of an oncoming vehicle. They should not react as though they honestly believe that apolitical behaviour is the corollary of professionalism. Such responses reflect the power of the Huntingtonian norm, not of reality. The US armed forces lobby on Capitol Hill in a way which would affront British liberal norms, and the link between success in high command and the presidency runs through every 'existential' war the United States has fought, beginning with George Washington and the American War of Independence, and embracing Ulysses S. Grant and the Civil War, and Dwight D. Eisenhower and the Second World War. The recent behaviour of

Colin Powell and Wesley Clark give the lie to the notion current in the United States, that American generals lack political ambition, one having taken office in a Republican administration and the other having sought the Democrat nomination for the presidency.[65] In Britain, officers have not been so identified with partisan politics, but the tradition that they are therefore apolitical in a more general sense is an invented one, out of step with historical reality.[66]

However, the norm has had its own consequences for behaviour. One is the convention that professional armed forces should not speak to the press. Its results are in practice unhelpful or even destabilising. Unhelpful are the opinions of retired senior officers, out of touch with current events, and often reflecting not only the values of a bygone generation rather than of those currently in uniform, but also the wars in which they fought rather than the conflict at hand. Destabilising are those in uniform who express their views to the press despite regulations to the contrary. Such press comment does not help the services or the public. Senior serving officers who speak on a matter of policy while in uniform are believed to have done so because their subordination to political control requires them to promote the government's line, not to vent their professional opinion. More junior service personnel are casti-gated for breaking ranks and being uncommandable. In Britain in 1997 Major Eric Joyce's Fabian Society pamphlet on the army's personnel policies attracted attention not because of its content but because a serving officer had breached apolitical norms. Thus his proposals were not debated on their own merits. We cannot expect a sophisticated and informed discussion on the uses of military force, when the information in the public domain is partial, in both senses of the word.

Of course, the fault lies not solely with the government, the armed forces and the Huntingtonian norm. The British Ministry of Defence still seems too often to be reactive, rather than proactive, in its management of debate, but it is dealing with a press that has the con-centration span of a day, that deals in headlines more than in analysis. The key feature of the 'Army 2020' reforms announced in July 2012 was the division of the army into a contingency capability and an adaptable force; the principal questions that arose from the restructuring concerned the capacity to 'regenerate' (or 'mobilise' in more old-fashioned lan-guage), the disproportionate cuts in logistics, and the effects on – and buy-in from – the other two services. Little of this was reflected in the press which focused almost exclusively on the second-order consequences for infantry battalions and regimental titles. British newspapers no longer sustain military analysts of the stature of Basil Liddell Hart or Cyril Falls, to name those of the inter-war years, or, in the United States, of Michael Gordon of *The New York Times* or of Tom Ricks and Dana Priest of *The Washington Post* today. This is not to say that the press does not give a great deal of attention to matters of strategic concern. The wars in Iraq and Afghanistan have produced more headlines and resulted in greater sustained public attention to military affairs than at almost any period in living memory (or at least since 1945). In some respects, the public is as a result both concerned and well informed; the trick which still eludes the press that informs this awareness is the move to nuanced argument. Britain has some excellent war reporters (Jason Burke, for example) and some well-informed defence correspondents (like Richard Norton-Taylor, James Blitz, Tom Coghlan and Deborah Haynes). However, they are responsible for the news; it is their editors who generate the comment – and very rarely, if at all, do they ask those correspondents to produce that comment.

These prescriptions are not adequate to meet the diagnosis. The management of civil–military relations in democracies is not susceptible to easy solutions. In recognising the need to harmonise the relationship between soldiers and politicians, Eliot Cohen has spoken of an 'unequal dialogue'.[67] Peter Feaver talks of the 'blurry line between advising against a course of action and resisting civilian efforts to pursue that course of action'.[68] This chapter too is 'blurry', posing more questions than it has provided answers. But getting the questions right is the first step to finding the correct answers. For too long, at least fifty years, we have started this debate with the answer, not the question. We have tended to assume that the danger is a military coup d'état, when the real danger for western democracies today is the failure to develop coherent strategy. A revised system of civil–military relations would re-empower the constitutional controls on the executive, help reintegrate armed forces and society, and – most important of all – enable an approach to strategy appropriate to the norms of liberal democratic government.

5 STRATEGY AND THE LIMITATION OF WAR

On 22 January 2003 the US Secretary of Defense, Donald Rumsfeld, angered by France and Germany's reluctance to embrace the war on Iraq, characterised them as the states of 'old Europe'. Those more familiar with the history of the continent were quick to point out that a refusal to go to war was in fact a truer reflection of 'new Europe'. In the first half of the twentieth century 'old Europe' had been far too quick to fight, with dire consequences for its member nations in 1914–18 and 1939–45, and as a result it had created institutions in the second half of the century, most obviously the European Union, designed precisely to prevent that eventuality. Rumsfeld's utterances have become the stuff of satire, but in this case we need to dig a bit deeper. However deficient his tact, however flawed his diplomacy and however inadequate his grasp of history, Rumsfeld had hit an exposed nerve. For Europeans, who grew up not only with the legacy of the two world wars but also in the shadow of the Cold War, the norm that war can be an instrument of policy, however compelling its apparent logic, is counter-intuitive.

The mix of the rational with the visceral in this opening paragraph is itself instructive. Because there was no war in Europe, Europeans became used to the idea that war itself had no utility. Even those, who, thinking historically, accepted that war against Adolf Hitler was justified, pulled back from embracing war against Leopoldo Galtieri or Slobadan Milosević. The incredulity which greeted the outbreak of war in 1982, when Britain fought to regain the Falkland Islands from Argentina, or in 1999, when NATO used air power to coerce Serbia over Kosovo, was not necessarily inspired by pacifism. Pacifists, however strident and impassioned their tone, also use powerfully articulated arguments. The overwhelming response was more emotional: it was one of surprise, even of shock. The dominant instrument of Cold War strategic thought, deterrence, had created the assumption that real wars were things of the past, not of policy.

The years since the end of the Cold War, and particularly since the 9/11 attacks of 2001, have therefore been ones of re-education for Europeans. Armed conflict has become much more frequent. The phrase 'new wars' (whether they are really new or not) and the doctrine of humanitarian intervention are both ways of making the frequency of war comprehensible and even logical for liberal middle classes accustomed to the norms of peace. But this process has not removed the sense of fear. This trepidation in regard to the use of war is not just a matter of war's casualties, of its destructiveness and its loss of life. It is an anxiety as to its political consequences. The great powers of the nineteenth century, for all that they may not be the great powers of the twenty-first, have not lost the habits of mind which gave them that status in the first place. The Duke of Wellington told the Military Secretary, Lord Fitzroy Somerset (who as Lord Raglan would command the British expeditionary force in the Crimean War in 1854), on the occasion of the 1838 rebellion in Canada: 'There is no such thing as a *little war* for a great Nation'.[1] He recognised the opportunity for exploitation given to lesser powers by the embroilment of a great power in armed conflict, and he also – and in consequence – appreciated the possibility of a small war escalating into a big one. Having been born in the eighteenth century, Wellington was only too well aware of how for Britain two wars in North America, the Seven Years War (1756–63) and the War of American Independence (1776–83), had both acquired European dimensions. Moreover, having won both his reputation and his title in the Napoleonic Wars, he also knew how a series of independent and self-contained conflicts, with different participants and with potentially independent conclusions, could merge into one larger and seemingly united struggle.

Wellington's admonition appeared particularly relevant in the summer of 2006. As Israel sought to escalate its confrontation with the Palestinians in Gaza to the south, it also resolved to tackle Hizbollah by invading Lebanon to the north. The reaction of two 'great powers', the United States and the United Kingdom, was not to restrain Israel but to let its armed forces have their head. Two separable conflicts, waged at opposite ends of the Israeli state, were conflated into one existential crisis. For Israel, unlike Europe, war had not lost its utility: its survival as an independent state had depended on its readiness to fight. But by 2006 what had been a genuine reason for war between 1948 and 1967 had now, in the eyes of some commentators, become a cover for colonialism. Israel had reacted disproportionately because it was seeking to expand its territory to its 'natural frontiers'. The rhetoric emanating from Tel Aviv in 2006 was that of escalation, not of limitation. Small-scale but persistent terrorist attacks were answered with the full conventional capabilities of the Israeli Defence Force, and Israel's posture was linked to global threats not just to regional ones. On the one hand this was a war 'to restore deterrence': the strategic theory of the Cold War was being used to justify war, not – as in the Cold War itself – to prevent it. On the other it was part of the US-led global war on terror. Conspiracy theorists, already sure that US foreign policy was too much in thrall to Israel, detected an effort by American neo-conservatives to re-launch their programme to reconfigure the Middle East. Finding their plan to establish Iraq as a democratic state checked, at least for the time being, they had now hatched a fresh plot. The way out of the Iraq imbroglio was not for US forces to withdraw from the region but to redirect and refurbish US policy by fashioning Israeli victories over its neighbours. Conflating, not containing, the conflicts of the Middle East would enable the Bush administration to maximise American power and so conjure success where regional defeat had seemed inevitable.

Once the fears that one small crisis could link with another took root, the scale of the possible conflagration grew. Those who in the Cold War would have expected containment now anticipated escalation. Europeans worked to defuse the tensions in the United States's relationship with Iran. America's readiness to use war as an instrument of policy did not seem to have been curtailed by the apparent failure of that policy in Iraq. Washington's apparent desire to confront Tehran, and Iran's refusal to be coerced, meant that the arc of conflict threatened to spread from the Middle East to central Asia, from the shores of the Mediterranean to the borders of Afghanistan. This geopolitical game (if that is not too trivial a word) having been put in motion, it was hard to see where its domino effect would stop. From Afghanistan to Pakistan, from Pakistan to India, animosities and tensions which were being contained regionally could be stoked when set against the broader backgrounds of super-power interests, 'clashes of civilisation' and religious fundamentalism.

Since 2006 the Middle East has not ceased to be a potential flash point for the aggregation of different conflicts, for the convergence of potentially separable struggles. For some time commentators have been saying that, if there is to be a Third World War, this is where it will break out. There are potential parallels. The world wars of the twentieth century did not necessarily begin as world wars; that was what they became. In July 1914 the Balkans served the function which the Middle East seemed poised to fulfil in 2006. Like Israel, Austria-Hungary believed that terrorism confronted it with a wider existential threat. As a multinational empire, it was a potential victim of irredentist nationalism, and it therefore took the opportunity of the murder of the heir apparent by Bosnian nationalists to launch what it hoped would be a limited war against their sponsors, Serbia. As it did so, it enjoyed the backing of a great power, Germany, but it did not give sufficiently serious thought to the possible expansion of the war on which it proposed to embark. It certainly did not imagine that, as a consequence of its actions, Japan would take the opportunity to seize Tsingtao, the German colony on the Shantung peninsula, and would use its victory there as the basis for imperialism both on the Chinese mainland and in the Pacific. Japan was not the only power to join what we now call the First World War for regional objectives. In Constantinople the Young Turks saw it as an opportunity for the Ottoman empire to throw off its subordination to great power control. In entering an alliance with Germany and Austria-Hungary, they were anxious not to remake the map of Europe but to create a regional security structure for the Balkans, by forging an alliance with Romania and Bulgaria in order to isolate Greece. In due course all three of these Balkan states entered the war, but they did so to advance their local ambitions, not to promote the broader claims of the great powers, the values of German *Kultur* or the rule of law or the rights of small nations. Interpreted through the eyes of these lesser powers, the First World War not only began as a Balkan war, the third since 1912, but it also continued as one – even beyond 1918. If it is seen as a war of Turkish independence it ran on until 1922. To get to the bottom of the First World War as a global war, we have first to disaggregate it into a series of regional conflicts.

Similar points can be made about the Second World War. A succession of distinguished historians, including A. J. P. Taylor, John Lukacs and, most recently, Ian Kershaw, have made the point that the Second World War did not begin until 1941. What happened between

1939 and 1941 was a series of bilateral campaigns waged by Germany to overrun each of Poland, Norway, Denmark, Holland, Belgium and France, before it turned on Romania, Yugoslavia, Greece and Russia. Moreover, the decisions taken in 1941 by each of Germany, the Soviet Union, the United States and Japan, while being informed by the wider strategic context and seeking to exploit it, were taken in isolation from the decisions taken by others. Ian Kershaw has described Mussolini's resolve to enter the war as a 'parallel war' or 'a war within a war', designed not to further the policies of the German–Italian 'pact of steel' but to take the opportunity to achieve Italy's foreign policy goals in the Mediterranean.[2] Here too, as in the First World War, time as well as geography can be used to conclude that what became a general conflict began as a series of distinct and separate wars. The war between Japan and China began not in 1939, but in 1937. The Japanese army hoped to be able to pursue its imperialist objectives on the mainland of Asia without the intervention of other powers. By the time Japan's navy struck Pearl Harbor on 7 December 1941, its army had already been engaged in a prolonged and costly war for approaching four and a half years.

What Philip Bobbitt has called 'epochal wars', including not only the two world wars but also the Peloponnesian War, the Punic Wars and the Thirty Years War, only became major wars in hindsight. In the midst of these aggregations of wars there were long periods of peace. Prussia did not fight France between 1795 and 1806 or between 1807 and 1813, despite the fact that France was almost constantly at war with other states in both periods. Similarly France was not formally at war with Germany between 1940 and 1944. Armistices, initially welcomed as the precursors to a more lasting peace when they were signed, were dropped from the dominant historical narrative when they failed to deliver. But this process was neither immediate nor inevitable: not every armistice led to a failure at the peace table and a renewal of hostilities. That too only became evident over time. Not until the nineteenth century were the wars between England and France, which ran from 1337 to 1453, given the collective title of the Hundred Years War.[3]

Historians have a lot to answer for. The desire of some to create a meta-narrative lumps rather than splits, aggregates rather than disaggregates. Two recent books concerning war as a historical phenomenon, both read widely beyond the historical profession, and indeed designed to be, are cases in point. Philip Bobbitt's *The shield of Achilles* (2002) and Niall Ferguson's *The war of the world* (2006) – however different in methodology, style and purpose – are united by their desire to provide general causal explanations for patterns within war and international relations. However uncongenial their authors may find the precepts of Marxism, they are its intellectual heirs in one respect at least: they are using interpretative tools to put a retrospective shape on events not only so that generalisations are possible but also so that political prescription can then follow. In pursuing generalisation they exclude the exceptional or inconvenient. Most decisions relating to war are not in fact taken in the light of the broad categories which such works seek to describe. Reading them may encourage us to think we gain in our understanding of the past, as in fact we do, but that comprehension is based on what is only a limited and selective set of insights. Above all, it eliminates the roles of personality and accident. As history is turned into political science, it makes a casualty of contingency.

This point matters – and it matters to the political scientist as well as to the historian. It matters above all in relation to war. In war the clash of two opposing wills in a resistant environment gives particular play to personality and accident. The job of strategy in war is to work with contingency. Of course strategy aspires to create a theory of war. It uses theoretical insights to question real events in a bid to shape them according to the needs of policy. But as soon as it allows the expectations of theory to obscure its vision of what is really happening, then strategy is not only no longer helpful, it is positively pernicious. Both in Vietnam and in Iraq sophisticated military thought created a construct which shaped the interpretation of what was happening on the ground. But its insights, however intelligent (and indeed their very intelligence exacerbated the problem as that made them even more seductive and persuasive), created a gulf between policy and practice. They ensured that the United States army's understanding of the war lagged behind reality. The most important single task for strategy is to understand the nature of the war it is addressing. Its next task may be to manage and direct that war, but it cannot do that if it starts from a false premise.

Strategy in practice is therefore pragmatic. For this very reason, most strategic theory – at least before the dropping of the atomic bombs in 1945 – was knowingly retrospective. It was grounded in military history. By putting shape on events that had seemed inchoate at the time, it provided interpretative and didactic tools for the future. Jomini and Clausewitz wrote after the Napoleonic Wars, in the light of their own experiences, and so provided the critical apparatus by which we can understand those wars and their influence on war's subsequent conduct. The same could be said of J. F. C Fuller, Basil Liddell Hart or A. A. Svechin in relation to the First World War. The theory of strategy therefore grew in step with the growth of war in the first half of the twentieth century. Confronted with a war which by 1917–18, for all that it might be seen in its causation as an aggregation of regional conflicts, became the prototype of 'total war', strategic theory responded with concepts that embraced not only the activities of armed forces but also the mobilisation of economies and the influence of propaganda. New phrases, such as 'total war', and then 'grand strategy' and 'national strategy', were coined to deal with what had happened. They served not only as explanatory tools in the 1920s and 1930s but also as prescriptions for the Second World War. They proved entirely appropriate to the task in hand.

From that fit between theory and reality was born a new orthodoxy. After 1945 the image of modern war was that of 'total war'. Strategic theory worked with this assumption and the invention of nuclear weapons seemed to confirm its relevance. As with the causes of the two world wars, the origins of the Cold War can be seen in regional terms: this 'war' too could have been split rather than lumped. The Soviet Union's push into eastern Europe and the United States's anti-communist response, specifically the Truman doctrine of 1947, embraced a number of conflicts that also had more local drivers, notably the Greek Civil War of 1946–9. Outside Europe, the challenge to the western powers in Asia came primarily from China, not from Russia, and indeed by the early 1960s the differences between the two communist states provided one abatement to the Cold War's challenges. Lumping threats in the 1950s and 1960s exacerbated problems that became more manageable when they were split. But by the same token since 1990 European joy at the end of the Cold War has served to obscure how much of the Cold War's architecture remains in place in Asia, not least in the Korean peninsula.

During the Cold War two factors in particular served to maximise the problems which strategy was designed to address, to encourage the aggregation of issues and to militarise international relations. One was political and the other technological. The ideological stand-off between the United States and the Soviet Union was presented in absolute terms, suggesting that democracy and communism were mutually exclusive, and that one would prevail only at the expense of the other.

Moreover, the conflict, whether it persisted at levels short of war or not, was seen as geographically unlimited: this was a global competition. Technologically, the advent of nuclear weapons meant the two sides had the potential to destroy much of the civilised world. Thus the primary task of strategic theory was to work with a vision of war that was so cataclysmic that war would be deterred.

Strategic theory usurped strategy: policy replaced practice. The fact that the Cold War stayed cold, at least in the sense that there was no third world war, meant that strategic theory did not develop pragmatically as it had done hitherto. In the two world wars the dialogue between practice and theory was constant, and expanding notions of strategy owed at least as much to statesmen and national leaders as to pundits, to what was done as much as to what was written, and to the conduct of war rather than its avoidance. In the absence of major conflict during the Cold War that relationship became less intimate. Nuclear deterrence theory was lampooned for its increasingly abstract qualities, but that did not prevent it becoming an academic gravy train, able to attract funds to sustain research departments and to ensure professorial tenure. By 1990 most strategic theory bore little relationship to what armed forces were designed to do or how they thought: indeed by the 1980s most uniformed practitioners were doing their own thing, forsaking strategy and focusing on what they called operational thought.

The end of the Cold War therefore confronted strategic theory with an existential crisis. Predicated on the possibility of a major war, it found itself in a world from which that threat seemed to have been lifted. The writings of John Mueller, Michael Mandelbaum and others on the demise of 'major war' (this now became the title of choice, not 'total war') were themselves revealing. Mueller was describing a process which he reckoned had begun after the First World War. When he published *Retreat from doomsday* in 1989 there had been no major war for forty-four years. Strategic thought did not confront a totally new situation in 1989; there had been real wars aplenty throughout the Cold War, but theory had not confronted them as fully as it should have done, preferring to see conflicts short of major war as exceptions to the rule rather than the norm. It tended to ignore those wars which had really been fought in favour of those which had not been but which might occur. And it continued to do so after 1989. The initial response to the end of the Cold War was to warn of the dangers of Russian resurgence or even of the expansionist designs of a reunited and revivified Germany, and so to deny that the threat of major war had been lifted and retain it as the 'gold standard' for armed forces.

As a result the stock of strategic ideas developed against the background of the Cold War has had greater longevity than perhaps we recognise. The most obvious driver is weapons procurement. Many critics of nuclear deterrence would argue that its theoretical underpinnings are no longer appropriate to the geopolitical threats which the owners of nuclear weapons confront, and that strategy has therefore become the prisoner of procurement. Similar arguments can be applied to conventional weapons as well. Fifteen- to twenty-year development cycles mean that technologies designed for one sort of war continue to shape expectations about future wars, and require them to be fought in conformity with those expectations even when those expectations run counter to the true nature of the war in hand. Tanks and aircraft intended for major conventional battles in Europe are not necessarily adapted to desert warfare in the Gulf or to counter-insurgency conflicts in Iraq and Afghanistan.

These are no more than outward manifestations of bigger and more consequential issues. Pre-emption became a principle of strategy within the context of nuclear deterrence. Although clearly aggressive in its effects, its employment was predicated on the evidence of an immediate and probable attack, and this was never forthcoming. Set within the framework of dissuasion, pre-emption was thus not used in practice. After the 9/11 attacks in 2001, it was placed in a different conceptual context, although the label remained the same. It became a free-standing element in the defence postures of both the United States and the United Kingdom. Now its application implied an early attack against threats that were latent, before they became imminent. A concept developed within one security structure was shoe-horned into another in order to give it a legitimating pedigree. Moreover, whereas in its earlier incarnation it was designed to prevent war, in its new format it was intended to provoke it.[4]

The mutation of pre-emption was replicated for deterrence as a whole. Deterrence relies on the threat that it invokes being credible. That requirement produced endless contortions in the Cold War, but they remained confined to the rhetoric and declarations of the two sides. It did not lead to war itself. When Britain's NATO partners declared that Mrs Thatcher's readiness to fight Argentina over the Falklands in 1982 enhanced the alliance's deterrent posture, they were passing a retrospective judgement, not proposing a reason for war in the first place. That changed with the loss of bipolar balance: freed from the threat of mutually assured destruction, powers felt able to use war to bolster deterrence. In 2006 Israel declared it was going to war precisely to enhance the credibility of its deterrent. Such statements are no longer unusual: the conceptual vocabulary of the Cold War is now being pressed into service to legitimate war, not prevent it.

One of the more misleading concepts in current strategy to emerge from Cold War thinking is that of the so-called 'long war'. When the Cold War ended, historians were attracted by the notion of what the Marxist Eric Hobsbawm called the 'short twentieth century', bounded by the outbreak of the First World War in 1914 at one end and the demise of the Soviet Union (itself a product of the First World War) in 1989–90 at the other. Philip Bobbitt put this idea into a more specifically strategic context in *The shield of Achilles*, when he lumped both world wars and the Cold War into one 'long war'. In some ways this was no more than a development of a more familiar notion that the two world wars were one, united by the ambitions of Germany, and driven by the simplistic belief that the second was the product of the failure of the 1919 Versailles settlement to resolve the issues of the first. At another it was an altogether more ambitious idea – that the 'long war' was fought to determine what kind of state would follow the 'imperial states' of Europe after the nineteenth century. For Bobbitt, the issues were constitutional – a struggle between fascism, communism, and what he called parliamentarianism.[5]

Both the historian and the strategist should take exception to Bobbitt's proposition. For the historian it does violence to the sequence of events: both fascism and communism were minority ideologies in 1914, and neither seemed to be at stake to the statesmen responsible for the outbreak of the war. Bobbitt's interpretation of the war's origins relies on an assessment of Germany's role which has now lost ground among specialists in the period. It also rules out the role of contingency both then and more generally. For the strategist the implications are far more serious, even dangerous. The 'long war' of 1914 to 1990 was not in fact a war at all. For all but ten of those years (1914–18 and 1939–45) the principal powers of Europe regarded themselves as at peace. For the United States the period of active fighting in the two world wars was even less. To be sure, most American citizens would add the Korean and Vietnam wars to the list of active hostilities in the course of the twentieth century, but at the same time these were wars that most European states would exclude from their national experiences of war over the same period. Bobbitt's interpretation of the twentieth century contributes both to the militarisation of international relations, since it interprets the absence of war not as real peace but as a temporary armistice, and to the aggregation of smaller wars into bigger ones. It serves the notion that major war is the dominant pattern to which strategic theory must pay attention.

Just as for Wellington's Britain there could be no small war for a great nation, so for the United States, because it is a global power with a sense of its democratising mission, there can be no wars that do not have universal implications. As Christopher Layne and Benjamin Schwartz have written (and they are quoted by Bobbitt): 'The continuity in US strategy was – and is – explained by the belief that preponderance prevents spiralling regional tensions by obviating the need for other powers to provide their own security.'[6] The effect is that regional clashes are maximised and become issues of global hegemony, with the result that the wars themselves become more intractable and the search for a strategy to manage them more problematic.

This is exactly the impasse which confronts strategy in the United States and – by extension – the United Kingdom (as the latter has reached a point where it seems incapable of thinking about strategy for itself). President Bush responded to the 9/11 attacks by declaring a global war on terror. The vocabulary of major war kicked in almost immediately. Both he and Tony Blair portrayed the struggle in which they were engaged as the defining conflict of the twenty-first century, a war for the values of civilisation and democracy. These were the rallying cries of the leaders of the Second World War: Bush's Wilsonian phrases harked back to Roosevelt, and Blair's to Churchill. Indeed they were not slow to liken Saddam Hussein to Adolf Hitler and Islamic fundamentalism to fascism.

The difference is that their publics did not believe them. The rhetoric of total war in 1941–2 was designed not just (or in some cases not at all) as a prescription for strategy but as a means of mobilising the nation and summoning it to make greater sacrifices. The words of each belligerent state's political leaders matched its people's perceptions of the situation – and that was as true of Nazi Germany and Soviet Russia as it was of Great Britain and the United States. In 2003 the peoples of the United States and of the United Kingdom were not ready to make greater sacrifices, and in reality they did not have to make many. The simultaneous waging of two overseas wars was achieved with no perceptible impact on levels of domestic consumption or of taxation; costs were deferred rather than confronted.[7] At home heightened security at airports was seen as an inconvenience, feeding accusations of bureaucratic incompetence rather than fear of home-grown terrorism. However severe the casualties suffered by the armed forces of the two countries, they were statistically insignificant in population terms and they would have been entirely acceptable to nations which were convinced that their ways of life and the values that sustained them were at risk. They were not convinced.

The speeches of Bush and Blair may have failed to rally their nations, but they became the basis for strategy. The rhetoric of the war on terror stepped in to the black hole created by the bankruptcy of strategic thought at the end of the Cold War. It provided the means to unite war and policy, and major war at that. Those who had made their careers through nuclear deterrence in the Cold War could shift to terrorist studies: the latter, from having been a fringe interest, moved to centre stage, confident that it would be central to the understanding of future war because the president and prime minister had said it would be. But there were significant differences. The Cold War, with its bipolar structure, created a security architecture of genuinely global significance. Moreover, nuclear weapons, for all that different nations developed their thinking in different ways, created some fundamental convergences in strategic thought. At bottom the threat of mutually assured destruction and the desirability of avoiding it concentrated minds wonderfully well. Terrorism, even when it uses suicide bombers or hijacked aircraft, does not generate such convergences. Today there are no assumptions within strategic thought common to both sides, for all the talk about globalisation and networked communications. The latter are a tool used by both, and they can affect the operational decisions that each takes. That is especially true of those belligerents who use terrorism, whose oxygen is publicity. But strategy is not influenced by, rather than grounded in, such capabilities. The west's own preoccupation with the consequences of real-time, world-wide communications has created a convergence with the universalism of American foreign policy but not with the nature of the wars that policy is asking America and its allies to undertake.

The war in Iraq was and that in Afghanistan is first and foremost a regional conflict. By aggregating them within a wider conflict we have made them bigger than they are, even less amenable to strategy in its pragmatic sense, and incomprehensible to the electorates of the demo-cratic states which are waging them. Iraq was a fractured society from its inception: in 2003, its population was divided by tribe and by faith, and its problems have roots that antedate the US-led invasion, and that had nothing to do with the so-called 'war on terror'. Afghanistan was also a tribal society, driven by an Islamic fundamentalism in a way that Iraq was not, and prey to violence and to poppy cultivation for decades. The west's fixation with major war has given the specific problems of both countries global resonances. Because it has used war to tackle these issues, the coalition has of course also changed their complexion; it has created a reactive relationship between regionalism and globalism, and so enabled local wars to grow into bigger conflicts. But by adopting the vocabulary of universalism, rather than that of particularism, the United States in Iraq and NATO in Afghanistan could not get near understanding the nature of the wars in which they were engaged, and until they did they were not able to develop an appropriate strategy.

In 2006, Afghanistan was presented as the supreme test for NATO and its future relevance as a military alliance. Just as the alliance's institu-tions were shaped and developed by its role in the Cold War, so they now had to be shaped and developed by this war. That process had slow beginnings: it was no coincidence that NATO still had no strategy for Afghanistan by 2009. One legacy of the Cold War is positive, that NATO's armed forces have a common set of operating assumptions; another is negative, that without the Cold War strategy struggles to marry those military capabilities to policy. Even if NATO had met this challenge successfully, its need for greater flexibility will be recurrent. By adapting itself to the specific demands of Afghanistan, NATO by definition has made itself less fit for operations elsewhere. One strategy will not fit all, particularly when its key instruments – counter-insurgency, counter-terrorism, political stabilisation and economic reconstruction – must be regionally determined.

This is not solely a NATO problem. Aware that 'the global war on terror' was not a helpful foundation for the development of strategy, the Pentagon's February 2006 Quadrennial Defense Review latched on to a new label, or rather to an old one in a new guise, 'the long war'. Bobbitt's title, having been applied to the short twentieth century, was now applied to the twenty-first. However, unlike Bobbitt's use of it, that of the Pentagon was prospective, not retrospective – a palpable absurdity since the definition of what is a long war is both inherently subjective and only clear in hindsight. Donald Rumsfeld, when being interviewed on 1 February 2006 about the new phrase, was asked whether he thought the war in Iraq was going to be a long war, and he replied, 'No. I don't believe it is.'[8] The war in Iraq went on longer than the First World War, a war which we are told was begun in August 1914 in the anticipation that it would be over within months and which accordingly we tend to see as long because it went on until November 1918 (although in reality it was of course shorter than many other 'epochal' wars). To reiterate, the notion of a long war is a way of lumping rather than splitting, of avoiding more specific and considered definitions in order to make simple points; it is not a serious analytical tool. As Ryan Henry, principal deputy under-secretary of defense for policy at the Pentagon put it, when asked to define the idea of 'the long war' in 2007, 'things get very fuzzy past the five-year point'.[9] His argument in favour of the phrase was: 'We in the defense department feel fairly confident that our forces will be called on to be engaged somewhere in the world in the next decade where they're currently not engaged but we have no idea whatsoever where that might be, when that might be or in what circumstances that they might be engaged.'[10]

As an expression of policy for the Pentagon or as a statement of the dilemmas of NATO defence ministries since the end of the Cold War that is unexceptionable; as a statement of strategy it is unacceptable. Strategy must address the nature of the war in which it is engaged; neither Ryan Henry nor the 2006 Quadrennial Defense Review did. Two points, both derived from Clausewitz, are relevant here. First, time in war tends to work to the advantage of the defender. In operational terms, the United States and its allies, especially if they are waging expeditionary wars, are the attackers. As the war lengthens, so protracted conflict saps the forces of both sides. By 2006 the armies of the United States and Britain were close to being broken by Iraq, regardless of the outcome. Clausewitz would argue that the war had long since passed 'the culminating point of victory' (it probably came when President Bush declared 'mission accomplished' in May 2003). Secondly, in long wars, the Clausewitzian norm, that war is an instrument of policy, is turned on its head in practice. Short sharp wars, like the German wars of unification in 1864, 1866 and 1870, have the best chances of delivering the political objectives of those who initiate them. In long wars, war shapes and moulds policy. In the United Kingdom, the debate on the powers to be conferred on the government to deal with terrorism in 2008, the division of the Home Office into two, with the creation of the Justice Department in 2007, and the repercussions of the Iraq War in the Scottish elections in May 2007 are all cases in point. And that is without factoring in the most obvious way in which war could shape policy: the possibility of coalition defeats in Iraq or Afghanistan. At the very least it is reasonable to say that the United States has not been fulfilling the political objectives set by the long war.

That is why governments do not deliberately embark on long wars. The United States did not in 2002–3. However, its adoption of 'long war' was not just a means of rationalising initial failure. It was also a way of coming to terms with the fact that it lacks a body of strategic thought to deal with regional wars. Conditioned by its own political inheritance, by the American 'mission' and by the legacy of the Cold War, its tendency to aggregate works against strategy's demand (in this case) that it splits. In 2004, before the Pentagon embraced 'the long war' in the Quadrennial Defense Review, US Central Command promulgated the idea, so shifting the focus from the war in hand in Iraq to a potential spectrum of conflict that swept across North Africa and into central Asia. It minimised the wars in which it was currently engaged by maximising the impact of other regional conflicts, with local dynamics, and projecting them on to a wider canvas. The instabilities in the Horn of Africa, at whose hands the United States had suffered in Mogadishu in 1993, were revisited in December 2006 in the name of the war on terror: a stable but Islamic government in Somalia was toppled by Ethiopian troops acting with US support. Military action was being driven less by realism than by theory. Significantly in April 2007, Admiral William Fallon, having succeeded General John Abizaid at CENTCOM, decided to abandon the phrase 'the long war' and told his command to focus on the real war, that in Iraq.[11] He escaped the straitjacket of strategic theory for the pragmatism of strategy in practice.

But Admiral Fallon had not thereby resolved the challenge confronted by strategic thought, at least for thought developed and moulded in the American tradition (which is most strategic thought in the western world today, and certainly within NATO). We do not have a coherent way of thinking about regional wars, and because of this deficiency we do not have a way of interrogating what we are doing and then validating it.

All actual wars since 1945 (and there have been a great many) have fallen short of generally accepted definitions of 'total war' or 'major war'. The 'general war' or 'central war' planned for in the Cold War never eventuated within Europe. Outside Europe, states, notably Israel in the first twenty years of its life, have fought existential conflicts, but these have still fallen short of the extremes set by the two world wars – in terms of weaponry, duration, geographical extent or the involvement of other powers. Within NATO a whole host of labels has been coined to describe wars short of major war – some of them, like low intensity conflict, out of fashion, and others, like counter-insurgency warfare, back in. But we are unsure about what separates such conflicts from others with different labels; we are not sure when peace-keeping becomes peace-support, or how both, at the stage when they move into peace-enforcement, then become counter-insurgency. Troops deployed in Iraq and Afghanistan were and are doing all these things: sometimes the operations on which they have been engaged could be described as low intensity and sometimes they most definitely could not be.

Such typological ambiguity is at one level a very sensible reflection of the fact that strategy is a pragmatic business, which must be responsive to the situation on the ground. But strategy is not simply reactive: its role is to direct the war, and to do that it needs to interact not only with policy but also with strategic theory. The dialectic tests out its conclusions, and that means that regional wars need a more sophisticated theoretical framework than that provided by the experience or expectation of major war.

The response of the Cold War warriors to this challenge was not in fact as unsophisticated as this chapter has so far suggested or as their apparent intellectual legacy conveys. Confronted with the fear of major war and its threat of an all-out nuclear exchange, but cognisant that the challenge which communism posed the democratic states of the west would be played out through proxy wars, they developed ideas about limited war. Many of the great names of strategic thought in the 1950s contributed to this enterprise, including William Kaufmann, Bernard Brodie, Morton Halperin, Maxwell D. Taylor and Thomas Schelling.

Limited war was one of the themes which Basil Liddell Hart was able to develop as he resuscitated a career which had faltered in the Second World War. After 1918, Liddell Hart's search for ways to limit war had to play second fiddle to the wider Wilsonian ambition to avoid it altogether. Gilbert Murray, writing not as Oxford's Regius Professor of Greek but as President of the League of Nations Union, declared in 1928 that, 'At the present day most nations realise that another first-class war would be the end of civilization.'[12] His words formed an introduction to a book by James T. Shotwell on the renunciation of war as an instrument of national policy. As the editor of the *Economic and social history of the World War*, a formidable edifice of around 150 volumes funded by the Carnegie Endowment for International Peace, Shotwell seemed well qualified both to comment on the links between war and economic development, and to conclude that the point had been reached when war could not be kept 'within bounds, as in the simple economy of the past'.[13] Liddell Hart's vision, which accepted the place of war in international relations but sought to restrain it, was – in the context of the 1920s – a secondary theme. Nor was he its most forceful and consistent exponent. That title probably belongs to the New Yorker Hoffman Nickerson, whose book, *Can we limit war?*, published in 1933, rested on the clear and unequivocal endorsement of a premise unacceptable to Shotwell, that 'war will continue as long as man is man'.[14] Nickerson, like Liddell Hart and that other great titan of inter-war British military thought, J. F. C. Fuller, sought to constrain war through the ending of conscription, the elevation of small, professional armies, and the equipping of this elite force with tanks and aeroplanes. 'Thoughtful readers', urged by Nickerson to reject the views of men such as Murray and Shotwell, 'will justly despise the materialist nonsense of those who say that the new *matériel* must make wars more savage and destructive than 1914–1918.'[15] But, while Hoffman's work rested on that of Fuller and Liddell Hart, his natural contrariness also led him to attack even them. Christopher Bassford has concluded that 'his patrician attitudes and prejudices removed him from the American mainstream, and some of his reviewers dismissed him as a harmless crank'.[16]

In any event, the Second World War suggested that both Liddell Hart and Nickerson had been wrong: neither tanks not aeroplanes served to limit the war. Sadly, so too were Murray and Shotwell: an awareness of war's increasing destructiveness did not in the end prevent its recurrence. Liddell Hart's determination to contain the war linked him first to appeasement and secondly to its wartime corollary, the need to seek a compromise peace. He believed that victory was impossible and the costs of pursuing it would be too great. However, after 1945, the advent of nuclear weapons gave such lines of thought fresh relevance. His immediate reaction, published in 1946, was that war would not disappear just because 'an unlimited war waged with atomic power would make worse than nonsense; it would be mutually suicidal'. Instead it would behove future leaders to pursue a form of warfare that 'will be less unrestrained and more subject to mutually agreed rules'. War would be likely to develop new forms within these limits, and it was more important to address 'the practical necessity ... of limiting war', rather than 'the perfectionist policy of preventing war'.[17] In 1953 Liddell Hart began to marshal his thoughts on limited war with a bibliography which began, reasonably enough, with his own writings, but also included those of Nickerson and Fuller, as well as Quincy Wright's *A study of war* (1942), Hanson Baldwin's *Great mistakes of the war* (1950), and a sequence of the later works on the French Revolution and Napoleon by the Italian liberal historian and journalist, Guglielmo Ferrero, who had died in Swiss exile in 1942.[18] Liddell Hart did not write a book devoted solely to limited war, as this preliminary sketch suggests that he perhaps intended, but he dedicated the last chapter of *Defence of the west* (1950) to the argument that the limitation of war had a long history, not least because the avoidance of extremes in war tended to produce a more lasting peace. His criticism of the manner in which the Second World War had been conducted remained unrelenting: 'it was ironical that nations who had entered the war to preserve civilisation should have come to practise the most uncivilising means of war that the world had known since those Mongol exponents of wholesale massacre'. However, precisely because '"Total Warfare", such as we have known it hitherto, is not compatible with the atomic age', so 'the limitless destructiveness of the weapon forms its own practical limitation'. For Liddell Hart, 'the best chance may lie in trying to revive a code of limiting rules for warfare'.[19]

In 1957, within four years of Liddell Hart's penning his hurried bibliography, Robert E. Osgood published the text which best embodied the ideas about limited warfare, *Limited war: the challenge to American strategy*. Osgood did not respond to Liddell Hart's call for rules, and to that extent the American proved less prescient than the Briton. From the perspective of the twenty-first century, the most obvious manifestation of the resolve to limit the conduct of warfare has been the determination to be vigorous in applying the laws of armed conflict, and to see adherence to them as a norm for civilised states and as a basis for their claims to legitimacy. The progressive adoption of the 1977 protocols additional to the Geneva conventions of 1949 has been a visible manifestation of the readiness to use rules, in the shape of international law, to limit war.

Some will argue that the laws of war restrain warfare most effectively when they are based on custom, and therefore history. This, after all, was – to all intents and purposes – the argument that Liddell

Hart had advanced. The history of war is not simply the history of violence, but is also itself the history of an effort to organise and channel that violence.[20] Although Osgood's historical range of reference was brief in comparison with that of Liddell Hart, it is nonetheless striking that the well-spring of limited war strategy, like the best of pre-1945 strategic thought, was not technological but historical. The Korean War demonstrated to a generation which had fought in the Second World War that a conflict which involved the United States, the Soviet Union and China did not have to be a 'general war'. Theory was a retrospective rationalisation of reality, and it argued that war could be limited geographically, militarily and politically. The critics of limited war theory will argue that the Korean War ended with a compromise settlement which rested on a partial victory and satisfied neither side. More importantly, however, it fulfilled the policy objective of the day, that of containment, and it obviated the real fear of a nuclear exchange. The outcome was an object lesson that security is relative, not absolute.

By 1962 limited war strategy had moved beyond academic discourse into the realm of policy. President J. F. Kennedy was persuaded that it presented an alternative to a third world war, that it provided a riposte to the use of proxy wars and nationalist insurgencies by communists, and that its effects would bolster the credibility of deterrence by linking conventional capabilities to nuclear in a ladder of escalation. Two National Security Action Memorandums of August 1962 recommended that the United States (in Osgood's words) 'adopt a strategy of integrating economic and political development along democratic lines with counterinsurgency effects in order to enable threatened governments to eliminate the roots of popular discontent and suppress guerrilla attacks upon their freedom'. There is a currency to these words; the relevance is reinforced by Osgood's further observation that this strategy might require the United States to strengthen 'beleaguered governments – even to reform them'.[21]

Vietnam was the testing ground of limited war strategy and it ended in failure. The concept has struggled to regain purchase ever since. But, Osgood argued, there were two approaches in seeking out the cause of the defeat. One was that the policy was wrong, and the other was that the armed forces of the United States were ill-adapted to the demands of limited war. By focusing on the former, the army avoided confronting the latter. Indeed it deliberately reconfigured itself, both physically and intellectually, to fight only major war. Its response was not to explore why its counter-insurgency practices had not worked or why it had been unable to implement limited war strategy; in other words, it did not develop strategic theory out of practice, using history by learning lessons with a view to future application. It preferred to turn its back on limited war and to revert to the model of major war, a response justified by the Cold War. It adopted the Total Force policy, which meant that it could not fight a war without mobilising its reserve, a concept that made sense for a conventional war on the scale of the Second World War, but which put strains on a voluntarily enlisted force committed to a war of lesser intensity with limited popular endorsement. In parallel, the Weinberger doctrine of 1984 and the Powell doctrine of 1992 both stressed that the United States should commit its forces only when national interests were at stake, that it should do so with all the resources available to it, with the support both of the American people and of Congress, and that it should have clear political and military objectives. Thus we confront the paradox of war today. Compared with our predecessors of fifty years ago (and it is more than half a century since the publication of Osgood's *Limited war*), the armed forces have the ability to use their firepower with discrimination and precision; often they do, but more often they use it in massive quantities, so vitiating the very virtue they are trying to exploit, and they do so because the context in which they wage war, and the purposes for which they wage it, lack clarity.

Strategic theory has therefore failed to provide the tools with which to examine the conflicts which are in hand. Osgood observed that the lessons of Vietnam were 'highly contingent, since so many of the military and political features of another local war are likely to be different or occur in different combinations'.[22] Major war is the preferred vehicle for the development of strategy, as the issues are absolute, the role of contingency diminished and the play of policy is less overt. But a phenomenon that is increasingly remote from the actual experience of war does not provide a sufficient template for the current debate on strategy. The result is a discussion in flux, without unifying themes or coherence. The concept of limited war may be too tarred by the brush of failure in Vietnam to be the appropriate label, particularly in the United States; for some too it is linked to the ideas of Herman Kahn and Henry Kissinger about limited nuclear, rather than conventional, war. However, it or its equivalent can provide the collecting box for a range of notions which at the moment lack unifying themes. What is striking about these is that those characterisations which try to encapsulate the nature of fighting short of major war (low intensity warfare, counter-insurgency operations and so on) are both contested and – like terrorism itself – descriptions of means not ends. Strategy aims to unite means to ends in war, and the labels which it uses therefore tend, and probably need, to be more wide-ranging and more inclusive. Certainly it has to link the use of military force to policy, and the rationales for war, whatever the rhetoric might suggest, are in practice more limited and the material conditions more local than the speeches which tend to accompany them.

Strategy, as opposed to strategic theory, has two principal tasks. The first is to identify the character of the war in hand. A misidentification is pregnant with consequences: it would be just as mistaken to fight a major war on the assumption that it is a smaller, more limited war, as the other way round. Moreover, what begins as one sort of war can, obviously enough, transmogrify into another. So recognising the character of the war and understanding it is a constant interrogative process (and one where strategic theory comes into play), not just something to be undertaken at its outset. But the second task of strategy, once the character of the war has been plumbed, is to manage the war and direct it. The first process is more reactive, the second more proactive. It is perfectly possible for the policy-makers of one belligerent to decide to escalate a war, to make a local conflict into a global one. But neither common sense nor common humanity suggests that that is very sensible.

6 EUROPEAN ARMIES AND LIMITED WAR

Since the industrialisation of Europe in the late nineteenth century, European armies have been able to trade firepower for manpower. The mass production of repeating weapons has made the battlefield more lethal, but it has also required fewer men proportionately to do the killing. As weapons have improved in quality, so they have reinforced the case against manpower in quantity. Technology was (and still can be) a force-multiplier.

This process did not initially result in smaller armies. Rather European states opted for both firepower and manpower: mass production enabled a large army to be equipped and supplied to a level and consistency that had defied the ambitions of less developed states. In August 1914 France mobilised eighty-two divisions and Germany eighty-seven, and each had almost three million men under arms. By late 1918 each of the three major allied armies on the western front (those of France, Britain and the United States, but not Belgium, which was cut off from its manpower pool) numbered in the region of two million men. These were conscript forces and represented the greatest numbers that their parent societies could bear. Although French and British divisions were smaller in manpower terms, and had fewer battalions than in 1914, they had increased their firepower ratio by the adoption of tanks, light machine guns, mortars and highly sophisticated artillery.

After the war, some strategic thinkers attributed the static character of the fighting which had dominated the western front specifically to this combination of firepower and manpower. The result, they argued, was a mass incapable of articulation through the processes of command and communication then available. In Britain, J. F. C. Fuller and (especially) Basil Liddell Hart came to see mass as the enemy of effectiveness. The armies of the First World War, Fuller wrote in 1923, became 'not more intelligent and scientific, but more brutal, ton upon ton of human flesh being added, until war strengths are reckoned in millions in place of thousands of men'.[1] Liddell Hart, by 1927, held it as axiomatic 'that the indigestible mass of infantry is the cause of our military nightmare'.[2] Nor were these simply the views of critics based in a country for which conscription was historically unfamiliar and constitutionally uncongenial. In France, the political home of the mass army, where conscription was aligned with notions of citizenship, Colonel Émile Mayer wondered in 1925 whether the nation even needed an army to wage modern war. Mayer's fans have traced a line from his thought to that of Charles de Gaulle, the advocate of a small, professional and mechanised army, and so a potential threat to those keen to cement the links between army and nation forged by the *union sacrée* in the First World War.[3] Even in Germany, Hans von Seeckt, head of the Truppenamt, Germany's substitute general staff, preached the virtues of mobility over mass. The fact that the size of the German army was limited to 100,000 men under the terms of the treaty of Versailles did of course leave him with no alternative.

In the event the Second World War, like the First, required mass and mobility, manpower and firepower. Germany was crushed between the anvil of the Soviet armies and the hammer of United States production. Unsurprisingly, after 1945 those who thought about conventional war in Europe were at first inclined to continue the same pattern. In February 1952 the North Atlantic Council met in Lisbon and resolved that by the end of 1954 the alliance should have created forty-two divisions ready for use, together with a further forty-five reserve divisions which could be capable of mobilisation within thirty days. The council increased the second figure to forty-eight divisions, giving a target of ninety in all.

The so-called Lisbon force goals were never met. The council was looking to old forms of war. The advanced weapons systems with which European armies were equipped in 1952 had finally so transformed the firepower to manpower ratios of their armies that mass had lost its dominance. Since 1952 Europe has steadily moved away from an image of war shaped by conscription and mass. By as early as April 1953 the North Atlantic Council had reduced its target to thirty ready divisions and thirty-six reserve divisions. These new goals were set by cost, but they were also rationalised in more directly military terms. The acquisition of nuclear weapons gave the alliance firepower without the need for manpower. States may have acquired nuclear weapons more to prevent war than to wage it, but their lethality and effectiveness marked the culmination of a process that had begun with the application of industrialised technologies to war a hundred years before.

Since 1945 the arguments deployed by the more radical voices between the wars have been progressively reinforced. If the Cold War in Europe had become hot, it would not have been limited except in one respect: it would have been (at least in most people's expectations) short. Armies became smaller because they were not expected to sustain resistance for more than a few days or at most weeks. Germany in particular, all too conscious both of the damage it had incurred through protracted conventional warfare in the Second World War and of the fact that it would be the principal European battleground in a Third World War, wanted to keep the ladder of escalation to nuclear release short and steep. NATO war games tended to end with a nuclear exchange within days. Germany's purpose was to reinforce deterrence, but if deterrence had failed its corollary would have been deeply destructive.

Those less close to the inner German border, and particularly the United States, wanted the ladder to be longer and the process of ascent more gradual. Their interpretation of the strategy of 'flexible response', adopted by NATO in 1967, stressed the initial use of conventional military capabilities as much as the final sanction of nuclear release. During the 1970s the deployment of short-range nuclear missiles, SS20s by the Soviet Union and Cruise missiles by the alliance, prompted anti-nuclear protests within Europe and demands for declarations that both sides cleave to policies which rejected the first use of nuclear weapons. The challenge for the armies of Europe was that the corollary of such thinking, even if it did not become policy, was the creation of greater conventional capabilities. Over the next decade they responded, at least to some extent, to this demand. In north Germany the British and German armies embraced the 'operational level of war', designed to interdict Soviet advances beyond the inner German border and to meet incursions across it with corps-led counter-strokes.

In the United States the army underwent a similar process with congruent outcomes, although its response had a significant additional source. It needed to re-find itself after the experience of defeat in Vietnam and it did so by stressing the value of doctrine. It developed ideas for manoeuvre warfare and what came to be called 'AirLand battle'. This sort of thinking found its battlefield application in the first Gulf War of 1990–1. That war, and particularly its ground component, proved shorter, quicker and more decisive than pre-war pundits had expected. Before the beginning of the ground attack, the commander of the British 7th Armoured Brigade, Patrick Cordingley, told the press that he anticipated that his formation would suffer 10 per cent casualties per day.[4] The press was horrified, but Cordingley was simply reflecting the planning assumptions embraced by NATO during the Cold War. The implication of Cordingley's calculation was that the initial ground forces would have lost two-thirds of their strength within ten days. The British army did not possess the effective reserves to fill the gaps which such losses would expose. The attention to the conventional capabilities of European ground forces had not prompted those armies that had abandoned conscription to reintroduce it; manoeuvre was meant to substitute for mass, quality to compensate for quantity. Cordingley had exposed the wishful thinking which had underpinned NATO planning since its rejection of the Lisbon force goals: that fighting would not be protracted because it could not be, as its armies were not renewable.

With the end of the Cold War, and the removal of the immediate threat of a major war of self-defence within Europe, that hope – implicitly at least – has become even more fervent. Britain's and America's allies have either followed their example in abandoning national service or so reduced the impact of conscription as to cease to make it an effective tool for the mobilisation of a mass army. One former Canadian general, Roméo Dallaire, who commanded the United Nations Assistance Mission for Rwanda in 1993–4, baldly declared in 2012 that, 'Conscription and the draft are mechanisms that spell defeat for any force that uses them.'[5] Most significant of all, France, the state which had given modern Europe the idea and even the ideal of the nation in arms, suspended national service in 1996–7. Today's European armies are simply unable to fight a long war of high intensity. They cannot command the manpower for 'total war'. The question that is more pressing is whether they can command the manpower for long wars of lower intensity.

One of the founders of modern counter-insurgency thinking in the teleological accounts favoured by today's armies is Joseph Simon

Galliéni, saviour of France in 1914 in at least some people's eyes, but above all the leading practitioner of French colonial warfare. In 1885, after the Franco-Chinese war for the control of Tonkin, the army asked for more men to complete France's pacification of Indo-China. Paris said it could not have them and so Galliéni, who was responsible for the area from Lao Kay in the north to Dien Bien Phu in the south, adapted his strategy to the forces he had available, proceeding more slowly but more methodically, and ensuring that he did not move on from a sector until it had been secured.[6] In some respects wars of colonial conquest were wars that required larger armies than the numbers of European troops revealed. The imperial powers often prevailed by dividing and ruling the indigenous population, and so were able to recruit from one tribe or ethnic group to fight another. The British held India principally through the agency of Indian troops, leavened with British regulars. France followed the same principles in Algeria and Morocco. Two consequences followed. The first was that, if troop levels were kept low, the spread of colonial authority was likely to be slow, and the war protracted. Colonial conquest, pacification and settlement took decades, not months. Secondly, the impact of these wars on metropolitan society masked their true scale as they sucked in manpower on a massive scale but did so locally rather than from Europe.

The analogy that compares the wars of colonial conquest in the late nineteenth century with NATO's interventions outside the area bounded by the North Atlantic Treaty in the early twenty-first is far from exact. Colonial powers saw themselves as sovereign authorities and were planning to stay; NATO's International Security Assistance Force (ISAF) operates in support of the Afghan government, is multinational in its composition and is beset by seemingly arbitrary timetables for withdrawal. But where the comparison works better is in terms of manpower. In both cases the peoples of Europe have seen these wars as 'small wars', and so failed to recognise their manpower demands as legitimate. In Afghanistan, the demand for more men has been met by private military contractors and by the expansion of indigenous forces.

Galliéni, like his most distinguished pupil and advocate, Hubert Lyautey, responded to limited resources by developing the idea of the 'tache d'huile' or 'oil spot'. The English language, when it adopts this concept, often replaces oil with ink, but the point is the same: that the spot will be secured and then widened as the indigenous population is drawn into the secure area by the need to trade and survive. Such thinking permeated ISAF in 2006. It was an approach which was adapted to the limited manpower available to fight the war, but it extended the time which the waging of the war would require. The spots, whether of oil or ink, depended on Afghan indigenous forces sufficiently capable and numerous to backfill the areas that had been secured. The need to hold what has been cleared of insurgents, particularly given the pressures to control the whole of Afghanistan simultaneously and to limit the use of firepower for fear of alienating the uncommitted or neutral population, meant that counter-insurgency warfare was in this respect less forgiving in its demand for men than 'hot war' in Europe. Current counter-insurgency theory regularly stresses optimum force to space – or force to population – ratios so high that they constitute a demand for a mass army. The 'surge' of an extra 100,000 troops in Afghanistan in 2010–11 is presumed to have had direct effects in bringing more security to more areas. At the same time Afghanistan was under pressure to create security forces which would peak at 320,000 men, three times the then-size of the British army despite the enormous disparity in their gross national products.

The war in Afghanistan demands a mass army but those European states that have retained conscription have not done so primarily in order to fight such a war, or indeed to fight wars at all. Neither Germany nor Norway any longer argues that it requires a reserve capacity so as to be able to generate a mass army to repel an invasion launched by a near neighbour. Now the case for conscription rests not on military utility but on domestic and internal values – on the need to ensure that the armed forces reflect society as a whole in order to minimise the threat of militarism posed by a professional army. Indeed in both countries societal expectations of the army can be at odds with its military effectiveness. In 2010 young German soldiers serving in Afghanistan, supported by their defence minister of the time, Karl Theodor zu Guttenberg, generated controversy because they described what they were doing as war rather than 'not international armed conflict'. They alarmed their seniors in the service who were used to associating the word 'war' with the generation and experiences of 1939–45. The former chancellor, Helmut Schmidt, when asked in January 2011 to comment on the fears within Germany of emerging military values and on the idea of the Bundeswehr as a separate community, responded that 'a special ideology would be life-threatening for our democracy'.[7] In 2010 Norwegian soldiers serving in Afghanistan, similarly anxious to promote military values, called

themselves Vikings.[8] The word was fraught not just for Norway's neighbours, whose societies were subject to raid and pillage a thousand years
ago by Norsemen in long boats. It also caused concern for those
Norwegians who remembered the Second World War: Viking was the
title appropriated by the Quislings who served in the SS.

At the heart of Europe's problem is the lack of a unifying conception of war – a conception which can tie the armies of Europe
and their parent societies into a common narrative. As both
the German and Norwegian responses show, public expectations of the
armed forces and their use of war adapt much more slowly than the
organisation and equipment of those forces. The European folk memory
of war is still shaped by the Second World War, by 'total war'. Two
consequences follow. The first is that armies exist only for purposes of
direct national self-defence in what the English language no longer calls
'total war', but 'major war' or increasingly 'existential war'. The corollary of a war for national survival should be an expectation that in such a
war armies should be both conscripted and large, reflective of their
parent societies in terms of their social composition and even more in
values. The second is the obverse of that position. Given the destructiveness for Europe of modern war, and particularly of the two world wars,
war is not in fact a continuation of policy by other means. War represents
the failure of policy, and so has no political utility.

Today Europe's armies are designed less to fight and more to
exercise diplomatic leverage. The inflation of Clausewitz's nostrum that
war is the continuation of policy by other means has had its effects: war
has come to be seen in terms less of destroying the enemy than of seeking
'influence'. Small contingents are a means by which a state pays its dues
to the international community and to the multilateral organisations,
principally the European Union, NATO and the United Nations, in
which most modern, westernised and democratic nations invest their
hopes of a stable international order. This 'tokenism' can extend to
bilateral relations, particularly given the possible long-term need to call
in aid from the United States. The real military strength of NATO lies
with America, and by sending forces to Afghanistan other states are
investing in a favour bank with the USA if their security is threatened
in the future. Alliances help keep armies small and serve to constrain the
circumstances in which they may be used.[9]

Arguably these aims are more diplomatic than military. Their
objectives address the overall efficiency of alliances, and the self-interest

vested in them. The very scale of a national contingent may be so small – say a hundred men – as to beg the question of whether that nation is at war. In other cases the state, even if its contribution is much more sizeable, may have legal difficulties in describing what it is doing as war. These problems may arise for domestic constitutional reasons, as they have for the defeated powers of 1945, or they may be the product of international law, the consequences of the Kellogg–Briand pact of 1928 or of the United Nations charter. Given that the UN charter reserves the unilateral resort to war for the extreme circumstances of national self-defence, it could be said to preserve major or existential war as the only national option. The result is that war must arise from dire necessity. So-called 'wars of choice' do not accord with the spirit of the charter; but the charter does of course allow the international community to use armed force provided it has the authorisation of a United Nations Security Council resolution, as in the case of Libya in 2011. If such use of war has a conceptual label it is limited war. This is the sort of armed conflict for which Europe's armies are for the most part currently con-figured. It is also the only sort of war in which Europe's armies have been engaged since 1945. But the theory of war has not adjusted to this reality. The phrase 'limited war' is one that does not have currency either in the study of strategy or in the rhetoric of policy. In terms of its intellectual pedigree there are two reasons for this, one most easily explained through the writings of Carl von Clausewitz and the other through those of Sir Julian Corbett.

In his note of 10 July 1827, published as the preface to *On war*, Clausewitz said war could be of two kinds. One sort aims to annihilate the enemy and so render him politically helpless; the other aims 'merely to occupy some of his frontier-districts so that we can annex them or use them for bargaining at the peace negotiations'.[10] Clausewitz's model for this second sort of war was not the fighting of his own generation, the Napoleonic Wars, but that of his father's, who had served in the army of Frederick the Great in the Seven Years War. It followed that this more limited form of war appeared to belong to the past and so seemed less likely to occur in the future. Indeed the more settled the frontiers of Europe, the less the cause for war over territorial objectives. The effect of the First World War was to associate Clausewitz with his first form of war, a strategy of 'annihilation'. When Liddell Hart castigated the effect of the mass army on the conduct of war, he also attacked Clausewitz whom he described as 'the Mahdi of Mass'.[11] Like some other western thinkers of his generation, Liddell Hart linked Clausewitz exactly with the sort of Prussian militarism whose resurgence the founding fathers of the Bundesrepublik were so anxious to forestall and which underpinned Helmut Schmidt's fears in January 2011.

The threat and the actuality of world war did not seem to make limited war a concept appropriate to European armies in the first half of the twentieth century, but it did make more sense to their navies, and particularly to that of Britain. In 1911, Corbett, in *Some principles of maritime strategy*, argued that an island state like Britain could engage in limited war, especially if it had a major ally on the continent of Europe and so could opt to exercise its influence on the periphery. The navy provided the security from invasion which meant that the war, however major, would never become for Britain a war of national survival. This was not what happened in the First World War. Britain had to raise a mass army, even adopting conscription in 1916, and to put it on the continent of Europe. By 1917–18, the British army was as big as that of France and doing as much of the fighting. The First World War discredited Corbett's argument for limited war, just as it had Clausewitz's.

What unites both concepts is not – or at least not in the first instance – the issue of policy, although we shall come back to that. Rather, their common feature is geography. Clausewitz's second form of war was limited because its means of achievement was territorial gain, and so its aims too were geographically limited. Today the geographical limits to Europe's wars are not primarily those of means and ends in quite the same sense. European states are not attempting to conquer neighbouring provinces in order to secure a different distribution of resources in a negotiated settlement. Corbett's definition of limited war, although also geographical, was not the same as Clausewitz's, and may be more helpful. His was a strategy appropriate only to maritime, not continental, states. In his thinking Britain, as an island, should adopt limited war as a means within a European war whose wider objectives were not limited. Today much of western Europe has begun to see itself in insular terms, cocooned from the great power rivalries emerging in the Pacific, and clothed in a regional bubble of atypical but seemingly eternal security. Its metaphorical island makes its position akin to that of Britain in the eighteenth century. Its wars are fought at increasing distances from the cockpits of the great European wars between the late seventeenth and the mid-twentieth century. Then the Low Countries and the Rhineland made war 'total' for Europe because its most advanced economic regions were also those most likely to be used for fighting. The same seemed likely to happen during the Cold War, but did not. Because today's fighting is itself at a distance from Europe's heartlands, Europe's wars are geographically more limited today than is suggested either by their rhetoric or by Europe's past.

Since the end of the Cold War, the only conflict to present Europe with serious internal disturbance has been on its south-eastern extremity, in the former Yugoslavia. Germany in particular was concerned about the wider repercussions for the continent, and European armies were deployed in order to contain them. The war was limited for NATO, which was able to encompass what it did under the umbrella of peace-keeping or, at most, peace-enforcement. This second phrase begged a number of questions about what is war and what not. When does peace enforcement shade into counter-insurgency? And, as the fighting mounted, what, apart from the precedent of UN peace-keeping, kept the word 'peace' in the title, as opposed to 'war'? 'Wider peace-keeping' has encapsulated the missions of some national contingents in Afghanistan, while others have been fighting a counter-insurgency campaign and yet have hesitated to describe what they are doing as war. These verbal sleights of hand themselves create expectations among Europe's populations which may not be reflections of the reality on the ground, and at the same time can generate doctrinal confusion for the troops required to implement national policies whose declared aims expect them to do one thing but whose deployments confront them with something else. Limited war provides a conceptual portmanteau to hold these competing but overlapping ideas, while retaining a clear distinction from major war, hot war or existential conflict.

Those in Britain or even in Germany, who during the Cold War and its immediate aftermath suggested that Europe's security rested on the Himalayas or on the Hindu Kush, were mocked – precisely because whatever happened there seemed so distant and so remote as not to present a viable security interest or to pose a threat within Europe.[12] There is both irony and paradox here. Irony that today European armies are fighting, killing and dying in Afghanistan, and paradox in that the geographical distance makes the war seem so removed that Europe's populations struggle to see themselves as being at war. Limited war cannot be more limited than that.

For Clausewitz, what united his two forms of war was policy, and it is policy that presents the greatest challenge in defining and shaping limited war. Corbett's vision of limited war was not an option for Clausewitz, a Prussian located in central Europe. It is true that, much to the fury and shame of Clausewitz, the king of Prussia tried to keep his state out of the wars which engulfed much of Europe. But the war came to Prussia nonetheless. By 1812 war against France was for Clausewitz a matter of German national survival. He, like the advocates of war in revolutionary France twenty years earlier, used the vocabulary of honour, freedom, nationhood, values and beliefs, rather than that of minor territorial gains, to justify fighting.[13] In both cases the military means and the political objectives were consonant. The challenge for Europe today is that the military means are limited but the political objectives are not. The result is strategic incoherence.

Europe's governments today pursue limited wars, consonant with the size and organisations of their armies, but can also follow the United States in using the rhetoric of major war to explain to their publics what they are doing. Robert E. Osgood's *Limited war: the challenge to American strategy*, published in 1957, set out to provide the conceptual framework for limited war. He appropriated Clausewitz as his principal intellectual inspiration, writing in the aftermath of the Vietnam War that Clausewitz had 'reacted against the wars of the French Revolution and Napoleon', and enunciated the principle that 'armed force must serve national policy' as the foundation of limited war strategy.[14] For Osgood – and for Henry Kissinger, whose *Nuclear weapons and foreign policy* was also published in 1957 – the Korean War was the example on which theory rested. The interests of three major states, the United States, the Soviet Union and China, had clashed on the Korean peninsula, but the war had not extended geographically and it had not triggered the release of nuclear weapons. Famously General Douglas MacArthur had wanted to use them but as a result was dismissed by the president, Harry S. Truman. Osgood's reading of Clausewitzian logic prevailed. War, as personified by MacArthur, had followed its own inherent trajectory towards escalation and 'absolute' forms, but policy had moderated and dampened that inherent dynamic and directed it into more sensible and contained channels.

The paradox of the war in Afghanistan was that this logic became reversed. Phrases like 'courageous restraint', coined by General Stanley McChrystal in 2009 to describe his expectations of the military use of force, and 'population-centric' counter-insurgency, show that in these sorts of war it is the armies which are using the ideas of limitation in war – albeit as a means rather than as an ends. By contrast some govern-ments, and particularly the United States in the aftermath of the 9/11 attacks, use the rhetoric of total war to articulate their objectives. George W. Bush spoke in terms of democracy, liberty and freedom, open-ended ideas, which themselves conjured up the Jeffersonian ideals which framed the foundation of the United States, and were used to underpin the idealism of American foreign policy by Woodrow Wilson and Franklin Delano Roosevelt. There are no inherent political limitations here. To be sure, Barack Obama has tried to damp down the rhetoric, but he cannot fully escape its consequences, since it both provided the initial rationale for the wars in Iraq and Afghanistan, and is still inherent in the thinking which shapes American politics, whether Republican or Democrat. Indeed, Obama's own Secretary of State, Hillary Clinton, continued to explain the United States's involvement in Afghanistan in terms of human rights, rather than the more specific objective of counter-terrorism.

Europe is not sure where it stands in this inversion of the political imperatives of limited war. Indubitably its military commitment is limited and the notions of 'courageous restraint' and population-centric counter-insurgency make as much sense to the armies of Europe as to that of the United States. Indeed in American eyes the principle of restraint is now so embedded in some European armies as at times to undermine their military value. But the political goals to which that military capability is being applied, even if they fall short of the ambition of 'the global war on terror', can still seem of fundamental importance, couched in terms of the threat to national security and linking al-Qaeda and even the Taleban to domestic terrorism.

That makes the war in Afghanistan 'a war of necessity'. Many western armies explain their mission there in terms not of counter-terrorism, but of human rights, of good governance in Afghanistan, and of security for its population. These humanitarian objectives, articu-lated by the British prime minister, Tony Blair, in his Chicago speech in 1999, and in the United Nations' ideal of the 'responsibility to protect', adopted in 2005, ought to prompt wars of necessity, but in fact have produced responses that are labelled 'wars of choice'.

In his 1982 speech to the National Defense College which first gave currency to the phrase 'wars of choice', Menachem Begin, the prime minister of Israel, presented 'a war of choice' as a war which was not waged in defence of the state's existence. This carried two implications.

The first was that, unless it was waged with the authority of a United Nations Security Council resolution, the war could be in breach of the United Nations charter. 'A war of necessity', waged for national survival, carried the implication that the war was inherently defensive; 'a war of choice', waged at a distance in somebody else's interest, that it was inherently offensive. In practice the distinction is not clear cut even in the case of 'a war of necessity'. Begin's speech began with a definition of 'a war of necessity' which rested on the Second World War. He argued that if France had not waited for the war of necessity but had opted for a war of choice and attacked Germany in 1936, 'there would have remained no trace of Nazi German power and a war which, in three years, changed the whole of human history, would have been prevented'.

Begin went on to argue that Israel had fought two unequivocally 'necessary' wars, that for its independence in 1947–9 and the Yom Kippur War of 1973. The latter did indeed begin with pure defence, as the Israeli Defence Force found itself surprised by the Egyptian army's crossing of the Suez canal and its advance into Sinai. The fact that six years before, in 1967, Israel had acted pre-emptively against a similar threat from Egypt meant that, in Begin's eyes, in that war Israel had exercised choice even if he believed that, as he averred in his speech, 'this was a war of self-defense in the noblest sense of the term'.[15]

At one level, as the 1967 Arab–Israeli War suggested, the distinction between a war of choice and a war of necessity is a false one. If France had attacked Germany in 1936, it would clearly have exercised a choice to do so: the threat to France from Germany was still more latent than manifest. Even in 1939 France and Britain chose to fight Germany over Poland, having refused to do so over Czechoslovakia, and in 1940 Britain 'chose' to carry on fighting, rather than to negotiate or even surrender as France had done. As Clausewitz pointed out, this argument can be taken even further: war begins not with attack, but in the choice of the defender to resist the attacker. If invasion remains unopposed, there is no 'clash of wills', and hence no war.

Begin's argument had particular purchase in the context of American foreign policy after 2001. The decision of the Likud government in 1982 to take war into Lebanon, 'Operation Peace for Galilee', was deeply unpopular – both with Israeli liberals and in some quarters of the Israeli Defence Force itself. Begin acknowledged that the terrorists' attacks, launched from bases in Beirut but conducted within Israel, 'were not a threat to the existence of the State'. However, he maintained that 'they did threaten the lives of civilians whose number we cannot estimate, day after day, week after week, month after month'.

The case advanced by George W. Bush for the invasion of Iraq in 2003 was not dissimilar, and became similarly divisive, initially abroad but progressively at home too. No link had been established between the 9/11 attacks and Iraq, but the American government's decision to invade that country piggy-backed both on the need to pre-empt further terrorist attacks after 9/11 and on its corollary, the 'war of necessity' to remove al-Qaeda bases in Afghanistan. Lawrence Freedman, whose original role in promoting the difference between 'wars of choice' and 'wars of necessity' found its reflection in Blair's Chicago speech, has subsequently pointed out that 'the problem with the distinction lay not in the idea of wars of choice but in the idea of wars of necessity'.[16] No responsible government is in fact going to argue for the opposite of a war of necessity, which is not in fact 'a war of choice', but an unnecessary war. Arguing that a war is one of necessity is a way of trying to close down domestic debate. Menachem Begin, by presenting a war to save Israeli lives as a war of choice, was in effect conceding ground to his political opponents in what was a deeply divisive internal debate for Israel. Bush sensibly took a different tack. He argued that the invasion of Iraq, like the war in Afghanistan, was a war of necessity, not least because it would have been political folly to have said anything else.

Freedman has argued that 'one way to think about the distinction therefore may be to take "necessity" as referring not so much to the actual decision but to the fact a decision must be made'. However, he sees this comparison in purely political terms, as Begin did in 1982 – even if Begin preferred to cloak the decision in terms of choice not necessity. What both approaches leave out of account are the ethical considerations which have become increasingly important in public debate since 1999. Freedman sees humanitarian interventions as wars of choice. The problem which liberal societies confront is whether a political choice is equivalent to a moral choice. The moral obligation to protect could trump the political choice not to intervene. The civil war which broke out in Syria in 2011 illustrates this dilemma in acute form. Even without the legitimisation of a United Nations Security Council resolution, the moral expectation created by the United Nations' endorsement of the responsibility to protect in 2005 could have created a coherent case for intervention. The loss of civilian lives and the suffering of non-combatants can exercise a moral obligation sufficient to make the case for a war of necessity.

So, two inherent contradictions bedevil the phrase 'wars of choice'. The first is that morally humanitarianism should leave no leeway for choice. The ethical imperative to act should be overwhelming, and not subject to national or other self-interest. This was the paradox that the European powers confronted in March 2011 as the rebels in Libya called for aid. Self-interest counselled against action both because Arab sentiment could resent European intervention and because the European powers could ill afford an entangling and protracted conflict while also being engaged in Afghanistan. On the other hand, the 'responsibility to protect' demanded intervention, to prevent war crimes, the deaths of innocent civilians and possibly humanitarian disaster. Those were all deeply moral reasons for action. Their ethical value points to the second contradiction in the idea of a war of choice. The title 'war of choice' implies a degree not simply of ambiguity but even of levity, which under-estimates the seriousness which should underpin the decision to go to war. Moreover, it is a title which is in danger (as Begin found out) of suggesting that no national interest is at stake. For the Mediterranean states of Europe, events in the Maghreb following the 'Arab spring' in 2011 had security implications potentially as serious as that which Germany feared in relation to the former Yugoslavia in the 1990s. In both places war's capacity to force migration cannot but have implications for neighbouring states – whether they lie across the Balkans or across the Mediterranean.

As Richard Hass, who served in the administrations of both Bushes, father and son, has pointed out, wars of necessity can easily become wars of choice.[17] He is of the view that the war in Afghanistan has gone through that process, in itself the consequence of the failure to limit the war in terms of time. But that evolution in itself has served to discredit both titles. The effort to distinguish a war of choice from a war of necessity, bound up as it was within the debate as to what constituted a war of national survival, and as to how the conceptual legacy of the Second World War was either relevant or even historically accurate, was a half-way house in an effort to shape the place of war within international politics after the end of the Cold War.

Political realities alone now demand that our conceptualisation of war is given fresh branding. The moral expectation which states have imposed upon themselves through humanitarian interventions leaves them little choice. Europe, with the possible exception of France, has not been good at developing its own strategic thinking since 1945, but it needs a fresh iteration of the idea of limited war both to explain how it structures its armed forces and to frame how it proposes to use them, not only for the guidance of its governments but also for the enlightenment of its peoples.

The United States is unlikely to lead the way, at least conceptually and at least for the moment, in part because the ideas of Osgood and of Henry Kissinger are associated with the determination of the Kennedy administration to commit itself to Vietnam. For Americans, limited war is now associated with failure. But that does not mean that it is not using something very like it in practice. Obama has turned his back on the rhetoric of his predecessor, that of global war; he is waging the campaign against international terrorism primarily with drones and special forces; he is imposing both manpower constraints and strict time frames on an army which is countering what in 2011 David Petraeus called an 'industrial-level insurgency'; he is getting his allies to deal with problems like Libya which are of more concern to them than to the United States; and he is using cyberwarfare, in the shape of the Stuxnet virus, rather than direct assault to curb Iran's nuclear capability.[18] Moreover, these solutions are going rather well, not least in the most obvious success of his presidency, the elimination of Osama bin Laden. As Dominic Tierney argued in 2010, 'in the current strategic environment, limited interstate war is an essential option in the military toolbox'; furthermore, from the American perspective it possesses a tradition that goes back to the founding fathers, to Thomas Jefferson and to John Quincy Adams.[19] Given Obama's re-election in 2012 the solutions could become entrenched in American strategic thought and so gain a label; if he had not been, the Republicans would presumably have carried out their promise to increase the military effort and to remove the pressure to contain the war in Afghanistan by setting a fixed timetable.

There is another point about American limited war thinking in the 1950s which is relevant to Europe today. Its nostrums were developed in the context of nuclear weapons; they were about constraining major war by proposing to engage in armed conflict with more limited means. Within Europe, the western states' insouciance about the danger of major, or even of inter-state, war should not be projected on to the future or on to their eastern allies. Those states that joined NATO after the end of the Cold War as part of the partnership for peace programme did so because their proximity to Russia meant that both – war and Russia – remained real dangers. NATO provided institutional support in circumventing them. The need to think about limited war is pressing not least because its disciplines should also lead us to think through the possible circumstances in which, thanks to the guarantee of common security provided by Article 5 of the Atlantic Alliance, major war too could edge its way back up Europe's agenda.

7 THE LIMITATIONS OF STRATEGIC CULTURE:THE CASE OF THE BRITISH WAY IN WARFARE

Few of the great thinkers on strategy who wrote before 1918 did so in English, and few of those who have done so since 1945 have been British as opposed to American. From Sun Tzu to Jomini, from Machiavelli to Clausewitz, most of the true originals in strategic thought have not hailed from the United Kingdom. But in one respect at least Britain can claim to have made an original contribution to strategic thought. Those who support the concept of strategic culture, the focus of much attention in contemporary strategic studies, have developed an ancestry for it which traces its roots to the British isles.

Not that the connection is immediately obvious. In 1977 an American, Jack Snyder, wrote a report on Russian strategic culture for RAND. Snyder defined strategic culture as 'a set of general beliefs, attitudes and behavior patterns with regard to nuclear strategy [that] has achieved a state of semipermanence that places them on the level of "culture" rather than mere "policy"'.[1] Snyder's piece was seminal: he asked strategic theorists to look at Soviet attitudes to war in the light not just of communism but also of Russia's geopolitical position and its Tsarist legacy. In a sense it turned the study of strategy away from its Cold War grooves, shaped by game theory and political science, and back to its more traditional disciplinary roots, geography and history. It was a point well made. Strategic culture has taken root in some university politics departments, and, although Snyder himself has since moderated his position, others – notably Colin Gray – have adopted it with increasing vehemence.[2]

Strategic culture explains why strategy does not change, not why it does. It contains strategy within a familiar framework, assuming that strategic culture limits choice and inhibits any adjustment in priorities, despite the fact that both are essential to the making of strategy. It is not a coincidence that its immediate origins lie in the Cold War, or that Snyder was specifically addressing the use of nuclear weapons. For many political scientists nuclear weapons had created a stability within strategy, a position which today seems increasingly untenable.

What followed from this fixation with continuity was a desire to give strategic culture a pedigree, and political scientists found it in the writings of the British military thinker, Basil Liddell Hart, who in 1927 first coined an expression, 'the British way in warfare', which can still shape debates on British strategy. The title, however nationally determined, has had international repercussions: in 1973 Russell Weigley adopted it for his study of military thought in the United States, *The American way of war*, and in 2005 Robert Citino produced *The German way of war*.

Both Weigley and Citino wrote as historians in works which were designed to be understood as interpretations of the past, not as prescriptions for the future. Weigley's last chapter addressed the United States's war in Vietnam and did so as it was drawing to its inglorious close. His final paragraph drew a line between the past and the future, between what he had just described and the direction he expected the United States to follow in the future. 'At no point on the spectrum of violence', it began, 'does the use of combat, offer much promise for the United States today.' This was a conclusion which reflected what he saw as the inutility of nuclear weapons. But he also reflected the prevailing views on the likely legacy from Vietnam: 'Because the record of nonnuclear limited war in obtaining acceptable decisions at tolerable cost is also scarcely heartening, the history of usable combat may at last be reaching its end.'[3]

Citino confronted an even more decisive break, that of 1945. It was hard to talk of a continuing cultural legacy in a state whose army had ceased to exist with the fall of Hitler and the division of the country between east and west. When the Federal Republic of Germany formed the Bundeswehr in 1955 it deliberately shunned the past and set out to create its own traditions and norms. The reunification of Germany, and the incorporation within the Bundeswehr of elements of the German Democratic Republic's Volksarmee in 1990, did not change the trajectory.

What is also striking about both the American and German 'ways of war' is that neither says very much about strategy in the sense in which Liddell Hart or the current proponents of strategic culture understood or understand the word. Liddell Hart's encapsulation of British practice, however tendentious, at least aspired to link the use of war to national policy. The subtitle of Weigley's book, 'a history of United States military strategy and policy', suggested that he would do the same. He did not. Although he began by acknowledging the value of an interpretation of strategy which linked war to policy, he then rejected it. He concluded that Clausewitz's definition, that strategy is the use of the battle for the purposes of the war, 'conveys better than any other concise one what Americans meant by strategy when they thought about the subject in its (to them) broadest sense from the beginning of their national history through the Second World War and even through the Korean War'.[4]

In other words the American way of war was concerned less with strategy as it was understood in the late twentieth century, and more with operational thought. Weigley's interpretation distinguished between a strategy of attrition, used by a weaker power to exhaust a stronger, and a strategy of annihilation, used by a stronger power for the direct over-throw and defeat of the enemy. He argued that, as the United States's wealth had grown, the latter had increasingly become its preferred option. Weigley's argument and even his history were confused, not least because the definition of attrition promoted by the German aca-demic Hans Delbrück before the First World War, that attrition was the strategy of a weak power manoeuvring to avoid battle, had been recast by the experience of that war, to mean exhaustion through the use of battle.[5] And so attrition in the second half of the twentieth century had become associated with economic strength, not weakness. Confusingly, Weigley, despite writing in 1973, had used attrition in the first sense, that of weakness, but in 2003 Max Boot, in an article provocatively called 'The new American way of war', used it in the second, that of strength. Boot's article was in part a celebration of the United States's (initial) success in Afghanistan and Iraq. He took these as an indication of the United States's prowess in small wars, its army's readiness to adapt, and as an alternative to the conventional association of the American way of war with 'a grinding strategy of attrition'.[6] Boot may have differed from Weigley on this point, but like him he did not address the link between war and policy. Antulio Echevarria took both of them to task in 2004. They tended 'to shy away from thinking about the complicated process of turning military triumphs, whether on the scale of major campaigns or small-unit actions, into strategic successes'. Echevarria's conclusion was damning: 'the American style of warfare amounts to a way of battle more than a way of war'.[7]

Exactly the same could be said of the German way of war. As Citino put it, the German solution 'was to emphasize an intermediate level known as the *operational*', which meant 'the maneuver of large units to strike the enemy a sharp, even annihilating blow as rapidly as possible'.[8] If the military achievements of Prussia or of Imperial and Nazi Germany have any resonance in strategic culture it is in the operational thought of armies other than Germany's, and especially that of the United States.[9] Significantly, when Boot argued that the invasion of Iraq in 2003 had created a new gold standard at the operational level, he used the Wehrmacht as his comparator. The 2003 invasion had replaced the 'Blitzkrieg' of 1940, making 'fabled generals such as Erwin Rommel and Heinz Guderian seem positively incompetent by comparison'.[10] Both armies had learnt how to deliver stunning battle-field successes; neither nation had developed 'a way of war' adapted to the pursuit of national policy goals.

Liddell Hart's British way in warfare was therefore very different on both counts. Operationally, he advanced the idea of the indirect approach, or attacking on the line of least expectation. Undoubtedly he saw this form of war as appropriate to the British military, but his account of the application of the indirect approach made abundantly clear that he did not regard it as an operational method that was particularly British. Strategically, the British way in warfare began not with operational methods but with national policy – with Britain's economic, maritime and trading position. Liddell Hart's concern with national military history was not solely, or even primarily, with the past. The challenge for strategy is how best to link past, present and future: how to apply the context of the past in order to understand the present and to inform an awareness of the future.

So Liddell Hart did not see the British way in warfare in the purely historical terms in which Weigley and Citino addressed the American and German versions. He employed history for didactic and prescriptive purposes. In 1927 he had extolled James Wolfe's capture of Quebec in 1759, the victory which gave Britain mastery of North America, as an example of the British way in warfare at the strategic level in *Great captains unveiled*, a book which – in Brian Bond's description – saw 'the past in terms of the present; to seek "a message and a moral"'.[11] The point was not lost on the book's reviewers at the time, and was made clearer five years later. Liddell Hart had developed a lecture, delivered in January 1931 at the Royal United Service Institution (as it was then called), on 'economic pressure or continental nation' into a full-blown book, called *The British way in warfare*. Liddell Hart's aim was 'to show that there has been a distinctively British practice of war, based on experience and proved by three centuries of success'. The practice was 'based above all, on mobility and surprise – apt to Britain's naval conditions and aptly used to enhance her relative strength while exploiting her opponent's weakness'. Britain's 'natural condition' was maritime and 'her relative strength' was naval; mobility and surprise were, however, not least in this context, associated with land warfare, even if they arose from Britain's domination of the seas. 'This naval body had two arms; one financial which embraced the subsidizing and military provisioning of allies; the other military, which embraced sea-borne operations against the enemy's vulnerable extremities.'[12] So, according to Liddell Hart, the British way in warfare was a marriage of maritime power, economic strength and expeditionary warfare. Developed in the aftermath of the First World War, it reflected Liddell Hart's reaction to that experience, and argued in essence that Britain, instead of creating a European mass army for deployment on the continent, should fight to the last Frenchman.

The trouble was that the British way in warfare did not reflect reality. In the twentieth century Britain's historic practice was not what Liddell Hart prescribed. France's military losses in the First World War were almost twice those of Britain, but Britain still created a mass army and delivered it to Europe. By 1917–18 the army was comparable in size to that of France and it could legitimately argue that it was doing at least as much of the fighting. Indeed this development was precisely that to which Liddell Hart took such strong exception. Britain put a mass army on the continent again in 1939 and in 1944, and it left it there after 1945; elements of it were still there when the twentieth century closed. Liddell Hart's model of the British way in warfare was derived from the eighteenth century, not his own. Moreover, it ignored the bulk of British military experience in the previous century, between 1815 and 1914, which had no relationship to Europe at all, and was directed to the acquisition and protection of empire.[13]

Strategic culture, and British strategic culture in particular, may therefore have a dodgy pedigree, but a central question is whether – despite that – Britain has made a distinctive contribution to strategic thought. It has. That contribution may indeed be shaped by Britain's geography, its island status and its empire, as well as by its history, but its importance lies not in its relationship to strategic culture, with its presumption of continuity, but to strategic thought proper. To be fair to Liddell Hart, that is exactly where he sought to place it. In an earlier book, *The decisive wars of history*, published in 1929, he drew conclusions from a review of the history of war up to 1914, on whose foundations he set out 'to construct ... a new dwelling house for strategic thought'. He rejected the notion that strategy was necessarily about the overthrow of the enemy's military power, and argued that a government might prefer 'to wait until the balance of forces can be changed by the intervention of allies or by the transfer of forces from another theatre', or 'even to limit its military effort, while economic or naval action decides the issue'. He rebuffed the notion that such a policy reflected weakness, not least because it was 'bound up with the history of the British Empire and has repeatedly proved a lifebuoy to Britain's allies, and a permanent benefit to herself'. He concluded that, 'there is ground for enquiry whether this military policy does not deserve to be accorded a place in the theory of the conduct of war'.[14] *The decisive wars of history*, which he regularly revisited and revised throughout his life (unlike *The British way in warfare*), became *Strategy: the indirect approach*. It has had an influence beyond the confines of the United Kingdom and yet it is shot through with themes derived from his reading of Britain's history.

Strategic thought requires a capacity to interrogate strategic practice, to reflect on the experience of the application of theory, and to do so in a way which produces ideas which are applicable beyond historical boundaries in terms of widening our understanding of war and its utility. Such an approach embodies the possibility of change, not just the straitjacket of continuity. Britain has made such a contribution, but its most original author was not Liddell Hart, who in this respect was no more than a populariser, a man who lifted ideas from others without acknowledgement.[15] The real originator of a distinctively British approach to strategy was Julian Corbett, and his principal insights are to be found in *Some principles of maritime strategy*, published in 1911.[16]

Corbett made a number of essential contributions to strategic thought which built on Clausewitz, whom he admired and quoted extensively, but which took the understanding of strategy far beyond

Clausewitz's (to our ears) narrow definition of it, 'the use of the battle for the purposes of the war'. Indeed Corbett was notorious in 1911 precisely for his scepticism about the importance of battle at all. He argued that command of the sea was a chimera, and rather that the aim was the command of its communications, both to enable and protect trade, and also to facilitate an invasion of enemy territory by the army. To do at least some of this a navy might have to disperse its assets, not concentrate them. It followed that fleet action could not be the principal goal of naval strategy. The notion that a battle squadron of the fleet was intended for battle only, he wrote, was 'an idea of peace and the study'.[17]

Corbett's central and distinctive departure point was of course clear in his title: it was maritime rather than purely naval. The great nineteenth-century thinkers, being continental Europeans, concentrated their attentions on armies which were determined to defend or to cross land frontiers. Corbett set out less to address naval warfare than to put it into the context of mainstream strategic thought, and he did so in a way that was much more productive (and still carries more current relevance) than did Alfred Thayer Mahan two decades earlier. Privately Corbett criticised Mahan for what he called his 'continentalist' modes of thought, by which he meant the determination to attack the enemy's battle fleet and to put that at the centre of naval strategy.[18]

Corbett saw maritime warfare as superimposed on naval warfare, because, as he put it, humans live on the land and therefore the issue is how sea power is brought to bear in human beings' principal medium of existence. Maritime strategy, he wrote, 'determines the part the fleet must play in relation to the action of land forces; for it scarcely needs saying that it is almost impossible that a war can be decided by naval action alone'.[19] Its prime function was to sort out relations between the army and the navy in a plan of war. The army's initial role might be to assist the fleet to achieve command of the sea as a preliminary to achieving effects on land; alternatively the fleet's task might be to forward military action, and to enable an island power to sustain a military contingent overseas.

It is Corbett's focus on maritime strategy which distinguishes him from Liddell Hart. The latter, despite his arguments about the British way in warfare, never devoted sustained attention to war at sea. The conclusion to his history of the First World War, *The real war*, first published in 1930, two years before his development of the idea of the British way in warfare, anticipated it by asserting that the Royal Navy, thanks to its blockade of

Germany, had done more to win the war for the allies than any other factor. 'The fundamental cause of the Armistice', he wrote, was 'Britain's sea power, her historic weapon, the deadliest weapon which any nation wielded throughout history'.[20] And yet neither the chapters of the book itself nor its bibliography reveal any sustained engagement with economic warfare or maritime strategy. Their focus is almost exclusively on the operations of land warfare, and Liddell Hart's own enthusiasms and expertise were concentrated on the army. Paradoxically, a man who above all studied the conduct of war on land wanted to contain and limit the British army's own practice of it.

Corbett's focus on maritime strategy led to four original contributions to strategic thought more generally, which continue to resonate to the present day. First, he introduced the idea of limited war. Modern strategic thought tends to see Robert Osgood as the father of this approach. Osgood, whose work has been discussed in the previous two chapters, does not seem to have been aware of what Corbett had said about limited war, although Corbett – like Osgood – had used Clausewitz's distinction between two sorts of war as his departure point. In his note of 10 July 1827, published as a preface to *On war*, Clausewitz had differentiated between a war 'to overthrow the enemy – to render him politically helpless or militarily impotent' and a war that ends in a negotiated settlement.[21] Clausewitz said little directly about limited war itself in the main body of his text, but Corbett developed the thought. Part of his thinking was moral. The less important the object, the less value a state attaches to it, and so the less the means (and the less the destruction) to be applied to its achievement. Morality therefore had a utilitarian value, reflected in economy of force: as Clausewitz too had recognised, not all war was 'absolute' war. But the principal justification for limited war was geographical. The distinction between the two sorts of war was more organic for maritime empires. Corbett argued that 'limited war is only permanently possible to island Powers or between Powers which are separated by sea, and then only when the Power desiring limited war is able to command the sea to such a degree as to be able not only to isolate the distant object, but also to render impossible the invasion of his home territory'.[22]

Limited war explained why Britain, possessing only a weak army, had been able to expand its empire at the expense of greater military powers. It also explained the value to Britain of what Corbett called 'wars of intervention'.[23] These could include wars in which Britain committed a force limited in size in a country in which it had no vital interest in order to aid the chief belligerent – what Corbett described as wars of 'limited interference in unlimited war'. The latter was of course what Liddell Hart would call the British way in warfare, which was itself in essence a form of limited war. Corbett wrote in terms which anticipated Liddell Hart by two decades: 'What may be called the British or maritime form is in fact the application of the limited method to the unlimited form, as ancillary to the larger operations of our allies – a method which has usually been open to us because the control of the sea has enabled us to select a theatre in effect truly limited.'[24]

Our modern use of the term 'wars of intervention' is couched in rhetoric which is derived from international law and international humanitarian law. Intervention in another state requires in most cases a United Nations Security Council resolution, and its justification often resides in the responsibility to protect innocent individuals from genocide or war crimes. So the political context is not that of coalition warfare between European powers, as it had been in the eighteenth century (a period which influenced Corbett's thinking as much as it did that of Liddell Hart). However, as in the eighteenth century, Britain in the first decade of the twenty-first was still projecting limited force at a distance, using air power as well as sea power, in conjunction with allies and in what was an ancillary mode. Kosovo, Iraq, Afghanistan and Libya were all wars of intervention: all were also – for Britain – limited.

Corbett was viciously attacked for his ideas about limited war in his own day, especially given the threat from Germany before 1914. Spenser Wilkinson, the first professor of military history at Oxford, in Corbett's terminology a 'continentalist' who, like Mahan, favoured fleet action, used his review of *Some principles of maritime strategy* in the *Morning Post* to warn naval officers of the dangers of reading the book.[25] However, unlike Liddell Hart, Corbett was not being definitive or dogmatic: he did not argue that limited war was applicable to all Britain's wars. Here he could call in evidence his second major contribution to strategic thought: his distinction between what he called minor strategy and major strategy. Minor strategy was what most of his contemporaries, following Clausewitz's definition, understood by strategy: the use of the battle for the purposes of the war. Today we would call this the operational level of war. Corbett identified major strategy as sitting above minor strategy. In 1923 J. F. C. Fuller, another Briton, would call major strategy grand strategy, and this title – which Corbett himself used on occasion[26] – has stuck. Liddell Hart in particular took it up and developed it.[27] Major strategy encompassed all the levers of national power, economic, social and political as well as military; it included relations with allies, the need to prepare for war in peacetime and, once at war, to coordinate operations in different theatres of war.

Today we more often call 'major strategy' simply 'strategy', and so use the latter word in a very different and much broader sense from what Clausewitz or Jomini meant by it. Again Corbett's point has contemporary resonance. Three British parliamentary committees addressed the issue of strategy between 2009 and 2012: the House of Commons Defence Committee, the House of Commons Public Administration Committee and the Joint Parliamentary Committee on the National Security Strategy. The second of these, whose report was published in 2010, enquired whether Britain still 'did' grand strategy, asking if not, why not, and, if it should do it, how it should.[28] The answers to the questions were negative, but successive governments made at least some progress in satisfying the parliamentary demand. In 2008 the Labour government under Gordon Brown drew up a National Security Strategy, and in 2010 the coalition government of David Cameron formed a National Security Council.

The third significant contribution which Corbett made to strategic thought was his recognition of the role of law in shaping strategy. Significantly Clausewitz had said almost nothing on the subject. Corbett was trained as a lawyer and was called to the bar. In 1909, by which time he had been lecturing on the Naval War Course at the Royal Naval College at Greenwich for seven years, Britain faced a critical moment in its capacity to use sea power in a future war. The declaration of London sought to curtail belligerent rights in war at sea, especially by tightening the definition of contraband and addressing the doctrine of continuous voyage. The latter covered the legal right to seize contraband carried in neutral ships to a neutral power but due for onward transmission to a belligerent. For Britain, if it were neutral in a future war, measures designed to keep the list of contraband short and to prevent the application of continuous voyage, would be advantageous. Its maritime supremacy and its merchant tonnage would ensure that it would reap commercial benefits as a cross-trader in war. However, if Britain were itself a belligerent, the reverse would apply. Its capacity to use its power at sea to wage economic warfare by establishing a blockade would be limited. Corbett threw his weight behind the move not to ratify the declaration of London in 1909, and eventually the House of Lords followed his course and rejected it.[29]

Corbett saw that law was central to British strategic thought. He appreciated that the fact that Britain possessed the maritime strength to do what it wanted to do on the high seas did not in itself warrant its putting international law to one side. Instead the reverse applied: Britain was required to respect the law and to apply it precisely because of its naval preponderance. Moreover, by doing so, Britain was better able to shape the law to suit its strategic priorities. His discussion of blockade was shot through with legal analogies and legal cases.

When Britain went to war in 1914 it gave as one of its reasons for doing so the need to uphold international law. By its invasion of Belgium, Germany had infringed both the rights of small nations and the obligations of international treaties. The members of the Oxford Faculty of Modern History declared in 1914: 'we must fight Prussia; and we fight it in the noblest cause for which men can fight. That cause is the public law of Europe.'[30] Once at war, Britain was therefore under a greater self-imposed pressure to observe the law. Admittedly the context was not the same as it had been in relation to the declaration of London: in 1914 international law did not have the power to prevent one sovereign state from going to war with another, but it did aim to modify the behaviour of one power in relation to another once war had broken out. So, whereas Germany could plausibly argue that Britain's reason for going to war lacked legal sanction, Britain knew that how it chose to fight that war should observe a growing body of international law.

International law was one component of the War Course on which Corbett had taught at Greenwich. Britain used the law to shape its conduct of hostilities and exploited its observance of the law and Germany's disregard of it for propaganda purposes. Before 1917 the effects of Britain's determination to harness international law for belligerent purposes were felt particularly in the United States. In its dealings with Washington, Britain's manipulation of neutral rights rested on the advice of international lawyers, and it stressed German breaches of the Hague conventions and the atrocities committed by the German army in Belgium. Nowhere was the appearance that Britain was conforming to international law more important than at sea. Britain's refusal to ratify the declaration of London and its imposition of orders in council to institute a blockade of Germany in 1915 enabled Germany to argue that Britain, not Germany, was the power which believed might was right. In some respects, therefore, the accusations levelled against German militarism were countered by German charges against British navalism. At the end of the war, therefore, J. A. Hall, naval officer and barrister, was at pains to argue that the British blockade 'was a lawful and reasonable application of the historical principles of international law to modern conditions'.[31]

Britain's need to conduct a blockade at all rested on the fourth of Corbett's contributions to strategic thought, the function of democracy in war. To end a modern war, Corbett argued, a state has 'to exert pressure on the citizens and their collective life'.[32] Clausewitz had recognised the role of the people in war in his manifesto of February 1812, when he hoped that at least Prussia and, ideally, the German nation as a whole would emulate the example of Spain and rise up against Napoleon and French tyranny. However, such ideas, with their empowerment of the people in relation to the monarchy, carried revolutionary implications, and after 1815, constrained by the king and his conservatism, he was more cautious in his utterings. He made reference to the role of the people in his section on the 'trinity' in war in book I of *On war*, and to the nation in arms and its possible future effect on war in book VI, that on the defence. However, his ideas on the mobilisation of the people found little resonance in mainstream strategic thought over the remainder of the nineteenth century. Most pre-1914 military writers focused their thoughts on the destruction of the enemy's armed forces, and marginalised the effect of popular insurrection.

In the First World War, however, Britain followed Corbett's injunction. It appealed to the German people over the heads of their government. The blockade was the stick with which to beat them for their loyalty to the Kaiser. It was accompanied by British propaganda which lampooned him, while recognising that his subjects could be agents of democratic change. The blockade proved to be a blunt instrument, unable to distinguish between genuine contraband of war and food supplies destined for non-combatants. It was increasingly designed to starve the population of Germany, rather than to deprive the German government of supplies vital to the maintenance of the war effort. But it therefore also fed on the hope that the German people would be pushed into revolution, so overthrowing the Kaiser, installing a democratic government and seeking peace with the allies.

On one reading of the events in 1918 that was indeed how the war ended. In Germany this interpretation suited the army, anxious to argue that it had not been defeated in the field but subjected to 'a stab in the back' from a population starved into socialism. In Britain the stab in the back suited the advocates of sea power and underpinned the 'British way in warfare'. Liddell Hart wrote in 1929, in an argument that he was to repeat but not develop in his histories of the First World War, that the blockade's 'existence is the surest answer to the question whether but for the revolution the German armies could have stood firm on their own frontiers. For even if the German people, roused to a supreme effort in visible defence of their own soil, could have held the allied armies at bay the end could only have been postponed – because of the grip of sea-power, Britain's historic weapon.'[33] So, somewhat improbably, German militarism and British navalism found themselves colluding in their explanation of how the war had been lost and won. In Britain, although the argument that the same process could be repeated next time round remained central to strategy in the inter-war years, it was the Royal Air Force which really appropriated the assumptions derived from Corbett's strategic thought. Corbett had seen the effects of blockade as slow to take effect,[34] and this need to develop a form of economic war which could achieve its results before they had been trumped by what happened on land drove much of the thinking on the subject in the 1930s. British intelligence sought to identify key commodities whose absence could cripple German production and so transform blockade from a blunt instrument into a rapier, agile and speedy.[35] The Royal Air Force had it both ways. Bombing promised precision effects (which in practice it struggled to deliver), while being able to hit the civilian population if it missed Germany's economic infrastructure. The latter, it was widely anticipated, would cause the sort of domestic chaos which reflected the hopes that many had pinned on naval blockade before 1914.[36] In 1925 Liddell Hart followed Giulio Douhet in arguing that bombing cities would precipitate first revolution and then a speedy overthrow of the enemy's government.[37] The strategic bombing offensive as conducted by Bomber Command rested on the presumption that if the German population suffered enough it would overthrow Hitler, just as it was believed to have turned against Wilhelm II as a result of the blockade.

It did not. However, the contribution of democratised societies to the conduct of war remained important to strategic thought. Nuclear deterrence rested on the idea that the civilian population could be held to account for the behaviour of the states of which they were members. Indeed, increasingly, deterrence relied on sparing the governments of nations under attack so that they could negotiate, while hitting their peoples with devastating strikes against cities. The perspectives applied by both sides to the wars since 9/11 have reflected their democratisation. Al-Qaeda and Islamic jihadist websites hold the peoples of democratic states accountable for the actions of their governments in order to justify their terrorist attacks. The United States's strategy for the invasion of Iraq in 2003 rested on the potential separation of Saddam Hussein from those he ruled, just as the allied blockade and then bombing of Germany had endeavoured to divide the people first from the Kaiser and then from Hitler. If the allies toppled Saddam Hussein, the belief ran, the Iraqi people would welcome their invaders.

So 'war among the people' has a much longer pedigree than the recent impact of that phrase as applied by another British strategic thinker, General Sir Rupert Smith, suggests.[38] And democratisation in war works both ways. Smith's attention was on the need for armies to recognise that their fight must win the support of the population in whose midst they are waging war. But in democratic societies, elected governments need also to consider the views of their constituents in 'wars of intervention'. In 2010 the British prime minister, David Cameron, said that Britain would end its war in Afghanistan in 2015, and on 20 November made a point that he made several times subsequently, that the British public expected a clear date for withdrawal and was right to do so. The impression he created was that domestic opinion in Britain was more important than the situation in Afghanistan itself.[39]

The place of democracy in strategic thought is of course not to be seen as an exclusively British contribution to strategic thought, nor should the idea of limited war be seen any longer in this light, or the importance of grand strategy, or the place of law in strategy. All of them play their part in the formation of strategies of other nations and of the coalitions to which they contribute. That is exactly why they cannot be subsumed under the heading of strategic culture. They are shared throughout Europe, and in the western world more broadly, precisely because the geopolitical strategic assumption on which Clausewitz rested his strategic thought, that Europe was the cockpit of war, no longer applies. Like Britain, all Europe now projects military power at a distance, and it does so to achieve greater objects than its limited means suggest are commensurate with its efforts. Law is fundamental to how that military power is applied, and democracy or democratisation is a tool of war as much as the object for which war is fought.

This conclusion does not mean that Corbett is today more influential in Europe than Clausewitz. Nor is it designed to set up Corbett as an alternative to Clausewitz: Clausewitz still matters if we are concerned to find a common strategic inheritance in Europe. Corbett's work is shot through with Clausewitzian influences, and Corbett did more than any other British thinker of his generation to think through Clausewitz's stress on the relationship between war and policy, as well as one of its most important consequences for strategic thought, the distinction between limited and unlimited war.

The central point to be extracted from Corbett's debt to Clausewitz is that what mattered to both of them was the relationship between theory and practice in strategy. We must be wary of assuming that current strategic practices are the norm, that they have the continuity of strategic culture. There is no guarantee, and indeed little probability, that what we do now will apply in future wars. To interrogate our current practices, and so to understand them, we need strategic theory, not strategic culture. This was the dialectic that mattered for Corbett, as it had done for Clausewitz.

8 MARITIME STRATEGY AND NATIONAL POLICY

Maritime strategy faces problems of definition even more acute than those currently confronting what some theorists call 'military strategy'. The latter is a tautology constructed to reflect the growth of grand strategy or national strategy, and is therefore some compensation for the sloppy, if currently fashionable, tendency to use the word strategy as a general synonym for policy. For traditionalists, all strategy is military. So what do modernists mean by 'military strategy'? How, for example, does it differ from the operational level of war? Is 'military' used in the narrow British sense, and therefore to refer only to armies? Or is its use more transatlantic, with the implication that 'military' encompasses all the armed services, including the navy? If the latter is the norm, is the expression 'naval strategy' redundant? To British ears, naval strategy implies that it is something that the Royal Navy does, and therefore carries the ultimate sanction of armed force. Maritime strategy by contrast is broader, potentially embracing all the nation's uses of the sea, economic as well as defensive. These questions are not hair-splitting. Words convey concepts: if they are not defined, the thinking about them cannot be clear, and there is also the danger that one person's military strategy is another's policy, just as one person's naval strategy is another's maritime strategy. Such ambiguity creates confusion within individual nations, let alone alliances ostensibly speaking a common language.

Strategy traditionally defined at the turn of the eighteenth and nineteenth centuries was what generals, not admirals, did. They applied strategy by employing their armies in particular theatres of war. Following a course set by the Enlightenment, by Joly de Maizeroy and the comte de Guibert, Jomini and Clausewitz sought, in the first place, to link tactics to strategy, and to provide a theoretical framework within which the practice of land warfare could be understood. To that extent the evolution of military thought is a story that starts at the bottom, with the practical and tactical guidance of the ancients, from Xenophon to Vegetius, and works its way up. Clausewitz defined strategy as the use of the battle for the purposes of the war: in other words, he aimed to link tactics to a wider objective and ultimately, of course, to link strategy to policy.

Naval and maritime strategy followed a very different evolutionary trajectory.[1] Those who wrote about land warfare said little (in Jomini's case) or nothing (in Clausewitz's) about war at sea. Although Clausewitz was reflecting on the experiences of the French Revolutionary and Napoleonic Wars, he did not mention Trafalgar. So what was Nelson doing at Trafalgar? Was he not using battle for the purposes of the war? He was, but he did not describe what he was doing as strategic. Nelson was a consummate tactician: he and his contemporaries focused on manoeuvring the fleet to maximise its firepower. Nobody who fought at sea in the Napoleonic Wars subsequently used those wars – as Clausewitz and Jomini, both veterans of the land war, used them – to develop thinking about strategy. Instead maritime strategy emerged less from the development of military theory, from the impact of the Enlightenment on military activity, and more from the need to codify practice.

The sea in the early modern world was a highway, used for the development of trade and empire. The theory that played a role in the development of thinking about war at sea was economic and legal, not military. Mercantilism, the argument that state control of overseas trade was vital to national wealth and national security, connected the protection of shipping and sea routes to governmental policy. The English navigation act of 1651, requiring English goods to be carried in English ships, encapsulates the linkage. The revenue generated through the customs levied on trade itself aided the development of a navy designed both to protect trade and to help secure colonies. In other words, the growth and application of sea power were intimately linked to economic practices in a way that land warfare was not.

Secondly, the origins of international law and the regulation of warfare through law lie, at least in the context of modern Europe, more obviously in developments at sea than on land. Hugo Grotius, the author of *De jure belli et pacis* (The law of war and peace), the founding text of the laws of war, published in 1625, became interested in the subject through international maritime law. He was employed by the Dutch East India Company to advise it on prize law at sea, and in 1605 argued, in *The freedom of the seas or the right which belongs to the Dutch to take part in the East India Trade*, that the sea was common to all. Grotius's case for freedom of the seas, which he further developed in 1609, rested on natural law, 'innate in every individual' and 'derived from nature, the common mother of us all'.[2] But this did not prevent him from also accepting the right of a belligerent to capture enemy goods at sea, even while aboard neutral ships. Those concerned with the exercise of maritime power in the seventeenth and eighteenth centuries had to contend much more directly with the legal framework for its exercise than did commanders in land warfare.

Practices at sea therefore combined naval (in the narrowly military sense) with maritime developments, peace with war, and economic and legal practices with national power. Nobody gave this the title strategy – and it wasn't, in the sense which most generals, at least until 1918, understood the word. It was not about the use of the battle for the purposes of the war. Significantly, however, John Hattendorf, having assessed Britain's wars with France over a span of 126 years, between 1689 and 1815, has concluded: 'One can see repeated strategic patterns emerging as Britain became involved in alliances and used her navy to support them, while at the same time protecting herself and her trade and extending her colonies and her markets.'[3]

Moreover, the same imperatives persisted after 1815. When Britain abandoned protectionism for free trade, most dramatically with the repeal of the corn laws in 1846, it changed the dynamic between sea power and the economy, but not the fundamental importance of the relationship. Britain adopted free trade not least because its position as the world's first industrial nation enabled it to export more effectively, at lower prices, than any other state. Its maintenance of the world's premier navy was the price it paid for that authority. Moreover, to echo Grotius, it also used the Royal Navy to further the principles of natural law by suppressing the slave trade. The word strategy was not used to describe any of this, partly because the level at which Britain was operating did not necessarily imply the use of war (between 1856 and 1914 Britain remained neutral in every international war except the South African War), and partly because the linkage that mattered was not that between strategy and tactics but that between naval capability and economic and geopolitical effect. Even as late as 1891 Vice Admiral Philip Colomb eschewed the word 'strategy' and did not directly address the concept in his book, *Naval warfare: its ruling principles and practice historically treated*.

Colomb and his brother John had by then been addressing what we would now see as the foundations of maritime strategy for more than twenty years, but by the time Philip Colomb published his big book he was too late to make his mark. In 1890, the year before, Alfred Thayer Mahan brought out *The influence of seapower upon history*. So at the very end of the nineteenth century Britain's eighteenth-century wars with France were employed to develop theories about the use of sea power, not only by Mahan but also in due course by Julian Corbett. This retrospective exploitation produced an obvious paradox: the achievements of sailing fleets were used to generalise about the applications of sea power in the age of steam and iron. Mahan justified this approach quite explicitly in his lectures at the US Naval War College: 'Based as Naval Strategy is upon fundamental truths, which, when correctly formulated, are rightly called principles, these truths, when ascertained, are in themselves unchangeable; but it by no means follows that in elucidation and restatement, or by experience in war, new light may not be shed upon the principles, and new methods introduced into their application.'[4]

The notion of unchanging principles is part of what has given classical strategy a bad name, particularly in an environment that is frequently historically illiterate and so can be quicker to condemn than to discriminate. It is, however, worth observing that Mahan, confronting the challenge of new technologies, emphasised continuity, not in order to deny the impact of those innovations but in order better to understand their consequences. It was precisely the fact of change that prompted naval thinking into life. Moreover, having been born, it soon realised that the theories of strategy developed for land warfare were not straightforwardly transferable to war at sea.

At one level of course both Mahan and Corbett, having recognised the existence of naval strategy, and having treated it as a distinct subject of its own, wanted to align it with military strategy. Mahan's father, Denis Hart Mahan, was a soldier who had taught at West Point and who thought in Jominian terms. Mahan himself stressed the importance of battle fleets and of fleet action. His view of strategy was set in large part by its relationships to tactics, 'when the fleets come into collision at the point to which strategic considerations have brought them'.[5] Because of changes in weapons technology, tactics were subject to change, but strategy much less so. Corbett, for his part, was impressed by Clausewitz and treated naval strategy as part of a much bigger whole, which also encompassed war on land. War was a continuation of policy. It was a branch of statesmanship. In practice, less divided Mahan from Corbett than some of the polarisations by later commentators have suggested. Like Corbett, Mahan saw strategic arguments as based on political economy. Maritime trade was vital to national prosperity, and naval superiority was essential to the protection of the nation's interests. He accepted that naval strategy had a role to fulfil in war as well as in peace.[6] Corbett's thinking, although different, was complementary. He contrasted 'minor strategy', by which he meant the strategy followed by a single service, with 'major strategy', by which he meant the use of all the nation's resources for the purposes of the war.

These historical points have a purpose. We now embrace a definition of strategy that is much wider than Clausewitz's, that is not just about the use of the battle for the purposes of the war. Strategy today is applied in peace as well as in war; it encompasses the preparation of plans and equipment for conflict, aspects which Clausewitz saw simply as ancillary; and it includes the economic capacity of a state and its people's political and social commitment to wage war. The intellectual roots of that definition derive from maritime power, not land power, and are a manifestation of the influence of sea power on strategic thought. Hattendorf's conclusion encompassed a period that ran from Louis XIV to Napoleon, from the late seventeenth century to the early nineteenth, to characterise British naval strategy against France. Like today's 'long war' against global terrorism, nobody knew when Britain's struggle with France would eventually end, and, because the British and French fought each other in the Americas and south Asia as well as in the narrow seas around Europe, it often seemed to lack a clear geographical focus. Nor could Britain's 'long war' with France be characterised as a genuinely continuous conflict: like today's 'long war', it was punctuated by periods of inactivity or even peace, both regional and general. But there is one crucial distinction between the 'long war' of the eighteenth century and that of today: nobody at the time gave it either that label or anything comparable. Britain in the eighteenth century was too pragmatic to use titles which inflated the problem, and which would make it even bigger in strategic theory than it was in practice. Strategy is a profoundly practical business: the application of the title 'the long war' has made the struggle against terrorism impractical, unfocused, and therefore 'astrategic' (if such an epithet exists).

In the eighteenth century, Britain and France were using sea power to further their economic and imperial objectives. Britain secured the sea lines of communication by controlling the world's maritime choke points. Mahan knew this, and he also knew that big battles were the dramatic and comparatively rare flash points in a much more mundane engagement with the realities of sea power, most of them having nothing to do with war. Trafalgar was the exception, not the rule: the rule was patrolling the West African coast to curb slavery or sending gunboats up waterways and rivers in support of land operations in colonial conflicts. In the latter context, the navy gave the army the range and the ability to sustain operations at considerable distances from the home base. Between 1815 and 1914, Britain dominated the world's waters. It implemented 'major strategy', but the Royal Navy did not fight a major action. Then, as now, the army, not the navy, got the headlines. Sea power served national policy, more than it served strategy.

There is an obvious and easy, if somewhat superficial, parallel with the Cold War. The army may have deployed significant elements to the British Army of the Rhine, but it did its actual fighting outside Europe, not inside it. Between 1945 and 1990, the Royal Navy was engaged much more directly in waging the Cold War than the army was. The Royal Navy, and other NATO fleets, constantly patrolled the Greenland–Iceland–United Kingdom 'gap'; its SSNs (nuclear-powered attack submarines) were involved in a continuous cat and mouse game with Soviet SSNs; and its SSBNs (submarines armed with ballistic missiles) exercised global power through nuclear deterrence.

The fact that all this changed in 1990, with the end of the Cold War, was a much greater revolution in strategy than the 9/11 attacks were. Its most striking manifestation was a negative one, the intellectual vacuum that assailed the services as they were robbed of the scenarios around which for four decades they had constructed war games and exercises, and which had driven technological innovation and defence procurement. After 1990, the removal of the bipolar balance and the reduced salience of nuclear deterrence allowed a much easier recourse to war. The effect on land strategy, although it seemed for the most part not to be recognised, was the resuscitation of very traditional approaches to strategy, and specifically the use of war for the purposes of policy. The effect on maritime strategy proved even more dramatic. Three shifts occurred: first, a shift from blue-water navies to brown-water navies, from operations in the oceans to operations on the littoral; secondly, a shift from operations under the water to operations on the surface, from being deliberately invisible to being often deliberately visible; and thirdly, a shift in emphasis in procurement from SSNs to aircraft carriers. But this too resulted in the resuscitation of a traditional form of maritime strategy. Navies are used to secure trade, to exercise political influence without necessarily resorting to war, and to apply sea power to sustain order at sea, particularly in the control of piracy and terrorism. These are very nineteenth-century approaches to maritime strategy, applied in the context as much of peace as of war; indeed, one might even call them 'policy'.

Moreover, within war itself, Corbett's observations on naval strategy, as opposed to maritime strategy, have resurfaced: 'Naval strategy is but that part of [maritime strategy] which determines the movements of the fleet when maritime strategy has determined what part the fleet must play in relation to the action of land forces; for it scarcely needs saying that it is almost impossible that a war can be decided by naval action alone.'[7] War, in other words, is joint, a point that was lost sight of when the Cold War did not involve fighting a war, at least not within the NATO area. 'There is no *naval* strategic warfare,' Captain Wayne Hughes of the US navy wrote in 1997: 'A maritime campaign by a maritime nation aims at sea control as the means not end, because strategy prescribes wartime goals and missions governed by purposes on the land.'[8]

These remarks have emphasised continuities, rather than changes, and that has been deliberate. Of course, there is a need to recognise change and respond to it. But it requires recognition first of what has not changed: far too much energy in current strategic thought goes into identifying 'new threats', which are in reality not very new. Advocates of maritime strategic priorities who stress either that the vast majority of the world's trade is moved by sea or that most of the world's population lives close to the coast are identifying not change but continuity: exactly the same points held true a hundred years ago, and were the axioms around which Mahan and Corbett developed their theories. Driven by the need to impress their political masters, and determined to secure their shares of scarce resources, ministries of defence are pressured into hyping threats as both new and growing. One must not confuse a necessary part of the political game in which they are caught with reality. Seeing what has not in fact changed is the precondition for appreciating what has – and that can involve a historical memory that goes further back than the declining years of the Cold War.

There is a further issue: the identification of new threats can be a means of conflict prevention. A threat, even one as great as that presented by the Soviet Union armed with nuclear weapons, does not have to become an opportunity for war. Today's challenges include globalisation, climate change, urbanisation, pandemics, and shortages of such vital resources as food and water. Are these challenges facing humanity threats, or can they become opportunities for cooperation? Will they be manifested in new wars or new forms of war? Will there be wars caused by the competition for wealth, living space or commodities? Of course, the answers to all these questions might be yes, but their very identification as a potential challenge to security could enable people to deal with them without their becoming causes for war. Water shortages do not have to become 'bellicised'; they can be dealt with, as they currently are in the Nile basin, by international agreements. In stressing 'new threats', and in making an easy jump from them to the notion that they will inevitably lead to wars, the evidence under our very noses is too readily ignored, that is to say the character of today's wars. Many of the wars fought in the early twenty-first century do not look very 'new' to the historian, particularly in terms of their causation: ethnicity, nationality and religion are much more significant drivers than urban slums or AIDs.

If imagined but largely putative maritime threats are allowed to drive us into customised responses and specific patterns of procurement, then the products are in danger of being totally unhelpful. Adaptability and flexibility must be the key words: in recent operations platforms, on both land and sea, have been used in contexts and in ways very different from those for which they were conceived. Moreover, much of the adaptation and flexibility may have to be in directions that look remarkably traditional. Although the Royal Navy's current deployments are different from those of the Cold War, they would be recognisable to the practitioners of Britain's global dominance one hundred and fifty years ago.

Geography provides strategy with an underlying continuity, a point that is generally true (nobody has moved Britain to a different location from the one it occupied in the past), but is especially important for the sea. Too many thematic and global refrains in current strategic debates fail to disaggregate regional pressures from wider concerns, and so miss the opportunity to make them more manageable, and even potentially soluble, if treated regionally rather than globally. The thrust of the 2010 British National Security Strategy was to emphasise that, in spite of the economic recession, Britain would retain a global role. It asserted that Britain has 'a global reach disproportionate to our size' and stated that 'Britain will continue to play an active and engaged role in shaping global change.'[9] Such ambitions do not sit easily with defence cuts driven above all by the need to reduce government spending. The National Security Strategy said, rightly, that strategy is about making choices. Such choices are more often driven by shortages, rather than by abundance. Publicly at least, the coalition government was clearer about choices in relation to the means available to implement its policies than it was about how the consequences have constrained the ends which it might seek to achieve, and therefore which ends it might choose to pursue and which it might abandon. Both the House of Commons Defence Committee and the Joint Parliamentary Committee on the National Security Strategy criticised the government on this count, effectively questioning how 'strategic' the National Security Strategy really was.

All three armed forces are potentially affected by the mismatch between ends and means, but the problem is particularly acute for a navy precisely because its roles lie across the axis of grand strategy, athwart the line between strategy and national policy. Maritime strategy, above all, has the task of ensuring that that line is not a fault-line but a form of linkage. Three specific areas of national policy illustrate the challenge for sea power and the understanding of its significance. They are: the stress in current defence policy on the prevention of conflict; the sorts of capabilities that are required to deliver on that aim, especially if it is to have a global remit; and the priority to be accorded to the Anglo-American relationship within that.

First, the National Security Strategy asserts that the United Kingdom 'will use all the instruments of national power to prevent conflicts and avert threats beyond our shores'.[10] Between 1815 and 1914 Britain used its sea power to maintain order on the world's seas, and did so in its own economic and colonial interests (primarily) but also in the interests of international order. In 2010 the Royal Navy recognised that its capacity to contribute to conflict prevention, not least in comparison with the other two services, was a possibly unique selling point. But four obvious questions arise. All four are central to any policy of prevention, but they are made more pressing by the diminution in the size of the fleet.

The first is where in the world the navy will concentrate its efforts, given its lack of ubiquity. Not even the Royal Navy of 1900 claimed to be everywhere all the time, and the issue of whether and how to concentrate its assets was the central dilemma confronted by Jackie Fisher when he was First Sea Lord between 1904 and 1909. In some respects the current British ambition, fed by the free use of the word 'globalisation', exceeds the ambition of the British empire at the height of its powers. So the first question in relation to prevention revolves around the issue of space.

The second question concerns time. For how long is the cost of prevention worth sustaining? When does it cease to be good value for money? During the Cold War, NATO felt the burden of a credible threat to deter a war with the Warsaw Pact was an expense worth bearing indefinitely rather than incur the destruction of an all-out major war which could, and probably would, have included the use of nuclear weapons. However, if the dangers consequent on war are more limited, and if the ongoing humanitarian consequences of not intervening or the national security risks of prevention begin to outweigh the costs, then the pressure to act becomes greater than the pressure to prevent.

Thirdly, and bound up with the question of time (or indeed of patience), there is therefore the place of deterrence within our notions of conflict prevention. Clearly Britain's capacity to prevent depends on its retention of the capacity to intervene on the ground if prevention fails or ceases to be useful. At that point the use of force, although initially limited, becomes subject less to the direction of national policy and more to the dictates of war itself. Reciprocity in armed conflict tends to lead to escalation – not least if it begins at a low level and increases gradually. Some would argue that that is exactly the problem with maritime intervention: that it takes time to deploy and to concentrate and so cannot strike an initial blow that is both overwhelmingly destructive and simultaneously demoralising. In 2011 the slow build-up, and even working up, of the task force in the Libyan conflict was made into a virtue, but it began as a necessity, as Britain had no other option.

Fourthly, after the issue of prevention, but related to it, especially if the responsibility to prevent is being interpreted as a global one, is the issue of capabilities. If the Royal Navy has become a more 'brown-water' navy since the end of the Cold War, does the stress on prevention now require it to regain some aspects of an oceanic capability? Geopolitical considerations suggest that, from the British point of view, sea power should find its more immediate application in waters that are adjacent to the United Kingdom. The North Sea, the Atlantic approaches and, as the polar ice cap melts, the Arctic are all obvious areas for maritime operations. Britain's alliance with France in 2010 and its commitment more generally to the security of Europe also give it a role in the Mediterranean. Its dependence on oil, its need to keep open the straits of Hormuz and its requirement that the maritime trade routes round Africa should be secure are all understandable priorities. But where does this leave the South Atlantic, with the ongoing commitment to the Falkland Islands, and what today are Britain's interests east of Singapore?

The largest and deepest ocean of the world, the Pacific, therefore raises in its most acute form the disjunction between the global ambition of national policy and the capacity of maritime strategy to deliver on that policy. The United States's maritime strategy is increasingly focused on the Pacific and the rise of China. The National Security Strategy is predicated on Britain's readiness to act in conjunction with the United States, but that commitment was forged during the Second World War, and then consolidated in the Cold War. It rested on American willingness to put the Atlantic and Europe ahead of the Pacific and Asia – a decision reached by Washington in 1941–2, albeit not without controversy, bitterness and heartache. On 5 January 2012, President Obama unveiled a 'Defense Strategic Review' for the United States, which said that 'Most European countries are now producers of security rather than consumers of it,' and declared that the United States would refocus its policy towards the 'Asia-Pacific'.[11] So the United States, with much greater capabilities, has realised that it has to adjust its policies in line with its resources, and to say where it needs to be stronger and where it can afford to be weaker. Britain has not.

In 1965 Britain did not follow the United States's interests in 'Asia-Pacific' to the point of involvement in the Vietnam War, despite the fact that Britain was still a player in south-east Asia. British national policy, to see the United States as its principal ally, was therefore potentially at odds with the means which underpinned British strategy. Britain's defence policy was increasingly predicated on the Anglo-American relationship, but Britain did not submit to American pressure to send troops to Vietnam, although its Commonwealth partners in the region, Australia and New Zealand, both did. In the event the expectations of the external relationship between the United States and Britain did not put to the test the internal relationship between British foreign policy and British defence policy, but the point is a salutary one. The relevance of the Vietnam example for 2012 relates to almost any British policy position with regard to states east of Syria. Is Britain prepared to follow up its diplomatic alignment with the United States to the point of war? In 2002–3 it was ready to do so in the cases of Afghanistan and Iraq, and current indications suggest that it would do so in the case of Iran. The big question arises in relation to China. In the event of a war between China and the United States, Britain might have no direct national interest, beyond that of a good relationship with the United States, and it looks almost certain that it would not possess the defence capabilities to make a meaningful contribution. So the third area of concern for Britain, after the unanswered questions of prevention and the matter of capabilities, is how far British maritime strategy should be shaped by, and subordinated to, the imperatives of the Anglo-American relationship and – hence – of American foreign policy.

The rhetoric which accompanies defence policy can too easily be allowed to obscure the pragmatism and hard-headedness which needs to underpin the making of strategy. Without the clarity which comes from context, whether geographical or historical, national security strategies can do more to aggregate threats than to discriminate between them. The Royal Navy has, reasonably enough, been at pains to emphasise its contribution to the war in Afghanistan, and not just through the deployment of the Royal Marines. The public's assumption that this is a war waged by land forces is logical enough: Afghanistan is, after all, a landlocked country. The fit between operations there and the expectations of maritime strategy can only be made by reference to the stock phrases of the Bush and Obama administrations, 'the global war on terror' and 'the long war', both of which put regional conflicts in a broader geopolitical context. Yet the problems which British forces confront on the ground in Afghanistan – lawlessness, poverty, drought, drugs and deeply traditional Islamic beliefs – were all evident forty years ago – long before 9/11, before the Soviet invasion and even before the toppling of the Emir. Long-standing local difficulties, profound and chronic but limited in their wider impact, have been overlaid with 'new threats' and so rendered more intractable, rather than less. By the same token, maritime trade did not suddenly become either 'global' or 'international' after the 9/11 attacks: it was both these things in 1900. The difference then was that the challenges to the security and development of global maritime trade were treated as regional and specific.

The conceptual challenge remains. If the web and woof of maritime strategy remain closer to policy than to traditional 'military' strategy, then this should be recognised for what it is, and not shoved under the carpet. At times, the Royal Navy seems to be in danger of denying its wider 'political' role. In their presentations to the RUSI 'Future Maritime Operations Conference' in 2006, both Amiral Oudot de Dainville and Vice Admiral John Morgan, representing the French and United States navies respectively, integrated nuclear deterrence in their remarks. The First Sea Lord, Admiral Sir Jonathon Band, did not. The determination of the uniformed armed forces, and especially the Royal Navy, responsible for manning the SSBNs which carry the Trident missile system, to treat the deterrent as a 'political weapon', is strategically counter-productive. This oxymoronic description implies (wrongly) that conventional military capabilities do not also have deterrent functions, and also suggests that there is a distinction – rather than a convergence – between the political and strategic roles of both conventional and nuclear capabilities. The function of strategy is to integrate the political and the military. If the nuclear deterrent is compartmentalised, separated from other military capabilities, then it is gradually robbed of utility and relevance. Three major consequences follow. First, the possession of nuclear weapons is divorced from thinking as to their applicability; nothing could be more irresponsible, since their use or the threat to use them becomes unpredictable and 'astrategic'. Secondly, the wider applications of deterrence within war, as well as outside war, particularly in the threat to escalate the use of conventional weaponry, tend to be forgotten. Thirdly, and consequently, deterrence loses its ability not just to prevent major war but also to limit most wars.

The key reason for the absence of inter-state war, especially in Europe, is the memory of unlimited inter-state war in 1939–45. Deterrence at this most basic level underpins the National Security Strategy's insouciance about the dangers of inter-state war, and yet it has been accorded a progressively lower profile in British defence policy as the memory of the Cold War has receded. By presenting terrorism as the principal existential threat facing the United Kingdom, British defence policy has robbed itself of coherence and of credibility.

Terrorism is a significant issue, but it is not the rationale for most of Britain's current defence capabilities. Because the latter do not serve to curb the former, they can seem redundant. Clearly capabilities should not shape strategy; the tail should not wag the dog. Thus the case against Britain's possession of the nuclear deterrent is that it will not deter terrorists, particularly suicide bombers. That is self-evidently true, but it is also silly. It gets hold of the tail, and then imagines that the dog is terrorism. The dog is war, and major war at that. During the Cold War the case for an independent British nuclear deterrent was weakened not by the nature of the threat, but by the strength of NATO and by the robustness of the American nuclear guarantee. Today both the latter look weaker and the effect should be to strengthen the case for a genuinely independent British deterrent. Paradoxically, however, many of those who were the most determined supporters of the British deterrent during the Cold War can now be numbered amongst its critics. Furthermore, British defence policy says very little about its deterrent functions – little, that is, by comparison with any statement on defence issued between 1957 and 1991, and little by comparison with what is still said by the United States in its quadrennial defence reviews. In part this is a reflection of the success of deterrence: the military threats which Britain faces are more remote than were those presented by the Soviet Union, but that is precisely because deterrence, often implicitly, has served and is serving its purpose, which is to prevent major war.

This is not solely a matter of nuclear, as opposed to conventional, deterrence, although the fact that deterrence is associated particularly with nuclear weapons has been one reason for its comparative neglect since 1990 and even more since 1997. The low public profile of nuclear deterrence, and the absence of public engagement with its nostrums, does not mean that there are not crucially important decisions to be taken around it. Three of those are imposed by technological considerations: the ageing of the submarines which carry the nuclear weapons, the United States's move away from the missile systems which deliver them, and the nature of their warheads. The fourth, and most immediate, consideration is indeed political: the consequences of the referendum on Scottish independence due to be held in 2014. The Scottish National Party has consistently opposed British possession of nuclear weapons. For too long the reaction of the Ministry of Defence was to ignore this 'political' problem. It can no longer do so: the British nuclear deterrent force is based at Faslane on the Clyde and its storage facilities are at Coulport, also in Scotland.

The future of the British nuclear deterrent is indeed a 'political' matter in the very direct sense of being subject to party political debate and immediate governmental input. But the Royal Navy is also colluding in the marginalisation of its role in the Trident question as it wants to avoid having to incorporate into its own budget both the direct and the opportunity costs of acquiring a successor system. By presenting the deterrent capability as 'political' rather than 'military' (in the broader American sense) the navy hopes to serve that objective. The renewal of the deterrent is thus made to appear as something falling outside the navy's interest. But at the same time as the navy separates deterrence from strategy, it obscures yet further the much broader policy objectives which maritime strategy specifically has aimed to serve. Moreover, as so often in strategy, these issues, although separable, and necessarily so if they are to be properly analysed, do not in fact stand in isolation. The United States has always been reluctant to tell its allies what particular capabilities it would like them to contribute to the alliance. However, when pushed in 2010, its response to the United Kingdom was more specific. The nuclear deterrent was one of three items that it hoped Britain would continue to contribute to the common weal. The imperative to integrate maritime strategy with national policy could not be stated with greater clarity.

9 TECHNOLOGY AND STRATEGY

The strategic contours of war in the early twenty-first century have not been as decisively shaped by technology as our own belief in the remorselessness and acceleration of innovation suggests. This is not to say that the machine has not had a public and highly charged impact on warfare. In the British case, claims that the British army in Iraq was forced to soldier with inadequate body armour, 'Snatch' Land Rovers rather than properly armoured vehicles and insufficient helicopters made equipment the stuff of headline comment and cross-party accusation.[1] These were issues because in Iraq and increasingly in Afghanistan improvised explosive devices (IEDs) became the major cause of deaths and serious wounds among coalition forces. What were initially quite crude devices became more sophisticated as coalition forces responded by improving their own measures for force protection, not least by increasing the armour on their vehicles and by travelling by helicopter rather than by road, and as counter-IED devices and detection improved. It can be argued that IEDs had a strategic effect.[2] The horrific wounds that they inflicted, particularly but not only to the lower limbs, fed the public image of the soldier as the victim of an unthinking and uncaring government, and so stoked the appetite for withdrawal regardless of whether the intended outcome of the war had been reached. But, in that case, the IED itself remained only a means, and the ways to its effectiveness were its propaganda effect. The transformation in media technologies (through the internet and mobile telephones), and the consequent democratisation of 'strategic communications', meant that the dissemination of news and opinion no longer occurred exclusively (or even principally) through the press and the politicians, but now belonged to the people.[3]

Although it can therefore be argued that both IEDs and mobile telephones are new technologies with strategic effects, it is less clear that those technologies have themselves changed strategy and strategic thought. Indeed, what is possibly more striking than their (visible) impact on the wars of the early twenty-first century is the less visible decision not to use much more destructive technologies in Iraq and Afghanistan. The most advanced military powers in the world have been waging war without using the full range of their technological capabilities, and that self-imposed restriction has not been confined only to nuclear or chemical weapons. Neither heavy artillery nor, once the initial battles of 2003–5 were over, main battle tanks played a major role in land warfare. The conditioning influences in shaping strategy in Iraq and Afghanistan have been less technological and more social, political and historical. Those responsible for the application of strategy have needed to understand the tribal structures of both countries, their religious affiliations and the long course of their troubled histories, more than the employment of revolutionary military technologies. On the ground armed forces have experienced a displacement effect, acquiring cultural awareness while no longer needing the expertise to plan and execute an artillery fire plan for a corps-level operation.

This observation, however trite, looks either remarkable or mundane, depending on one's perspective. If judged against the background of twentieth-century military history, with its sequencing of new technologies designed to mass fire and to deliver more of it more accurately, it is remarkable. If judged in the context of classical strategic thought, it is mundane.

Nineteenth-century strategic thinkers did not see technology as a central consideration in strategy. Neither Jomini nor Clausewitz gave it independent consideration. Since the weaponry employed by the armies in which they had fought had changed little during the course of the previous century, that was hardly surprising. What mattered to them was social and political change, effected above all by the French Revolution. Clausewitz's understanding of the dramatic ways in which the character of war had changed in his own day rested precisely on the level of popular participation in war which the revolution had enabled.[4] Nor, in the context of land warfare, did the progressive industrialisation of Europe radically change the existing contours of strategic thought over the course of the nineteenth century.

The railway was the product of European heavy industry with the most obvious strategic effects. It enabled large bodies of troops to be moved and supplied, and it enabled a commander to concentrate his forces more quickly, for defence as much as for attack. Helmuth von Moltke the elder, the chief of the Prussian general staff, showed how it had changed the relationship between time and space in mobilising his armies more quickly than did either Austria in 1866 or France in 1870. Moltke himself was under no illusion as to the effects of railways: 'They enormously increase mobility, one of the most important elements in war, and cause distances to disappear,' he wrote in January 1870. Moltke not only expected railways to shape 'the organic and tactical arrangements of armies', but also demanded that in future Prussia's commercial interests be 'unencumbered' to enable their full development.[5] With effects that ranged from the tactical to the economic, and which were likely to shape both military structures and the state management of industry, the railway was clearly a technology with revolutionary implications for strategy. And yet that was not how Moltke or other strategic thinkers saw it.

Strategy, Moltke wrote in 1871, involved 'the transfer of knowledge to practical life, the continued development of the original leading thought in accordance with the constantly changing circumstances'. In the process the railway had the capacity to emphasise or de-emphasise the component parts of strategy, but not to dominate it as a whole. 'An invention', Moltke opined, 'is not what it is itself; all depends on its future development.'[6] All European armies before 1914 were well aware that the weapons with which they were now equipped, breech-loading magazine rifles, machine guns and quick-firing artillery, all of them products of science's application to mass production, had irrevocably changed tactics. Writing half a century after Moltke, in 1913, General Max Schwarte, in an encyclopaedic survey of technology's impact on warfare, wrote that 'it is not possible fully to separate the art and science of war from technology; they are too tightly bound in with each other and stand too closely alongside each other in their very strong and unbreakable mutual effects'.[7] Schwarte observed that the technological changes in the business of war since the French Revolution had been particularly significant in the previous few years, stoked as they had been by great power rivalries.[8] So Schwarte had moved a long way from Clausewitz. However, he was much less certain that technology had changed strategy: indeed, he did not use the word 'Strategie', let alone address it, preferring 'Kriegführung' (or the conduct of war).

Schwarte's response was not unusual. When Alfred von Schlieffen, who had retired as the chief of the Prussian general staff at the end of 1905, wrote an article on 'the war of today' in the *Deutsche Revue* in January 1909, his vision of warfare was indubitably materialist, shaped by the impact of science on the battlefield.[9] To that extent little separated his thinking from the much fuller and better-known description of the effects of modern weaponry on modern war by the banker I. S. Bloch, published in six volumes a decade before. However, whereas Bloch's conclusion was that war had now become effectively impossible, not only because of the changes wrought on tactics by technology but also because of the problems for credit, production and trade that major war would generate, Schlieffen's was that strategy, defined largely by its capacity to maintain an army's capacity to manoeuvre, had to triumph over tactical constraints. Schlieffen could not follow Bloch's reasoning to its conclusion precisely because as a professional soldier he had to give war utility. Strategy therefore continued to operate on some enduring but largely unexplained plane where it was unaffected by technical innovation. The great controversy over strategy in Wilhelm II's army, that between the Prussian general staff and Hans Delbrück, pivoted after all on competing interpretations of Frederick the Great's strategy a century and a half earlier, in the Seven Years War.[10] Schlieffen regretted that Moltke had not written a theory of war, regarding his famous aphorism that 'strategy is a system of expedients' as insufficient.[11] But Schlieffen himself did nothing to fill the gap.

Even those in the German army who took issue with Schlieffen's materialism, as General Friedrich von Bernhardi did in 1912, found themselves on converging courses with him when it came to strategy. Bernhardi accused Schlieffen's article of privileging the experience of the Russo-Japanese War of 1904, arguing (reasonably enough) that 'it is inadmissible to deduce the character of modern war from a special case'. War, Bernhardi thought, does not have 'a uniform strategic character, because the whole strategic situation changes with the conditions of the ground and its cultivation, the formation of the frontiers, the railway system, as well as the size and character of the masses employed'. He rejected the notion that modern strategy depended above all on the concentration of forces, and that therefore the railway's capacity for assembling armies would be decisive in a future war. For him, 'the mechanical conception of war cannot after all be convincingly substantiated by theory'. Bernhardi closed his critique of Schlieffen with a ringing and neo-Clausewitzian endorsement of the enduring factors within strategy: the role of politics in the conduct of war; the nature of generalship; the utilization of time and space; and, above all, 'the superior influence of spiritual and moral forces'.[12] Bernhardi's was a frequent refrain in pre-1914 military circles. In Britain, Major General E. A. Altham, asked to write a commentary on the recently issued *Field service regulations* (published for the first time in 1909), produced a volume on *The principles of war* in 1914, which argued that success or defeat in modern war 'depend not so much on the size of armies and fleets' as on 'their fighting efficiency', which 'is directly proportionate to the moral force of the nation'.[13]

So, for soldiers before 1914, the industrialisation of Europe and its attendant technological innovations had changed tactics, and had consequently effected change from the bottom up, but they had not caused a revolution in strategy. During the war which followed, that upward pressure would force them to begin to acknowledge the effects within the making of strategy, but they saw little need to do so before the war. For sailors, the story could and should have been very different, but in the end was not.

The application of steam propulsion to ships in the 1840s, the emergence of the ironclad warship by 1859, and the ultimate development of the steel-hulled, big-gun battleship, the Dreadnought, by 1905, meant that navies underwent an even more dramatic change at the tactical level but in an area of operations where the separation of tactics from strategy and even policy was much harder to sustain than on land. The commander of a fleet in action was both directly engaged at the tactical level, and himself in mortal danger (to that extent Jellicoe at Jutland in 1916 was relatively as vulnerable as Nelson had been at Trafalgar), but at the same time took decisions with more immediate strategic consequences than any land commander. Bernard Brodie (of whom more anon) wrote in 1942 that, 'The warship, which is still the chief instrument of sea power, has no counterpart among the implements of land warfare for mobility and for tactical and strategic independence.'[14] Therefore the changes which the warship underwent in the nineteenth century, the adoption of steam, shell guns, screw propellers, rifled ordnance and armour, had strategic as well as tactical effects.[15] For a maritime power like Britain, they fundamentally altered its geopolitical relationships both with Europe and with its colonies.

In 1845 Lord Palmerston told the House of Commons from the opposition benches that 'the Channel is no longer a barrier. Steam navigation has rendered that which was before impassable by a military force nothing more than a river passable by a steam bridge.'[16] Two years later, with Palmerston back in office as Foreign Secretary, the Duke of Wellington concluded that, because steamships could navigate independently of wind and tide, 'every coast of these islands is open to attack'. The prime minister wanted to keep up to 70,000 regular soldiers at home and to create an army reserve, and the military engineers called for the fortification of the south coast. British fears of a French steamborne invasion, so acute in 1847–8, 1852 and 1859–60 that the Radical politician Richard Cobden dubbed them 'the three panics', did not disappear with Prussia's defeat of France in 1871. They recurred as late as 1898, and after 1904 fear of France was replaced by fear of Germany. The Committee of Imperial Defence, created in 1902, conducted three major inquiries on the invasion threat, in 1903, 1907–8 and 1913–14.[17] That sense of danger persisted throughout the First World War and surfaced again in 1940.

The risk was that the Royal Navy, even if stronger in overall terms, would not be able to concentrate to meet an enemy invasion fleet at short notice: steampower had changed the relationship between time and space at sea, just as its application to the railway had done on land.[18] If that happened, if an enemy fleet crossed the Channel or the North Sea overnight, the defence of Britain would rest with the army, most of which spent most of its life stationed not at home, but in the colonies abroad. If more of the army were held at home to guard against invasion, it would not be free to police the empire. On the other hand, if the Royal Navy were to be relied on to prevent an invasion of Britain, it would have to concentrate more in home waters and so would itself be less able to police the world's oceans or to reinforce or support the army in the event of war abroad. Of course steam gave the Royal Navy greater flexibility and added speed in the event of its having to juggle these competing requirements, but the very success of the steamship added a further strategic responsibility. The growth of Britain's merchant fleet, fuelled by Britain's excellent reserves of coal, and its corollaries, the growth of international trade and its reliance on coal bunkers throughout the world, gave the Royal Navy a further task. Its job was to protect British trade from attack, not least because the credit of the London banks, and London's status as the world's premier shipping and insurance market, depended on it.

The naval rivalries generated by those powers which challenged British maritime supremacy provided the prototypes for the arms races of the nuclear era. Moreover, alongside the principal arms races, that between Britain and France from the 1840s until the 1880s, and that between Britain and Germany between 1905 and 1914, subordinate and regional arms races developed. The improvements in ship design provided a materialist push to naval strategy. In France in the 1880s, the Jeune École argued that torpedo boats could deny battleships command of the sea by avoiding fleet action and by waging a 'guerre de course'.[19] In Germany after 1897, Alfred von Tirpitz used his position as head of the Reich's naval office to drive through a programme of ship construction whose tempo was set by naval laws agreed by the Reichstag and whose rationale rested on the idea that numbers would deter Britain from action against the imperial fleet.[20] In Britain, Jackie Fisher, who became First Sea Lord in 1904, saw the Dreadnought as the first in a series of technological steps in which it would be replaced by the battle cruiser, capable of greater speed and a longer radius of action, and then be finally trumped, at least for inshore and coastal defence, by the submarine.[21] Clark G. Reynolds has argued that 'this technological capacity led to the domination of the material school of strategy in the years 1867 to 1914 in all countries'.[22]

Reynolds, however, acknowledges that this was not a school of strategy to which the best-known naval strategic thinkers of the day, Mahan and Corbett, subscribed. For them, 'the idea of super-warships with improved naval guns, propellers and armor deciding command of the sea with only perfunctory notice of principles of naval strategy grounded in historical experience appeared as anathema'.[23] In 1874 John Knox Laughton, who had served as a civilian with the Royal Navy but ended his career as professor of modern history at King's College, London, delivered a paper at the Royal United Service Institution on 'the scientific study of naval history'.[24] His argument, that history could be the basis on which the theory and the principles of naval strategy could be grounded, was one which Mahan and Corbett accepted and developed. Both the latter, when writing their most important theoretical books, *The influence of seapower upon history* (1890) and *Some principles of maritime strategy* (1911), used illustrations derived exclusively from the British experience in the age of the sailing ship. Both saw sea power as resting on geographical position, trade and maritime shipping, not on industrialisation and technological innovation. Clark argues that the clash between the two approaches to strategic thought, materialist and historical, generated 'a golden age of naval thought'. But the officers with a predisposition to materialist ideas did not prevail. In France, the Jeune École lost out to conventional battleship construction after the battle of Tsushima in 1905; in Germany, Tirpitz found himself without a viable strategy for actual war in 1914; and in Britain, Fisher could not easily break the stranglehold that the battleship exercised on the imagination of the public or of the government. The influence of Mahan and Corbett was pervasive because both occupied central positions at the heart of their two navies' educational systems. In addition, rather than beginning from scratch given that the sea provided a very different environment from the land, both looked to the strategists of land warfare for inspiration and system – Mahan to Jomini and Corbett to Clausewitz. Mahan even argued that 'the fundamental principles of warfare are the same on land or sea'.[25]

So, by the outbreak of the First World War, although technology had raised fundamental questions about the relationship between naval strategy and national policy, it had not shaped maritime strategic thought. Instead a gap had opened up between national policies, particularly but not exclusively that of Britain, and technological innovation, which had indeed transformed naval warfare but whose strategic effects had been so ill digested. The evidence for this gap is the lack among all the belligerents of coherent and accepted naval war plans to match the detail and development of those of armies. In 1914 war planning was the activity which had the potential to bring the armed forces' strategic intentions into line with national policies. In the German case, institutional competition within the navy compounded intellectual confusion. Plans for a naval war with the United States were more coherent, however fantastic the overall scenario, than those for the more likely eventuality of a war with Britain.[26] In the British case, although Corbett was involved with such planning as did occur, and in particular was close to Captain Edmond Slade, appointed to be Director of Naval Intelligence in 1907, the results were undermined by the emasculation of the Naval Intelligence Division in 1909. The latter had been a naval staff in embryo, but never fully recovered from the consequences of the clash between the first sea Lord, Fisher, and his arch-protagonist, Lord Charles Beresford, who in calling for the creation of a proper naval staff damned the idea in Fisher's eyes. Although a naval war staff was created in name in 1912, it had not fulfilled its functions by 1914.[27] The opposite could be said of army general staffs, even in Britain, the laggard in the process of their establishment. It can be argued that by the outbreak of the war almost all armies had developed operational plans which to varying degrees usurped the deliberations of the policy-makers. The coordination of war plans with national polices was not without friction, but no comparable clashes emerged in the case of the navies, partly because both their thinking about how they would wage a major war and their structures for giving those ideas effect had remained so fluid.

In the First World War, technology's impact on tactics would, in many respects, trump the making of strategy, albeit less obviously at sea than on land, precisely because the distinction was not so firmly etched. To that extent technology revolutionised strategy, because its dominance in the war created intellectual confusion for those who cleaved to a classical and historically driven approach to the subject. At its conclusion, Douglas Haig, the commander-in-chief of the British Expeditionary Force in France, stressed the continuing validity of the 1909 *Field service regulations*, whose principal author he had been, while as early as 1916 the Chief of the Imperial General Staff, Sir William Robertson, said that they would 'require a tremendous amount of revising when we have finished with the Boche'. He was right and Haig was wrong: the *Field service regulations* went through four revisions in fifteen years.[28] This was the context into which the theorists of air power stepped. Because of the doubts about the historical approach which the experience of the war had generated, and because of the scepticism as to the solutions which the generals had embraced, they were able to exercise considerable leverage. Foremost among them, and effectively the earliest, was Giulio Douhet.

Douhet's input to strategic thought is interesting for three reasons. The first, and seemingly the least important, is that he has good claim to be the foremost Italian to make a really significant contribution to the understanding of war since Machiavelli. The crucial distinction between the two was that, whereas Machiavelli was addressing the problems of a city state struggling for power within the Italian peninsula, Douhet was concerned with the strategy of a united Italy which confronted threats from outside Italy itself, and particularly from north of the Alps. His response to this geopolitical shift of focus was to embrace a new technology, the aircraft. Here was a means by which Italians could jump over an obstacle which Hannibal and Napoleon had had to negotiate, and whose passes had confounded many less gifted commanders. This, the second reason for studying him, is the best-known facet of his thought. It opened the way to the third. By predicating his arguments on the changes likely to be wrought in warfare by new technologies, Douhet shifted the dialectic within strategy, from a discussion between the present and the past, to a discussion between the present and the future.

In the later Middle Ages and early modern period, of Italy's city states only Venice had been a truly successful exponent of sea power, maximising its situation on the Adriatic coast to ensure an entrée to the eastern Mediterranean, and challenging the Ottomans for hegemony in the region. The unification of Italy in 1859 at once revealed Italy's exposure to the pressures of sea power, and particularly its vulnerability to British naval dominance. Here, as much as in Italy's pursuit of its territorial ambitions at the expense of Austria-Hungary, can be found a reason for Rome's decision to abandon the Triple Alliance in 1915, and to enter the First World War on the side of Britain, France and Russia.

Although the First World War shaped Douhet's thought decisively, it did not in itself give it life. Douhet's father was a soldier and he himself trained for service in the artillery. He made a study of the Russo-Japanese War of 1904–5, but his early ideas were shaped not by the titans of war on land, such as Jomini or Clausewitz, but by Mahan. Mahan's most famous book, *The influence of seapower on history*, was published in 1890, when Douhet was twenty-one: a convenient coincidence of public impact on the one hand and personal maturation on the other. Although Mahan had used history as the experiential basis for his strategic thought, Douhet applied Mahan's thoughts about maritime power, and especially his concept of the command of the sea, to a new environment, that of the air. In 1911, Italy invaded Libya, as the springboard for its own Mediterranean empire, and for the first time in the history of war aircraft bombed targets on the ground. In 1912 Douhet wrote a report on the use of air power in the Libyan War. Mahan had stressed the links between an economic and civilian capacity for seafaring, on the one hand, and naval strength in a military sense, on the other. Douhet applied these insights to the air, arguing that Italian military aviation would flourish if Italy developed a strong civilian aviation sector, and urging the state to cooperate with the Italian aircraft manufacturer, Giovanni Caproni.[29]

What Douhet meant by command of the air at this stage of his development was not the bombing of civilians but aerial combat against enemy air fleets. He saw the bombing of cities as barbaric and likely to prove counter-productive if used in the context of what he and his contemporaries called 'civilised war', or in other words war between European powers as opposed to colonial war. Instead he wanted his air fleets to fight each other, a war of combatant against combatant, in order to establish control of the air, on the grounds that the air – like the sea – derived its value from its use as a route. He was not alone at this stage in the development of air power thinking, in seeing command of the air as procurable on some sort of lasting basis. At sea, such an expectation rested on the ways in which straits and currents, and their relationship to land masses, created set routes, whose command through the establishment of ports and bases could be controlled in the interests of one power or its allies. This was not possible in the air. The First World War showed how contested the air space over the battlefield was to become, and made clear that domination by one party or another was likely to be temporary and even fleeting. Control of the air had to be fought for continuously and, once gained, had to be exploited before it was again challenged or imperilled.

The war of 1915–18 also revealed to Douhet another insight central to much maritime thought and reflected at least in part in the writings of Clausewitz: the place of public opinion. In his famous passage on the 'trinity', Clausewitz had identified three elements in war – passion, the play of probability and chance, and reason – and he had associated each of these with the people, the armed forces and the government. In the case of Clausewitz's Prussia, public readiness to fight was more noticeable by its absence than by its force, but Clausewitz knew enough of what Napoleon had encountered in Spain, Switzerland and even Italy not to underestimate the power of the people in a war in which the whole nation was engaged. Clausewitz, unlike Douhet, was cautious in his engagement with the future, but he did suggest that, if war was to become 'absolute' in the future, one reason why it would be so would be because of national passion.

Douhet agreed. He realised that industrialised societies could generate the means to wage long and costly wars, in which economic strength would ultimately prove decisive. But he also believed that industrial power did not stand on its own. The nationalisation of war required states to generate social and political coherence as well as industrial might. For Italy these issues were fraught. The country was economically backward and politically divided; entry to the First World War had not united Italy as it had the original belligerents, and so Douhet knew from first-hand experience that public debate could divide a nation at war as well as unite it. He therefore realised that the nation was both a means to win the war and a potential source of vulnerability.

Julian Corbett had made the same point at the conclusion of his book, *Some principles of maritime strategy*, published in 1911. The use of economic warfare through blockade at sea would strike directly at the citizens in whom the political power of the democratic state was ultimately vested.

In 1815 the peacemakers of Europe had been anxious to separate the idea of war from that of revolution. Theirs was a conservative vision of Europe, designed to ensure great power cooperation to limit war and even – through the use of the Congress system – to forestall it. The efforts of the British Foreign Secretary, Sir Edward Grey, to do exactly that in July 1914 failed, and he, Tsar Nicholas II of Russia and the German chancellor, Theobald von Bethmann Hollweg, were all agreed that once the war broke out it was likely to end in revolution. Both Britain (in the Middle East) and Germany (throughout the empires of its enemies) were ready to ride the whirlwind, to promote revolution not for its own sake but to enable victory in the war. So was Douhet: he wrote as early as 7 August 1914, '[This war] will end with exhaustion, tiredness, with the rebellion of one people against a state of prolonged pain and excessive anguish.'[30]

The British used their naval blockade to this end, and believed that the revolution of November 1918 in Germany eventually proved its efficacy, so much so that for much of the inter-war period this remained a British weapon of choice for the next war in Europe. Douhet argued that air power was a more effective way of achieving the same end in shorter order. He no longer believed that bombing from the air defied international norms. Instead he used the arguments of democracy against itself, just as the maritime thinkers did, and as Islamic fundamentalists would also do after the 9/11 attacks. Those who voted had the power to topple regimes which behaved in illegitimate ways, and so were complicit in the crimes of their governments. In Douhet's eyes, the best way to punish them was to bomb them. After Italy's entry to the war in May 1915 Douhet called for the creation of a fleet of heavy bombers, and by 1918 the allied powers, Britain and France as well as Italy, moved to the creation of independent air forces to hit Austro-Hungarian and German cities.

This was the context in which Douhet wrote *The command of the air*, first published in 1921 and then revised and radicalised in 1927, after its author had retired. Douhet took the independent air forces of 1918, embryonic and limited in their effectiveness, as models for something much more ambitious. A force of one thousand bombers, with a range of 200 to 300 kilometres and capable of ceilings which would take them over the Alps, would strike the enemy's industries. The bombers would be accompanied by combat units, whose task was solely to clear the path for the bombers. The opposing air force would no longer be destroyed in the air but while it was still on the ground.

Inherent to Douhet's vision were a number of principles which were entirely familiar in strategic thought. One was that of concentration. In the 1921 edition of *Command of the air* Douhet had allowed for what he called auxiliary air forces, which were to remain under the control of the army and the navy, and be available for reconnaissance, artillery spotting and so on. By 1927 Douhet dismissed these as representing diversions of effort. Another principle was that of the primacy of the offensive. Command of the air now meant preventing the enemy from flying through attacking the factories that manufactured their aircraft and the bases that serviced them.

Douhet's view of strategy was not without precedents, in both military and maritime strategy; it was also directly shaped by the experience of the First World War. And yet it broke with traditional strategy in quite explicitly rejecting the role of history in its formation. Both Jomini and Clausewitz had used the campaigns of Frederick the Great to measure what had changed under Napoleon and what had not: history provided context, and they – just like Mahan and Corbett at the turn of the nineteenth and twentieth centuries – saw one of their functions as the assimilation of current practice with past precedent. This is not to say that they were blind to change; they simply realised, as any professional historian does, that the understanding of true novelty depends on an appreciation of what had gone before. Douhet did not. 'Future wars', he stated with the combativeness so distinctive of his style, 'will be radically different from wars of the past.' And, he went on, 'Clinging to the past will teach us nothing useful for the future.'[31]

Such dogmas created severe analytical challenges. Douhet believed that 'victory smiles upon those who anticipate changes in the character of war, not upon those who wait to adapt themselves after the changes occur'.[32] There was an illogicality here: Douhet was himself extrapolating from the experiences of the First World War, but was claiming that he was not. His argument was that Italy should base its national defence not on those experiences but on 'the character and form future wars may assume', and that its procurement decisions should then follow from those assumptions.[33] So, to say that Douhet was linking present to future in his approach to strategy may be stretching a point; what Douhet actually said he was doing was picking some point in the future and reverse-engineering back to the present.

Given that much strategic thinking since the First World War has followed Douhet's precedent, particularly with the advent of nuclear weapons, it is necessary to stress that what Douhet was proposing was not entirely free of all disciplinary rigour, despite its jettisoning of history. The new basis for strategic thought was to be technology and the expectations vested in its likely development and potentially perfect performance. This vision of the future was based, Douhet insisted, 'not on idle imaginings', but 'upon the reality of to-day, out of which grows the reality of to-morrow'.[34]

Much of Douhet's encapsulation of the problems which aviation faced and of how they might be overcome was perspicacious, but his expectations of the capabilities of combat aircraft dismissed the 'friction' of war. Douhet assumed that aircraft had complete freedom of action and direction, and almost 'limitless' (his word) range. The bomber, he averred, can travel 'without restriction over the whole surface of the globe, needing only a point of departure and one of arrival'. He suggested that units of ten bombers, each of them carrying a load of two tons of bombs, could destroy a circle 500 metres in diameter. So a thousand-bomber force could generate a hundred such units, and, if fifty flew per day, they would destroy fifty city centres per day. These bombs, thanks to gravity, would be accurate: 'Aerial bombs have only to fall on their target to accomplish their purpose.' Douhet assumed that the targets would not be hardened, and as they would be big the chances of missing them would be minimal. 'Bombing targets', he said, 'should always be large; small targets are unimportant and do not merit our attention here.'[35]

Douhet dismissed the possibility of an effective defence against such attacks. Defensive air forces would lack the intelligence to be able to intercept an incoming air force, and (in another throwback to traditional principles of war) they would have to disperse to cover all possible targets. So they would be individually overwhelmed as the defender would have divided his forces while the attacker concentrated his. Anti-aircraft fire was discounted for similar reasons, and Douhet urged states to put more resources into aircraft and their offensive properties rather than waste their money on ground-based guns.

Underpinning the whole structure was a paradox. The aim was to end the war quickly and if that aim were fulfilled war would cost fewer lives (an ambition which provided yet another illustration of how the history of the First World War loomed larger than Douhet cared to admit). But the way to achieve this seemingly humanitarian objective was to make the civilian population the principal target. Douhet, a fascist (he had joined Mussolini's march on Rome in 1922), was not alone in using this argument: so too did the British liberal, Basil Liddell Hart, in *Paris: or, the future of warfare*, published in 1925. Both rationalised the paradox by saying that total war had made all citizens combatants. So Douhet's responses to Germany in 1914–15 found their place in an argument that was both moral in an ethical sense and designed to have moral effects in a psychological sense. Douhet reckoned that urban targets would be softer and therefore bombing would have greater effect: 'We should always keep in mind that aerial offensives can be directed against objectives of least physical resistance, but against those of least moral resistance as well.'[36]

Douhet developed this point, to conclude that the effect on morale could be more significant than the material effects. News reports and rumours would spread panic after the first attack, and lead to revolution. 'A complete breakdown of the social structure cannot but take place in a country subjected to this merciless pounding from the air.' And the effects would be rapid: people 'would rise up and demand an end to the war before the army and navy will be defeated'.[37] So the aim of bombing moved from the destruction of the enemy air force on the ground to the dissemination of terror. Bombers would drop high explosive to destroy buildings; they would then switch to incendiaries to create fires; and finally they would spread poison gas to hamper the operations of the fire services.

This was a vision of technology which rested on a one-sided view of what technology could deliver. It underestimated the problems in aircraft design of matching power-to-weight ratios, especially for long-range bombers loaded with fuel as well as bombs; it neglected navigational hazards such as cloud, wind and weather; and it assumed perfect intelligence as to target sets. Above all, it did not allow for technology's own response to technological innovation, not least radar which would enable the coordination of aerial defences in a fashion which Douhet had simply discounted.

What Douhet's work also reveals is the inadequacy of an approach to strategic thought that rests on technology but fails to analyse with similar scientific rigour the social and political assumptions on which the employment of that technology is predicated. Douhet's presumption that air attack would promote revolution seemed to be as forward looking as any of his technological assumptions. Like much else that he wrote, it rested on the lessons of the First World War more than his rejection of history suggested. His belief that civilians would panic under attack from the air owed not a little to what soldiers had done when strafed in 1918, but unlike civilians they had had to stay in the open to fight. Civilians, able to flee and actively encouraged to take cover in cellars, proved more resilient under aerial bombardment than allowed for by inter-war theory. Douhet illustrated his argument by reference to the so-called 'stab in the back', the belief that it was the German revolution which had taken Germany out of the war, but he failed to ask which was the cart in this relationship and which the horse. Many, even as Douhet was writing, were arguing that Germany had revolted not least because it was defeated, not that revolution caused the loss of the war.

Douhet's advocacy of the aeroplane and its revolutionary effects on warfare at the strategic level as well as the tactical were reflected in the writings of others. In the United States, Billy Mitchell, first demoted and then court-martialled for his heterodox views on air power and the American armed services, published *Winged defense: the development and possibilities of modern air power* in 1925. He, like Douhet, located the revolutionary effects of the new technology on strategy at two levels. The first was geographical, and was directly reflected in the choice of title for his book. Mitchell acknowledged that the United States was secure from air attack for the time being but pointed out that, as the range and load-carrying capacity of aircraft developed, America's cities and industrial centres would become as vulnerable as those of Europe. 'The former isolation of the United States is a thing of the past,' he wrote, but he then argued that air power would also provide the answer to this new threat: air power not only 'can hold off any hostile air force which may seek to fly over and attack our country, but it can also hold off any hostile shipping which seeks to cross the oceans and menace our shores'. And that led to his second line of reasoning. In describing the allied air attacks on German industry in the Ruhr in 1918, Mitchell argued in 1930 that, 'This phase of air force work is the one outstanding development that occurred in the European war. It is the thing that will bring about victory or defeat in future military contests.'[38]

This second argument was more about economic effect, the impact on a country's war-making capacity rather than on its will to fight.

Mitchell did not discount the horrors that an air attack would inflict on an urban population, but his justification of them rested less on the moral rightness of holding a population democratically accountable for its leaders' actions or that in 'total war' all were combatants, and more on the perverted humanitarianism which Douhet had anticipated and which Basil Liddell Hart also embraced. Because 'an attack from an air force using explosive bombs and gas may cause the complete evacuation and cessation of industry in these places [i.e. cities]', Mitchell argued, it 'would deprive armies, air forces, and navies of their means of maintenance'.[39] The terrorisation of civilians would shorten a war, and so prevent the loss of military lives from armies condemned to protracted and indecisive trench warfare. The perversity of the argument was that non-combatants had to be killed to save the lives of combatants. In *Paris*, Liddell Hart asserted that, if one country possessed a superior air force and the other a superior army, 'there is no reason why within a few hours, or at most days from the commencement of hostilities, the nerve system of the country inferior in air power should not be paralysed'.[40] Liddell Hart argued that government would collapse not so much because of revolution (although even in his vision 'the slum districts [would be] maddened into the impulse to break loose and maraud'), but because of the destruction of the infrastructure which would remove its ability to command and direct the nation in war. The arguments advanced for air power in the 1920s collectively contended that a new and still evolving technology would revolutionise strategy geopolitically, temporally, morally and politically. In Mitchell's words, 'a whole new set of rules for the conduct of war will have to be devised and a whole new set of ideas of strategy learned by those charged with the conduct of war'.[41]

Liddell Hart never again wrote anything so extreme about air power, and by the late 1930s his advocacy of mechanised warfare on land seemed at times to neglect the air threat to the tank's physical safety or to its capacity for undetected manoeuvre. Both he and his senior, J. F. C. Fuller, claimed to have influenced the German army's thinking on the use of armour. They did, although the degree to which they did so is contested.[42] However, in the inter-war German army the adoption of new technology was socially constructed, that is to say it was made to fit within the officer corps' existing world view – which remained remarkably unaffected by its catastrophic defeat in 1918. It also had to serve doctrine rather than become doctrine's building block.[43] The approach of Liddell Hart and Fuller to new technology was of a different order, with neither of them underestimating the impact of new technology on warfare. They sought to shock and provoke, to change and not to conform, often caricaturing and criticising the army in which they had served and whose greater effectiveness they sought. As a staff officer serving with tanks in the First World War, Fuller had been the author in 1918 of a futuristic and unrealisable plan to win the war in 1919 with deep, mobile tank attacks directed against enemy headquarters. He believed absolutely that technological innovation and progressive industrialisation would shape future warfare, and it was a theme which recurred in his writings, from *The reformation of war*, published in the wake of the First World War in 1923, to *Armament and history*, which appeared after the Second in 1946. But Fuller's focus when addressing technology was on the character of war, on its tactics and operations, not on its strategy. For both Fuller and Liddell Hart the understanding of change was historically rooted, and it did not discount continuity. Change could be change back: Liddell Hart's identification of the strategy of the indirect approach rested on examples drawn from a survey of the history of war from the ancient world to the present. 'Unless history can teach us to look at the future', Fuller wrote in one of his most purely historical works, 'the history of war is but a bloody romance.'[44] For him and for Liddell Hart, unlike Douhet, military history was still central to strategic thought. 'To understand the past and to judge the present is to foresee the future,' Fuller said when he was awarded the Royal United Service Institute's Chesney Gold Medal in 1919.[45]

When the two atomic bombs were dropped on Japan in August 1945 Liddell Hart was completing a book which he had begun in 1944. Called *The revolution in warfare* and eventually published in 1946, it was more a critical survey of allied strategy in the Second World War against the background of history than a response to the advent of nuclear weapons. The word 'revolution' in the title was to that extent misleading. Liddell Hart added an epilogue which began, 'nothing could have been more effectively designed to reinforce the argument in the preceding pages, which were written beforehand, than the advent in warfare of the atomic bomb in August 1945'. In saying that 'past experience has shown that no development is ever quite so overwhelmingly potent as it appears in anticipation, or even on the promise of its first performance', Liddell Hart acknowledged that he was in danger of underestimating rather than exaggerating the break with the past that the atomic bomb represented. As a result the book showed a maturity and balance which *Paris* had not. Liddell Hart embraced the fact that a new set of circumstances existed but used history to provide context the better to understand them. If both sides possessed a nuclear capability, 'total warfare' would make no sense. The challenge would be to develop new forms of war given that 'any future warfare will be less unrestrained and more subject to agreed rules'.[46]

Fuller's attempt to come to grips with the same challenge, in *Armament and warfare*, also published in 1946, compared the losses at Hiroshima and Nagasaki with those at the Somme in 1916 and Ypres in 1917: the numbers were similar but in 1945 the victims were civilians, not combatants, and they had been killed in seconds, not months. He then went on to ask, 'How far does the power of this new weapon affirm or disprove what I have already written?' His answer was that in some respects he felt vindicated and in others not. Fuller's conclusion, like that of Liddell Hart, was 'not to abolish war; but, so long as the urge to fight remains part of human nature, to impose the will of the victor upon the vanquished with the least possible destruction to either, because destruction is never more than a means to the end'.[47] Liddell Hart and Fuller were not professional historians, and were quicker to use history as a didactic and utilitarian resource than proper scholarship might allow, but like earlier strategic thinkers they realised history's disciplinary value in determining the relationship between continuity, which they did not exaggerate, and change, which they saw as much in evolutionary and cyclical terms as in revolutionary. Things had changed in 1945, and technology had changed them, but not everything had changed.

That was not the line taken by another strategic thinker equally well versed in the historical approach to the subject, the American, Bernard Brodie. Whereas the pedigrees of both Fuller and Liddell Hart were in land warfare, Brodie's lay in war at sea. His doctoral thesis, published in 1941 as *Sea power in the machine age*, examined the effect on naval warfare of the technological innovations in ship construction in the nineteenth century that had so influenced what Clark Reynolds called the materialist school of maritime strategy. Brodie was clear that 'a military invention, though designed for a specific tactical effect, may also have strategic consequences'. The steam warship had changed strategic geography by being able to sail independently of the wind, by introducing naval dependence on fuel supplies (and hence bases), and by modifying the problem of distance through faster sailing times. The trouble was that statesmen, although often acutely aware of technological change, could be slow to recognise 'changes operated through effects on tactics, or on strategy in its more restricted sense'. This was a particular problem for democracies, which left such matters to the professionals, but 'at the same time denied the military chief the influence on the determination of foreign policy granted him in autocratic countries'.[48] Brodie was therefore convinced that 'the pursuit of military ends has always been determined by the inherent potentialities or limitations of the machines with which war is waged', and drew a distinction between changes in the weapons with which war is waged and 'the effect of specific inventions ... and their impact on world politics, past and present'. To fulfil the latter task Brodie had to reintroduce Mahan, whom Americans of his generation had neglected, but whom in 1941 Brodie called 'the apostle of modern sea power'.[49] During the Second World War Brodie, not least thanks to his observation of the United States's use of sea power in an oceanic context in the war against Japan, achieved the fusion of the materialist and historical schools in maritime strategy which had eluded the pre-1914 generation of naval thinkers.

On 7 August 1945, or so the story has it, Bernard Brodie was travelling in a car with his wife, and stopped to buy a copy of *The New York Times*. He read the report of the dropping of the atomic bomb on Hiroshima and immediately declared that 'Everything that I have written is obsolete.'[50] Over the next year he set out to think through the implications of his own reaction, and to give it an intellectual foundation. Based at Yale, he coordinated and edited *The absolute weapon: atomic peace and world order*, published in 1946. His own essay described the Second World War, a truly global war requiring the coordination of allied resources, as 'the conflict in which sea power reached the culmination of its influence on history'. That 'mighty power' had now become redundant because of the atomic bomb, which made 'clear that our military authorities will have to bestir themselves to a wholly unprecedented degree in revising military concepts from the past'. He declared comparisons between the atomic bomb and 'any military invention of the past' to be 'ridiculous', and memorably concluded that: 'Thus far the chief purpose of our military establishment has been to win wars. From now on its chief purpose must be to avert them. It can have almost no other useful purpose.'[51]

Brodie's doctoral thesis on sea power had been written under the supervision of Quincy Wright at Chicago, and had formed part of the latter's monumental two-volume *The study of war*. Wright, a professor of international law, had begun the book in 1926, when hopes for the League of Nations were still strong and two years before the Kellogg–Briand pact had outlawed the state's recourse to war. He signed the foreword on 11 November 1941, not only the anniversary of the armistice which ended the First World War in France but also less than a month before the Japanese attack on Pearl Harbor. By the time the book was available to the public, in 1942, its theme – the prevention of war – was not calculated to find a ready audience, despite its scale and ambition. However, Wright had secured a receptive pupil in Brodie. In 1938 Brodie wrote an essay for Wright on 'Can peaceful change prevent war?', in which he argued that 'a method must be devised of establishing procedures for allowing changes in the international system, of avoiding war by accomplishing peacefully the ends for which nations might otherwise despairingly resort to war'.[52]

Brodie's 1946 vision – that of both sides acquiring nuclear weapons and so establishing mutual deterrence – was therefore not as much of a revolution as he himself presented it to be. The idea of deterrence had been evident in maritime strategy before 1914, not least as expounded by Tirpitz and Fisher, and it was also given an airing in a nuclear context by a third great naval strategist who also synthesised the material and historical approaches, Raoul Castex, in an article published in October 1945.[53] In another sense Brodie was responding to Wright's ambition. Whereas Liddell Hart and Fuller, with their greater readiness to stress continuity amidst technological change, had argued that nuclear weapons required war to be limited, Brodie, with his belief in the capacity of technological change to recast the international order, saw the opportunity to prevent it. Brodie's piece was scathing about the sort of history peddled by Liddell Hart and Fuller, as well as many other strategic thinkers: 'History is at best an imperfect guide to the future, but when imperfectly understood and interpreted it is a menace to sound judgment.'[54] However, Brodie was not rejecting the value of history itself; his objection was to its use in seeking enduring principles, in stressing continuity in order to deny revolutionary change. Implicit in this criticism was a point that would become increasingly clear over the next three decades. Brodie's engagement with nuclear weapons did not mean turning his back on history as a constituent discipline of strategic thought as completely as his 1946 statement on 'the absolute weapon' had suggested; what it did require was a capacity to be sufficiently historically aware to recognise revolutionary change when it occurred. His more mature reflections on the atomic bomb, contained in

Strategy in the missile age (1959), paid lip service to change, while resting on a foundation of classical strategic thought. Its inspiration was ideas about air power, not sea power, and their principal exponent was Douhet, not Mahan. The latter was 'essentially a scholar and historian', whereas the former represented a 'violent break with the past'. For Douhet 'Every war *must* be total war, regardless of the character of the powers waging it, the causes of the conflict, or the original objectives of the statesmen who have let themselves be drawn into it.' Although Brodie conceded that strategic bombing in the Second World War had not delivered all that Douhet had anticipated, 'the framework of strategic thought he created is peculiarly pertinent to any general war in the nuclear age'.[55]

Brodie's argument, that nuclear weapons meant the object of military force was now to prevent war, not wage it, was more revolutionary than the weapons themselves. The destruction that they could wreak was no different, he argued, from the destruction of which the United States had been capable in the Second World War, a point which Thomas Schelling would reiterate in *Arms and influence*, published in 1966 – in other words even after the hydrogen bomb had increased the destructive effect of the atomic bomb one thousand times. What was different, both agreed – and so had Liddell Hart and Fuller – was the speed with which this damage could be done. That in turn affected 'the control of events, the sequence of events, the relation of victor to vanquished, and the relation of homeland to fighting fronts'.[56] The challenges were therefore those of time and – especially after the nuclear warhead was allied to a more effective delivery system, the intercontinental ballistic missile – space, both hardy perennials in strategic thought.

Brodie had studied Socratic philosophy and been trained as a historian. These were in some senses the traditional disciplines of strategic thought, but were now in retreat. Schelling was (and is) an economist and game theorist. Herman Kahn was a physicist who had worked on the development of the hydrogen bomb. In urging the United States 'to think the unthinkable' in 1960 he used history in a very different way from his predecessors, constructing alternative and counter-factual scenarios alongside his version of the 'real' events. A combination of science fiction and systems theory underpinned what were essentially unprovable hypotheses. For him, the strategist was left with no other methodology, since nuclear weapons meant that doctrine consistently lagged behind the pace of technological change.

> These doctrinal lags will in themselves be dangerous; leading to important gaps in our preparations, the waste of badly needed resources on obsolete concepts, the neglect of possible strengths, the overuse of especially glamorous tools, and, possibly most important of all, heightened possibilities of serious miscalculations or accidents because we have not had time to understand and make provisions for the requirements of the newly installed systems.[57]

Kahn, with his ample girth and thick glasses, and his determination that the United States must be serious about waging nuclear war, not just deterring it, was lampooned, as Groteschele in Eugene Burdick's and Harvey Wheeler's novel, *Fail-safe*, and as Dr Strangelove in Stanley Kubrick's eponymous film. However, his influence has been more persistent and more pervasive than the caricatures suggest. For him, 'virtual' strategy prevailed over strategic practice, and strategic thought became increasingly subordinate to predictions for the future rather than informed by the experience of the past. The rationale that drove this approach was the pace of technological change, despite the fact that during the Cold War nuclear weapons had a deadening effect on change more generally. They were used, not in anger, but to generate a remarkable stability in the system of international relations constructed around them. The challenges arose after the end of the Cold War, when nuclear deterrence lost its salience and actual wars introduced real fluctuations in international politics.

By then the presumption of technological perfectibility was hard-wired into operational thought, and so was deemed capable of delivering strategic effect. For the United States and its NATO allies, both the Gulf War of 1990–1 and the Kosovo campaign of 1999 confirmed this image of what had happened to warfare. Its principal vehicles were the so-called 'revolution in military affairs', network-centric warfare and then 'transformation', all of which rested on a presumption of technological dominance which ensured (in the title of an official history of the United States army in the Gulf War) 'certain victory'.[58] Control of the electronic spectrum and the possession of satellite technology enabled the Americans to communicate, to acquire targets and to strike them with precision, in ways that their enemies could not match. Technological superiority revolutionised strategic thought in that it seemed to remove chance and reciprocity from war; now the link between intent and outcome would truly make war a continuation of policy by other means. Typical of this hubris were the claims of air power theory. 'Today', Richard Hallion wrote in 1997,

> the traditional notion of massing a large ground force to confront an opponent, particularly on a 'field of battle', is largely rendered archaic. The precision air attacker overcomes the battlefield by attacking at ranges far in excess of the most powerful artillery. What can be identified can be targeted so precisely that unnecessary casualties are not inflicted. Thus, increasingly, war is about destroying or incapacitating *things* as opposed to *people*. It is now about pursuing an *effects-based* strategy, rather than an *annihilation-based* one, a strategy that one can *control* an opponent without having to *destroy* him.[59]

Some of these assertions survived contact with the enemy in 2003; most did not. In that very year, when the United States was still flush with what seemed to be a sufficiently easy victory not to have dented the confidence of the 1990s, Major General Robert Scales, the author of *Certain victory*, and Williamson Murray, a military historian, wrote an account of the invasion of Iraq which was not so triumphalist as not to utter a note of warning. They dismissed the notion that technology could either lift the 'fog of war' or remove its Clausewitzian friction. 'The arguments in support of technological monism echo down the halls of the Pentagon,' but such policies, they warned, 'rest on a profound ahistoricism', which 'misses the lessons of the past, much less even a reasonable examination of recent events'.[60] Defence ministries across the world, struggling with the rising proportion of their budgets devoted to equipment, and anxious to manage the procurement process for the sake of economic efficiencies (an inherently difficult task given that they are buying products which have not been fully developed and tested), can mistake the acquisition of capabilities for development of strategy.

The biggest change in warfare at the operational level since the first Gulf War in 1990–1 has been in what are often called 'joint-enablers', a title which itself reveals their essentially supportive as opposed to strategic role. Armed forces have a greater capacity to conduct reconnaissance, to use the intelligence that they so acquire to identify targets (and to do so correctly), and then to kill or destroy them with relatively little collateral damage. The irony is that these very capacities to deliver fire with precision can encourage their excessive use, particularly given the propensity of small arms (or least the British SA 80 rifle) still to jam in a fire-fight, given the reluctance to use heavier ground weapons like artillery and tanks mentioned at the beginning of this chapter, and given the political pressure to ensure the security of one's own forces. Their techno-logical sophistication and their effects as force-multipliers can be forgotten as NATO forces focus on the cultural and social challenges in Afghanistan, but come more sharply into focus as they transfer their responsibilities to Afghan security forces that do not have them or at least are dependent on ISAF for them. 'I could see and then imagine the war in the sky,' wrote an observer of British operations in Helmand conducted on 5 August 2010:

> wee hand-launched drones checking what was round the corner; larger Reaper drones scanning a wide area; the Attack Helicopters, support and casualty evacuation helicopters; the Spectre Gunships looping lazily like the first fly of spring and pregnant with death; Electronic Warfare planes intercepting and jamming insurgent communications; A-10 tank busters; the French, American, British and other jets, providing another set of eyes and ready with bombs if you were really in a tight spot; American Awacs but no longer Nimrods; the B-1 bombers; the U-2 spy planes out of the UAE, scanning the ground for IEDs from 70,000 feet; above all the satellites – a link with home via the phones men had half an hour a week. A firmament of support.[61]

The emerging technology with the greatest current capacity to have strategic effect is the unmanned aerial vehicle. Its claims rest on two characteristics, which transcend its tactical effects, one legal and the other moral. The first is its use to fly over and strike targets in others' sovereign territories. Since 2009, the United States under President Obama has increasingly employed 'drones' to target and kill terrorists in Pakistan. The unmanned aerial vehicle therefore raises issues of inter-national law, although whether these are any different in kind from those raised by manned aircraft undertaking reconnaissance and attack missions is less clear. The second is that the 'drone' is remotely piloted. The person flying the vehicle may be based thousands of miles away, and is not himself or herself exposed to danger, so undermining the reciprocity inherent in the nature of war. Again, there are elements here which are familiar. The one-sidedness of being able to kill at a distance is an attribute which all belligerents naturally desire. Henry V used his longbow-men to achieve victory at Agincourt in 1415. In late nineteenth-century colonial warfare, European armies possessed a capacity to generate fire which could produce extraordinarily one-sided results. At the battle of Omdurman in Sudan in 1898, the British and Egyptian forces, using Maxim guns and breech-loading rifles, inflicted more than 10,000 deaths on the Mahdi's forces while themselves suffering only 47; the action was completed in five hours. Similarly, in most counter-insurgency campaigns since the Italian campaign in Libya in 1912, one side has enjoyed a monopoly in the use of the air. Two observations follow. New technologies create advantages which may be only temporary – either because the enemy acquires similar technologies himself or because he devises counters which can mitigate the advantages which enhanced or advanced technologies confer. Already reports are emerging that suggest that the monopoly which the drone has created will not last long – and clearly it would not exist at all in an inter-state war between major military powers.[62] Secondly, those responses can be tactical rather than simply technological. Unmanned or remotely piloted vehicles, on the ground as well as in the air, do raise important legal and ethical questions; but what is less certain is that the answers will necessarily have strategic effect.

None of this is to say that technology does not help strategy, but two points are clear. First, the principal contribution of new technologies is to enable tactical and operational effects, and much of what air power has contributed to warfare is to be understood in these terms – as a force-multiplier and rarely as a benefit that is independently and strategically decisive. However, for a generation scarred by the exaggerated claims of the 'revolution in military affairs', and reeling from the effects of wars in Iraq and Afghanistan in which 'low tech' solutions have allied themselves to social and political levers, it is too easy to say that this is all that technology contributes to strategy. It is, at least arguably, a land-centric view of warfare: from Jomini and Clausewitz to Liddell Hart and Fuller, classical strategic thought has been dominated by armies, which naturally put human qualities, morale and manpower, on a par with technology. Both navies and air forces exist for and are organised around the machines they serve, and on which they depend to master the element in which they fight. It is therefore unsurprising that those strategists who have seen technology in more revolutionary terms have tended to come from those two backgrounds. The technologies for which they claim strategic effects, the steamship, the manned aircraft or the rocket, have triumphed over geography, changing the relationship between space and time, and thus have a geopolitical effect as well as a directly operational one.

So it is patently absurd to deny that the impact of new technology can be strategically significant. The First World War makes this point in its own right: the war was shaped by the tactical effects of new technologies (including air power) and those effects then conditioned and even determined what strategy could achieve and limited the goals it could set itself. Even more striking was the impact of nuclear weapons, the devastating effects of which, if they had been used in the Cold War, would have trumped strategy completely, and which needed strategy in the shape of deterrence thinking to rationalise their existence. Air power between the wars, not least thanks to Douhet, acquired some of the same qualities. In claiming more than it could deliver, it achieved a political effect, for example prompting Britain to commit itself to the forward defence of Europe for fear of an air attack launched against the United Kingdom from the Low Countries, and also shaping, to a disproportionate extent, public expectations of what the next war would be like. Moreover, after 1940, once Britain had been forced off the continent, strategic bombing fulfilled the promise inherent in its grandiose title by drawing the German air force into a defensive battle over the Reich. Air power therefore had an operationally enabling effect for the armies converging on Germany's frontiers from east, south and west, and a strategic effect in ensuring that the western allies made their contribution to a coalition war in which the Soviet Union saw itself as fighting a lone battle. However, none of these were effects which Douhet had anticipated. As Brodie observed in 1946, 'It is already known to us all that war with atomic bombs would be immeasurably more destructive and horrible than any the world has known … But as a datum for the formulation of policy it is in itself of strictly limited utility. It underlines the urgency of our reaching correct decisions, but it does not help us to discover which decisions are in fact correct.'[63]

10 WAR IS WAR: IMPERIAL LEGACIES AND CURRENT CONFLICTS

Cool and steadfast under fire. Sound tactical ability. In operations in Greece & Crete showed ability to meet unexpected situations. In command of the 10th Brigade in Crete he showed confidence, aggressiveness, power of command and an undefeatable spirit. His deep distaste of showmanship has given him a somewhat retiring manner, which tends to obscure his great ability. Has a deep knowledge of military history.[1]

This is the report on New Zealander Howard Kippenberger after the battle of Crete, the action in which 'Kip' earned the first of his two DSOs. Written by Edward Puttick on 25 July 1941, it recommended Kippenberger for promotion to brigadier, the rank in which his reputation was made and from which he took the title of one of the classic memoirs of the Second World War, *Infantry brigadier*. Two qualities in particular attributed to 'Kip' in the report are important for what follows – the ability to meet the unexpected and a deep knowledge of military history.

The standard wisdom is that the latter is the enemy of the former. The British military theorist Basil Liddell Hart used to say – in his characteristically snide manner – that generals spend too much time thinking about what happened in the last war and not enough thinking about the one they are actually fighting. In reality Liddell Hart, who became a *bête noire* for Kippenberger when he was the editor in chief of New Zealand's official history of the Second World War, used military history just as extensively as Kippenberger did. In criticising the abuse of military history, we can too easily dismiss its use – indeed its essential and vital utility. Without the context which it provides, students of war are like ships at sea without charts and for which the stars are obscured by cloud (at least in a pre-GPS era). We have no reference points by which to judge what is new or to frame the questions to be asked of what seems to be new; as a result we are disproportionately disconcerted and even frightened by its unfamiliarity. Nor, without it, can we understand how and why Kippenberger, a provincial lawyer, gained his reputation not in the courts of Christchurch but on battlefields more than half a world away from the direct defence of New Zealand.

Kippenberger was a Territorial soldier. In 1885, the Russians occupied Pendjeh in northern Afghanistan, so pre-empting negotiations with the British over the limits to Russian expansion in central Asia and prompting fears for the security of India. London had already alerted Australia and New Zealand to the possibility that, if there were hostilities between Russia and Britain, Russian warships might raid New Zealand harbours. New Zealand's response was not just to attend to its own defences but also to offer troops for imperial service. This particular crisis was resolved by arbitration. However, the challenge presented to coastal defence by steam-based navies meant that even the most remote of British dominions became aware both of its reliance on the Royal Navy for its security and of the need to set that security within a collective imperial framework. In 1899 New Zealand decided to send troops to serve in the South African War, and after the war was over, like the other countries of the empire, it reviewed both the strategy for imperial defence and its own contribution within it. In 1909 the New Zealand Defence Act remodelled the country's armed forces, creating the Territorial Force, establishing a liability for compulsory military training, and incorporating the principle that New Zealand might despatch an expeditionary force overseas in support of the British empire. Both elements of the act have shaped the military history of New Zealand from that day to this. A hundred years after the passage of the New Zealand Defence Act, in 2009, New Zealand Territorials were serving in Afghanistan – in exactly the same theatre as that for which New Zealand first offered troops for imperial service in 1885.[2]

The Defence Act established that the training of the New Zealand Military Forces would be conducted according to lines set out in the *Field service regulations*, the British army's first ever formal statement of doctrine.[3] Creation of the *Regulations* had begun five years previously, when the British army had finally (it was the last major European army to do so) set about the formation of a general staff, a process completed in 1906. The general staff was tasked to do the army's thinking and planning in peacetime, as well as being responsible for its command and administration in wartime. In 1908, General Sir William Nicholson had been appointed its first proper chief. 'Nicholson's career', the 'old' Oxford *Dictionary of national biography* remarks, 'was as peculiar as it was brilliant, for though he never commanded a unit in peace or war he became a field marshal, and though he never passed the Staff College he became chief of the general staff.'

This observation is not quite correct, for Nicholson was appointed not Chief of the General Staff, but Chief of the Imperial General Staff. His responsibility was the defence of the empire. The general staff was to be a body whose task was to ensure that all British imperial forces could operate together. The Territorial Force in New Zealand needed, if necessary, to be able to take the field alongside the Grenadier Guards from that other Wellington (the barracks in London). To do that the armies of the empire required a common doctrine, a common way of thinking about war, and a common method of applying those thoughts in practice.

Before 1914 this was the principal purpose of studying military history. Academic military history was in its infancy: the chair of the history of war at Oxford was also established in 1909, and it was designed as much to address current defence issues as to study past wars. On 19 January 1910, at the general staff's third annual conference, that body discussed the possibility of introducing a course in military history for junior officers. 'The only remark I can make about this', Nicholson (himself an engineer) said, 'is that, I think, taking people generally, there are few who for the love of it will study military history just the same as there are few who study mathematics out of love for this branch of study. People study both subjects, in nine cases out of ten, for the hope of professional advancement.'[4] In 1909, as opposed to today, when military history is read because it is massively popular, military history was studied because it was believed to be useful – a belief which was almost completely removed from the British army's educational system after 1970.

The challenge for the British army was that its history seemed to make it inherently very difficult to produce doctrine. In 1909 France knew that its most probable enemy was its immediate neighbour,

Germany, and that it was therefore likely to fight on its northern or eastern frontier, as it had done in 1814–15 and in 1870–1. Britain had no such historical or geopolitical framework against which to set its thinking about war. Colonel G. F. R. Henderson, who had read history at Oxford, was the professor of military art and history at the Staff College between 1892 and 1900, and as such taught most of the generals of the First World War – including Douglas Haig, William Robertson, the Chief of the Imperial General Staff between 1915 and 1918, and Edmund Allenby, the victor in Palestine. Henderson had written in 1900:

> It is useless to anticipate in what quarter of the globe our troops may be next employed as to guess at the tactics, the armament, and even the colour ... of our next enemy. Each new expedition demands special equipment, special methods of supply and special tactical devices, and sometimes special armament. Except for the defence of the United Kingdom and of India, much remains to be provided when the Cabinet declares that war is imminent.[5]

Henderson's views were not only widely shared, they were also a fair reflection of the truth. The British army studied European warfare but practised colonial campaigning, which on the whole it did not study. The first proper publication on the wars of empire was C. E. Callwell's *Small wars*, first published in 1896 and best known in its edition of 1906. In other words the army encapsulated its thinking on colonial wars just when the practice was about to stop being imperial campaigning and start being European warfare. The challenge which therefore confronted the British army was not only doctrinal – not only how it should think about war when it did not know whom or where it was most likely to fight, but also how it should be equipped and organised.

For the war with France in 1870 the Germans had mobilised more than a million men. In 1863, seven years earlier, for the biggest operation of the New Zealand Wars, the invasion of the Waikato, the British had reckoned that they needed a force of 10,000. The Prussian army was recruited through short-service conscription; the British through long-service voluntary engagements. In New Zealand it was the Maori, not the Pakeha, who had to adopt a system for war which embraced an entire society.

Confronted with this contrast, those who earned their spurs under the command of Garnet Wolseley in Africa or of his great rival,

Frederick Sleigh Roberts, in India and Afghanistan, divided war into two categories, civilised war and uncivilised war. Civilised war was war in Europe, fought against armies uniformed and disciplined like one's own, where the laws and customs of war applied. Uncivilised war was war outside Europe. The principal problems here were those of transport, supply and geography. The great advantages which a regular army possessed in uncivilised war were discipline and organisation. The security which they provided meant that, in the words of Major General Patrick Macdougall writing in 1864, 'in irregular warfare, generally received military rules must often be violated, and may be so with comparatively small risk, provided such violation be methodical'.[6] Macdougall was referring to rules in terms of tactics, but armies in wars outside Europe also broke other rules – both sides often killing rather than taking prisoners, both sides attacking women and children, and both sides in general committing atrocities which would have triggered outrage within Europe.

Implicit here is what we might call a binary vision of war: regular versus irregular war; European versus colonial war; civilised versus uncivilised war. It is a division which has resonance for the coalition armies deployed in Afghanistan at the beginning of the twenty-first century.

Since 1945, and particularly since the late 1960s, the British army and the New Zealand Defence Forces have pursued increasingly divergent courses in terms of both policy and politics. During the Cold War, British defence policy focused on Europe, beginning with Duncan Sandys' defence white paper of 1957, which confirmed nuclear deterrence as the United Kingdom's principal means of defence against the Soviet Union, and which abolished conscription. This was a process confirmed by 1969, when the British completed their withdrawal from east of Suez. The 1982 Falklands War was an echo of the past – 'the empire strikes back' – not a pointer to the future. By contrast New Zealand defence policy, although still inherently expeditionary, focused increasingly on the Pacific and south-east Asia, as the wars in Korea, Malaya and Vietnam all showed.

But the armed forces of the United Kingdom and New Zealand continue to share some core assumptions, beyond those simply of a common history and the joint legacy of the two world wars. For both powers real soldiering has become focused on counter-insurgency warfare. The British may not have fought in Vietnam, but between 1945 and the end of the twentieth century their campaigns were above all campaigns of so-called low intensity fought mostly outside Europe – from Malaya to Northern Ireland, via Cyprus, Kenya, Oman and Aden. As a result during the 1960s the British army was increasingly divided according to a binary vision of war. On the one hand part of the army, focused in the British Army on the Rhine and located in Europe, stressed armour, artillery, and divisional and corps levels of command. On the other the infantry, its thinking shaped the counter-insurgency operations of colonial withdrawal, stressed platoon and even section tactics. This division deepened in the 1980s, as the British army (as well as that of New Zealand) aped and was shaped by the army of the United States.

The United States also inherited a binary vision of war from the nineteenth century. European models were embodied in the experience of the American Civil War, and they contrasted with the frontier wars against native North Americans. The United States had its own wars of empire (even if it did not use that term) in Cuba and the Philippines. The Vietnam War reawakened that legacy, but the lesson that the US army took from Vietnam was not how to win the next counter-insurgency campaign, but how to avoid ever fighting such a war again. The norm was to be major war, fought with overwhelming force for unequivocal objectives, with a clear exit strategy – a response driven by Colin Powell both when he was military adviser to Caspar Weinberger (and reflected in the Weinberger doctrine of 1984) and when he was Chairman of the Joint Chiefs of Staff (and reflected in the Powell doctrine in 1992). The consequences were ones from which the US army struggled to emerge in Iraq and Afghanistan.

As a result in the 1980s the US army refocused on major conventional operations in Europe, and it used doctrine to drive change and to recover a sense of professional self-worth. NATO armies followed in its wake, with a stress on the operational level of war, 'AirLand battle', manoeuvre and the corps counter-stroke. Although a trail whose start point was to defend northern and central Germany from a Soviet invasion, it led, through the first Gulf War of 1990–1, to the 'revolution in military affairs', 'transformation', network-centric warfare, and ultimately to the successful invasion of Iraq in March and April 2003. It culminated on the deck of USS *Abraham Lincoln*, where George W. Bush hubristically appeared beneath a banner declaring 'mission accomplished'.

What became important for NATO armies in the 1990s was matching themselves against the United States, not against the enemy.

They wondered whether they could keep pace with the United States technologically, straining their defence budgets to remain interoperable with the world's military super-power. Meanwhile most of their enemies were perfectly happy with equipment that represented not the highest common factor of warfare but the lowest common denominator – the AK47 rifle and the hand-held rocket-propelled grenade, available to and useable by all fighters, including children.

The British army both was part of this trend and promoted it. Its most conspicuous success since the Falklands War of 1982 has been in Northern Ireland. But Northern Ireland was piggybacked on to the continental commitment to Europe. It never became the driving factor in British defence policy. In the 1990s, and up until – and including – the tenure of General Sir Mike Jackson as Chief of the General Staff, the gold standard for British doctrine remained the conduct of major war, not the waging of counter-insurgency campaigns. The army fought to maintain a corps headquarters through the ARRC (Allied Rapid Reaction Corps) in NATO, and it argued that an army which was equipped for major war, and prepared and trained for it, could also fight lesser forms of conflict. These 'lesser' forms of conflict went under an increasing and bewildering array of titles. Nomenclature became all: counter-insurgency and low intensity conflict; peace-enforcement, peace-keeping, and peace-support operations; and then, more recently, asymmetric warfare, and by 2009 stabilisation operations.

One pillar of the binary vision of war was becoming endlessly sub-divided and re-categorised, and each of those categories of 'small war' depended on the notion of so-called major war for its intellectual coherence. A common understanding of major war, or a common assumption as to what it was, was crucial to the intellectual coherence of the rest. This was the pole around which they circled. The 'lesser' forms of war defined themselves by their relationship to, and in opposition to, major war.

Small wars were inherently under-resourced, whereas major wars required the full mobilisation of the nation. In major wars command was united, but in the operations in the 1990s in Bosnia and elsewhere it was often divided, as it was initially in Afghanistan, with the US-led Operation Enduring Freedom and the NATO-led International Security Assistance Force operating in parallel. Only in 2007 was a single US commander appointed for both components. In small wars the objectives were also small, scattered, and often not decisive when gained, and forces were dispersed and not concentrated, as they would be in major wars. In small wars operations could often be deliberately protracted; in peace-keeping the aim could even be to postpone a decision by holding the ring between conflicting parties. Finally, in small wars the need for full force protection, to avoid casualties, tended to work against the principles of manoeuvre and operational flexibility.

The binary vision of war has the effect of pulling armed forces apart, not providing coherence. The tension can become insupportable. In the autumn of 2008, the British Chief of the General Staff, General Sir Richard Dannatt, organised his annual staff ride as a battlefield tour to look at the Russo-German war of 1944–5. In the late 1970s the eastern front in the Second World War used to be the sole purely military historical study provided in the war studies course at the Royal Military Academy Sandhurst, but that was during the Cold War, when the British army might reasonably expect to have to fight a defensive battle against Soviet armoured divisions as the Germans had done in the final months of the Third Reich. Dannatt's purpose in 2008 was different: he felt that it was important that the pressures of current operations should not cause the army to forget other sorts of warfare. But for many who had served or were about to serve in Afghanistan it seemed more important to win the war in hand than to prepare for a future war which might never come.

New Zealand is not exempt from similar pressures. The public consultation document issued in 2009 as part of the first defence review for a decade said that current defence policy required the New Zealand Defence Force to be 'appropriately equipped and trained for both combat and peacekeeping' (p. 16). Combat remained the gold standard for the Defence Force, but nothing more was said about it. Instead, the paper went on to state, reasonably enough, that 'participation in peace support operations has become a major element of the Defence Force's role over the past two decades' (p. 18). Its failure to say more about war-fighting was significant. As the Royal New Zealand Returned and Services' Association's report on *Defending New Zealand*, published in 2005, put it: 'we do a great disservice to the nation if we size, shape and equip the armed forces of New Zealand as though civil assistance were their dominant purpose'.[7]

The issues therefore are not only conceptual, they are also budgetary. Small armed forces – which mean those of both the United Kingdom and New Zealand, however comparatively large those of the

UK might seem to a Kiwi – cannot afford any longer to pursue balance, however much they might want to do so. In January 2009, Robert Gates, the US Secretary of Defense, wrote an article in *Foreign Affairs* entitled 'A balanced strategy: reprogramming the Pentagon for a new age'. This was not so much a plea for the retention of major war capabilities as a signal to the dinosaurs of the US armed forces that they had to accept the long-term need to retain the capacities generated by and for the conflicts in Iraq and Afghanistan. Gates was refusing to let the United States army do again what it had done after Vietnam. But balance of Gates's sort, generating the skills for 'small wars' while keeping the practitioners of 'major war' in business (and up to speed intellectually as well as in terms of high-end equipment), assumes massive resources, possibly too massive even for the United States and certainly so for its allies. In the United Kingdom, even before the economic recession, it was clear that British defence spending was carrying one major equipment programme too many. Another British writer who, like Liddell Hart, has straddled military history and the study of contemporary conflict, Sir Max Hastings, argued in *The Guardian* on 30 April 2007 that the British army should become de facto the senior service, that the Chief of the Defence Staff should always be a general, and that the other services should be restructured to support the army in what will be its sole function for the foreseeable future – irregular war. In other words the aircraft carriers so ardently wanted by the Royal Navy should go, and so too might the renewal of the British nuclear deterrent. This would be not so much the abandonment of the binary vision of war as the unilateral embracing of a singular vision of war.

At this point it is pertinent to refer back to the 1909 *Field service regulations* for a bit of context. The British general staff was caught between the daily demands of colonial garrisoning with an over-stretched and under-funded army, and simultaneously needing to prepare for a possible war with Germany in north-west Europe – or even with Russia on the north-west frontier of India. Its solution was to embrace not a binary vision of war, but a unitary one. *Field service regulations, part I: operations* contained a chapter on 'warfare against an uncivilized enemy'. Paragraph 1 began: 'In campaigns against savages, the armament, tactics, and characteristics of the enemy, and the nature of the theatre of operations, demand that the principles of regular warfare be somewhat modified; the modifications in this chapter are such as experience has shown to be necessary.'[8]

Note that the emphasis was on modification, not on polar opposites. The Director of Staff Duties in 1909, Douglas Haig, had wanted the
Field service regulations to begin with a note 'at the top of the first page,
which said that these Regulations were not intended for small campaigns'. There is no such note in the published version. Haig's ambition,
in his words 'the creation of an National Army ... based on European
and not Asiatic conditions', had run into a wall erected by Henderson
before his premature death in 1902.[9]

Henderson too had wanted an army capable of engaging in
European warfare, but recognised that the primary requirement was
for an army that was flexible and adaptable, that could use its judgement
to meet the circumstances that confronted it. Regular and irregular
warfare, European and colonial wars, were therefore subsumed within
the same publication, and were united because they rested on the same
general principles. Henderson, confronted with the diversity of war, did
not abandon the effort to find coherence. His answer was to stress the
principles of war – principles which might conflict with each other, which
were 'neither to be so rigidly applied nor over-scrupulously respected',
which were 'to be obeyed rather in the spirit than in the letter'. 'The
strategist, to be successful,' he wrote, 'must know exactly how fast he can
go in disregarding them or modifying them.'[10]

Henderson therefore embraced a unitary view of war, not a binary
one, and this was the philosophy that permeated the army in his day and
which found its way into the *Field service regulations*. In 1897, Brigadier
General Reginald Clare Hart, late director of military education in India,
published the second edition of his book, *Reflections on the art of war*.
Like most such books, Hart's discussed the great commanders of European
history – Turenne, Marlbrough, Eugene, Frederick and Napoleon.
However, Hart himself had won the Victoria Cross in the second Afghan
War, rescuing a wounded sowar of the 13th Bengal Lancers in the Bazar
valley. It had been suggested to him that he write 'a separate chapter on
savage, mountain, or jungle warfare', but he had decided against it 'because
the principles are the same in all kinds of warfare'.[11] William Robertson,
the future Chief of the Imperial General Staff, and one of Henderson's most
loyal pupils, taught, when commandant of the Staff College in 1912, that
the aim of the *Field service regulations* was 'to train the judgment of all
officers so that when left to themselves they may do the right thing'.[12]

In other words the British army before the First World War
responded to the challenge of war's diverse character by embracing a

unitary view of war's nature. It stressed that fighting lay at the heart of war; that war therefore depended crucially on moral factors; and that war was waged against an enemy who should be presumed to be adaptable, resourceful and not an inanimate object. War was a reciprocal act where seizure of the initiative and the ability to do the unexpected were the essentials in delivering victory.

A criticism often levelled against the *Field service regulations* of 1909 is that it made frequent reference to general principles, but that it did not list the principles of war in precise and aphoristic fashion (a defect corrected in the later editions of the 1920s). That too is a criticism levelled at Clausewitz. *On war* contains many references to the need for principles and system, but never delivers them in a way designed to be learnt by the parrots of military crammers and spoon-fed examinees. Just as *On war* aims to promote understanding by debate and dialectic, so the 1909 *Field service regulations* aimed to teach judgement and discrimination. Clausewitz's unitary view of war, like that of the *Field service regulations*, was a matter of morale, *coup d'oeil* and military genius, all of which found their expression in the resistant medium of fighting and battle. It is embedded in books III to V of *On war*, with their graphic descriptions of what he himself had seen and experienced in the wars against Napoleon.

The underlying point is simple: one war is more like another than it is like any other human activity, and that is sufficiently true across time for us to identify the nature of war as possessed of enough enduring characteristics to be a common phenomenon.

Is that a helpful observation, or is it merely trite? Self-evidently each war in practice possesses different characteristics, so much so that the presumption that the last war can teach you about the next has too often proved to be wrong, particularly in the eyes of superficial critics. This brings us back to the beginning of this chapter – and to Liddell Hart. The generals of the inter-war British army were often criticised, not least by Liddell Hart, for being too caught up in the experience of the First World War to recognise the impact of armour, mechanisation and airpower. But in fact, as Howard Kippenberger himself made abundantly clear in *Infantry brigadier*, the experience of 1941–2 in North Africa revealed that British military thinking in the 1930s had become too subject to the fads and enthusiasms of Liddell Hart and others to be able to retain a sense of context. It so emphasised the independent use of armour that the capacity to coordinate it with infantry and artillery was thrown away. Kippenberger wrote: 'It seemed to me that Libya '41, or the Winter Battle, or Auchinleck's offensive, or "Crusader", as it was variously called, was fought with total disregard of what one had understood to be the principles of war.'[13] As Kippenberger's own accounts made clear, from October 1942, and beginning at El Alamein, the British and Commonwealth forces fought their battles in ways that owed much more to the attritional fighting and heavy artillery preparation characteristic of the allied victories of 1918 than the vainglorious Montgomery, despite being their author, was ever wont publicly to acknowledge.

So what had happened between 1918 and 1942? In the early 1920s when Liddell Hart was a callow captain writing about infantry tactics and hanging on to the coat-tails of J. F. C. Fuller, the fashionable books to read in the British army still included works whose origins predated the First World War. One author represented by three volumes in the Kippenberger library in New Zealand's National Army Museum in Waiouru was G. F. R Henderson, who remained as well studied after 1918 as he had been before 1914. Another was Ferdinand Foch, whose *The principles of war*, although written in 1903 by the man who ended the First World War as the allied generalissimo, was not translated into English until 1918. Foch justified the 1918 edition, despite the immense changes wrought on warfare in the interim, by saying that, 'it is always necessary to establish the principles of war'. And, his preface went on, 'The present work, although dating from 1903, can still serve for the formation of men called to lead troops or simply anxious to reflect on the demands of war.'

That was the aspiration of the Territorial Force officer in Canterbury, Howard Kippenberger, and his citation of the principles of war in reference to the North African campaign in 1941 may have been an unconscious tribute to Foch, as Foch's book too was in his library.[14] So too was the second edition (1925; the first was published in 1920) of Major General W. D. Bird's *The direction of war: a study of strategy*. Bird's book, like Foch's, had begun its life before the First World War, its broad outline and arguments taking shape in *A précis of strategy*, published in 1910. Like Foch, Bird saw little cause to revise his basic assumptions about the nature of war in the light of what had happened in the intervening period. Indeed he quoted Foch on exactly this point in the preface to the second edition of *The direction of war*: 'The rules and principles of war are always the same. It matters nothing whether your soldier is on his feet in the open or shut up inside a tank ... The development of the art of war is like that of architecture. The materials you use for your buildings may change. They may be wood, stone or steel. But the static principles on which your house must be built are permanent.' As Bird went on to explain, the principles of war were what enabled the soldier to balance continuity with change: 'The principles, then, that govern the direction of war are constant, although their application varies with the means at the disposal of a government or commander, and with the conditions prevalent during a campaign. The exact conditions on which any campaign was fought are unlikely to be repeated, and reliance on the experience of one war is liable to lead to false conceptions.' Kippenberger was particularly taken with Bird's stress on the importance of geography, a point entirely in conformity with the 1909 *Field service regulations*, which had divided 'uncivilised war' not according to the changeable characteristics of its belligerents but according to the more permanent factor of the terrain over which it was fought.

In 1909 uncivilised war was categorised according to whether it was fought in mountains or in jungle. The post-1918 editions of the *Field service regulations* added desert. The development was symptomatic of a broader trend: successive editions, greater in bulk, fell victim to complexity and lost clarity. As doctrine became increasingly sophisticated, theory swamped reality. The *Field service regulations* tried to do more but in the process delivered less. Some soldiers took doctrine as prescriptive, not inquisitive; as providing solutions more than prompting questions; and so they stopped thinking for themselves.

We confront a similar problem today. We recognise, I hope, although I sometimes wonder, that the war in Afghanistan is different from the war in Iraq, because each is a different country, with different political, economic and social structures, and different geographies. But if that point – that each small war is different – is clearly understood, then what is less clearly recognised in the typologies embraced by most soldiers today is that each major war has also been different. The major war which strategic pundits use as their benchmark – an existential war for national survival – depends on the Second World War for its construction. Deterrence theory during the Cold War extrapolated from the Second World War to make a truly global war, with deaths – civilian as well as military – in the millions, a theoretical norm rather than an exception.

This leaves the inter-state wars waged since 1945 in a limbo. They do not fit into the paradigm of major war because they have been limited – in the British case from the Falklands War in 1982 via Kosovo in 1999 to Iraq in 2003. That point is also true of wars fought more recently by other powers, including the Russian invasion of South Ossetia and Israel's attack on Gaza in 2008. The limits have operated in various ways – in terms of geography, weaponry or time – but those limitations have been sufficient to ensure their exclusion from our notion of major war. But nor do those wars fit comfortably into norms developed for small wars.

The problems posed by definition and categorisation are more complex still. Many small wars have taken place within big wars: guerrilla war in Spain, Italy and Switzerland during the Napoleonic Wars; revolutionary war in the Middle East and central Asia, as well as in Ireland, in the First World War; and partisan war in central and southeast Europe in the Second World War. And, furthermore, those major wars swept up within them many inter-state wars which were themselves limited, including Japan's war against Germany in 1914–18 and the Soviet Union's war with Japan in 1945.

The challenge which students of war confront, whether pure historians or those who study war as a practical business of immediate, albeit terrifying, relevance, is how to bridge the divide between the nature of war more generally and the specific character of each war in particular. What is striking about the British army's response to this problem in 1909, and about its continued application of the 1909 *Field service regulations* throughout the First World War, was that it focused on the relationship between strategy and tactics, and not on that between strategy and policy.

In plumbing the nature of war, as opposed to the characterisation of each war, the relationship between war and policy is frankly secondary, not primary. Policy determines which wars are fought, where they are fought and why they are fought. The function of policy is pervasive but it is proximate. It is policy which makes it so hard to anticipate future wars and what they will be about. The salience of policy in war, the belief that it determines the nature of war, is very largely a product of the Cold War, because policy shaped deterrence. Of course this is profoundly nonsensical as the Cold War was not a war and, if it had been, policy might not have remained so pervasive. But the duration and stability of the Cold War themselves created a sense of continuity which experiences since 1990 have been slow to slough off. The fact that the wars since 1990 have been wars of lower intensity rather than higher has played its part here, because political effects are disproportionately more important in wars of lower intensity. In past wars of higher intensity corps commanders have operated in what was to all intents and purposes a policy-free zone. Policy in major wars of national survival works with the grain of war and its drive to escalation. In wars that are more restrained policy can find itself at odds with war's nature, a point observed by Clausewitz when contrasting the wars of the eighteenth century with the Napoleonic Wars. As a result political effects stand out more distinctly in wars of lesser intensity. The strain on civil–military relations becomes more pronounced and the activities of somebody like Lynndie England while guarding Iraqi prisoners at Abu Ghraib in 2003 can have dire political consequences.

Fashionable titles (at least in the United Kingdom), such as stabilisation operations and the comprehensive approach, with their emphasis on the fact that the military is not necessarily the most important element in the war in Afghanistan, reinforce this notion of policy's logical supremacy. However, the bread and butter of what most soldiers do, in small wars as in big, lies not at the interface of policy and strategy, but at that between strategy and tactics, and in the vast majority of cases at the purely tactical level. In Geneva in September 2008, General Sir David Richards, the former ISAF commander in Afghanistan and at that time Commander-in-Chief Land Forces in the British army, asked, 'If it is decided that our armies need to be capable of succeeding in both [wars against non-state actors and wars against states], do [those charged with designing and equipping armies] believe that the two types of conflict would in practice look surprisingly similar, at least to those actually charged with fighting them at the tactical level?'[15]

The implied answer was that they would. At the 2009 Land Warfare Conference, an annual event held at the Royal United Services Institute in London on behalf of the British Chief of the General Staff, Richards spoke of 'generic future conflict' and a 'single version of war'. Nor was he alone. The outgoing Chief, Sir Richard Dannatt, now voiced similar views, and at the same event General George Casey, Chief of the Staff of the US Army, and General James Mattis of the Joint Forces Command made related points. By 2013, in the view of one German newspaper, the experience of sustained combat in northern Afghanistan had taught the Bundeswehr how to fight – and not just against the Taleban but also in whatever context it might be asked to act by the German government.[16] Général Vincent Desportes, formerly director of the French armed forces' doctrine centre and head of the Collège Interarmées de Défense between 2008 and 2010, put it as clearly as anyone. 'War is war,' he wrote, continuing: 'For centuries, we have had the feeling that we are fighting new wars, unrelated to previous conflicts, [but] with the benefit of hindsight, it is surprising to see the stability of the general characteristic of conflicts, their unchanging logic and the error that could have been avoided if the "trendsetters" of the period had simply had longer memories.'[17]

The binary vision of war has two illogical consequences. First, it treats current operations as exceptional, as deviations from the norm of major war. Secondly, it can make many long-term procurement projects look irrelevant and sometimes irrational. It then presents national armed forces with an unpalatable choice. Either they make massive investments in order to maintain balanced forces capable of prevailing in both sets of options, a cost which seems disproportionate to the threats, or they concentrate on specific roles. All armies worth their salt fear the threat that they will become a gendarmerie. A decision to prepare and sustain armed forces specifically for what have come to be called stabilisation operations, or even for counter-insurgency warfare, looks to those opposed to such ideas like an acceptance of an inability to fight and win what they would see as real war.

A unitary vision of war, with its focus on war's nature, can offset this. It treats short-term, not long-term, procurement in the immediate build-up to war, and within the war itself, as the prevailing pattern. And in situations where there is no imminent likelihood of war it should treat flexibility and adaptability as the sine qua nons, not just of the doctrine embraced by the armed forces but also of the weaponry which flows from that thinking. As General Sir Rupert Smith has pointed out, equipment used in most operations since 1990 was designed with the Cold War in mind.[18] Embracing the unitary nature of war as a departure point is not a substitute for hard thinking about the character of wars which are either imminent or in hand, but it does mean that that hard thinking rests on a secure, rather than a superficial, foundation.

The binary vision of war creates a ready-made characterisation of wars based on theory but often insufficiently flexible to reflect reality. A model derived from British counter-insurgency in Malaya or in Northern Ireland was not ready-made for Afghanistan; nor were the first or second Afghan Wars of the nineteenth century appropriate models for the Afghan War of the twenty-first century. A war having been slotted into one envelope can jump into another but the change can then go unrecognised for too long, as armies remain caught in the web of their own theoretical expectations. The United States, having fallen victim to this in Vietnam, ran foul of it again in Iraq in 2003–4. A recognition of the nature of war in its broader sense can self-evidently only be theoretical and therefore demands that those who profess it go on to ask fundamental questions of the war that actually confronts them, and do so on that basis – in a spirit of enquiry – rather than on the basis of a flip and easy solution, pulled off the shelf of ready-to-wear clothing.

On 24 August 1941, two months after Edward Puttick had written his report on Howard Kippenberger, the latter wrote to his wife, Ruth: 'The fact is that I've read & studied & thought about war so much that almost automatically I know the right thing to do in a crisis.'[19] Military history had enabled a Territorial Force officer, who had spent most of his service in the Canterbury hills of the South Island, to be able to respond to the unexpected. For the historian, there is a further and final point: a distinction between the nature of war and the character of particular wars will prevent the impact of short-term issues from swamping a sense of perspective on long-term continuities.

11 STRATEGY AND THE OPERATIONAL LEVEL OF WAR

On 23 June 2010, President Barack Obama recalled General Stanley McChrystal to Washington, and relieved him of his command in Afghanistan. In the view of most commentators, the president had little choice. As quoted by Michael Hastings in an article in *Rolling Stone*, McChrystal and his immediate circle of military advisers had criticised and disparaged the United States's ambassador in Kabul, Karl Eikenberry, the president's special representative for the region, Richard Holbrooke, and the vice-president, Joe Biden. Their scorn had gone further: it had embraced the president himself. Had Obama failed to act, the norms of civil–military relations would have been overthrown. As the president put it, the article had undermined 'the civilian control of the military that's at the core of our democratic system'.[1]

But McChrystal had not set out to challenge that norm. This was a cock-up, not a conspiracy. His dignified response, and his refusal to try to justify or explain away the remarks attributed to him, confirmed his disciplined acceptance of his own constitutional position. What he had done was something rather different: he and his colleagues had vented their frustration at the lack of clear political guidance within which McChrystal's own operational concepts were meant to sit. The operational level of war is the level of command situated between the tactical and the strategic, between the company or battalion commander in the field and the president in the White House. It is in the exercise of operational art that today's senior generals, like McChrystal, hope to reach the acme of their professional careers. The bulk of the planning done by their staffs is devoted both to preparing for that opportunity and then to applying their skills in order to manage the characteristic chaos of war. But to do that operational art needs direction; it requires of policy a degree of clarity and a consistency of purpose which can frequently be at odds with the realities and contingencies of politics. In 1952, when General Douglas MacArthur was recalled by President Harry Truman, his sin was to have called for a change in strategy; by contrast McChrystal just wanted a strategy.

President Obama declared, 'I don't make this decision based on any difference in policy with General McChrystal.'[2] But McChrystal's complaints derived in large part, at least by implication, from a lack of clarity as to what that policy was. The intractability of the war in Afghanistan, even more than in most wars, precluded the formation of simple and clear goals, or of the consistent objectives which the operational commander not only craves but also needs. And so strategy, the place where operational art and policy meet, became the focus for the clash between the soldier's pursuit of operational goals and the politician's desire for flexibility amidst shifting and uncertain scenarios. Such tensions were not in themselves new, and this particular iteration of them had a back history that extended over the three previous decades.

Strategy is about the relationships between means and ends. It has become common currency to talk about the plan of the campaign in Afghanistan as a 'counter-insurgency strategy'.[3] If that is the case, then it rests on an old-fashioned and narrow definition of strategy. When Clausewitz defined strategy as the use of the battle for the purposes of the war, he was thinking along not dissimilar lines, but that is a characterisation of strategy which has not carried much weight since the First World War.[4] As Chapter 2 has argued, twentieth-century descriptions came to see strategy as linking war to policy. The ideas of counter-insurgency do not operate at this level, either geopolitically or institutionally. They are means to an end, not an end in themselves. To paraphrase Clausewitz, they explain the use of armed force for the purposes of the war, but they do not explain the purpose of the war itself. Général Vincent Desportes, formerly director of France's Collège Interarmées de Défense, went to the heart of the problem when he observed that McChrystal's removal had relaunched two debates: 'one tactical – how one fights in Afghanistan – and the other strategic – what does one do beyond that'.[5]

Tactics are not spoken of much these days, although one immediate response among many American soldiers to the news of McChrystal's departure was to hope that the tight controls on the use of firepower would be eased. During the Cold War, thinking about war neglected tactics to focus disproportionately on strategy. The stand-off between NATO and the Warsaw Pact provided a clear strategic context within which the utility of force could be considered and a firm geopolitical framework within which it could be set. But the Cold War also meant that force, because it found functions short of war, became divorced from actual fighting; deterrence theory, strategic thought's principal output by the 1960s, was largely shaped by civilian strategists. The effects of this evolution were twofold. First, during the Cold War the actual conduct of war was little studied, with the result that strategy did not put much weight on war-fighting itself. Secondly, and consequently, soldiers were left without a clear role in the shaping and development of strategy.

The early strategic thinkers, those of Clausewitz's generation, would have been flabbergasted: the very factors which drove the need for strategy in the first place had been ripped from strategic thought. It was an unnatural void, and one that was likely to have dire consequences if armed force were actually applied in war. In the 1980s the operational level of war filled it. Operational art, which could be defined in just the same terms as those used by Clausewitz to define strategy, 'the use of the battle for the purpose of the war', both focused on the conduct of war and was clearly the province of uniformed thinkers, rather than of academics and politicians. Two separate impetuses drove this process. The first was the need of the United States army to recover its *amour propre* after the war in Vietnam: doctrine became one device by which it sought to reassert its professional self-worth.[6] The second was the pressure in the 1980s to raise the nuclear threshold, to respond to the Soviet declaration renouncing the first use of nuclear weapons, and to exploit the increasing effectiveness of precision-guided munitions which promised the ability to check a Soviet invasion and even to enable a NATO counter-attack. The source here was as much European as American: in the Northern Army Group (NORTHAG) Anglo-German forces developed ideas for a corps counter-stroke.[7]

The operational level of war and its bundle of associated ideas, including manoeuvre and then 'manoeuvrism', spread through NATO armies like wildfire, and remain in their doctrines today. Although presented as the bridge between strategy and tactics, the orientation of the operational level in the late 1980s was towards the interface with tactics, not strategy. After all, in the late 1980s, with the Cold War still running, the political context was clear enough. Furthermore, any discussion of the operational–strategic interface, particularly in the context of European war, was soon likely to become mired in issues of nuclear release, with the implication that the military would lose control of the war's conduct to civilians.

Indeed, that was precisely the attraction of the operational level of war, that it was developed in a policy-free zone, in which military expertise was unfettered and where armies reasserted their authority over war's conduct. It soon established its own intellectual pedigree, not least through the selective use of military history.[8] The most thoughtful of the analysts, like Richard Simpkin and Shimon Naveh, found the origins of operational thought in the inter-war Soviet Union, in the ideas of V. K. Triandafillov and M. N. Tukhachevskii, in 'deep battle' and (by the late 1980s) 'operational manoeuvre groups'.[9] But most of those who used history in this way paid less attention to the Soviet Union's contribution to operational thought, and rather more to Germany's.[10] The invasion and rapid defeat of France in May 1940 was elevated to the status of role model, an example whose force was amplified by the absence of a broader strategic context – which would of course have pointed out that in the end Germany lost the war. The invention of operational art was pushed even further back in time – to another loser, Napoleon, and Michael Howard and Peter Paret inserted the words 'operations' and 'operational' into the text of their English translation of Clausewitz's On war in 1976, despite the absence of their equivalents in the original German.[11]

Operational art in the 1980s was an intellectual construct, a product of military doctrine more than of direct battlefield experience: hence its tendency to reach back in time for its ideas. Much military doctrine developed in such circumstances is vilified for its tendency to focus on the last war, not the next – with the implication that an acquaintance with the past would prove inimical to the future. That was not the case – or so it seemed – with the military doctrines developed in the later stages of the Cold War. Operational art found its pay-off on the battlefield in Operation Desert Storm in 1991. NATO armies applied the thinking of the 1980s to the Middle East, not to Europe, and achieved victory in short order. In retrospect the campaign looked increasingly like the culmination of a process, as the end of a line of development, but at the time it seemed to be the dawn of a bold new future. Between then and the invasion of Iraq in 2003 most fashions in military thought grew, in linear progression, from the desire to conduct conventional operations on land with even greater tempo, and with an increasing ability to concentrate fire to enable manoeuvre. Their route passed through the 'revolution in military affairs', 'network-centric warfare', 'effects-based operations' and transformation.[12] All were ways of waging war that exploited new technologies for tactical effects, which were so sequenced and staged that they had operational outcomes.

Operation Iraqi Freedom, launched in March 2003, was therefore a sort of denouement, standing on an apparent continuum from the lessons learnt in the aftermath of Vietnam and passing through the first Gulf War of 1990–1. But there had also been a change. On 28 February 1991, as the broken Iraqi army streamed back along the so-called 'highway of death', President George Bush (senior) called a cease-fire. In the eyes of his critics, he had stopped short: 'Saddam Hussein was defeated on the battlefield and discredited in the eyes of military professionals. But the Iraqi leader held fast to the reins of power in Baghdad.'[13] In 2003, two spokesmen for those 'military professionals', Williamson Murray and Major General Robert H. Scales, the former a distinguished military historian and strategic commentator, and the latter the principal author of the US army's official account of the 1991 war and responsible for the Army After Next programme from 1995, produced a somewhat premature and even hubristic account of the invasion of Iraq. They described what had happened in 1990–1 as 'tactical victory, operational failure'. Although they rather confusingly went on to concede that 'the US military had conducted a successful campaign at the operational level', they concluded that in 1991 'missteps at the operational level ensured that the coalition's brilliant tactical performance on the battlefield would not achieve the kind of strategic and political victory that could have toppled Saddam and his regime'. The 2003 war with Iraq was 'a different story', their history of the war claimed, displaying 'a combination of tactical and operational virtuosity that obliterated the Baathist regime'.[14]

Murray and Scales were using 'the operational level of war' in two different ways, and hence the ambiguity in their assessment of what had happened in the first Iraq War: the context to which they applied the phrase in 1991 was tactical, that of 2003 was more strategic. The orientation and expectations of the operational level had changed over a decade. The strategic expectations vested in operational thought had expanded as strategy itself lost direction. In the 1980s the operational level of war could focus on its tactical applications because it had been developed in a strategic or even grand strategic context which could be taken for granted; after 1989–90 those strategic certainties were removed by the end of the Cold War. As a result NATO's strategy became increasingly confused and strategy itself progressively lost precision – in terms of what it meant, who did it and where it was made. Strategic thought, such as it was, continued on the trajectory set for it by nuclear deterrence, becoming a synonym for policy, not the means to link policy to the waging of war. National leaders could be clear about their policies, but that did not make them masters of strategy, despite their frequent references to it. President George W. Bush and the British prime minister, Tony Blair, were able to articulate policy goals in 2001–3, but they did not understand the nature of war, and therefore did not appreciate the reciprocal, interactive and often unpredictable relationship between war and policy.

In the 1990s this trend did not matter too much as many armed forces, especially those of Europe, began to see their functions in terms of 'softer' effects, such as internal security, peace-keeping and peace-support operations. Not only were these commitments not war as it was understood in the light of the two world wars, they were also not counter-insurgency as it has come to be understood since 2003: they were not violent enough for that. The United States army only engaged in peace-keeping and state formation reluctantly, if at all, and continued to emphasise the operational level of war which it associated with major war. Since other armies within NATO had few enemies against which to match themselves, they measured themselves against the US army, and so, despite their experience of peace-keeping, kept alive the operational level of war as their intellectual gold standard. The key criterion for military effectiveness within NATO in the 1990s became the capacity to be able to operate alongside the United States. Successive British Chiefs of the General Staff, up to and initially including General Sir Richard Dannatt, who was appointed in 2006, stressed the need to keep alive the 'war-fighting' flame. The British determination to run the Ace – later Allied – Rapid Reaction Corps (ARRC), set up in 1992, was a further manifestation of that priority.

The ARRC was, and still is, a NATO headquarters, so this particular operational imperative had a political impact. Operational thinking had political consequences in the United States as well. In 1992 the Chairman of the Joint Chiefs of Staff, Colin Powell, adapted the 1984 Weinberger doctrine for the use of the armed forces to the circumstances prevailing after the Cold War, effectively demanding that the United States should only go to war if the US armed forces concluded that the political circumstances were conducive to operational success. Powell seemed to ignore the need to bend operational capabilities to political imperatives, as the Secretary of State, Madeleine Albright, somewhat testily pointed out.[15]

What was happening was that, subliminally, the operational level of war was moving into the space created by the absence of strategy. From being concerned with the operational–tactical interface, it was increasingly preoccupied with that between operations and strategy. In Britain in 1993, Brigadier (later Lieutenant General Sir) Alistair Irwin produced a pamphlet that was indicative of the trend. It committed to print two lectures he had delivered to the Higher Command and Staff Course (which the British army had set up in 1988 specifically to focus on the operational level of war), entitled 'The levels of war: operational art and campaign planning'. Irwin stressed that the operational level applied not just to corps command but to all forms of war, including counter-insurgency. However, most of his examples were derived from corps-level battles and concerned regular and conventional warfare. He argued that the political dimension was an important element in the operational level of war, precisely because an operation should achieve an outcome which has a material effect, and so it should assist in the achievement of strategic goals. However, in saying this, he assumed that the commander would be guided by top-down direction. When he went on to describe the functions fulfilled at the operational level, he reckoned that the strategic objectives would be clear, with the result that the operational commander would be able to convert them into operational and tactical actions. He envisaged a cascading effect from policy, so that it would be possible to deduce from the goals of policy what military conditions were desirable, how to sequence events and what resources would be required. All this was entirely logical, but it begged a very important question: what would happen if there were no strategic goals?[16]

Grand strategy is a pragmatic business; it needs a war or at least a crisis for the head of state of a democratically elected government to give it full consideration. Without a war, it tends to be neglected as it is above the pay grade of generals who are the products of democracies. Shaped by the norms for the conduct of civil–military relations set by Samuel Huntington, they see themselves as apolitical, and so do not embrace the political repercussions of their actions.[17] These were the norms that Obama invoked on 23 June 2010, and to which McChrystal duly deferred. Those generals who have been and are most aware of the political ramifications of military involvement are those who exercise multinational command in regions like the Balkans, responsibilities which require them to use political skills to understand and manipulate their allies, or to broker deals between ethnic groups in theatre. But even the impact of that sort of insight can be limited because of the association of major conventional war with the operational level of war, and because of the consequent tendency to see irregular war, counter-insurgency warfare and peace-keeping operations as occupying a separate analytical compartment.

Generals who have fought actual wars have found that the presumption that war was a continuation of policy – axiomatic for Huntington and re-emphasised through a one-sided and selective reading of Clausewitz – has created as many problems as it has solved. Policy, as Clausewitz acknowledged, can be like an alien element in war.[18] General James Jones, President Obama's National Security Advisor in 2009–10, was fond of quoting the third lesson of *Lessons in disaster*, Gordon Goldstein's book on the Vietnam War (where the young Jones had served with the US Marine Corps): 'Politics is the enemy of strategy.'[19] The two converge in a major war of national survival, but they diverge all too easily in wars presented as limited or 'discretionary' (to use the current word of choice). Even the Kosovo campaign in 1999, the classic example of a recent and successful war of intervention, generated deep tension along the civil–military fault-line. The political and legal problems of that conflict undercut the military preparations of General Wesley Clark, the Supreme Allied Commander Europe, leading him to conclude: 'any first year military student could point to the more obvious inconsistencies between our efforts and the requirements posed by the principles of war'. Clark's military experience is recent, but his refrain sounds familiar, even if old-fashioned: 'Using military force effectively requires departing from the political dynamic and following the so-called "Principles of War" identified by post-Napoleonic military writers a century and a half ago.'[20]

Clark may not always have commanded the admiration and approbation of his peers, but such thinking had become commonplace by 2003. In the planning for the invasion of Iraq, General Tommy Franks told Paul Wolfowitz, Donald Rumsfeld's deputy at the Pentagon, 'Keep Washington focused on policy and strategy. *Leave me the hell alone to run the war.*'[21] Franks was stressing his desire to focus on the operational level of war, his professional comfort zone; he did not want to be concerned with strategy, precisely because it lay at the civil–military interface. Nor was Britain's approach any more coherent, even if it did not reap the consequences of its insouciance, at least in the first instance. The original intention, to insert a division from the north through Turkey, was largely guided by operational considerations, the need both to open a second front and to isolate Saddam Hussein's heartland, Tikrit. It took little account of the possible consequences of entering Kurdish territory at the borders of Turkey, Iran and Iraq. Political imperatives, in this case Turkey's refusal to cooperate, trumped operational considerations, and in the event the British entered Iraq from the south, but the point remains. In 2003, as became increasingly clear after Murray and Scales had published their account of the invasion, there was no strategy that united the military and the civilian, the operational to the political, with the result that the operational level of war also became the de facto strategy, and its focus meant that there was little wider awareness of where the war was going. In the immediate post-invasion phase of the war, policy and the war's conduct proceeded on two parallel tracks which (by definition) never converged, the first run by Ambassador Paul Bremer and the second by General Ricardo Sanchez.

That represented a nadir, but it was not untypical. The close (and convergent) relationship established by Ambassador Ryan Crocker and General David Petraeus in Iraq in 2007 contrasts with the rockier dealings between Ambassador Karl Eikenberry and General Stanley McChrystal in Afghanistan in 2009. Arguably strategy has been absent throughout the wars in Iraq and Afghanistan. In part that is because the political objects have been unclear, or variable, or defined in terms too broad to be deliverable in strategic terms. Because there has been no clear relationship between the ends and the limited (and often inappropriate) means, strategy is simply not possible. The result has often been war shaped by platoon and company commanders, a series of ill-coordinated tactical actions, where killing and casualties define success – not the objectives of securing the population, establishing law and order, and delivering aid and reconstruction.[22] Counter-insurgency theory has stepped in to give shape to what has happened. The US army's Field Manual 3–24, published in December 2006, is a clear illustration.[23] But, while positive in so many ways, counter-insurgency doctrine has only served further to complicate the relationship between the operational level of war and strategy.

In counter-insurgency the distinctions between the levels of war, tactical, operational, strategic and political, are much less clear than in major war. The former can establish a direct link between low-level, comparatively minor actions and significant political outcomes which is very rare in major war. The conflicts waged since 2001 provide abundant evidence, in examples which have embraced the United States, Britain and Germany – from the treatment of detainees at Abu Ghraib and Camp Breadbasket in Iraq in 2003 to the Wikileak film of an Apache helicopter attack on civilians in Baghdad in 2007 and the Kunduz airstrike in Afghanistan of 2009. For General McChrystal, the outcome of the German decision to call in an American airstrike on two fuel trucks captured by the Taleban, resulting in more than a hundred civilian deaths, was particularly frustrating. His own directive had made clear the direct link between tactics and strategy in counter-insurgency: 'We must fight with discipline and *tactical* patience. We must balance our pursuit of the enemy with our efforts to minimise the loss of innocent civilian life. Every Afghan civilian death damages the *strategic* effect of our operations.'[24] To talk of 'strategic corporals' is misleading if it implies that junior non-commissioned officers are now required to think strategically, but it is entirely apposite if it refers to the possible consequences of their decisions.

Political effects are therefore part of the immediate framework of military action in counter-insurgency warfare. The delivery of security and good governance in Afghanistan may be an objective of counter-insurgency, but it is also itself one of the means to effective counter-insurgency. This leads to calls for whole-of-government approaches, in which the standard rule of thumb (at least in military manuals) is that political or non-military effects will outweigh military by 80 percent to 20 percent. In practice they don't. The military has to make much more than 20 percent of the effort to achieve political effect, and much that it does will not be directly military. As a result 'political' generals – such as David Petraeus for the United States in Iraq and David Richards for Britain in Afghanistan – do better in counter-insurgency than 'gung-ho' warriors. 'Political' is used here in a non-partisan and entirely unpejorative sense: it just means that officers have to be able to negotiate as well as to fight, to be sensitive to others' culture as well as to the morale of their own units. Nor are generals the only soldiers who have to be politically aware: as McChrystal's strategic guidance for the Afghanistan campaign of August 2009 made clear, 'Every soldier must be empowered to be a StratCom [strategic communications] messenger for ISAF.'[25]

It is thus very easy, in the continuing absence of strategy – of political goals to which the military effort is to be adapted – for counter-insurgency doctrine to fill the gap, for operations to double as strategy. Crudely put, Field Manual 3–24 took the place of a coalition strategy for Iraq in 2007. Doctrine worked out at the operational level was used by the military to exert pressure on civilians and politicians. The 'surge' in Iraq in 2007, as its opponents made clear at the time, was a change in operational method which lacked a framework of political objectives.[26] The aim was to flood manpower into Iraq in order to create security; the hope was that the political solution would step into the space which effective military action had created. As General David Petraeus, the hero of 2007 and CENTCOM commander in 2009, put it when advising President Obama on his strategy for Afghanistan: 'You have to recognize also that I don't think you can win this war. I think you keep fighting. It's a little bit like Iraq, actually Iraq is a bit of a metaphor for this.' As he went on, 'All we have to do is begin to show progress and that'll be sufficient to add time to the clock and we'll get what we need.'[27] The surge in Iraq worked, arguably a result as much of a change of mood within the Iraqi people, 'the Sunni awakening', as of US planning and Petraeus's pursuit of reconciliation. It was a May 1940 moment. The operational level of war delivered despite the absence of strategy.

The Germans defeated France but still lost the Second World War. It behoves the United States to remember that fact, as it tries to turn a one-off victory into a blueprint. 'Population-centric COIN [counter-insurgency] may be a reasonable operational method to use in certain circumstances', Colonel Gian P. Gentile wrote somewhat testily in 2009, 'but it is not a strategy.'[28] Specifically, references to the surge in Iraq underpinned the arguments used in relation to the strategy for Afghanistan, especially by Petraeus. His view was that this was a long war, 'the kind of fight we're in for the rest of our lives and probably our kids' lives'. Obama's intention for the war in Afghanistan was different: he rejected the long war as not being in the national interest, so confronting what for Petraeus were operational realities with political impera-tives. But Obama still cited Iraq as a model when he delivered his speech on the strategy for Afghanistan at West Point on 1 December 2009.[29]

Nor has the USA been alone in building strategy from the bottom up more than the top down. In the United Kingdom, the Joint Doctrine and Concepts Centre, created as a result of the 1997 Strategic Defence Review, and rebranded as the Development, Concepts and Doctrine

Centre (DCDC) in 2006, has become the Ministry of Defence's principal agency for long-term thinking. Originally responsible for doctrine primarily at the operational level, and to that extent an outgrowth of the trends established in 1989, the year that the army published *British military doctrine*, the DCDC has gradually broadened its remit, especially with *Global strategic trends*, a publication which tries to capture the broader security picture by identifying emerging threats up to three decades in advance. The operational level of war may be DCDC's bread and butter but its work has aspirations which are both strategic and, ultimately, political.

In November 2009 DCDC produced a totally new manual, *Security and stabilisation: the military contribution*, Joint Doctrine Publication 3–40, to sit above the army's doctrine on counter-insurgency (which was also finally revised in that year). Chapter 4 was called 'Operational guidance', and began with 'the practical application of operational art', but the succeeding chapters rapidly broadened the framework to 'security and security force capacity building' (chapter 5), 'governance and institutional capacity building' (chapter 6) and 'economic and infrastructure development' (chapter 7). All these fall within part 2, 'The *military* contribution to stabilisation' (emphasis added). Part 3, 'Campaigning *in* stabilisation' (again emphasis added), contained a chapter on 'political and social analysis', which was then followed by chapters on planning and execution, the latter of which was subdivided into 'the conduct of operations' and 'measuring campaign success', titles which brought the doctrine back to functions and frameworks that fall within the comfort zone of the operational-level commander. The publication, a direct product of recent experience in Iraq and Afghanistan, was in many respects a major achievement. Nonetheless it is not so much doctrine as aspiration, an effort to co-opt other government departments, outside the Ministry of Defence, as well as the host nation, in the implementation of operational goals. Its key sections both addressed the civil–military relationship and assumed that generals have political functions. After all, the armed forces are not designed specifically to build government capacity, to sustain economic development or to drive political analysis, but JDP 3–40 is a manual which demands that they acquire these capabilities.

Doctrine seeks general principles, and it engages with strategic theory (as opposed to strategy in practice) to find continuities. It does this best at the operational level; the tactical level is too influenced by changing technology, the political level is too subject to contingency. So doctrine strives to establish generic views of war, not just of counter-insurgency warfare. In 2008–9 a number of officers, including General Sir David Richards, who became the Chief of the British Defence Staff in October 2010, and General James Mattis, one of the fathers of the US Field Manual 3–24 who succeeded David Petraeus at CENTCOM in August 2010, argued for a vision of war-fighting shaped by its tactical continuities, independently of its political context.[30] These encapsulations by senior officers of how war is being and will be waged, the operational level, are entirely proper in professional terms, but their effects shape defence policy. As with Field Manual 3–24 and Joint Doctrine Publication 3–40, the operational level of war is hijacking its political direction.

There is nothing unconstitutional, unprofessional or improper in what senior officers are doing: they are addressing issues which they more than anybody else are qualified to address. The fact that military operations have political consequences is part and parcel of war. But, when the political consequences of professional wisdom become evident, the public reaction too often mistakes cause for effect. General Sir Richard Dannatt's unguarded interview with the *Daily Mail* in October 2006 is a case in point. Some criticised the Chief of the General Staff for behaving politically by speaking publicly. They addressed what they saw as an issue of principle, arguing that a serving officer should not communicate directly to the press, but in doing so they were in danger of mistaking Dannatt's motivation, which was at bottom professional more than it was political. The Chief of the General Staff declared that the army was 'running hot' and that the demands created by waging two wars concurrently were too great for a small army to bear over a sustained period. The army's head was concerned for the welfare of the institution for which he was responsible. Not least for that reason he believed that Britain should leave Iraq by the end of the following year, 2007.[31]

In effect, the British army, although motivated by professional and operational considerations, was setting the public timetable for withdrawal – in other words it was trumping the government and setting strategy. But as the army reached up into the strategic sphere from the operational level, it created dissonance at both levels. At the strategic level, the United Kingdom was set on reducing its force levels in Iraq and establishing a timetable for withdrawal just as its major and senior ally, the United States, was doing exactly the opposite by implementing the 'surge'. At the operational level, British troops in theatre were devising a plan whose aim was not withdrawal but success, but which was predicated on increasing the resources in Iraq, not decreasing them. 'Operation Sinbad', planned and implemented in Basra in 2006, was conceptually sound enough – it aimed to convert operational effects into strategic outcomes, but it assumed that it had greater numbers of troops available than it possessed, and that it could take a longer-term view than that being entertained in London.[32]

These consequences, for the operational level to shape strategy and for the outcome to confuse not only strategy but also the operations themselves, were even more evident in 2009. On 27 March Barack Obama delivered a speech, which was his first significant statement about Afghanistan since taking office as president of the United States. In announcing 'a comprehensive, new strategy for Afghanistan and Pakistan', he made three principal points, of which that statement was the first: that the war embraced both countries, not just the first. Thus for operational reasons Washington created a new entity – 'Afpak' – calculated to affront the sensibilities of both states and so to have unfortunate political repercussions. Secondly, the president argued that the war in Afghanistan was a war of necessity, not – by implication – a war of 'choice'. The Iraq War, partly because its justification was the pre-emption of a geographically distant threat from weapons of mass destruction before it had become imminent, had come to be seen as 'discretionary'. Neither 'choice' nor 'discretion' played well in democracies educated to see war's justification only in terms of existential threats. Thirdly, Obama stressed that the war's aim was counter-terrorism, 'to disrupt, dismantle and defeat al Qaeda'. In other words Obama hoped to revert to the original *casus belli* of 2001, the 9/11 attacks on the United States.

Obama's strategic grasp – in the sense of his capacity to relate war to policy – was, on the evidence provided by Bob Woodward, both sure-footed and shrewd. What guided him was the national interest of the United States and its allies, 'not just any piece of insurgency in Afghanistan'. He was determined to define that priority before he settled on troop numbers. He was also well aware that war has its own dynamic, which can lead its participants in directions which they have not anticipated, with costs and consequences that cannot be determined in advance. He saw clearly enough that his role as president was to remain focused, and to set targets which were realisable rather than simply the products of war's own momentum. Refusing to think in terms of victory or defeat, he preferred to concentrate on 'a strategy that results in the country [i.e. the USA] being stronger rather than weaker at the end of it'.[33]

This was encouraging. He had taken up office at a stage when the United States had no clear strategy in Afghanistan, as Admiral Mike Mullen, the Chairman of the Joint Chiefs of Staff, acknowledged.[34] However, Obama's own aims contained a potential, if understandable, contradiction. He wanted to limit the war, which was creeping out of control as it pursued divergent objectives, but he dared not say so publicly. For Americans, the phrase 'limited war' was associated with the Vietnam War. Moreover, by stressing the national interests of the United States over the good governance of Afghanistan or the human rights of its peoples, he had put himself between a rock and a hard place. He had reduced the aim of the war, effectively to one of counter-terrorism, and so returned to the task which the United States had originally set itself after the 9/11 attacks. But at the same time he had committed himself to an aim – that of the direct defence of America – which by definition he could not reduce further. In other words, he had left himself little room for manoeuvre. His problem was that between 2001 and 2009 the war had acquired its own momentum, and – given the absence of clear strategy during that period – most of that momentum was driven by operational thought.

Powered by Field Manual 3–24, and fuelled by the success of the 'surge' in Iraq, some US generals had developed a belief in what they called 'fully resourced counter-insurgency'. General David Petraeus was the public face of a doctrinal current supported by several others, including General Jack Keane. For them, counter-terrorism, which privileged precision air strikes, did not change the situation on the ground. The base from which al-Qaeda was operating was the Taleban, who were themselves rooted in the Pashtun population of south and east Afghanistan. So, to defeat terrorism, the United States had to defeat an insurgency. It had to protect the Afghan population while providing the time for indigenous Afghan security forces to grow. In March 2009, the president was told that 'fully resourced counter-insurgency' would require additional troops – numbered between 33,000 (the figure proposed by Bruce Riedel in a report commissioned by Obama) and 100,000 (the figure proposed by the National Security Advisor, General James Jones). Obama claimed that by sending 17,000 additional troops to

Afghanistan and by supplementing them with a further 4,000 he had responded to the request for more troops from the US commander in theatre, General David McKiernan. In fact McKiernan had asked for 30,000. Within less than two months, McKiernan was on his way home, replaced by General Stanley McChrystal, who had a special forces background entirely consonant with the stress in Obama's March speech on counter-terrorism. McChrystal's skills, in the views of the counter-insurgency fraternity, 'seemed to reside in the art and science of killing bad guys', not in 'winning hearts and minds'.[35] In fact he had studied revolutionary warfare at West Point and learnt from Iraq in 2007 that aggressive counter-terrorism produced only tactical gains; fully resourced counter-insurgency was required for strategic victory. The president simply accepted the recommendation of Admiral Mullen (endorsed by Robert Gates, the Secretary of Defense) that he appoint McChrystal to Afghanistan without meeting him in person. In June 2009 McChrystal told the Senate Armed Services Committee that he wanted 21,000 additional troops by October; in September he called for 40,000, and in November 85,000.[36]

On 30 August 2009, when General McChrystal delivered his initial assessment as the commander of ISAF, he began by embracing the president's aim: 'NATO's Comprehensive Strategic Political Military Plan and President Obama's strategy to disrupt, dismantle, and eventually defeat al Qaeda and prevent their return to Afghanistan have laid out a clear path of what we must do.' But what he then addressed was not counter-terrorism but counter-insurgency, talking specifically of a 'counter-insurgency strategy'.[37] ISAF needed to shift its 'operational culture to connect with the people'.[38] What was set out as an operational method – and therefore could be seen as the means to a strategic objective – very quickly became an end in itself, 'The new strategy: focus on the population'.[39] That new strategy was described as having four pillars, two of which could probably be described as operational because they were means to an end (to improve the Afghan national security forces and to gain the initiative 'in a series of operational stages'). One was more strategic because it could be seen as an end in itself (to establish good governance in Afghanistan) – even though it too could be seen as a means to an end, because without good governance insurgency would continue, and possibly with it terrorism. The fourth pillar, to gain more resources for the campaign, although clearly a means to an end, became in the febrile political atmosphere of Washington an end in itself. Indeed it was the core of the debate between Obama and his advisers, and the one for which the president's support proved most transient and conditional. The president's focus in March on 'Afpak' found at best limited recognition in COMISAF's initial assessment. Although McChrystal acknowledged the importance of Pakistan, he put the weight on Afghanistan, saying quite explicitly that 'most insurgent fighters are Afghans' and that 'the insurgency in Afghanistan is predominantly Afghan'.[40]

Undoubtedly General McChrystal saw his 'new strategy' as a means to achieve a political end: effective counter-insurgency in Afghanistan could be a route to effective counter-terrorism. However, his was a view of strategy shaped by operational considerations, naturally enough because at bottom a general is an operational commander. One critic concluded after McChrystal issued his commander's guidance on 13 June 2009: 'Currently, US military strategy is really nothing much more than a bunch of COIN principles, massaged into catchy commander's talking points for the media, emphasizing winning hearts and minds and shielding civilians.' While such an attack carried the danger that it would throw out counter-insurgency best practice, there was surely truth in its conclusion that 'the result is a strategy of tactics and principles'.[41] Indeed McChrystal's subsequent COMISAF assessment provided direct evidence that that was the case: 'GIROA [the Government of the Islamic Republic of Afghanistan] must sufficiently control its territory to support regional stability and prevent its use for international terrorism. Accomplishing this mission also requires a better understanding of the nature of the conflict, a change in the basic operational culture, concepts and tactics, and a corresponding change in strategy.'[42]

McChrystal's strategy, as he presented it at the end of August 2009, was shaped from the bottom up; without a clear articulation by NATO or the United States of their political objectives and hence of their strategies, it could not be anything else. The planning flow ran in one direction only. As McChrystal said, 'ISAF's new approach will be nested within an integrated and properly-resourced civilian military counter-insurgency strategy.'[43] There was little to explain how the achievement of those objectives would fit in with wider political objectives or what those objectives were. COMISAF's initial assessment was the best and fullest statement of what ISAF was seeking to do in Afghanistan in 2009. However, its attention was on the how rather than on the why; its focus was on means, as the ends with which it was concerned were – in the standard hierarchy of military plans – essentially operational, not strategic, even if they posed as strategic.

McChrystal reiterated the manpower demands of his predecessor and restated the case for effective counter-insurgency. In doing so, because his was the report that was leaked, he made the most effective and publicly significant statement on US and NATO objectives in Afghanistan for 2009–10, itself a turning point in the war. On 15 September 2009 McChrystal told the Senate Armed Services Committee that he supported 'a properly resourced, classically pursued counter-insurgency effort', and two weeks later, speaking at the International Institute for Strategic Studies in London, he publicly rejected the counter-terrorism option in favour of that for establishing stability in Afghanistan.[44] The speech provided the precedent for the *Rolling Stone*'s revelations the following year: McChrystal had acquired form in trespassing on political terrain. The aims of the war were being defined by a theatre general, not by the president. By late 2009, the latter, at least from a European perspective, seemed increasingly hesitant and still unclear in his strategy, caught on the one hand by domestic political issues like health care and assailed on the other by the competing logic of counter-terrorism as the basis for operations as well as strategy.

A rift had opened up between the White House and the military, with the former objecting to the latter briefing the press, and the latter being resentful that they were being excluded from vital meetings. Strategy and operations were on divergent courses. McChrystal said at the beginning of October that he had only met the president once in the previous seventy days.[45] Obama himself objected less to McChrystal, whom he respected as a professional soldier, and more to his need for 'strategic communication'. Borrowing an idea from Petraeus, McChrystal had brought in a team of academic advisers and think-tank experts to assist in his review process. His aim was not just to help with 'out of the box' ideas but also to create a community who could communicate his intentions, and the logic behind them. In a war which was becoming increasingly contentious at home, the development of wider public understanding was critical, and McChrystal – like Petraeus – was good at it. The trouble was not just that McChrystal's communications had filled the void left by the painfully slow and divisive process of presidential decision-making, it was also that the messages were not ones to which the president subscribed. He did not accept that the defeat of al-Qaeda required a 'counter-insurgency strategy', and particularly not one that could demand an eight- to ten-year commitment. By the end of the year any notion that the United States had a united strategy had been shattered. The president re-emphasised that his approach was 'not fully resourced counter-insurgency and nation building', and he refused to use the phrase in public.[46] He would only commit himself to what was necessary to attain the goals of the United States. On 25 November 2009 he told the national security team that, 'This needs to be a plan about how we're going to hand it off and get out of Afghanistan. Everything that we're doing has to be focused on how we're going to get to the point where we can reduce our own footprint.'[47]

So within a year the national security interest of the United States had become that of withdrawal. Obama selected the lowest increase in troop figures given him by the Department of Defense, that of 30,000. He accepted a 'surge' but said that the numbers in theatre would begin to be reduced from 2011.[48] So it should have been no surprise to the generals when he announced on 22 June 2011 that 10,000 troops would be home by Christmas and a further 23,000 by summer 2012. But it was. The soldiers had planned on defeating the Taleban, in a campaign whose design presumed a counter-insurgency model that was not only fully resourced but also open-ended. They had seen counter-insurgency as an ineluctable method which would eventually create sufficient security for a political outcome to emerge; Obama had seen it as a short-term 'gamble'.[49] In 2011, the generals were on the back foot, a political decline accelerated in 2012 by the scandals concerning their private lives that engulfed not only Petraeus but also his successor in Afghanistan, General John Allen. It was a far cry from the dominance which the military had enjoyed in the first year of Obama's presidency. As one of Obama's advisers had told him at the end of November 2009: 'I don't see how you can defy your military here. We are kind of where we are. Because if you tell General McChrystal, I get all this, I get your assessment, get your resource estimates, but I have chosen to do something else, you're going to probably have to replace him. You can't tell him, just do it my way, thanks for your hard work, do it my way.'[50]

The whole episode highlights the United States's urgent need for a more sophisticated understanding of civil–military relations if it is to make effective strategy. In the long term the United States has probably undermined its own opportunity to succeed in Afghanistan, however illusory some of its critics have felt that objective to be. In the short term, the lapse of time between the delivery of COMISAF's initial assessment at the end of August 2009 and the president's statement on strategy for Afghanistan on 1 December created an expectation which was not met. By then the strategy had either failed, because it was too focused on President Karzai's bid for legitimacy through an election process which proved flawed (as realists always assumed it would be), or had become compromised by the tensions between counter-terrorism and counter-insurgency. For Vice-President Joe Biden, as for President Obama in his speech of 27 March, counter-terrorism was the strategy: Americans were present in the region so as to reduce the possibility of an al-Qaeda attack on the United States. However, by 2009 the majority of the United States's allies were in Afghanistan to promote the better government of Afghanistan, the security of its population, the removal of corruption from its administration and the delivery of basic human rights to its people. Indeed such objectives were not just embraced by other powers, they were also stressed by the State Department. For those committed to a strategy of counter-terrorism, these aims, however laudable, were like counter-insurgency, no more than means to another end. The chairman of the US Joint Chiefs of Staff, Admiral Mike Mullen, captured these tensions, and both their inevitability and function, when he sagely observed on 3 March 2010:

> Policy and strategy should constantly struggle with one another. Some in the military no doubt would prefer political leadership that lays out a specific strategy and then gets out of the way, leaving the balance of the implementation to commanders in the field. But the experience of the last nine years tells us two things. A clear strategy for military operations is essential; and that strategy will have to change as those operations evolve.[51]

Showing his own political skills (in this case in diplomacy), Admiral Mullen went on to select the Australians as particular experts in counter-insurgency warfare. The evidence to support his case came not just from the advice and writings of a former Australian infantry officer, David Kilcullen. In 2009, Lieutenant Colonel Mark O'Neill, tasked by the Australian army to revisit its counter-insurgency doctrine, wrote a pamphlet which quite explicitly called for counter-insurgency to be developed as a strategy, not an operational method. O'Neill stressed information operations and whole-of-government approaches. Implicit here was the same point: the upwards pressure from the armed services to shape strategy which spills over into the political domain

What controls and legitimates all these demands from the uniformed services is strong political leadership which both asserts clear political control and recognises that effective strategy combines wisdom from both sides of the strategy divide, from politicians and generals, from policy and operations. O'Neill quoted Colonel Peter Mansoor of the United States army on the early days of the insurgency in Iraq: 'Without an operational concept to guide the conduct of the war, Lieutenant-General Sanchez and CJTF-7 lacked the link between strategic ends and tactical means that would ensure a successful outcome to the struggle, or even a calculation as to the necessary means to wage it.' But in the very next sentence O'Neill jumped a level: 'This view that *strategy* is lacking has widespread support.'[52] In other words, by introducing a further point, he conflated the operational level of war with the strategic.

The issue here is not just that the United States and its allies (like the Germans in 1940) were in danger of making the operational level do duty for strategy, nor that they lacked a strategy, although both were true. It goes further: the understanding of operational art has become so stretched, from the strategic corporal to the political general, that it ceases to have specific meaning and so is of diminishing value. As two more Australians, Brigadier Justin Kelly and Dr Michael Brennan, have written, 'The term "operational art" can mean anything we decree it to mean, but it cannot usefully mean everything we presently think it does.'[53] If everything is operational, then nothing is. Admiral Mullen recognised the danger, even if he did not reach his conclusion by way of the same diagnosis. 'US foreign policy', he said, 'is still dominated by the military, too dependent upon the generals and admirals who lead our overseas commands. It's one thing to be able and willing to serve as emergency responders; quite another to always have to be the fire chief.'[54] Mullen reflected an increasingly familiar, but to some paradoxical, refrain when he asked for more money not for his own department, that of defence, but for the State Department. It was the armed forces, not the other government departments, that said that the war in Afghanistan required a 'whole-of-government' or 'comprehensive' approach. It was the military, not the politicians, who tended to acknowledge the weakness of a set of operational concepts that were being stretched too far. 'Counterinsurgency is not a strategy,' one of the most thoughtful of its American military practitioners, Colonel

Christopher Kolenda, has written: 'Insurgency–counterinsurgency, like conventional war, is a type of conflict.'[55]

When General Ray Odierno, the United States commander in Iraq and the so-called 'Patton of counterinsurgency,'[56] was asked by the press in late March 2010 if the war in Iraq was effectively over, he replied, after some hesitation, 'War is a very different concept,' and went on, 'I call it more of an operation, not a war.'[57] War in practice is a whole, not a series of separable levels organised in a hierarchical sequence to suit the Huntingtonian norm of civil–military relations. Both the levels of war and the nostrums of *The soldier and the state* make sense as theory and are enormously helpful diagnostic tools; once they become prescriptive methods for interpreting reality, they exceed their station. Kelly and Brennan conclude: 'operational art is not the entirety of warfare. Operational art is not the design and conduct of campaigns. Operational art is not an interagency problem. Operational art *is* the thoughtful sequencing of tactical actions to defeat a component of the armed forces of the enemy.'[58]

Some British army officers today have come to question the stress on the operational level of war as inappropriate to their experiences of war in Iraq and Afghanistan. In 1988, when the Higher Command and Staff Course was set up by the army at the Staff College at Camberley for those destined for senior posts, its focus lay on the operational level as Kelly and Brennan understand it. It prompted one of the most powerfully creative moments in British military thought since the end of the Second World War. It was also a sensible response to the political and strategic conditions of the day. But those conditions have changed, and the character of war has done so too. Today the Higher Command and Staff Course, now located at the Joint Services Command and Staff College at Shrivenham, gives more attention to strategy than to operations. It does so precisely because the original course was predicated on the basis of a possible major war in Europe, but today's is not. The prevalence of limited war, small wars and counter-insurgency campaigns, in other words forms of conflict where policy intrudes more directly into operations, exposed the deficiencies of a body of thought based on a very different expectation of war. However, the problem lies not with our understanding of the operational level; it lies with our understanding of strategy and even more our approach to its direction. Operational art has been stretched hither and yon because it is not contained by a sure grasp of the relationship between war and policy, and by proper structures to debate and guide strategy. Once they exist, operational art and the operational level of war may rediscover both their true purpose and their proper place.[59]

General McChrystal's failing was not that he had behaved 'politically'. If that were a sin in itself David Petraeus would not have been appointed to succeed him in Afghanistan. Of all those who had lobbied for a fully resourced counter-insurgency campaign in 2009, the CENTCOM commander stood out as the most publicly influential, both within the United States and internationally.[60] McChrystal's problem was that his management of civil–military relations lacked the finesse required of command success today. In his Kermit Roosevelt lecture for 2000, General Montgomery Meigs, having just completed a stint as the commander both of the US 7th Army and of the NATO Stabilization Force in Bosnia and Herzogovina in 1999–8, said that he was sceptical about the traditional view in the US army 'that the senior leaders should stick to their own knitting'. One of Petraeus's obvious qualifications for the COMISAF job was precisely that he would 'probably distinguish himself from his predecessor with the political skills that carried him through the most difficult months of the counteroffensive in Iraq'.[61] Presidents and prime ministers, Meigs believed, 'want to be confident that the military advice they receive is as competent as possible and sensitive to what they see as political reality'.[62] At no stage did President Obama say that he was unhappy with the specifically military advice given him by General McChrystal. The quarrel was (to use Meigs's phrase) with its political reality, an understandable failing given that some military officers 'truly don't know where the President stands'.[63]

McChrystal's dismissal revealed a more profound set of issues than perhaps the *Rolling Stone* realised when it set his downfall in train. The president as commander-in-chief exercised his constitutional rights over an American officer. However, McChrystal also exercised a NATO command. NATO was not (at least publicly) consulted over his removal; given that NATO has effectively no role in the formulation of strategy that was unsurprising, but it also confirmed how little Obama had done in 2009–10 to shape and lead the alliance at whose apex he and the United States stood. Obama's choice of Petraeus as McChrystal's successor was also unsurprising. But, like George W. Bush before him, Obama made himself 'beholden to the most celebrated soldier of his generation'.[64] He had therefore done nothing to resolve the tensions which had arisen over civilian control of the military. He had also still not resolved their corollary, and the source of those tensions: the absence of an effective and clear strategy for Afghanistan.

Lacking guidance in 2010, the United States's allies were pulling forces out while the United States was still pushing forces in; they were also setting different and divergent dates for withdrawal. Those enamoured of a counter-terrorist approach claimed that the losses inflicted on al-Qaeda by drone attacks within Pakistan were doing irreparable damage to the organisation's capabilities, while advocates of counter-insurgency believed that the strikes were no more than the equivalent of decapitating a hydra. Indubitably, too, they infuriated the government of Pakistan, whose national sovereignty had been infringed, and called into question the United States's own respect for the laws of war, an issue of central importance to the doctrine of counter-insurgency. Within Afghanistan, therefore, some sought to negotiate with the Taleban, arguing that their ranks contained reconcilable elements, while others countered vehemently that these 'moderate' Taleban were a figment of the imagination, generated by wishful and even sloppy thinking. So, while the logic of counter-insurgency took the United States army in one direction, the logic of human rights took the State Department (and other organisations) in another – since they argued that negotiations with the Taleban were incompatible with education for women and therefore with concepts of human security. As NATO made efforts to mentor and promote the Afghan National Army, expanding it faster than its funds, equipment levels or training regimes for senior and staff appointments could bear, it tried to secure Afghanistan from within. Here was another operational method, another means, which was in danger of becoming an end in its own right, that of enabling NATO withdrawal. In the process NATO could seem to ignore the counter-insurgency efforts of the one really strong and ready-made army in the region, that of Pakistan. However, the Afghan government did not, because for it Pakistan, not Afghanistan, was the home of the insurgency with which it was dealing, and Islamabad, not Kabul, was the author of its problems. Operations which failed to work with the grain of political realities, however intractable, were unlikely to succeed.

British policy in relation to Afghanistan in the nineteenth century, so often denigrated as a failure, was in reality a relative success: confronted with an intractable problem, it limited its ambitions, seeking internal compromise and regional containment. Broadly speaking the policy worked across three Afghan wars, all of which ended victoriously even if there were major tactical setbacks in the winter of 1841–2 and in 1880, and even if the corollary was persistent engagement on the north-west frontier of India. If an American president really is to marshal his generals (not to mention his allies), he must have a policy which meets and channels operational effects. True, they are only one facet of the challenges which he confronts, and he will not be able to give his operational commanders clear and consistent guidance without significant opportunity costs – costs which will be borne in both regional and domestic politics. These are the issues which the McChrystal affair brought into sharp relief. Resolving the latter has not removed the pressures of the former. As Henry Kissinger observed of McChrystal's dismissal, 'America needs a strategy, not an alibi.'[65]

12 STRATEGY AND CONTINGENCY

Strategy is oriented towards the future. It is a declaration of intent, and an indication of the possible means required to fulfil that intent. But once strategy moves beyond the near term, it struggles to define what exactly it intends to do. Part of the problem is generated by the conceptual shift from what current NATO jargon calls 'military strategy' to what Americans increasingly call 'grand strategy' (and which other states, as the USA once did, have come to call 'national strategy'). The operational plans of military strategy look to the near term, and work with specific situations. Grand strategy, on the other hand, can entertain ambitions and goals which are more visionary and aspirational than pragmatic and immediate. It is as much a way of thinking as a way of doing. By using the same word, strategy, in both sets of circumstances, we create an expectation, each of the other, which neither can properly fulfil. The shift from 'military strategy' to 'grand strategy' is particularly fraught: it suggests that the latter, like the former, is underpinned by an actionable plan. If strategy is a matter of combining means, ways and ends, what are the ends towards which a state, nation or group is aiming when it cannot be precise about the future context within which its means and ways are being applied? Answering that question is the central conundrum of grand strategy, and being able to do so sensibly is correspondingly more difficult the more extended the definition of the future which grand strategy uses.

National strategies tend to look at least ten years ahead, not least because that is the minimum normal procurement cycle of most defence equipment. The French white paper on defence and national security of

2008 aspired to set out France's strategy for the next fifteen years – or, more accurately, seventeen, as its reference point was 2025.[1] The Australian defence white paper of 2009 set its sights twenty years ahead, to 2030 and beyond.[2] The United States's Joint Forces Command, in *The joint operating environment (JOE)*, approved for release on 18 February 2010, chose a period twenty-five years into the future, which took it to 2035,[3] and the New Zealand defence review published later in the same year followed suit.[4] In Britain the Development, Concepts and Doctrine Centre's Strategic Trends Programme looks forward thirty years. So its 2010 report aimed 'to provide a detailed analysis of the future strategic context for defence out to 2040'. Unsurprisingly, since the report said that it would be 'an essential input into policy and concept development',[5] the Chief of the Defence Staff, General Sir David Richards, when giving evidence to the House of Commons Defence Committee on 17 November 2010, provided a description of grand strategy which was unequivocally long term: 'the grand strategy, as we would define it, is looking at the world as it is going to be in 2030 or 2040 and deciding what Britain's place in that world is'.[6]

That is exactly what the prevailing orthodoxy, predominantly preached in the United States, says grand strategy is. Paul Kennedy, who along with John Lewis Gaddis and Charles Hill has presided over the grand strategy course at Yale since its inception in 1998, has written that 'the crux of grand strategy lies therefore in *policy*, that is, in the capacity of the nation's leaders to bring together all of the elements, both military and non-military, for the preservation and enhancement of the nation's long-term (that is, in wartime *and* peacetime) best interests.'[7] Kennedy penned those words in 1991, as the Cold War ended, a process hastened by the economic penalties suffered by the Soviet Union as it sought to match US defence spending. With the Soviet Union in dissolution, the United States was the dominant and indeed only global power. Only three years before, in *The rise and fall of the great powers*, Kennedy had highlighted the pressure on failing empires to increase defence expenditure beyond their economic resources. However, his final chapter, which he called 'The problem of number one in relative decline', suggested that these were challenges which confronted Washington, not Moscow. In 1991 Americans who took a short-term view of grand strategy could scoff at such pessimism. But a longer-term view of strategy makes him look extraordinarily prescient. Twenty years on, in 2011, the United States had accelerated its own relative decline by military spending which had served to increase its debt, and engaged in wars whose course and outcomes had lowered its prestige rather than enhanced it.

If the wars to which the United States has committed itself since 9/11 are part of a grand strategy that is oriented towards some distant future, then grand strategy is in danger of proving to be a delusion. The presumption within grand strategy is not just that it is oriented towards some distant future, but also – at least if it is to have purchase in policy – that it is designed to avert decline, and even that it can make the future better. Emerging states have less need of grand strategy as they forge their empires than do satiated states anxious to hold on to what they have acquired. It is not at all clear that China, let alone India or Brazil, has a grand strategy.[8] British strategic thought was almost non-existent while Britain enjoyed the equivalent of its unipolar moment after 1815. It began to flourish from about 1870, as the country confronted relative economic decline, growing international competition and the strains of imperial overstretch.[9] In 1902 Britain gave its concerns institutional effect by forming the Committee of Imperial Defence, a sub-committee of the cabinet. By 1914 it was a status quo power confronted by a newly unified and emerging Germany, which saw the contribution of *Pax Britannica* to international order as a constraint on its development. London therefore used strategy to manage change, to dissipate its effects and to mitigate risk. The logic of grand strategy forced it into two world wars that it would have rather not fought. On the one hand, the economic consequences of those wars hastened decline rather than forestalled it. On the other, the logic of grand strategy was correct. If Britain had not fought Germany in 1914 and 1939, its credibility as a European actor would have been forfeit, and geopolitically an over-mighty Germany on Europe's north-western seaboard would have left its global status vulnerable. Grand strategic thinking did not avert the dilemmas of decision-making, as Britain was caught both ways. On this interpretation the use of grand strategy is not to avert decline but to manage its impact, and slow down its onset. Britain played its cards as best it could, using strategy to do so. It is perhaps no coincidence that the term 'grand strategy' was developed by two of the best-known British strategic thinkers of the twentieth century, J. F. C. Fuller and Basil Liddell Hart.[10] Germany, by 1914 the greater economic power, with a stronger army if not navy, played its cards badly, and lost: institutionally it had no central body to make strategy, and it failed intellectually, unable to see how to use its military assets to best advantage or how to harness war (if it made sense to use it at all) to further its national objectives.

When Kennedy defined grand strategy in terms of the long-term future, his aspirations were neutral or even negative: for the United States to preserve what it possessed. Thomas P. M. Barnett, who between 1998 and 2005 taught at the US Naval War College, the body which inspired Yale's teaching on grand strategy, served in the Department of Defense in 2001–3, and wrote *The Pentagon's new map* when he left it in 2004. His blog defines grand strategy in terms that also stress the long-term future, but go further in their ambition, speaking not just of the preservation but also of the enhancement of the nation's strength:

> As far as a world power like America is concerned, a grand strategy involves first imagining some future world order within which the nation's standing, prosperity, and security are significantly enhanced, and then plotting and maintaining a course to that desired end while employing – to the fullest extent possible – all elements of our nation's power toward generating those conditions. Naturally, such grand goals typically take decades to achieve.[11]

This vision of grand strategy is open to three sets of observations. First, Barnett's definition, while long-term in outlook, is also opportunistic. In practice, the United States, confronted with threats, has come to define its strategy in terms of managing and controlling risk in the pursuit of national interest. General Jim Mattis, when Joint Forces Commander, wrote in the foreword to the *JOE*, 'In our guardian role for our nation, it is natural that we in the military focus more on possible security challenges and threats than we do on emerging opportunities.'[12] The United States is not the only status quo power to define strategy in this way. Chapter 3 of the 2009 Australian defence white paper is titled 'Managing strategic risk in defence planning'.[13] The principal innovation in the British National Security Strategy of 2010 was a risk register. Western powers are using strategy to seek effects which mitigate the impact of change in the interests of stability. The cynic might argue that strategy therefore also represents the triumph of hope over experience. A grand strategy which becomes implicitly defensive and inherently reactive contravenes the standard orthodoxies of 'military' strategy, which stress the value of taking the initiative, not least through the offensive. The military approach to strategy exploits risk, rather than sets out to minimise it.

Secondly, for the United States in particular, such a utilisation of grand strategy confronts it with a logical absurdity. As Barnett's definition of grand strategy makes clear, Americans still see themselves as the democratic and progressive power *par excellence*. This creates a tension between its domestic self-definition and its external status. Its use of strategy today supports an agenda that is conservative, not least because it recognises that change may not be in the national interests of democratic powers dependent on the workings of the free(ish) market. Unable or unwilling to shoulder the full burden of global responsibilities itself, it looks to allies to do more of that work for it.[14] But America's friends have already had to handle their own decline, and now have less appetite for thinking in terms of grand strategy in the first place: indeed they have been told by some Americans that mid-ranking states cannot craft grand strategy, since – in Williamson Murray's words – 'grand strategy is a matter involving great states and great states alone'.[15] The British Cabinet Office, when asked in 2010 by the House of Commons Public Administration Committee to define grand strategy, responded by saying that it was no longer 'a term that is in widespread usage'.[16] Europeans have less difficulty in imagining the United States's need to manage its own relative decline than do Americans themselves, whatever their political persuasions. But in respect to grand strategy the Americans are more right than the Europeans. The coyness of the latter, and particularly of Britain, with regard to grand strategy is at odds with their global ambitions. The successive editions of the British National Security Strategy have continued to assert London's global ambitions, despite its diminishing resources. It is this relationship which lies at the heart of the dilemma confronting the status quo power: if ambition outstrips resources, the need for grand strategy, and for it to be coherent, is all the greater because waste is both unaffordable and unforgivable.[17]

Thirdly, establishing too close a relationship between strategy and the very long term does not allow for the unexpected, for the 9/11 attacks in 2001 or 'the Arab spring' ten years later. Of course prudent and intelligent men and women, like the authors of *Strategic trends* or of the *JOE*, anticipate this criticism. The former has a section devoted to what it calls 'strategic shocks'. Mattis continued his foreword to the *JOE* by saying, 'None of us have a sufficiently clear crystal ball to predict fully the changing kaleidoscope of future conflicts that hover over the horizon, even as current fights, possible adversaries' nascent capabilities, and other factors intersect.' The *JOE* began by citing the younger Pitt telling the House of Commons in February 1792 that it could reasonably expect fifteen years of peace, just as Britain was about to embark on more than twenty years of almost unbroken conflict.[18]

'Strategic shocks', the possibility of the unexpected appearing in short order, are part of the stock in trade of the policies designed to give effect to grand strategy. No defence white paper or its equivalent produced in the western world is deemed to be complete without a reference to the 'uncertainties' (invariably increasing) in a rapidly changing and tautologically 'globalised' world. The driver in much defence policy is that procurement is a long-term process intended to deliver insurance against an uncertain future.[19] It is also accepted that equipment is increasingly likely to be used in roles which are different from those for which it was first designed.[20] Ironically, therefore, one of the pressures in the escalation of procurement costs is the very need to produce equipment flexible enough to cope with the expectation of the unexpected. So the tail wags the dog.

A somewhat different but related example is Britain's possession of nuclear weapons: the standard rationale for the British deterrent used by British governments is that it is not required to deter any immediate or identifiable danger but is a final guarantee of national security against a low-probability but high-level threat. In other words it rests on a strategy which identifies the means but those means lack any clear relationship to ways and ends: the strategy which underpins Britain's possession of nuclear weapons is currently not expressed in a coherent fashion (which is not at all the same thing as saying that it cannot be coherent). One reason for the incoherence is precisely and paradoxically the place of nuclear weapons in a grand strategy which is trying to be long term in its focus and yet simultaneously ready for the unexpected.

The 'Arab spring' and the UN-authorised intervention in Libya in March 2011 highlighted this tension. The long-term strategy of the United States, the United Kingdom and NATO did not envisage intervention in Libya in the short term, and Britain specifically had not identified Libya as an area of significance in its strategic review of October 2010. The Labour opposition, and indeed many supporters of the Royal Navy and RAF, all of which supported intervention, claimed that Libya rendered the British government's Strategic Defence and Security Review (SDSR) out of date within six months of publication. Libya required the very air and maritime assets which the SDSR either removed (Nimrod) or mothballed (aircraft carriers). The coalition government's pre-emptive response to this line of attack was contained in the foreword to the National Security Strategy signed by the prime minister and his deputy: 'in an age of uncertainty, we need to be able to act quickly and effectively to address new and evolving threats to our security'. So without a clear vision of a specific threat to the United Kingdom, the SDSR focused on the means to meet a range of threats, which it called 'the adaptable posture'.

Not much was new here. This is what every other national strategy or national defence policy aspires to do. Since the end of the Cold War, adaptability and flexibility have been the watchwords which have accompanied most attempts to produce a long-term strategy in most western countries. In the United Kingdom, the coalition's SDSR of 2010 looked very similar in philosophy to the Labour government's Strategic Defence Review of 1998, which it had set out to replace: both rested on a maritime–air expeditionary capability, and assumed interventions of short duration. However, none of the west's national strategies has looked very adaptive in practice. Confronted with the unexpected, the customary refrain of all governments is to emphasise underlying consistency, just as the British government did in the first half of 2011. The United Kingdom did not conduct a defence review between 1998 and 2010, limiting its response to the 9/11 attacks to a so-called 'new chapter' to the 1998 review. Throughout the years 2003 to 2007 it fought two wars simultaneously while sticking to a procurement policy designed for European collaboration and 'high-end' capabilities. Long-term strategy became the road block to short-term adaptability.[21] More serious was the slow evolution of the armed forces of the United States. They rejected peace-keeping and nation-building in the 1990s, and failed to see the change in the character of the war in Iraq in 2003–4, as the insurgency developed, or in Afghanistan as the tempo of fighting was rekindled after 2006. By 2009 it had become fashionable, at least in British military circles, to commend the United States army for its subsequent shift, manifested in the reception and status accorded to its Field Manual 3–24 on counter-insurgency, published in December 2006.[22] This reinvigoration of the mythic aura of American military excellence needs to come with a health warning. If the US army had taken as long to change in the Second World War, the war would have been almost over by the time it had completed the process. The desire to copper-bottom adaptability for long-term insurance against the anticipation of the unexpected handicaps the flexibility to meet the reality of the unexpected in the short term.

At the same time the acceptance that the unexpected will happen seems to drive a coach and horses through the delivery of the grand strategy in the long term. So should we cynically conclude that, if grand strategy is oriented to the long term but nonetheless has only limited predictive value, it is in fact without value? Should we put strategy alongside economics as a pseudo-science, bounded by theory and incapable of validation through experiment? If we do those things, we find ourselves in a position where strategy effectively abandons responsibility when confronted with a 'strategic shock'.

To understand the problem, we need to unpack strategy a bit more, and bring it back to its roots in war itself: to move from grand strategy, which Paul Kennedy's definition stresses is political, to strategy in its original and military sense. When Sir David Richards defined grand strategy, nobody presumed that deciding Britain's place in the world three or four decades hence was the sole responsibility of the professional head of the armed forces. But equally, precisely because strategy is a specifically military competence, and implies the use of military means, nobody disputes that his views on the subject are important or deserve a hearing. That presumption of authority derives from the armed forces' grasp of traditional definitions of strategy, of 'military strategy', rather than of grand strategy. Strategy as it was understood by nineteenth-century generals was not vulnerable to any of the three observations entered in relation to current US definitions of grand strategy. It was not reactive, but proactive; it was about changing the status quo, not preserving it; and because it was applied in war, it flourished specifically in the realm of uncertainty.

The strategic thinker who best captured this approach to strategy was Clausewitz. He would not have understood the United Kingdom's National Security Strategy as strategy; he would not have called strategy what Kennedy or Barnett call strategy. For him strategy was the use of the engagement for the purpose of the war.[23] In other words strategy was consequentialist for Clausewitz: one thing followed another, and outcomes and events shaped the next step. Strategy drew on what had happened in order to decide what to do next. As he put it: 'Only great tactical successes can lead to strategic ones.'[24]

It is worth remembering, as current exponents of grand strategy rarely do, that these were very important facets in the exercise of grand strategy in the Second World War. Churchill and his chiefs of staff were certainly conscious that what they were doing was grand strategy, even if they omitted the epithet 'grand'.[25] One, but not the only, element in their thinking consisted of what to do each day in the light of that day's events, of the situation on the ground and of real-time intelligence. They made a clear distinction between public statements and private grief. They did not become victims of their own story of success, but squared up to defeat (of which Britain had its fair share between 1939 and 1942, not least in Libya) and used long-term strategy to overcome it. Grand strategy was then as much reactive as prudential; as much an exercise in flexibility and adaptability in the short term as a narrative projected into the future. It is this aspect of strategy which current strategic thinking seems to have lost. This is the sort of strategy which shapes events in Libya, or reacts to them. Those who say there is no strategy in Libya miss the point. There is strategy: the question is whether it is good or bad. The narrative of success, of making progress, which has characterised not only public statements but private discussions in the wars fought since 9/11, can become the enemy of good strategy. It can also make the strategy hard to divine or define: when British Ministry of Defence press releases focus solely on tactical events without strategic context, much comment has by default to be speculative.

As well as strategy more traditionally and narrowly defined, Clausewitz helps us to think about the understanding of grand strategy, even if he did not call it that. He did not see war just in terms of confusion, chaos and chance. The most important book of *On war*, at least on this point, is not book I but book VIII.[26] The latter, not the former, contains Clausewitz's mature thoughts on the relationship between strategy and policy, the domain within which grand strategy sits, rather than the domain around which the majority of *On war* is focused, that between strategy and tactics. Book VIII is called 'War plans'. In other words, like grand strategy today, its intention is purposive and prudential. It considers how Prussia might engage in a European war if France once again were to upset the balance of power, as the revolutions of 1830 suggested it could. We know about the intellectual origins of this book. In December 1827 Carl von Roeder asked Clausewitz for his comments on two operational problems. Clausewitz replied: 'Every major war plan grows out of so many *individual* circumstances, which determine its features, that it is impossible to devise a hypothetical case with such specificity that it could be taken as real.'[27] As General Victor d'Urbal, writing after another major European war and from the perspective of a different nation, put it in 1922: 'one does not prepare for war in general, but for a specific war, waged in order to obtain a given result, in a defined theatre of operations, against a given adversary, who deploys or is able to deploy in a given time period, given means'.[28] Book VIII took a real plan and set it in a specific set of circumstances. So the conclusion of *On war*, the most important book on strategy ever written, is a plan – an attempt to put order on chaos, to give direction to war – or at least a campaign within a war.[29]

This stress on planning is not a feature of Clausewitz's writing which many contemporary commentators highlight; instead it has become fashionable to follow Clausewitz's attention to friction and to what Alan Beyerchen calls 'the non-linear nature of war'.[30] Planning is generally linked to the second of the two strategic thinkers whose interpretations were forged by their interpretations of the Napoleonic Wars, Antoine-Henri Jomini. Jomini was certainly the more influential figure in his own day, and arguably he has remained particularly so in the United States – for three reasons.[31] First, long breaks between wars (at least up until 1941) have made the United States more dependent on theory than on concrete cases in their approach to the study of war. Secondly, Clausewitz wrote on the back of the devastating defeat at Jena in 1806, whereas Jomini wrote in the expectation of victory – as he served with Napoleon up until 1813, and then switched to the allied side as Napoleon lost. These facets of Jomini's background conform with the self-image of the US armed forces, confident not only of their invincibility but also of the value of a rational and managerial approach to war. This is the third attraction of Jomini for Americans. His thinking about strategy is about how to wage war; it is prospective and purposeful. Clausewitz's is about how to think about war; it is more descriptive and analytical.[32] Jomini declared that his aim was to formulate rules hitherto held in the heads of great commanders. For him strategy was less a theory which linked tactics to policy by the exploitation of the outcome of battle and more a self-contained and separate entity. Jomini saw strategy as a science, subject to a set of maxims or principles, and so he thought that much could be done to settle the outcome in advance. For him, it found expression in a theory of decisive strategic manoeuvre, set by the army's line of march, related to its base of operations and its ability to control the enemy's line of communications. One principle dominated all the others: the application of superior forces on the decisive point. The effect of his military history was to read the sequence of events in reverse so as to show the guiding effect of these principles as they led back to the original plan of campaign.[33]

So, following this logic, if the plan was right, it would lead to victory; even if the battle itself was in the realm of chance and contingency, at least it was set in a strategic narrative. This was how strategy was taught at most military academies in the nineteenth century. As Jomini had put it, the soldier had to begin his professional education not with tactics, not from the bottom up, but with strategy, with the business of the general, as this was scientific and subject to rules.[34] It was expressed in the stylised maps of campaigns contained in Jomini's best-known work of theory, *Le précis de l'art de la guerre* (1838).[35] You need a map to read Jomini; you don't need a map to read Clausewitz. Jomini's maps suggest that strategy can master geography and terrain, and he went so far as to propose that the general should choose the theatre of war according to its operational potential not according to its political priority or even military necessity.

The war plans of European armies in 1914 were Jominian. They were not grand strategy as we would now understand it, since there was no allowance for economic mobilisation or political direction, and not much for coordination between allies and theatres of war. These were operational plans for single campaigns, designed to achieve decisive success through manoeuvre according to certain principles; like Jomini, they largely ignored the impact of tactics and the contingent effects of battle. From today's perspective they were campaign plans, not war plans (but then, significantly, so were the plans for Afghanistan in 2001, Iraq in 2003 and Libya in 2011).

Despite the outcome of the campaigns in 1914, planning has remained an integral part of our understanding of strategy. It was how strategy found expression in peacetime; it provided an occupation for general staffs, not only before 1914 but also between 1919 and 1939. Moltke the elder famously said no plan survives the first contact with the enemy,[36] but that did not mean that he did not plan in peacetime.[37] And the tools which he and the Prussian general staff developed, like war games, staff rides and tactical exercises without troops, encouraged all staffs not only to prepare for mobilisation and initial deployment but also to try to envisage what they might do after their first contact: in other words to plan the war right through to a victorious denouement.

After 1945, the possession of nuclear weapons increased this tendency. In one sense the United States's successive Single Integrated Operational Plans were Jominian.[38] Thanks in part to the impact of Michael Howard's and Peter Paret's fresh translation of *On war*, which came out in 1976, the Cold War can be seen too easily as the moment when Clausewitz finally became the dominant text on strategy, at least in the Anglo-American tradition. Clausewitz's ideal of absolute war was elided with twentieth-century definitions of total war, and both concepts were given immediacy by the memory of the Second World War and by the threat of even greater and more instantaneous destruction through the unrestricted release of nuclear weapons. The fears of nuclear holocaust were contained by the utilitarianism of the Clausewitzian nostrum, that war is an instrument of policy. Although Clausewitz's focus was to explain how war was conducted, nuclear deterrence saw the relationship in terms of how war was to be prevented: a shift from course to cause. The corollary of this focus on the 'Clausewitizian dictum' was to be found in two publications which appeared in 1957, nearly two decades before the publication of the Howard and Paret translation of Clausewitz, and both of them robust evidence of the burgeoning health of American strategic studies after the Second World War. First, Samuel Huntington conscripted Clausewitz in support of his theory of civil–military relations, and adduced him as evidence for the subordination of military professionals to civilian control.[39] Secondly, and simultaneously, Robert Osgood developed his thinking on limited war, taking Clausewitz as the founder of the idea that war could be fought for more restricted objectives than 'annihilation'. This interpretation of *On war* depended on Clausewitz's introductory note of 10 July 1827, in which he argued that wars could be of two kinds, wars of annihilation and wars for more limited (and geographical) objectives – an approach to strategy which had been developed amidst much controversy in pre-1914 Germany by the military historian Hans Delbrück.[40]

Both Huntington's concern with the growth of military professionalism, a phenomenon to which Jomini contributed much more than Clausewitz, and Osgood's with limited war suggest that the Cold War should be seen as Jomini's era at least as much as Clausewitz's. The possibility that war can be limited is a theme which runs through the *Précis de l'art de la guerre*, where it commands considerably more attention than it does in *On war*. Clausewitz seemed to doubt whether humans could really turn the clock back now that Napoleon had given reality to 'absolute war'; Jomini developed ways in which that aspiration might become reality. He presumed that rationality could be applied to war precisely because he saw strategy as a science governed by unchanging principles. Reasons for criticising this approach to strategy are not dissimilar from one of the standard objections applied to nuclear deterrence: that it presumes rationality in engaging with threats that are irrational and disproportionate. In ascribing rationality to both parties, deterrence theory too easily treats the enemy not as an independent actor, likely to adopt divergent courses of action, but as a party which adopts strategies which conform to the expectation of the United States and its allies. Just as the United States was criticised for this sort of mirror imaging, so was Jomini. Both were taken to task for failing to appreciate sufficiently that the enemy was a reactive entity, whose aim was to frustrate the other side's plans, not to fall in with them.

Nuclear planning, precisely because it aspired never to be put to the test of reality, placed even more weight than had Jominian strategy on plotting the links between its initial premises and its desired outcome. Both therefore endowed operational decisions with political significance, without at the same time engaging with policy. This is not to repeat the *canard* that Jomini neglected the role of policy in war. The opposite was true: indeed he even told his pupil, the Tsarevitch and future Alexander I of Russia, to read his book *La vie politique et militaire de Napoléon*, as it formed 'the most complete guide to grand strategy'.[41] But he did see the functions of policy as standing outside the functions of strategy. Similarly, the mechanics of deterrence, counter-force and counter-city targeting, first and second strikes, were vested with an increasingly self-referential meaning, that could seem to ignore the really salient political fact, that nuclear war would tear up all previous assumptions.

Operational thinking finds its intellectual focus in doctrine. Today, by virtue of its use of predominantly (if not exclusively) conventional means, doctrine is seen as largely a professional military matter. But during the Cold War it had sufficient political impact to be seen in strategic terms. The origins of this causal chain lay in the apparently revolutionary and irreversible effects of one set of weapons on international relations, but the consequences were interpreted more broadly, using historical analogies to support its arguments. In 1984 Barry Posen published a pioneering work, *The sources of military doctrine*, a study of France, Britain and Germany between the two world wars. Its underlying assumption was that 'military doctrines are critical components of national security policy or grand strategy'. Posen summarised his argument as follows: 'A grand strategy is a chain of political and military ends and means. Military doctrine is a key component of grand strategy. Military doctrines are important because they affect the quality of life in the international and political system and the security of the states that hold them.'[42]

The sources of military doctrine ended with policy-relevant conclusions for the United States, NATO and the Soviet Union, particularly in regard to nuclear weapons and the inherent danger that they would be used offensively. Posen was not alone in his approach. Jack Snyder's *The ideology of the offensive*, a study of war plans in 1914 and also published in 1984, and Elizabeth Kier's *Imagining war*, which again focused on the inter-war period and appeared in 1997, similarly pursued the argument that the preference in 'military strategy' for the offensive could have destabilising consequences at the strategic level, even when (in Snyder's words) 'military technology ... favoured the defender and provided no first-strike advantage'.[43] Kier began: 'choices between offensive and defensive military doctrines affect both the likelihood that wars will break out and the outcome of wars that have already begun'. Kier differed from Posen and Snyder in seeing the choice between offence and defence as being exercised through the domestic balance of power rather than the international one, through 'the interaction between constraints set in the domestic political arena and a military's organizational culture'. Her work was therefore shaped by the growing enthusiasm of the academic strategic studies community for strategic culture, a fashion set in train by Snyder himself in 1977. But her conclusions did not obviate the overall point that national styles in the conduct of operations had determining effects on the policies which the governments of those nations then adopted.[44]

Two consequences followed for strategy as it was understood by the end of the Cold War. First, Jomini's understanding of strategy, which was located in what we would now call the operational level of war, was applied in the context of what was by then commonly referred to as 'grand strategy'. Secondly, strategy became located above all in the business of planning, and, moreover, in plans which were never tested by reality or – despite the enthusiasm for war games – by approximations of reality as testing as those encountered by some armies during war games and manoeuvres before 1914 or 1939. The conflation of NATO's military strategy with grand strategy, and today's belief that strategy has a long-term and predictive quality, are both, above all, products of the Cold War. During the Cold War, grand strategy and military strategy were united by a clear enemy and an explicit geographical focus, and so provided a form of continuity that ran for more than forty years. The Cold War created the expectation that grand strategy had predictive, stabilising and long-term qualities. Strategic studies in the sense which Kennedy or Barnett understood them grew out of that experience. And although operational experience and real war had little corrective effect, the potential operational applications of the use of nuclear weapons underpinned the whole edifice. So 'military strategy' was assumed to have similar qualities and even effects to those of grand strategy. Nuclear planning lay at the heart of strategy in the Cold War. The possibility that planning could deliver effective strategy followed.

Harry Yarger has challenged these assumptions, arguing that strategy is not planning, and that we have confused the two: 'Planning makes strategy actionable. Planning takes a gray world and makes it black and white. Planning is essentially linear and deterministic.' Yarger follows the logic of the Cold War legacy in locating planning in the realm of operations: 'In modern war, winning battles is a planning objective; winning wars is a strategic objective.'[45] But there has been another influence which has elevated planning within strategy, and that has been the export of strategy to business schools, its reinterpretation for a non-military, non-lethal context, and then its re-importation back into the military environment whence it originally came. Business theory 'assumes that strategic planning will deliver strategy mechanistically', dividing the creation of strategy from its execution, and reckoning that '"analysis will provide synthesis"'. Steven Jermy has pointed out that a strategic-planning process is not the same as a strategy-making process.[46] In war, the creation and execution of strategy are locked into an iterative relationship, which rests on an inherently dynamic and changing situation and has to respond to the counters of the enemy.

The ability to produce operational plans is what distinguishes military personnel from their civilian counterparts, and even defence ministries from other government departments. But such plans are not the same as the sort of planning implicit in Thomas Barnett's view of grand strategy. They are located in real time and focused on specific geographical theatres, neither of them attributes of national strategies looking twenty-five or thirty years into the future. Major General Jim Molan, an Australian officer who served as deputy chief of staff for strategic operations in Multi-National Force – Iraq (a corps command) in 2004–5, 'owned every operation that either had an agreed plan, was currently running as an operation, or would start in the near future'. His description of life at the interface between planning and execution captures the difference between the 'military' understanding of strategy in relation to planning and the presumption that long-term planning is possible in grand strategy:

Original plans were prepared in a separate division, but when a plan
was ready for execution, it would be passed to me. Getting the
timing of this right was critical because if the plan was passed too
late or in an incomplete state, I did not have the manpower to do
anything more than minor adjustments on the run. This created
many raised voices, not because I was right and others were wrong,
but because the link between what has to be done in the future and
those that have to do it is a point of maximum stress in any modern
headquarters.

In describing his approach to 'strategic operations', with its need to
respond to contingency, Molan used terms which were reminiscent of
Clausewitz's consequentialist definition of strategy: 'One thing happens
because other things have happened: military planning must retain an
infinite flexibility.'[47]

Clausewitz captured Molan's point in book I of *On war*: 'Since
all information and assumptions are open to doubt, and with chance
working everywhere, the commander continually finds that things are
not as he expected. This is bound to influence his plans, or at least the
assumptions underlying them. If this influence is sufficiently powerful to
cause a change in his plans, he must usually work out new ones.'[48]
Planning may not be strategy but we certainly need an awareness of
strategy in order to be able to plan. Clausewitz's doubts about the value
of intelligence, which are frequently used to feed the 'chaotic' interpretation of *On war*, make a similar point: information derives its value
precisely from its self-contradicting qualities, as they enable the general
to differentiate what may be true from what may not be true by a process
of comparison.[49] Clausewitz seems to have influenced Mao Tse-tung on
this point:

Because of the uncertainty peculiar to war, it is much more difficult
to prosecute war according to plan than the case is with other
activities. Yet, since preparedness ensures success and
unpreparedness spells failure, there can be no victory in war without
advance planning and preparations ... We are comparatively
certain about our own situation. We are very uncertain about the
enemy's, but there too there are signs for us to read, clues to follow
and sequences of phenomena to ponder. These form what we call a
degree of *relative certainty*, which provides an objective basis for
planning in war.[50]

We need planning to embrace chance, chaos and the 'unexpected', knowing that it will not remove any of these things from war, but appreciating that it will minimise their part in it and allow for their effects. Napoleon is reported to have said, 'The science of war consists of effectively calculating all the chances first and then working out exactly, mathematically, the part which luck will play. It is on this point that you must not be wrong, and a decimal point more or less can change everything.'[51]

Finally, if strategy is oriented towards the future, and yet planning is not strategy, what is the role of strategy? This is where we come back to Clausewitz's evocation of war as a total phenomenon in which friction competes with planning. In 2004 Gary Hart defined grand strategy as 'a coherent framework of purpose and direction in which random, and not so random, events can be interpreted, given meaning, and then responded to as required'.[52] Hart's definition, unlike Kennedy's or Barnett's, recognised that strategy may be proactive but that it cannot be prescriptive. This is where it differs from policy, to which it offers options not a straitjacket. Indeed, without political buy-in, it has no purchase: significantly Hart served on the bi-partisan commission set up to look at US homeland security in 1998, which warned of the possibility of a terrorist attack, but whose recommendations were not heeded before 9/11. Strategy occupies the space between a desired outcome, presumably shaped by the national interest, and contingency, and it directs the outcome of a battle or of another major event to fit with the objectives of policy as best it can. It also recognises that strategy may itself have to bend in response to events. Essential here is the need for flexibility and adaptability, the need for real-time and short-term awareness, as well as long-term perspectives, and the need to balance the opportunity costs of both.

A long-term view of strategy is of course precisely what keeps powers in a war despite setbacks, mounting casualties and even defeats. In that sense it is the counter-narrative: the one that says that it is precisely because of losses that the fight must be continued rather than ended. Strategy has also to integrate short-term shocks and the interactive effects of enemy action. To return to Churchill and Alanbrooke: they looked to the long term in their planning, but they moderated their views in the light of daily news and real-time intelligence, and by the same token they adapted and changed long-term objectives in the light of short-term considerations. They accepted both that war was chaotic and confused, and that the best way to master it was through planning. Strategy was the sum of both, not just the latter. As Yarger has put it: 'strategy provides a coherent blueprint to bridge the gap between the realities of today and a desired future'.[53]

If we see grand strategy so much in terms of ends, we neglect the ways and means, and so reverse-engineer from potential outcomes back to today. At the operational level that way of thinking produced effects-based operations. The armed forces of the west emerged from the Cold War with legacy equipment that was not necessarily the best means for the ends which governments sought. As a result, so the argument ran, they tended to design plans around what they had, often seeking to give roles to capabilities which were not necessarily appropriate to the objectives being sought, rather than to generate force designed specifically to address those objectives. Effects-based operations sought to plan by beginning with the desired outcome, with the implicit assumption that it might be gained by means very different from those suggested by capability-based plans. The whole concept was extraordinarily woolly and was largely driven by the United States Air Force as a way of promoting its capabilities.[54] Contained within it was the aspiration implicit in counter-insurgency and discussed in the previous chapter: a desire to give operational outcomes the purchase of strategy. In the present context, however, the trouble with effects-based operations was similar to that which can beset grand strategy. It reverse-engineered from a desired future without making sufficient allowance for what might happen en route, or indeed for unintended consequences. Thanks not least to its robust rejection by General James Mattis in 2008, it is now discredited and largely abandoned. Until we wake up to the same fallacy within strategy we shall continue to see events in more 'unexpected', 'revolutionary' and 'destabilising' terms than we should. We shall also not obtain the value from strategy that we can or which we need.

13 STRATEGY: CHANGE AND CONTINUITY

For the historian strategic studies today present an interesting paradox. Thirty years ago strategic studies was a hybrid, a disciplinary mix of history, politics, law, some economics and even a little mathematics. Today the subject has been increasingly appropriated by departments of political science, its identity often subsumed under the amorphous title of 'security studies'. As a result the study of strategy has been largely divorced from the historical roots in which it first flourished. This is not to say that history has no value for political scientists. They use case studies all the time, but they tend to choose those topics which prove or disprove a thesis, not subjects which are to be studied in their own historical contexts. Stories told without context obliterate the woof and warp of history, the sense of what is really new and changing as opposed to what is not.

This is not a historian's diatribe against a discipline other than his own. Historians can be just as guilty of tunnel vision, too readily feeding the caricatures of themselves painted by political scientists. They are the party poopers who respond to claims that all is new and different by saying the reverse (and the perverse), claiming precedents which stress continuity, not change. So, for example, if the character of war is changing in the twenty-first century, those changes can be associated with non-state actors and private military companies, both of which are familiar to early modern historians, or with terrorists and insurgents, also equally well known to historians, in this case of Napoleonic Europe or of nineteenth-century imperialism.[1] If this difference in disciplinary approach were uniformly true, what follows should stress continuity, saying that not much that is really new is likely to appear in the twenty-first century (and in some respects it will do that). Following the same logic, if the chapter had been written by a political scientist, it would have predicted dramatic changes, presenting major threats in that recurrent cliché, 'an increasingly globalised world'.

The challenge for the historian is much harder than the identification of continuity. That is the easy bit. The next stage is to use that as the bedrock from which to identify what is really new, as opposed to what merely seems to be new, to distinguish the revolutionary and the evolutionary from the evanescent and ephemeral. After the fall of France in 1940, Marc Bloch, the great French economic historian and co-founder of the *Annales* school, joined the resistance, a decision for which he was to pay with his life when he was executed by the Gestapo in 1944. Having served in the victorious French army of the First World War, as well as that of the Second, he was keen to explain what he called a 'strange defeat'. Part of his answer addressed the educational system of the École de Guerre. He accepted entirely that it should be based on military history. 'The military art is one of those', he wrote, 'which precludes the possibility of experimenting', and so 'the only sensible thing is to fall back on the lessons of the past'. The problem in 1940 had not been the decision of the French army to use history to train its officers; its problem was that it had not understood that 'History is, in its essentials, the science of change.' For the army history had been about recurring patterns in warfare running back in a continuous line to Napoleon, but history 'knows ... that it is impossible to find two events that are ever exactly alike, because the conditions from which it springs are never identical'. Bloch did not dispute that there were long-lived aspects to the story of human evolution, 'but the lesson it teaches is not that what happened yesterday will necessarily happen to-morrow, or that the past will go on repeating itself. By examining how and why yesterday differed from the day before, it can reach conclusions which will enable it to foresee how tomorrow will differ from yesterday.'[2]

Bloch's claim for history did not lack ambition: it is, 'in its truest sense, an experimental science, because by studying real events, and by bringing intelligence to bear on problems of analytical comparison, it succeeds in discovering, with ever-increasing accuracy, the parallel movements of cause and effect'. For the historian who looks at current strategic studies what is striking is the apparent loss of this capacity within political science. Empiricism seems to be out of fashion. Theory, having been granted primacy, creates expectations of reality and so prevents the hard-headed interpretation of events, blocking rather than refracting the light shed on theory by change. The result, paradoxically, is that historians can be readier to identify change than are students of strategy.

Most inimical to the idea of change in strategy is a relatively new conceit (another paradox), the concept of 'strategic culture', already discussed in Chapter 7, and which – in the words of one historian – 'has gradually gained support within the ranks of political scientists studying international relations', but 'has attracted few followers outside of political science'.[3] Jack Snyder, whose report on Soviet strategic culture in 1977 for the Rand Corporation is credited with launching the concept within the political science community, acknowledged that strategic culture could develop and adapt, but he argued that it would do so only slowly. 'We also assume a large residual degree of continuity,' he wrote: 'Culture is perpetuated not only by individuals but also by organizations … Rationales can outlive the conditions under which they were developed and to which they were most appropriate.'[4]

Although Snyder has since distanced himself from the body of ideas to which he gave birth, two things are noteworthy about his original formulation. The first is its association with nuclear weapons, and the second is the presumption that strategic culture inhibits change.[5] These two themes are linked. In 1982 Laurence Martin, the BBC's Reith Lecturer in 1981, and professor of war studies at King's College, London between 1968 and 1977, attributed to nuclear weapons what he called 'the deceleration of history'.[6] The Cold War both created strategic studies and then imposed on it a sort of stasis through its stress on the use of nuclear deterrence to prevent major war. The inner certainties of the strategic studies community between the 1960s and 1980s provide a healthy reminder of the dangers of hubris, especially when contrasted with the uncertainty (but also volatility and hence creativity) surrounding the subject at the start of the twenty-first century.

Since the end of the Cold War, nuclear deterrence has lost its state of semi-permanence, at least in its more evident forms, and as a result strategic culture too, at least in the formulation originally offered by Snyder, has lost some of its explicatory power – not entirely, not as an interpretative tool for the past, but in terms of its predictive value. Military historians have long been familiar with the idea that nations have particular 'ways of warfare', and the father of national ways of war is Basil Liddell Hart's 'British way in warfare', first articulated in 1927 and itself a product of the marriage of history to politics. What his theory could not cope with was reality. British strategic practice throughout the first half of the twentieth century and beyond defied Liddell Hart's model, despite the fact that it was precisely because of its prescriptive value that he had formulated it in the first place.

Strategic culture may (like many theories) raise important questions about strategy for the twenty-first century, but its lack of predictive power suggests that it will leave us short of answers. This is not the view of Colin Gray, who has argued vehemently for the links between strategic culture and strategic behaviour. Gray sees strategic culture as nationally and geographically determined, the product of history and place, and therefore internalised 'within us'.[7] Gray, a student of politics, uses history to argue that not much changes. 'There is an essential unity to all strategic experience in all periods of history', he asserted (in 1999 and in italics) on the opening page of *Modern strategy*, 'because nothing vital to the nature and function of war and strategy changes.'[8]

One thing that has changed a great deal over the past two centuries is what we understand by the word strategy, as Chapter 2 has outlined. The word was not used by Napoleon until he was defeated and in exile. Instead he spoke either of grand tactics or of policy, with nothing in between,[9] and yet it was his practice in war which inspired the writings of Clausewitz and Jomini, the first theorists to give currency and even primacy to strategy in military thought. Clausewitz's definition of strategy, 'the use of the engagement for the purposes of the war', was sufficiently close to what became the orthodoxy in the nineteenth century to be the sort of definition used by the generals of the First World War. They saw the goal of strategy as the achievement of the decisive battle, but like Clausewitz and Jomini they located it in its relationship with tactics. However, the definition of strategy which gained currency in the light of that war, and with increasing force as the twentieth century proceeded, was very different. Its focus was not on the relationship between tactics and strategy, but on that between strategy and policy. So at the start of the twenty-first century the word 'strategy' has come to carry very different connotations from those with which it was associated at the end of the eighteenth. Gray rides roughshod over change across time and assumes that there can be a concept of strategy, and a practice derived from it, for epochs and civilisations which had no word for it.[10] His hero, Clausewitz, knowing that strategy was a recent phenomenon, did not.

Nor is Gray alone. In 1979 Edward Luttwak, the author of *Strategy: the logic of war and peace* (1987), one of the most influential works on the subject of recent times, wrote a book on the grand strategy of the Roman empire. The initial reactions of ancient historians were hostile. They stressed that Luttwak had appropriated a concept developed in, and designed for, the twentieth century, and so was in danger of imposing a coherence and logic on the empire's designs which were not necessarily present at the time. This reaction has been modified over time, as ancient historians have become more comfortable with the use of concepts from modern military history when addressing the ancient world, even when the contemporary vocabulary is lacking to give those concepts clarity.[11] When, thirty years later, Luttwak gave Byzantium the same treatment, he did so both with more reason and with greater modesty. The emperor Maurice (AD 582–602) had at least written a treatise called *Strategikon*. The chapter entitled 'Strategy' in the English translation begins with instructions for blessing the flags and includes advice on watering horses and what rations should be carried in saddlebags; there is little here that could be described as strategic in the modern sense.[12] Luttwak, while acknowledging that the idea of a Byzantine grand strategy was hard to follow in the sources, argued that the Byzantines, like the Romans before them, knew what they were doing even if they did not speak of what they knew.[13] This sort of thinking, that grand strategy rests on an instinctive understanding as to how to handle the instruments of power, and is therefore universal rather than specific, has taken firm root in American military circles. It treats as its founding text Thucydides' *The history of the Peloponnesian war*, which as a result has been embraced by the curriculums of American war colleges.[14] That American officers read Thucydides is to be welcomed. However, they do so not in the ancient Greek, but in the translation of Richard Crawley, published in 1874. Crawley sought to simplify the complexity of the original text, not least by introducing ideas which would make it more immediate to a late nineteenth-century audience.

Implicit in this reading of strategy, and therefore in its application to our expectations for the twenty-first century, is the idea of continuity, the expectation that strategy, not least because it enshrines eternal verities, has a predictive and prudential quality. It may not enable us to see to the end of the century, but it should at least help us along its next three decades or so. Conveniently, as the previous chapter has pointed out, this is the sort of timeframe set by current procurement cycles and – probably for related reasons – embraced by official think tanks. But for the military historian, inherently reluctant to leave the past for the present and certainly not ready to embrace the future, there is a worrying naivety here, a rejection of contingency and of the role of surprise and shock. Particularly striking is the implicit contradiction between two recurrent claims of strategic studies, that strategy possesses an underlying continuity and that strategy is the use of war for the purposes of policy.

Policy occupies the domain of contingency. Of course, nations have policies which aspire to be long term and generic, but they are subject to the competing dynamics of politics. For democratic states in particular, policy has to be adaptive and reactive as well as purposeful and deliberative. If strategy is today defined as operating on the boundary between war and policy, then it is being expected to be prudent and far-seeing while also being contingent and adaptive. To that extent strategy as it is understood by purists has a paradoxical tendency to become a peacetime business: the result of the efforts of one polity to shape international affairs, including through the threatened and actual use of armed force, in its own national interest. In the competitive and fast-moving environment of armed conflict, where neither side can monopolise control, however much each struggles to do so, the dynamic and reciprocal nature of war shapes strategy more than strategy shapes war. The 1997–8 process in Britain which led to the Strategic Defence Review was trumpeted for being 'strategy-led', as though that quality gave it an underlying consistency and coherence. Over the medium term, it did no such thing. Its assumptions were completely wrong-footed by the political decisions, incapable of adequate prediction before the 9/11 attacks in 2001, to invade Iraq in 2003 and then to deploy British forces to Helmand in 2006.

To square this circle, to reconcile the contrast between strategy's long-term aspirations and its need for flexibility, we need to distinguish between strategic theory on the one hand and strategy in practice on the other. Nineteenth-century strategic thinkers were better at this than those of the twenty-first century. The Cold War, precisely because it remained cold, never required us to confront that distinction: theory could run riot because its confrontations with reality were so restricted. Clausewitz sought systems which would enable him to understand war as a general phenomenon. His self-education in philosophy as an adolescent officer left its mark, prodding him to seek an explanatory theoretical framework which would be constant across time. He was constantly frustrated by his own intellectual and historical rigour: hence practice intruded, resulting in his recognition of exceptions to his own rules, and producing the slipshod conclusion by lazy readers of *On war* that he rejected systems, despite that being his ultimate goal.

By following Jomini, other nineteenth-century strategic thinkers adopted a different tack when addressing the same set of problems. They stressed the principles of war, ten or so leading ideas to be used as an interrogative basis for looking at the character and conduct of individual wars. In 1909, as discussed in Chapter 10, the British army published its first ever official manual on war, the *Field service regulations*. Confronted with the imminence of colonial war, which meant fighting on the north-west frontier of India or in Áfghanistan, while preparing for the more remote (but in practice not very distant) contingency of major war against Germany in Europe, it responded with a set of generic principles of war. This first edition of the *Field service regulations*, unlike those published after the First World War, has been attacked for not actually spelling out what those individual principles were. But this misses the most important principle of all: that all wars, whatever the geographical conditions and the identity of the enemy, required the application of similar considerations – whether it was that of economy of force or the concentration of mass on the decisive point.

Two points emerge out of the consideration of strategic thought, as opposed to strategic practice. The first is its basis in history. When Clausewitz hit a methodological problem he went back to military history, of which he wrote a great deal alongside and at the same time as he was developing the arguments of *On war*; this was not a separate creative process but integral to it. The use of history for strategic theory was not so much to stress continuity but to assess and assimilate change: to provide the context that enabled the most recent experiences of war to be understood, to sort out what reinforced existing thinking and what did not and therefore demanded that strategic thinking adapt. This was, and is, why strategic thought is rooted in history.

The second point is that what strategic theory hoped to develop from this use of history was doctrine. Clausewitzian and Jominian solutions grew out of the need for strategic theory to generate precepts that were of practical application, that were of use to soldiers. However, the outcomes were very different when strategy proceeded from practice, not from abstract conceptions. There is no universal character to war, however true it may be that war has its own nature. Strategic theory, beginning in Clausewitz's and Jomini's day, and continuing right up until the mid-twentieth century, remained much more interested in the relationship between strategy and tactics, not only because industrialisation's reshaping of the technologies of war confronted tactics with constant and increasing change, but also because battle (a tactical event) could determine the outcome of a campaign, however good the strategy within which it was set. So what would now be called the operational level of war but our predecessors called strategy mattered. It attempted to collate change from below, at the tactical level, with the need for a conceptual framework directed from above. Herein, it seemed, lay consistency across time, despite the impact of industrialisation on war. It required the experience of the First World War to highlight just how difficult, if not impossible, that task of integration had now become. The conditions of the battlefield swamped strategy: it was dominated by artillery, trenches and barbed wire, and those who fought in it themselves called it industrialised warfare. At one level, therefore, strategy could not give shape to the bottom-up drivers of tactical and technological change. At another war required a new understanding of strategy, which embraced the relationship between strategy and policy, and spawned the terms 'grand strategy' or 'national strategy'. Both phrases were legitimated by the conduct of the Second World War and the advent of the Cold War, and so strategy in practice became much more concerned with the relationship between strategy and policy than with that between strategy and tactics.

Politicians, that is to say those in democratic states who practise strategy in this twentieth-century sense, do not on the whole engage with strategic theory. However well and shrewdly they use war to fulfil the ends of policy, they are unlikely to have read Clausewitz. They have not been to staff colleges and military academies, the only places where strategy traditionally understood is likely to be studied. They are driven by the real-time concerns of intelligence and by daily developments on the ground. Precisely because strategy is in the hands of politicians, not of generals, it is even more pragmatic and even less theoretical than it was in the nineteenth-century. Politicians can be in immediate and simultaneous contact both with their forces on the ground and with their electorates at home. They can intervene at the operational and even tactical level, while doing so in ways designed to achieve domestic political effect. In the war to retake the Falkland Islands in 1982, the decision to fight a battle at Goose Green is a case in point: although the position and its garrison were deemed militarily irrelevant by the commander on the ground, it 'was vital to register a British success to win back the headlines'.[15] However, if the wars in which a state is engaged are not 'existential' and especially if (unlike the Falklands War) they are protracted, the attention which national leaders give them can prove intermittent, as they turn their focus to domestic politics and economic crises. In such circumstances war becomes both peripheral and inconvenient. For states committed to democratic norms, which include the (historically naïve) assumption that democracies are inherently peace-loving, the decision to go to war is both paradoxical and discontinuous. So the heads of democratic states are unlikely to be 'Clausewitzian' in another very specific sense: they go to war not as a 'continuation' of policy, but because the policy which they have followed hitherto is no longer sustainable.

That is the departure point for any analysis of strategy in the twenty-first century: the need to differentiate not only between the longer-term aspirations of strategic theory and the more immediate and contingent preoccupations of strategy in practice, but also to recognise that the normative statement that war is a continuation of policy is in fact an acknowledgement that strategy in practice must always struggle to possess consistency and longevity. The statement that war is a continuation of policy, however helpful to our ability to understand and define strategy, creates an entirely false sense of stability. The very use of the word 'continuation' implies a persistence and endurance which works against the recognition of change.

When Clausewitz discussed the relationship between war and policy (which in fact he did not do very much), he did so the better to understand the phenomenon of war, and in particular to understand wars which did not obey what he saw as war's inherent logic, its drive towards absolutes, its escalatory dynamic. In the wars he had experienced, the wars of the French Revolution and of Napoleon, the role of policy, although obviously present, was less evident in the conduct of war than it had been in the more limited wars of the eighteenth century. His interest was in war itself and its conduct; he did not write about the causes of war. What led him to stress the role of policy in relation to war was that for Frederick the Great policy had prompted restraint in the conduct of the war, whereas for those who followed the French Revolution policy removed limitations: as he put it, 'we might doubt whether our notion of its absolute nature had any reality, if we had not seen real warfare make its appearance in this absolute completeness right in our own times'.[16] Today we too often use his normative statement about war's relationship to policy as though it applied to the causes of the war, and so fail to recognise how often states go to war not to continue policy but to change it. The declaration of war, and more immediately the use of violence, alters everything. From that point on, the demands of war tend to shape policy, more than the direction of policy shapes war. This volatility in the relationship between war and policy is what deprives strategy in practice of its consistency.

During the Cold War, the relationship between war and policy lost its dynamic quality precisely because it was used to prevent war, not to wage it. The Clausewitzian norm became a statement about war's causes, and because there was no war it became an argument that underpinned the stable balance of terror created by the threat of mutually assured destruction. By the same token, strategy became applicable to situations without war, a virtual synonym of foreign policy, and its most obvious focus was deterrence. Deterrence conflated strategic theory, with its aspirations to continuity and unchanging principles, with strategy in practice, and so that distinction too became forfeit. Strategic culture was one product of this hybridisation. Half a century or so is long enough for such approaches to be deemed customary, for the distinction between strategy in theory and strategy in practice, and for the awareness of war's discontinuous effects on policy, to be forgotten or neglected – particularly in a strategic studies community less disposed to think historically.

The effect of policy is what creates uncertainty for states in relation to the use of war. Armed forces and their capabilities crave and create long lead-times. Hierarchies establish stable organisations, their more ambitious members are encouraged to plan careers in phases of twenty years or more, and procurement cycles for the technologies that shape those careers last even longer. So armed forces demand an element of certainty from strategy in practice which strategy in practice cannot provide. Policy generates decisions to go to war over much shorter lead-times. 'While policy can turn on a dime, as the old saying goes,' Colin Gray wrote in 2009 (and to quote him with approbation), 'the major capabilities available to strategy to advance policy will have lead-times that typically are measured in several years'.[17]

The spread of democratic government (if that remains a long-term object for the west and if the project is itself successful) is more likely to increase this unpredictability than reduce it. In democracies domestic political imperatives to act can exercise greater leverage on decision-makers than may be the case in totalitarian regimes. Mrs Thatcher's decision to retake the Falkland Islands in 1982 is a case in point. Would another Conservative leader have made the same decision, given the views of senior cabinet ministers, the absence of the Chief of Defence Staff in New Zealand, and the hesitations not only of many senior civil and armed servants but also of her own defence minister? Her action, which proved to be right after the event but seemed deeply hazardous and even counter-intuitive at the time, was widely interpreted as having turned her premiership round, giving her a domestic authority which she had hitherto lacked and which was not exhausted for nearly a decade.[18] George W. Bush's decision to invade Iraq in March 2003, not least while the war in Afghanistan had still not delivered on its initial objective, the capture or elimination of Osama bin Laden, prompts similar questions. Political pressures, albeit in this case applied by close governmental associates from the vice-president down, trumped strategic sense. Would a Democrat president have been more or less resistant to such pressures? In this case the political calculation proved wrong, and the United States was saddled with a lame-duck leader (albeit one it re-elected) for almost six years. In both cases the armed forces found that the strategies to which they had subscribed were trumped by what civil–military relations theorists call 'objective' political control. Having committed themselves to a coalition within Europe, in 1982 the British mounted a major expeditionary campaign on the other side of the Atlantic for which its armed forces were not prepared. In Washington in 2001–2, the Joint Chiefs of Staff, having similarly planned for a different sort of war, found themselves cut out of the decision-making loop by the vice–president and the Secretary for Defense,[19] and, while the initial invasion of Iraq was brilliantly executed at the operational level, plans for the subsequent phases of the war were deliberately stifled for political reasons.[20]

Empowerment through the media is a second way in which democracy has added to unpredictability in political decision-making in the use of war. The comparative silence of political opposition in the mainstream democracies in time of war is not new; nor is the assumption by the press of the role of critic and chorus-leader in its stead. Both were phenomena evident in Britain in the First World War. Without a free(ish) press many wartime leaders would have had a comparatively easy ride, however incompetent their administrations. What is newer is the role of the media, and especially the visual media, in creating a public appetite for and acceptance of the decision to use military force in wars unlike the First World War: wars of intervention, 'wars of choice', and wars fought at a considerable distance in areas of the world largely unknown to the public. Wars that are the product of the 'responsibility to protect' or of humanitarian need rely on television pictures to legitimate the determination to intervene. National self-interest at the governmental level can be fused with humanitarianism, so uniting right and left. The notion that human rights can trump the sovereign rights of the state, articulated by Tony Blair in his Chicago speech on 24 April 1999, was the justification of the Kosovo campaign then under way. Increasingly, and retrospectively, the same argument has been used to legitimate the wars in Afghanistan and Iraq. In 2011 it was used prospectively in relation to Libya, but with mixed consequences. Only small numbers of non-combatants were killed by either side, but it has therefore been possible to argue that there was never a threat to them, even from the Gaddafi regime. Such wars, commenced as campaigns intended to remove specific threats, became struggles to create economic and human security through the establishment of good governance (so showing once again how war changes policy). The challenge which confronted President Obama in March 2009, when he announced his strategies for the conflicts in Iraq and Afghanistan, and indeed the challenge for any Democrat in the United States and all liberal interventionists everywhere, was how to limit them by redefining their objectives in terms of national self-interest without robbing them of their rationale in the courts of liberal and international public opinion.

Herein is a tension which seems set to become a fault-line, particularly for western democracies, both as the twenty-first century unfolds and as they confront recession and economic austerity while also absorbing the lessons of Iraq and Afghanistan. Most populations within NATO countries have increasingly interpreted both these wars as evidence of war's inutility. Their governments may not have gone so far, but they have concluded that, if they do decide to intervene overseas, protracted counter-insurgency operations on the ground are not the best method to pursue their objectives. The alternative method increasingly preferred by the United States, after its decision to end the 'surge' in Afghanistan, is to rely on remotely piloted vehicles, an approach which is just as bent on making operational methods do duty for strategy as counter-insurgency became. The fact that drones are unmanned is seen as an ethical problem by philosophers as it is in danger of eliminating the reciprocity inherent in war, and so removes the mutual vulnerability which they see as defining it. But this is its big political attraction: drones remove the risk that domestic support for the campaign will be undermined through casualties to one's own side. They also have the merit of being more accurate than earlier methods of killing at a distance, like aerial bombing or artillery fire, and so minimise collateral damage. But within the growing deployment of drones (now possessed in various forms by at least eighty states) are two potentially negative consequences. Neither is a product of the legal dimensions of their current use, particularly in Pakistan, by the United States: the legal concerns, which pivot on the infringement of state sovereignty, would be the same if the United States were using manned aircraft or howitzers. The first consequence is that greater accuracy can provide greater temptation to employ weapons, precisely because of the reduced risk to one's own side and of the increased certainty that the deaths that follow are those of the enemy and not of non-combatants. In other words improvements in technology, ironically when combined with direct legal advice, can create a more permissive environment for the use of possibly excessive amounts of firepower. The second is that there has emerged, in step with the reluctance to put 'boots on the ground', a resolve to use 'proxies' in support of action from the air. The focus in the war in Afghanistan on the build-up of indigenous security forces as the intermediate step in the creation of surrogate forces for western manpower has obscured the full implications of this development. They became clearer in Libya and by 2012–13 were immediate in Syria. In both countries western powers, in relying on proxies to achieve the effects that they are not prepared to implement themselves by putting forces on the ground, have found themselves promoting insurgency, not countering it: this is where the special forces and intelligence agencies began their lives when confronting the German and Japanese occupations in Europe and Asia in the Second World War. As then, so now: there is little guarantee that what will emerge as a result will be western liberal democracy. Moreover, there is something paradoxical in western armed forces, with their current commitment to 'stabilisation forces', deliberately becoming agents of instability.

So, if policy's part in the formulation of strategy in practice generates change and unpredictability, what can give continuity to strategy – and particularly the sort of continuity that makes it even worth talking about future strategy, particularly over as long a time frame as the course of the twenty-first century? One answer is to turn back to strategic theory, and to acknowledge that what lies at the heart of strategic theory is not policy but war itself.

War's character changes, and it does so for reasons that are social and political as often as they are technological, but war's nature still provides sufficient fixed points to make the study of war as a discrete historical phenomenon a legitimate activity. The differences between the historian's approach to war and the political scientist's can be recast to clarify the point. War shows both change and continuity, reflected in the distinction between its character and its nature. The forms of individual wars are of course profoundly affected by the circumstances of their own times, but the dynamic generated by the decisions of two sides to use armed force against each other generates recurrent features – many of them too easily forgotten because they have become clichés: the fog of war, the play of friction, the role of chance, the importance of will, the function of courage and fear. Most important of all is the reciprocity in war created by the clash of wills. War cannot be the unilateral continuation of policy by other means because both sides are using war to thwart, subvert or change each other's policies. The clash of wills creates a clash of policies, which themselves become subject both to the requirements of waging war and to what the military is actually capable of delivering.

Strategic theory sets out to put shape on what can be chaotic and unpredictable, to apply rationality to what is disordered. But it can only do that effectively if it proceeds from an appreciation of war's nature, a point which the emphasis on war as a continuation of policy tends to downplay. The cry during the wars in Iraq and Afghanistan that strategy – both strategic theory and strategy in practice – had been neglected, not only by governments, particularly those of the United States and the United Kingdom, but also by multilateral organisations, like NATO, is a reflection of the fact that strategy has submerged itself within policy; in the process it has failed to recognise the nature of war, which lies at the heart of strategy in both its forms. By stressing the apparent rationality and logic of policy, strategy has downplayed the seeming irrationality and frequently different logic of war. During the Cold War, strategy too often left the business of actually conducting war to one side, and it has still not recovered.

A clear indication of this last point is the fact that by 2008–9 the challenge confronting the state in relation to the making of strategy was not normally seen in these terms. Strategy was required to predict the future. The tendency, at least in government, was to regard the failure of strategy since 1990, or even more since 2001, in terms of its failure to respond to new threats. The real issue was the lack of flexibility, and the problem was pragmatic and methodological; strategy needed to become better at asking questions, and also at responding to answers which were different from those that were expected. But the actual response veered towards futurology. A succession of high-level documents, beginning with the European Security Strategy in 2003, spoke of 'global challenges', rolling unverified statistics into a mix of issues predicated on the catchphrase that 'security is a precondition of development'.[21] In the United Kingdom the first National Security Strategy, published by the Labour government in March 2008, said little about war or the use of armed force but a great deal more about climate change, migration, disease and other long-term threats to security broadly defined. The British had taken their concerns about climate change to the United Nations in March and April 2007 (although it was not always clear whether countering climate change was deemed to be akin to the waging of a global war or not countering it would result in global war).[22] At the beginning of 2009, James Jones, on his appointment as Obama's National Security Advisor, announced that he planned to widen the role of the United States's National Security Council from its traditional areas of responsibility in defence and foreign policy to embrace over-reliance on fossil fuels, poverty, disease, corruption and the global economic crisis.[23] In other words the western world, and especially Britain and America, seemed bent on reconfiguring strategy to deal with most of the globe's long-term ills as well as many of the responsibilities already entrusted to other government departments.

Such statements represent either a utopianism, which smacks of hubris and borders on unreality, or paranoia. Governments have imported into policy the academic world's determination to redefine strategic studies as security studies, have consequently confused national security with human security, and are in danger of disregarding one of the more obvious truisms of the early deterrence theorists – that security can only ever be relative, never absolute.[24] Creating litanies of threats that lack specificity makes it inherently difficult to produce operational solutions. In other words there can be no national strategy – no means for action – contained in statements about global security.

However, what was also striking about Britain's 2008 National Security Strategy, especially given the date of its composition, was its pragmatism and good sense on terrorism and its implicit rejection of the so-called 'global war on terror'.[25] One of the merits of listing so many other dangers, therefore, was the consequent ability to put into perspective those to which the press headlines and the government's own actions had given greater urgency. After all, the Foreign Secretary, David

Miliband, did not get round to renouncing the phrase for another ten months,[26] and in 2009 Gordon Brown's government continued to justify Britain's involvement in the war in Afghanistan in terms of countering terrorism at home. By then, the British scepticism about the 'global war on terror' was also mirrored across the Atlantic.[27] In the United States, the Obama administration sought to distance itself from the phrase; the important and much more difficult question was whether it had rid itself of the thinking which underpinned it. To do that effectively it would have had to go back to the drawing board of strategy.

The 'global war on terror' was simultaneously symptomatic of a lack of strategic rigour in the opening decade of the twenty-first century and a principal driver in the desire to produce 'security strategies'. Because so little strategic thinking had gone into counter-terrorism, the threat from terrorism failed to produce adequate strategies to counter it.[28] Instead the problem was 'securitised', and so was linked to economic backwardness, governmental weakness and religious fundamentalism, all of them bigger and more amorphous challenges which are not themselves terrorism. The effect was further to empty out the strategy from the statements on security, since without terrorism the principal threats to security came less from conflict than from natural disasters and man-made environmental mismanagement. The security strategies tended to be blithely dismissive about the danger of inter-state war, and thus they lacked scenarios for war traditionally defined sufficiently credible to under-pin defence budgets, many of which were still often shaped by Cold War assumptions.

So the most striking feature about statements on strategy at the outset of the twenty-first century is less their predilection for terrorism and more their near certainty that certain sorts of war belong to the past. The hypothesis is very hard to test as it is not clear exactly which sort of war is being considered: is it a war defined by its aims, in other words a war between states, or is it a war defined by its conduct, a so-called 'regular' war as opposed to a guerrilla war? After all, states can fight each other using guerrilla, rather than regular, methods, as the partisans of the Soviet Union did Germany in 1941–5, just as non-state actors can form regular forces, as countless civil wars have demonstrated. Or is the apparent disappearance of some sorts of war a regional issue? It is true that certain neighbours who were at one point ready to fight each other – the United States and Canada, or France and Germany – seem increasingly unlikely to do so. But to extrapolate such pregnant examples from either an American context or a European one to the rest of the world, to Asia and Africa in particular, seems fanciful. The threat of inter-state war remains latent between Russia and its neighbours, and Israel and its, not to mention between India and Pakistan and between North and South Korea. Moreover, those whose thinking is shaped by the western tradition have almost no historical evidence to support a belief in the obsolescence of certain sorts of war, despite its near orthodoxy. Europe enjoyed relative peace between the end of the Napoleonic Wars in 1815 and 1848 or 1914, according to your taste on what is a major war, but the peace-makers of 1815 were never guilty of believing that they had put the problem of war behind them. It was their very lack of hubris that made them particularly vigilant for the first thirty years of what some have seen as a century of European peace, and, as we now know, they were right to be so. True, inter-state war has declined in frequency and in intensity since 1945, and the United Nations Security Council can probably take some credit for this.[29] But it has not entirely disappeared: with the exception of a couple of years in the early 1990s, it has continued at a constant, even if low, level ever since 1945. For a time civil wars (which are of course frequently about statehood and nationality) took their place, but that surge was above all generated by the aftermath of colonial withdrawal and the end of the Cold War, and it abated during the 1990s as the newly formed states established their monopoly of armed force.[30] The evidence for such optimism with regard to the likely incidence of 'traditional' or modern (as opposed to 'post-modern) war in the future seems to derive largely from another hypothesis developed by political scientists but about which historians are deeply sceptical – that of the 'democratic peace'. The thesis that democracies do not fight each other either rides roughshod over differences between types of democracy or has to operate with so many exceptions that it is really unsustainable. But, instead of being thrown out, it has been widened into more general norms, including the self-evidently bogus notion that democracies are inherently reluctant to wage war. As the French Revolution made clear, and the Arab spring of 2011 has re-emphasised, democratisation is a process that mobilises citizens, for domestic political participation certainly but for conflict if need be.

There is a paradox locked in the heart of the national security strategies. Before the 9/11 attacks, when defence departments engaged in scenario building designed to imagine where wars might occur in twenty or thirty years' time, and over what (themselves classic illustrations of the use of strategy for predictive purposes), they focused on the possibilities of conflict generated by scarcities of resources. The twin phenomena of climate change and urbanisation seemed likely to create competition for water, fuel and food. The presumption was that if assets like health, wealth and nutrition were in short supply we would fight for them rather than distribute what we have through multinational organisations or by some form of global government. But, if this scenario building is followed through to its logical conclusion, it suggests that free trade will be abandoned and economic autarchy will be prevalent: the haves will hold on to what they have, and the have-nots will have to fight to get what they need. Control of territory will be an important indicator of relative wealth and will also be a crucial ingredient in economic capacity. As the twenty-first century unfolds, the big states physically – the United States, China, Brazil and India – look set to prosper because of the resources they can command within their own land masses, more than the small ones. The proliferation of small states, particularly within Europe, is only possible within a collective security framework and rests on a presumption of free trade.

So-called 'resource wars' were remarkably familiar before the stabilisation of national frontiers, and even persisted after them. In the eighteenth and nineteenth centuries, they were waged, according to one interpretation of imperialism, by European powers bent on the acquisition of wealth, land and labour from elsewhere in the world. In the twentieth century, the Second World War in particular was fought at least as much in pursuit of economic autarchy as because of fundamental ideological difference. Unlike communism, neither Nazism nor the Samurai tradition was intended for export; the first was rooted in ideas of Aryanism and *Deutschtum* which were culturally as specific as Shinto and Bushido were in the second. Both the German search for *Lebensraum* (living space) and the Japanese wish to create a Greater East Asia Co-Prosperity Sphere were more important precipitants of war than were political beliefs, or the racism and the genocidal policies which accompanied them and which progressively shaped the war once it had begun.[31] Indeed, in both cases the latter were not separable from the former: for the Nazis, clearing the lands to the east of people was the preliminary to their settlement and exploitation by Germans, just as the racism manifested by the Japanese towards the Asian peoples they conquered was linked to the need to extract labour and resources from their lands.

The fact that the Second World War was a 'resource war' is simultaneously both helpful and misleading in terms of thinking about the place of climate change in twenty-first-century strategy. On the one hand it is an argument against change and for continuity: it says that wars have often been fought for the control of food and fuel, and we should not be surprised by the possibility of their recurrence in the future. But what such assertions deny is the qualitatively and quantitatively distinct aspects of the Second World War. In future, the states which will be most likely to resort to war to resolve their economic inadequacies are unlikely to possess the resources to wage war on a scale that could be characterised as 'total'. Indeed the historical argument in relation to war since 1945 associates war with poverty and backwardness. People fight – literally – to survive, and a weak state structure, which both distributes resources inequitably and cannot control or police its peoples, permits them to use violence to get both food and resources more quickly and in greater quantity than any other method of acquisition. In 2011 a report from Columbia University argued that 50 of 250 civil wars between 1950 and 2004 were 'triggered' by the El Niño cycle, which brought drought and cut food production in tropical countries.[32] The Oxford economist Paul Collier has similarly argued that 73 per cent of those living in the poorest countries in the world, 'the bottom billion' whose incomes fell in the 1990s by 5 per cent when global incomes were rising, simultaneously experienced civil war.[33] Early modern European states experienced conflict between those who had wealth and those who were caught by cyclical collapses in food supply: it required changes in agricultural practices in the eighteenth century and the advent of industrialisation in the nineteenth to ensure consistent food supplies. The incidence of much violence in early modern and even nineteenth-century Europe was obscured because it was not dignified with the title 'war', but was called rebellion – or at best revolution. These are distinctions which we should not lose sight of: civil war, like revolution, may have an economic driver, but it also assumes a more narrowly political superstructure shaped by a desire to form or reshape a state.

The big question for states which can wage 'total' war, like China and the United States, is whether for them, unlike the poorer states of the world, war can make sense in terms of cost–benefit calculations. Of course the fact that war did not make economic sense for the great powers in 1914 did not prevent them fighting, but they did not go to war in the first place in order to secure resources or for economic reasons.[34] Both China and the United States need raw materials and markets in order to sustain their own growth but, provided global free trade does not give way to autarchy, they can secure them without recourse to war.

The demand for commodities, and the consequent pressure to fight for territorial control, suggest that battles will be fought between neighbours along and across their mutual borders. The possibility of cross-border conflict is a reasonably immediate issue not just for states in areas becoming subject to desertification, but also for more northerly (and highly sophisticated) states which abut the Arctic. The need to control sea lanes and natural resources is producing competing claims to the land mass under the melting ice-cap and has already led to the assumption that the region will be 'militarised'.[35] If these issues are not resolved without war (and of course they may be: so far the states irrigated by the Nile have managed to agree on the use of its water without conflict), then the wars that follow seem likely to be remarkably traditional – wars fought between states for control of territory or their equivalent, the control of territorial waters and the assets beneath them.

In this context the revival of the vocabulary of geopolitics is instructive.[36] During the Cold War geographical self-interest and the pursuit of ideological purity marched in step. The very expression 'the west' makes the point: those states committed to liberal democracy and capitalism were also geographically contiguous, and united by the Atlantic. Since 1990 they have not been. Their interests have diverged, with the United States being the least equivocal in asserting the consequences. Obama's presidential statement on strategy in January 2012 prioritised the Pacific and Asia, arguing that at least some European states were now net exporters of security. As American policy in the Libyan campaign made clear, he saw security in areas adjacent to Europe, including the Mediterranean and the Middle East, as the responsibility of the Europeans themselves. The United States's progress towards self-sufficiency in fossil fuels thanks to the 'fracking' of oil can only promote this current in its grand strategy, as it makes its own wealth less dependent on the stability of the Persian Gulf and its adjacent states. But the result is potential confusion for those who continue to align their ideologies with their geopolitics. In the Pacific Australia's economy has coped well with recession because of its booming commodity exports to China; nonetheless it still welcomes a closer defence relationship with the United States, as the latter seeks to create a ring of allies in the western and southern Pacific in order to contain China. In the Atlantic, British defence policy remains predicated on its presumption that the United States is its major ally, despite the fact that the United States's own defence is 'pivoting' to areas where the United Kingdom abandoned a direct geopolitical interest in 1969 when it withdrew from east of Suez.

Confronting the separation of ideology from geopolitics has the potential to change how we see both strategy and its use of war, particularly in view of their intimate links to the pursuit of national self-interest. The biggest challenge that confronts strategy today and tomorrow is not terrorism; it is, as it always has been, war, and possibly even war in its more traditional form, inter-state war. Strategy is the only tool we have for conceptualising armed conflict and – if war breaks out – for directing it, but strategy in the absence of actual war cannot be certain of where such a war will occur, between whom and for what ends. So, if strategy is a science, it is a very imprecise one – and, in the vocabulary of the physicist or chemist, the matter with which it deals is both very volatile and unpredictable in its effects. Strategy aspires to control and direct war, but will always struggle to do so, because war has its own dynamic, which is independent of the rational calculations of any one actor. True, from the perspective of western Europe and even of North America, as well as of the Antipodes and of some other places in the world, inter-state war appears to be the least of our worries. But that is precisely the challenge. Can we in the west therefore go one stage further and consign more traditional definitions of war to the rubbish bin of history? The focus on terrorism, which may be a more immediate and recurrent problem, obscures the fact that, were an inter-state war to occur, it would be a far more serious issue. Strategy therefore matters: however imperfect it is as an intellectual tool, it is the best we have for the task available.

States – or, rather, some states – remain the most powerful military actors in the world, and the issues surrounding statehood still generate more wars than the issues surrounding resource availability or climate change. Britain's insouciance about inter-state war is remarkable given that it has fought against another state five times since 1982 – to retake the Falklands from Argentina in that year, to drive Iraq out of Kuwait in 1990–1, to protect the Kosovars from Serbia in 1999, to topple Saddam Hussein in 2003 and to bring about the fall of the Gaddafi regime in Libya in 2011. Moreover, the deployment of British troops to Sierra Leone and Afghanistan were both examples of armed conflict where the issues were ones of governance and state formation. If Britain is an example, states have not abandoned using war as an instrument of policy. Moreover, what we see as new phenomena within war may be something else: fresh manifestations of more traditional behaviours. The growth of private military companies has been the consequence, above all, of the state's continued desire to employ armed forces, albeit without retaining national capabilities commensurate with that intention. An increasing reliance on mercenaries may be at one level the product of post-heroic societies, which do not see military service in as honourable or patriotic terms as did their more nationalistic predecessors, but the private military companies themselves are employed overwhelmingly by states which use them for state objectives, and which by definition possess state structures sufficiently sophisticated to pay them.[37]

All this does not mean there has not been change in the state's use of war. States have, at least for the time being, stopped using total war or major war as an instrument of policy. This is where strategic theory has been slow to adapt to the tenets of strategic practice. The doctrines of the armed forces of NATO rest on the idea of the 'spectrum of conflict', and at one end of the spectrum is 'general war' or all-out nuclear exchange. Strategic theory has still not adequately responded to the absence of 'general war', not just since 1990 and the end of the Cold War, but since 1945 and the end of the Second World War.[38] The world has suffered only one total war, defined as such while it was being waged by those who fought it, and that was the Second World War after both the Soviet Union and the United States entered it in 1941. The First World War was not generally identified as a total war until after it was over.[39] The theoretical force of the Second World War has been with us ever since, partly because the idea of total war was present in the literature of warning produced in the 1930s, partly because the total war of 1941–5 was then found to have precedents, and partly because the conclusion to the war – the dropping of the atom bombs on Hiroshima and Nagasaki – carried its own warnings. As a result total war became the foundation stone for strategic theory in the second half of the twentieth century, and its contribution to that theory was deterrence.

Nor was it just the advent of nuclear weapons that confronted major wars with redundancy after 1945. Many states, both in Europe and Asia, remain reluctant to use military force because of the memory of the Second World War and its horrors; it may be the 'good' war for the countries that fought fascism, but for those they defeated (and even for some of those that did the defeating) the scale of the war has become an argument for preventing wars not waging them. Self-deterrence, although often not declared, is crucially important to the more general success of deterrence. For central Europe, and for Japan, war lacks political utility: they have, in some senses, become profoundly un-Clausewitzian.

Deterrence works because of the danger that actual war will result in massive destruction. Like most of the basic nostrums of deterrence, this one is absurdly simple. The fact that deterrence became a driver in the design and procurement of nuclear weapons in the Cold War resulted in a determination to over-theorise, and the additional and occasionally unnecessary intellectual baggage of deterrence may have been one reason why it was too readily ditched from the vocabulary of strategy after 1990, especially on the Atlantic's eastern seaboard. But deterrence is still in play, albeit in ways that are largely unrecognised and therefore unsung. The principal function of deterrence is to prevent total or major war, not to provide the excuse for lesser wars. This is not to say that deterrence cannot operate to prevent lesser wars or that deterrence cannot operate within war. But wars initiated in order to 'restore deterrence', an argument used in the United States to justify pre-emption and in Israel to explain the use of force against its neighbours, represent a failure of deterrence. One reason why so much attention has shifted to terrorism and to non-state actors in the discourse on war is that deterrence is one of the factors that has made major war between states an ineffective tool of policy.

The success of deterrence since 1990, however unacknowledged, has not in fact denied military force its utility. Some states remain robustly ready to use military force in the pursuit of policy goals. To name only the most obvious and immediate, Russia did so in South Ossetia in 2008, Israel in Gaza in 2008–9, and the United States in Iraq and Afghanistan in 2001 and 2003. But all these states have used military force within constraints. Geographically, wars have remained more regionally focused than the rhetoric of globalisation and especially of the 'global war on terror' suggests. Temporally, despite the prolongation of many wars, the timetable for withdrawal frames strategy. Militarily, major states do not bring their full resources to bear and do not mobilise either their economies or their peoples for war. Most significantly of all, nuclear powers treat each other with restraint: neither India nor Pakistan used the Mumbai terrorist attacks of November 2008 as an excuse to expand the latent hostility between them.

Therefore, as well as deterrence, there is another concept which has also gone out of fashion but which – as Chapter 5 has argued – needs rethinking, and that is limited war. During the Cold War, the wars in

Korea and Vietnam and the proxy wars fought in Africa or Latin America, which melded colonial withdrawal with communist-inspired revolutionary warfare, had at their roots ideas which were capable of expanding wars, not contracting them. But the participants often had an interest in curbing the effects of these ideas. Global revolutionary war, however beloved in the 1960s by communist theorists and by the writers of counter-insurgency textbooks, was trumped by those who waged it. For the belligerents themselves, the objective was less the waging of a 'global cold war' and more the pursuit of national independence.[40] For their sponsors, the super-powers, the balance of terror created by the possession of nuclear weapons provided an incentive for containment, not expansion. The imposition of a global framework on to localised conflict gave it greater international resonance while curbing its consequences. If what is now called 'globalisation' has replaced the 'global cold war' as the international context within which wars are set, it too could limit future wars. If fought over resources between neighbours, wars could be stripped of ideological content and so be limited by more than simple geography. In this way, the character of war could change through a reversion to older forms of war as well as through genuine innovation.

For the moment, however, the United States seems determined to pursue a security policy which is predicated on the need for others to think as it does.[41] Like the limited conflicts within the Cold War, the wars of the early twenty-first century have not been ideologically constrained. The objectives for which wars have been waged – for the advancement of democracy, for the furtherance of Islam, or for the protection and promotion of human rights – have been remarkably grandiose and open ended. In the wars waged after the 9/11 attacks both sides actively pursued the globalisation of their causes, so that the issues at stake were at odds with the means employed. If states are genuinely engaged in a 'long war', as Philip Bobbitt has argued,[42] or a 'global insurgency', the term which David Kilcullen has used,[43] or even the war of the twenty-first century or the 'global war on terror', the two phrases employed by George W. Bush, then they have been setting about it in a very strange way. The mismatch between ends and means suggests that strategy in practice is flawed. Nor has the difficulty in implementing America's strategy produced a change in the underlying political intent which drives it. The humiliation which the United States has incurred as a result of the wars in Iraq and Afghanistan, not to mention the costs in blood and (albeit less explicitly accounted for) treasure,[44] have produced a refocusing of the appropriate means but not of the ends. With the election of President Obama in 2009, the United States became more wary about its own use of war, but not about war's utility in effecting change. In 2011 it took a back seat in the NATO campaign against Libya, but it still provided key assets, especially in intelligence and target acquisition. That war was authorised by a United Nations resolution, and summoned up images from Rwanda and Srebrenica to argue that we have global humanitarian responsibilities which demand pre-emptive action on humanitarian grounds. The failure to secure any comparable resolution for Syria in 2012 suggested less that we live in a 'globalised world' and more that the 'global cold war' still persisted. Russia and China supported the Assad regime, while the United States and its allies supported the 'Free Syria Army'; these national divisions harked back to older ideological cleavages, reflected in the Cold War, and the provision of arms by each group to its favoured party sustained war and deepened divisions, rather than laid the basis for conflict termination and resolution. The members of the United Nations Security Council pursued policies which, although fed by the fear that the civil war in Syria would not remain geographically limited, at the same time made it harder to limit it in other respects – and so stood in danger of undermining their core objectives.

In the first decade of the twenty-first century policy and the use of war were at odds with each other. The United States fought its wars in Afghanistan and Iraq under the banner, first, of the 'global war on terror' and, then, of 'the long war'. Even within the United States, the substance did not necessarily follow the rhetoric. The Bush government avoided confronting Congress or the American people with the true financial cost of the war, in terms both of immediate funding mechanisms and of long-term debt burdens. When Obama came to office, his Defense Secretary, Robert Gates, said that not even the Pentagon was on a war footing, so focused was it on future procurement to the detriment of current conflict.[45] Broadly speaking, the United States's allies, despite declaring their solidarity with America after the 9/11 attacks, were even slower to follow its lead. They rejected the use of the word 'war' in relation to countering international terrorism. In Britain in early 2009, both the prime minister, Gordon Brown, and the Secretary of State for Defence, John Hutton, stressed that British troops were fighting in Helmand in the national interest, but at the same time the Ministry of Defence refused to say that Britain was at war.[46] From the public's perspective, the evidence of killed and wounded soldiers, brought to them by the media and also by charities like 'Help for Heroes', implied the opposite, that Britain was indeed at war. The same discontinuities between thought and action, between policies and within policy, were played out across other states in Europe, in different ways and at different tempos.

Some of these differences have been evident in the clashes between politicians and their senior service advisers. Our image of strategy is that it is formed at the interface of the civil–military relationship, whose weight in most democratic strategic theory rests on the relationship between the governments and their armed forces. But absent from the theory, certainly as it was developed in the Cold War and particularly in the work of Samuel Huntington, is the role of what Huntington called 'subjective control'.[47] In one of his most important passages, Clausewitz used the metaphor of the Christian trinity to capture the nature of war, the three elements being passion, the play of probability and chance, and logic or reason. From this he derived a secondary trinity, the actors in a nation at war, more than the characteristics of war itself – the people, the armed forces and the government. Western norms concerning the formation of strategy at the beginning of the twenty-first century focus on the armed forces and the government but neglect the people.[48]

Where are the people in strategy today? Counter-insurgency strategy, as expressed for example in the US Army Field Manual 3–24, published in December 2006, is well aware of the people as the object in war, of the need to gain the support of the population in the country where insurgents are active.[49] The United States armed forces are also determined to ensure the support of the American people for the war, having concluded after the Vietnam War that it had lost the war on the television screens of American citizens. However overdrawn that is as diagnosis of the reasons for America's defeat, its legacy was evident in the determination to have retired officers appear on television as pundits during the war in Iraq.[50] Also influential here is the phrase used by General Sir Rupert Smith in *The utility of force*, published in 2005, that wars today are 'wars among the people'. That particular insight is not as new as the frequency with which it is cited, especially in relation to the sorts of counter-insurgency campaigns and peace-keeping operations of which Smith and other British soldiers have so much experience. Both Northern Ireland and Bosnia taught that lesson. Much more challenging for strategy is another of his insights, that contemporary warfare is a form of theatre, played out by a small, separate group (i.e. a professional and not a conscript army), orchestrated by a team of unseen directors, stage managers and lighting engineers, but watched by many more.[51]

The people are the audience for war. Colin McInnes has used the analogy not of theatre but of 'spectator-sport warfare'.[52] Sporting events, for example the 2012 London Olympics or a World Cup football match played out by two teams of eleven players, command global television audiences of millions. Similarly, the limited wars of today are rendered unlimited by the mechanisms of their reporting. Moreover, the technologies now employed – blogs, websites, mobile telephone images – mean that the distinction between combatant and reporter is removed. The combatant is his own reporter, and because the reporter interprets the events which he or she observes, almost in real time, the reporter is no longer a neutral but a participant.[53]

The newness of the challenge posed by non-state actors in war to our understanding of strategy is less the fact that they do not belong to states than the fact that they have displayed a better understanding of the 'trinity' of strategy. Like Maoist guerrillas, at least in Maoist theory, they recognise that the people must be participants, even if only passive and secondary ones, not neutral onlookers. One of the most enduring criticisms of NATO strategy in Afghanistan has related to its public communications, where the Taleban has enjoyed the advantage of tempo and also, at times, of content. But the means by which propaganda (the word is not pejorative, but accurate: another example of how western states loosen their grip on ideas by relaxing their use of language) is disseminated ensures that the message to the people of Afghanistan is also potentially the same message to the people of the United States, however different their economic circumstances or their religious or political beliefs. Thus the people in the audience are not just the people in the war zone, nor even the populations of all the belligerent states, but the court of world opinion. It really is like a World Cup match. What has perplexed western governments is less the fact that they have struggled to win over the other side's potential supporters, which is always going to be a struggle, and more that they have not got their own crowd cheering them on. The populations of NATO states can support the players, that is the armed forces, but they withhold support for the team managers and for the war itself.

There may be a danger here of mistaking the specific for the general: reluctance to support an unpopular war may not be the same as a refusal to support all wars waged in the name of the nation. But there is still a general observation to be made, which is that – paradoxically – democratic states seem to be frightened or confused by the democratisation of war reporting. News travels with a speed which gets inside the reaction cycle of governments. The British government controlled the story in the Falklands War, although as a result reporting seemed slow and ponderous. In 1999, during the Kosovo campaign, it could still in general do so, and with much more lightness in its footwork, not least thanks to the efforts of Alastair Campbell, Tony Blair's press adviser. On 16 April Campbell saw both NATO's Secretary General, Javier Solana, and the Supreme Allied Commander Europe, General Wesley Clark, to tell them that 'we needed a strategic approach to communications'. Campbell, although alarmed by the degree to which Clark was counting on him, concluded, 'If you are fighting a war, it has to be fought like a war at every level.'[54]

Like operational art in the first Gulf War, the management of the press in the Kosovo campaign now looks like a climax rather than the beginning of a new era. In less than a decade governments, despite the fact that they desire to shape the story as Campbell did, find themselves fighting wars on the back foot, with news sometimes surprising them as much as their own publics. The solution adopted by the US government in 2003, that of 'embedding' journalists with front-line units in the invasion of Iraq, meant that the force earmarked for the assault on Fallujah on 7 November 2004 had sixty media outlets and each company of United States Marines had an embedded media crew. General George Casey's team believed that 'public information turns tactical success into strategic victory'.[55] But control of information has become as contested as control of the battlefield. Not all reporters are committed to the 'strategic victory' of the forces with which they are embedded, opting instead to honour their callings as professional and therefore objective journalists, and in any case they themselves no longer have a monopoly on reporting. All participants now possess the capacity to be able to communicate instantaneously, and to do so with images to support their reports or claims. The presence of television monitors throughout the main building of the British Ministry of Defence, playing 24-hour news programmes, is symptomatic: a ministry which should be making news is passively and continuously receiving it.

Governments can be lured into premature reactions before the full situation is known to them, or they can give mixed messages as they fight for time. The function of strategy, while of course remaining adaptive and flexible, is to provide a context within which shocks and surprises can be set; strategy has the capacity to enable governments to regain control, if it is well handled, but to deepen their problems if it is not. A contradictory response may be worse than a delayed response or no response at all. On 1 May 2012, President Obama visited Kabul to promise Afghanistan the cooperation of the United States after the completion of the withdrawal of NATO forces from front-line operations in 2014. In the early hours of the following morning, while still in Afghanistan, he broadcast to the American people to tell them that the war would end in the same year. In other words he tried to convey different and in some respects incompatible objectives to what he saw as distinct audiences, despite the fact that those audiences live in an era when the media have become globalised and interconnected. The first message struggled to reach the people of Afghanistan, and if it did they were not reassured; the second message was heard but not necessarily believed. Delivering different messages to different audiences confounds not just strategic communications but strategy itself. If democratic states believe that their armed forces are fighting for democratic objectives, then the democratisation of the popular battle space should in the long run produce better coordinated strategy; indeed it has to. People, armed forces and government need to become three in one in reality as well as in Clausewitzian theory.

So far strategic theory has yet to get its head round this aspect of twenty-first-century strategic practice. This is potentially a classic illustration of how strategic theory is developed. Experience, and the experience of failure, is fed back into theory in order to give it purchase on the future by its incorporation of the lessons of the past. Above all, strategy provides the strategic narrative (and there can be no such narrative without strategy in the first place) within which government and army can understand what is going on and communicate that understanding to the people. That narrative then gives the context into which specific episodes in a war can be placed. When the western, democratic state can do that better than it was doing it in 2009 or 2012, it will have reconsolidated its position in the strategic firmament.

For a historian, to argue in terms that combine change and continuity is no more than a matter of sticking to his last. Much of the change suggested here is a change backwards, a reversion to the ideas of deterrence and limited war, and such changes – particularly when they refer to ideas which were current in strategic theory until comparatively recently, can therefore also be seen as forms of continuity. The wars waged at the start of the twenty-first century were still predominantly the products of national, religious and ethnic identity; their aims remained governance and state formation. Paradoxically, however, they have been seen as wars of a new variety, principally because we have mistaken the character of individual wars for war's normative nature. The wars of the later twenty-first century may well be waged for assets, to which we feel in theory all humanity should have equal access but for which in practice we compete. But if we cannot share resources without war, then we are most likely to fight for them as members of states or multinational alliances, since only thus will we have the leverage to use war effectively. But, if what therefore happens is indeed another change backwards, a reversion to the sorts of wars waged in Europe at least until 1648, and in some respects to 1789, and to the sorts of wars waged outside Europe until the end of empire, then there is hope that they can also be limited. If wars for resources replace wars of ideologies, if the notion of the 'global war on terror' and the 'long war' prove as locked in the circumstances and timing of their coining as seems likely, then the wars of the later twenty-first century have a chance of being ideologically empty and geographically contained. For that optimism to be also realism (and so to mix schools of international relations theory), then the strength of the state remains not only a sine qua non, but also central to the coherence of deterrence. Deterrence is not just about nuclear weapons, but short of an effective non-proliferation regime it remains the most effective envelope within which their possession can not only be contained but also contribute to world security. However, that thought, like everything else written here, assumes that security is relative, not absolute.

NOTES

1 War and strategy at the beginning of the twenty-first century

1. Gerhard Ritter, *The sword and the sceptre: the problem of militarism in Germany* (4 vols., London, 1970–3), vol. II, p. 197.
2. *The Herald* (Glasgow), 9 March 2007.
3. From Clausewitz's note of 10 July 1827, in *On war*, ed. and trans. Michael Howard and Peter Paret (Princeton, 1976), p. 69.
4. See below, pp. 00–00.
5. Sami Ramadani, 'In Iraq, public anger is at last translating into unity', *The Guardian*, 20 March 2007.
6. Julian Corbett, *Some principles of maritime strategy*, ed. Eric Grove (Annapolis, MD, 1988; 1st edn London, 1911), p. 308.
7. J. F. C. Fuller, *The reformation of war* (London, 1923), p. 218.
8. Clausewitz, *On war*, book VIII, chapter 6A, p. 606.
9. Colin Powell, with Joseph Persico, *My American journey* (New York, 1996; 1st edn 1995), p. 576.
10. Thomas E. Ricks, *The generals: American military command from World War II to today* (New York, 2012), p. 412.
11. Clausewitz, *On war*, book I, chapter 1, p. 127.

2 The meaning of strategy: historical perspectives

1. See reports in *The Times* and *Daily Telegraph*, 20 November 2003. What follows was delivered as my inaugural lecture as Professor of the History of War in Oxford on 4 December 2003.
2. CM 6052, December 2003.
3. CM 6041, December 2003.

4. CM 5566, July 2002.

5. Carl von Clausewitz, *On war*, ed. and trans. Michael Howard and Peter Paret (Princeton, 1976), p. 177, see also pp. 128, 227.

6. Xenophon and Polybius both used στράτηγημά, or stratagem, to cover the art of the general. Xenophon uses στρατηγία, or strategy, to mean plan in *Anabasis*, book II, chapter ii, 13; but contrast I, vii, 2, where a Persian council of war discussed 'how he [Cyrus] should fight the battle', and II, ii, 6, which speaks of the 'wisdom which a commander should have'. Onasander, Στρατηγικός (or *The General*) discussed 'the principles of generalship' and 'the art of the general and the wisdom that inheres in the precepts' (Proemium, 3), but used the word 'strategy' in chapter XXXII, 5. I am grateful to Martin West and Brian Campbell for discussing these points with me.

7. Azar Gat, *The origins of military thought from the Enlightenment to Clausewitz* (Oxford, 1989), p. 39.

8. Quoted by J.-P. Charnay, in André Corvisier (ed.), *A dictionary of military history and the art of war*, English edn ed. John Childs (Oxford, 1994), p. 769; see also Gat, *Origins of military thought*, p. 42.

9. Napoléon, *De la guerre*, ed. Bruno Colson (Paris, 2012), pp. 147–9.

10. Quoted by Charnay in Corvisier, *Dictionary of military history*, p. 769.

11. Antoine-Henri Jomini, *Summary of the art of war*, trans. G. H. Mendell and W. P. Craighill (Philadelphia, 1862), p. 137.

12. Ibid., p. 13.

13. Ibid., p. 69.

14. Gerhard Ritter, *The sword and the sceptre: the problem of militarism in Germany* (4 vols., London, 1970–3), I, pp. 187–260.

15. Friedrich von Bernhardi, *On war of to-day*, trans. Karl von Donat (2 vols., London, 1912–13), II, pp. 187, 194.

16. Jean Colin, *The transformations of war*, trans. L. H. R. Pope-Hennessy (London, 1912), p. 343.

17. Commandant [Henri] Mordacq, *Politique et stratégie dans une démocratie* (Paris, 1912), pp. 214, 237.

18. Julian Corbett, *Some principles of maritime strategy*, ed. Eric Grove (Annapolis, 1988; 1st edn London, 1911), p. 10.

19. Ibid., p. 17.

20. Ibid., p. 30.

21. 'The Green Pamphlet', printed as an appendix in ibid., p. 308.

22. Jon Tetsuro Sumida, *Inventing grand strategy and teaching command: the classic works of Alfred Thayer Mahan reconsidered* (Washington, 1997), p. 27.

23. Raoul Castex, *Théories stratégiques* (5 vols., Paris, 1927–33; the quotation is from the revised edition of vol. I, published in 1937), I, p. 9.

24. Ibid., vol. III, p. 115.

25. Cameron Hazlehurst, *Politicians at war, July 1914 to May 1915: a prologue to the triumph of Lloyd George* (London, 1971), p. 176.

26. J. F. C. Fuller, *The reformation of war* (London, 1923), p. 218; see also Fuller, *The foundations of the science of war* (London, [1926]), pp. 105–7.

27. Basil Liddell Hart, *When Britain goes to war* (London, 1928), p. 83; see also Liddell Hart, *Thoughts on war* (London, 1944), pp. 151–6.

28. J. R. M. Butler, *Grand strategy* (London, 1957), vol. II, p. xv.

29. Michael Howard, *Grand strategy* (London, 1972), IV, p. 1; see also Michael Howard, 'Grand strategy in the twentieth century', *Defence Studies*, 1 (2001), pp. 1–10.

30. Liddell Hart, *When Britain goes to war*, p. 83.

31. Edward Mead Earle (ed.), *Makers of modern strategy: military thought from Machiavelli to Hitler* (Princeton, 1943), p. viii.

32. Clausewitz, *On war*, p. 606.

33. Herfried Münkler, *Über den Krieg. Stationen der Kriegsgeschichte im Spiegel ihrer theoristchen Reflexionenen* (Weilerswist, 2002), pp. 91–115; Andreas Herberg-Rothe, *Das Rätsel Clausewitz* (Munich, 2001), pp. 31–4, 102–24.

34. See the political manifesto of 1812, cited in Carl von Clausewitz, *Historical and political writings*, ed. and trans. by Peter Paret and Daniel Moran (Princeton, 1992), p. 290, and below, pp. 59–60.

35. See the discussion 'Concerning violence', in Franz Fanon, *The wretched of the earth* (1961; Penguin edn, London, 2001), esp. pp. 57–8.

36. Erich Ludendorff, *The nation in arms* (London, [1935]), trans. A. S. Rappoport, pp. 19, 22, 23; see also Hew Strachan, 'Clausewitz and the First World War', *Journal of Military History*, 75 (2011), pp. 367–91.

37. Lawrence Freedman, *The evolution of nuclear strategy* (London, 1981), p. 193.

38. Eric de la Maisonneuve, *Incitation à la réflexion stratégique* (Paris, 1998), p. 6.

39. André Beaufre, *An introduction to strategy* (London, 1965), pp. 14, 23.

40. Interestingly Bernhardi explicitly used the phrase 'political strategy' in *War of to-day*, II, p. 454, but only once and without defining it.

41. Castex, *Théories stratégiques*, I, pp. 17–18.

42. Beaufre, *Introduction to strategy*, pp. 11, 13.

43. Edward Luttwak, *Strategy: the logic of war and peace* (Cambridge, MA, 1987), p. 4.

44. Barry Posen, *The sources of military doctrine: France, Britain, and Germany between the world wars* (Ithaca, NY, 1984), pp. 13, 220.

45. Aleksandr A. Svechin, *Strategy*, ed. Kent Lee (Minneapolis, 1992), p. 69.

46. For books which stress the Russian pedigree in operational thought, see Richard Simpkin, *Race to the swift: thoughts on twenty-first century warfare* (London, 1985), pp. 37–53, and Shimon Naveh, *In pursuit of military excellence: the evolution of operational theory* (London, 1997), pp. 164–208. For a comparison, consider the German focus of the essays in Richard D. Hooker, jr. (ed.), *Maneuver warfare* (Novato, CA, 1993).

47. Erich Ludendorff, *Kriegführung und Politik* (Berlin, 1922), pp. 320–42; see also Otto von Moser, *Ernsthafte Plaudereien über den Weltkrieg* (Stuttgart, 1925), pp. 6–14; Ein Generalstäbler, *Kritik des Weltkrieges. Das Erbe Moltkes und Schlieffens im grossen Kriege* (Leipzig, 1920).
48. Hermann Franke (ed.), *Handbuch der neuzeitlichen Wehrwissenschaften* (3 vols. in 4, Berlin, 1936–9), I, pp. 181–2, also p. 195.
49. Ibid., pp. 175, 549–53.
50. See, above all, Karl-Heinz Frieser, *Blitzkrieg-Legende. Der Westfeldzug 1940* (Munich, 1995).
51. Martin van Creveld, *On future war* (London, 1991; published in the USA as *The transformation of war*); John Keegan, *A history of warfare* (London, 1993); Mary Kaldor, *New and old wars* (London, 1991).
52. Stephen Launay, *La guerre sans la guerre: essai sur une querelle occidentale* (Paris, 2003), p. 334.
53. Bob Woodward, *Bush at war* (New York, 2002), pp. 174–6, 192.
54. James Fallows, 'Blind into Baghdad', *Atlantic Monthly*, January/February 2004. I am grateful for the comments on the last section of those who heard me speak at the Olin Institute of Strategic Studies, at Harvard, and at the Triangle Institute for Security Studies, North Carolina, in April 2005, and especially to Stephen Rosen, Peter Feaver, Richard Kohn and Jacqueline Newmyer. They forced me to sharpen my argument, even if they do not necessarily agree.

3 The case for Clausewitz: reading *On war* today

1. Colin Powell, with Joseph Persico, *My American journey* (New York, 1995), pp. 207–8.
2. For a discussion of the 'trinity', see Christopher Bassford, 'The primacy of policy and the "trinity" in Clausewitz's mature thought', in Hew Strachan and Andreas Herberg-Rothe (eds.), *Clausewitz in the twenty-first century* (Oxford, 2007).
3. Harry G. Summers, jr., *On strategy: a critical analysis of the Vietnam War* (Novato, CA, 1982); on his influence, see Dominic Tierney, *How we fight: crusades, quagmires and the American way of war* (New York, 2010), p. 179.
4. Daniel Moran, 'Clausewitz, Carl von', in John Whiteclay Chambers II (ed.), *The Oxford companion to American military history* (Oxford, 1999), p. 143.
5. Cited in Keith L. Shimko, *The Iraq wars and America's military revolution* (New York, 2010), p. 22.
6. Alvin and Heidi Toffler, *War and anti-war: survival at the dawn of the 21st century* (London, 1994; first published New York, 1993), p. 8.
7. Bill Owens with Ed Offley, *Lifting the fog of war* (New York, 2000), pp. 12, 14; it is perhaps symptomatic of Clausewitz's use as a straw man in these

arguments that Owens believed *On war* was published in 1812; it was actually published in 1832–4, after Clausewitz's death.

8. The classical account of the Mogadishu operation is Mark Bowden, *Black Hawk Down* (London, 1999); for its effects, see Tierney, *How we fight*, pp. 203–16; Robert Patman, *Strategic shortfall: the 'Somalia syndrome' and the march to 9/11* (Santa Barbara, 2010).

9. John Keegan, *A history of warfare* (London, 1993), pp. 3, 391; for a sustained response to Keegan, see Christopher Bassford, 'John Keegan and the grand tradition of trashing Clausewitz: a polemic', *War in history*, 1 (1994), pp. 319–36.

10. Mary Kaldor, *New and old wars: organized violence in a global era* (Cambridge, 2001; first published 1999), pp. 15, 21; for criticisms of Kaldor's thesis, see Mats Berdal, 'The "new wars" thesis revisited', in Hew Strachan and Sibylle Scheipers (eds.), *The changing character of war* (Oxford, 2011; Ole Jørgen Maaø, 'Mary Kaldor's new wars: a critique', in Karl Erik Haug and Ole Jørgen Maaø (eds.), *Conceptualising modern war* (London, 2011).

11. Carl von Clausewitz, *On war*, trans. O. J. Matthijs Jolles (Washington, DC, 1950), p. 18; I have used the less fluent but more literal translation of Jolles, rather than the better known one of Michael Howard and Peter Paret, as it is closer to the original German.

12. Raymond Aron, *Penser la guerre, Clausewitz* (2 vols., Paris, 1976), vol. I, p 169; vol II p. 139.

13. Clausewitz, *On war*, trans. Jolles, p. 16

14. Liddell Hart's most forceful attack on Clausewitz, although it is to be found scattered throughout his writings, is contained in *The ghost of Napoleon* (London, 1933), pp. 118–29.

15. On some of the problems which have arisen as a result, see Jan Willem Honig, 'Strategy in a post-Clausewitzian setting', in Gert de Nooy (ed.), *The Clausewitzian dictum and the future of western military strategy* (The Hague, 1997), and Honig, 'Clausewitz's *On war*: problems of text and translation', in Strachan and Herberg-Rothe, *Clausewitz in the twenty-first century*; Hew Strachan, 'Clausewitz en anglais: la césure de 1976', in Laure Bardiès and Martin Motte (eds.), *De la guerre? Clausewitz et la pensée stratégique contemporaine* (Paris, 2008), esp. pp. 94–122.

16. See on this issue, in English, Azar Gat, *The origins of military thought: from the Enlightenment to Clausewitz* (Oxford, 1989), pp. 169, 213–30; Hew Strachan, *Clausewitz's 'On war': a biography* (London, 2007), pp. 71–6.

17. Clausewitz, *On war*, trans. Jolles, p. 570.

18. Honig, 'Clausewitz's *On war*', p. 65; see especially Michael Howard, *Clausewitz* (Oxford, 1983), p. 47.

19. Strachan, 'Clausewitz en anglais', pp. 114–16.

20. Carl von Clausewitz, *On war*, ed. and trans. Michael Howard and Peter Paret (Princeton, 1976), p. 608.

21. Clausewitz, *On war*, trans. Jolles, pp. 45, 81–2.

22. Carl von Clausewitz, *Preussen in seiner grossen Katastrophe* (first published 1880; reprinted, Vienna, 2001), p. 12.

23. Clausewitz, *On war*, trans. Jolles, p. 599; emphasis in the original.

24. The full texts can be found in Carl von Clausewitz, *Schriften-Aufsätze-Studien-Briefe*, ed. Werner Hahlweg (2 vols. in 3 parts, Göttingen, 1966–90), Vol. I, pp. 226–588. Although Christopher Daase has promised an English translation of the lectures, it has yet to appear, but see his 'Clausewitz and small wars', in Strachan and Herberg-Rothe (eds.), *Clausewitz in the twenty-first century*.

25. In the third of the manifestos of February 1812, Clausewitz, *Schriften*, vol. I, pp. 740–1.

26. The first manifesto only is available in an English translation, in Clausewitz, *Historical and political writings* (Princeton, 1992), ed. and trans. Peter Paret and Daniel Moran; here p. 290; the full texts are in Clausewitz, *Schriften*, vol. I, pp. 682–750.

27. Clausewitz, *On war*, trans. Howard and Paret, p. 483.

28. Stephen L. Melton, *The Clausewitz delusion: how the American army screwed up in the wars in Iraq and Afghanistan (a way forward)* (Minneapolis, 2009), pp. 12, 17 and 116 (quoting Franks).

29. Ibid., p. 12.

30. John A. Nagl, *Learning to eat soup with a knife: counter-insurgency lessons from Malaya and Vietnam* (2nd edn, Chicago, 2005), p. 19; on Nagl's influence and his link to Petraeus, see Fred Kaplan, *The insurgents: David Petraeus and the plot to change the American way of war* (New York, 2013).

31. Paula Broadwell, with Vernon Loeb, *All in: the education of General Petraeus* (New York, 2012), p. 68; see also David Cloud and Greg Jaffe, *The fourth star: four generals and their epic struggle for the future of the United States army* (New York, 2009), pp. 62–6.

32. Wolf Kittle, 'Host nations: Carl von Clausewitz and the new US Army/Marine Corps Field Manual, FM 3–24, MWCP 3–33.5, *Counterinsurgency*', in Elisabeth Krimmer and Patricia Anne Simpson (eds.), *Enlightened war: German theories and cultures of war from Frederick the Great to Clausewitz* (New York, 2011), p. 282.

33. Ibid., pp. 284–5.

34. Clausewitz, *On war*, trans. Howard and Paret, p. 88.

4 Making strategy work: civil–military relations in Britain and the United States

1. Colin Gray, *Another bloody century: future warfare* (London, 2005), p. 111.

2. Lord Butler of Brockwell (chairman), *Review of intelligence on weapons of mass destruction: a report of a committee of privy counsellors* HC 898 (London, 14 July 2004).

3. Michael Gordon and Bernard Trainor, *Cobra II: the inside story of the invasion and occupation of Iraq* (London, 2006), p. 81.

4. Gray, *Another bloody century*, 53.

5. Ewen Mackaskill, 'Rice and Rumsfeld bury the hatchet for Iraq visit', *The Guardian*, 27 April 2006, p. 24.

6. Donald Rumsfeld, 'Transforming the military', *Foreign Affairs*, May/June 2002, pp. 20–32.

7. On 'non-linearity' in war, see Alan Beyerchen, 'Chance and complexity in the real world: Clausewitz on the nonlinear nature of war', *International Security*, winter 1992–3, pp. 59–90.

8. Bob Woodward, *Bush at war* (New York, 2002), pp. 128–9; see also pp. 84, 174.

9. Ibid., pp. 135, 321.

10. Andrew Bacevich, *The new American militarism: how Americans are seduced by war* (New York, 2005), p. 148.

11. See James Fallows, 'Blind into Baghdad', *The Atlantic Monthly*, January/February 2004.

12. Thomas E. Ricks, *The generals: American military command from World War II to today* (New York, 2012), pp. 399; see also Seymour Hersh, *The chain of command* (London, 2005), pp. 134–42.

13. Tommy Franks, *American soldier* (New York, 2004), p. 440.

14. Ibid., p. 441.

15. H. R. McMaster, *Dereliction of duty: Lyndon Johnson, Robert McNamara, the Joint Chiefs of Staff and the lies that led to Vietnam* (New York, 1997), esp. pp. 328–9.

16. Deborah D. Avant, *Political institutions and military change: lessons from peripheral wars* (Ithaca; NY, 1994), p. 49; see also p. 10.

17. Lt Gen. Greg Newbold, 'Why Iraq was a mistake', *Time*, 17 April 2006, pp. 40–1; Evan Thomas and John Barry, 'Anatomy of a revolt', *Newsweek*, 24 April 2006, pp. 24–9; see also *The Guardian*, 14, 15 and 17 April 2006; *International Herald Tribune*, 17 and 24 April 2006.

18. Sherard Cowper-Coles, *Cables from Kabul: the inside story of the west's Afghanistan campaign* (London, 2011), p. 178.

19. House of Commons Defence Committee, session 2009–10, 3rd report, *National security and resilience*, 16 December 2009.

20. Joint Committee on the National Security Strategy, 1st report of session 2010–12, *1st review of the National Security Strategy 2010*, HL paper 265, HC 1384, published 8 March 2012; the oral evidence is available online.

21. Bill Jackson and Dwin Bramall, *The chiefs: the story of the United Kingdom chiefs of staff* (London, 1992), p. 426.

22. Ibid., p. 433.

23. John Kampfner, *Blair's wars* (London, 2003), pp. 23, 305.

24. Jackson and Bramall, *The chiefs*, pp. 432, 433, 436.

25. Douglas Hurd, 'This is more like Major's nosedive than Thatcher's fall', *The Guardian*, 18 May 2006, p. 34.
26. Jackson and Bramall, *The chiefs*, p. 448.
27. Nick Hopkin, 'Angry Cameron dresses down First Sea Lord', *The Guardian*, 16 June 2011; Allegra Stratton, 'Separate bunkers fighting the same war', *The Guardian*, 7 July 2011.
28. Marquess of Salisbury, Douglas Slater and Alixe Buckerfield de la Roche, *Clear and accountable: institutions for defence and security* (London: Politeia, 2009).
29. See especially Peter D. Feaver, *Armed servants: agency, oversight and civil–military relations* (Cambridge, MA, 2003), and Eliot Cohen, *Supreme command: soldiers, statesmen and leadership in wartime* (New York, 2002). Cohen summarises the criticisms of Huntington on pp. 225–51.
30. Samuel P. Huntington, *The soldier and the state: the theory and politics of civil–military relations* (Cambridge, MA, 1957), p. 456.
31. Ibid., p. 71.
32. Ibid., p. 329.
33. Cohen, *Supreme command*, p. 8; for the implications of this for Britain, see Hew Strachan, *The politics of the British army* (Oxford, 1997), pp. 1–19.
34. Carl von Clausewitz, *On war*, trans. O. J. Matthijs Jolles (Washington, DC, 1950), p. 599.
35. Feaver, *Armed servants*, p. 145.
36. Nicholas d'Ombrain, *War machinery and high policy: defence administration in peacetime Britain 1902–1914* (London, 1973), here esp. pp. 8–9.
37. Julian Corbett, *Some principles of maritime strategy* (Annapolis, 1998; first published London, 1911), p. 8.
38. Hilary Synnott, *Bad days in Basra: my turbulent times as Britain's man in southern Iraq* (London, 2008), p. 10.
39. Hersh, *Chain of command*, p. 177.
40. Feaver, *Armed servants*, p. 215.
41. H. R. McMaster, *Dereliction of duty: Lyndon Johnson, Robert McNamara, the Joint Chiefs of Staff, and the lies that led to Vietnam* (New York, 1997).
42. See John Reid, 'Twenty-first century warfare – twentieth century rules', *Journal of the Royal United Services Institute for Defence Studies*, 61, no. 3 (June 2006), pp. 14–16.
43. *Independent*, 14 April 2006.
44. Richard Dannatt, *Leading from the front: the autobiography* (London, 2010), pp. 237–40.
45. Jonathan Powell, *The new Machiavelli: how to wield power in the modern world* (London, 2011; first published 2010), pp. 89, 269–70.
46. Frank Ledwidge, *Losing small wars: British military failure in Iraq and Afghanistan* (New Haven, 2011), pp. 2, 128–32.
47. Cowper-Coles, *Cables from Kabul*, pp. 176–7.

48. House of Commons Foreign Affairs Committee, *The UK's foreign policy approach to Afghanistan and Pakistan*, minutes of evidence, 2 March 2011, Q. 99; Richard Norton-Taylor, 'Former top diplomat delivers broadside against Helmand strategy', *The Guardian*, 14 January 2011.

49. Deborah Haynes, 'Helmand dangers "not helped by US and political meddling"', *The Times*, 12 May 2011.

50. *Guardian*, 13 and 14 January 2011.

51. Ledwidge, *Losing small wars*, p. 124.

52. Avant, *Political institutions and military change*, pp. 103–26 uses the Malayan example in a similar way.

53. Gordon and Trainor, *Cobra II*, p. 39.

54. Hersh, *Chain of command*, p. 178.

55. Bob Woodward, *Obama's wars* (New York, 2010), pp. 35–8, 289, 343–4.

56. Clark A. Murdock et al., *Beyond Goldwater–Nichols: defense reform for a new strategic era*, Center for Strategic and International Studies, March 2004, p. 10. See also Martin J. Gorman and Alexander Krongard, 'A Goldwater-Nichols act for the US government: institutionalising the interagency process', *Joint Forces Quarterly*, no. 39 (2005), pp. 51–7. I am grateful to Dr Audrey Kurth Cronin for drawing my attention to both pieces.

57. Patrick Wintour, '"Greeted with a yawn:" how embassy wrote off PM', *The Guardian*, 3 December 2010.

58. Richard Teuten, 'Stabilisation and "post-conflict" reconstruction', talk to the Royal United Service Institute, 31 January 2007, www.stabilisationunit.gov.uk/.../RTs_speech_to_RUSI_Jan_07.doc; see also the negative verdict in Synnott, *Bad days in Basra*, p. 260.

59. Gordon and Trainor, *Cobra II*, p. 47.

60. Murdock et al., *Beyond Goldwater–Nichols*, pp. 7–8.

61. Bacevich, *The new American militarism*, p. 210.

62. Murdock et al., *Beyond Goldwater–Nichols*, p. 10.

63. *Sixth report from the expenditure committee. The future of the United Kingdom's nuclear weapons policy*, HC 348, session 1978–9; *Fourth report from the defence committee. Strategic nuclear weapons policy*, HC 36, session 1980–1.

64. *The Guardian*, 30 June 2006, p. 10.

65. For a much fuller exploration of the politicisation of American officers, see Peter Feaver and Richard Kohn (eds.), *Soldiers and civilians: the civil–military gap and American national security* (Cambridge, MA, 2001), esp. pp. 289–324.

66. Strachan, *The politics of the British army*, esp. pp. 269–71 for recent cases.

67. See not only Cohen, *Supreme command*, but also Cohen, 'The unequal dialogue: the theory and reality of civil–military relations and the use of force', in Feaver and Kohn, *Soldiers and civilians*.

68. Feaver, *Armed servants*, p. 62.

5 Strategy and the limitation of war

1. Wellington to Somerset, 5 January 1838, Wellington papers, Southampton University Library; he made a similar observation to the House of Lords on 16 January 1838: 'A great country cannot wage a little war.'
2. Ian Kershaw, *Fateful choices: ten decisions that changed the world 1940–1941* (London, 2007), p. 147.
3. Philip Bobbitt, *The shield of Achilles: war, peace and the course of history* (London, 2002), p. 21.
4. For a fuller discussion of these points, see Hew Strachan, 'Preemption and prevention in historical perspective', in Henry Shue and David Rodin (eds.), *Preemption: military action and moral justification* (Oxford, 2007), pp. 22–39.
5. Bobbitt, *Shield of Achilles*, pp. 24, 38–9.
6. Christopher Layne and Benjamin Schwartz, 'No new world order: America after the Cold War', *Current*, December 1993, quoted in Bobbitt, *Shield of Achilles*, p. 251.
7. Joseph Stiglitz and Linda Bilmes, *The three trillion dollar war: the true cost of the Iraq conflict* (London, 2008).
8. See www.sourcewatch.org/index.php?title=The_Long_War, downloaded 27 April 2007.
9. See www.washingtonpost.com/wp-dyn/content/article/2006/02/03/AR2006020301853, downloaded 27 April 2007.
10. See www.guardian.co.uk/usa/story/0,,1710062,00.html, downloaded 27 April 2007.
11. See www.nytimes.com/2007/04/24/washington/24policy.html; www.tbo.com/news/metro/MGBJ651OOoF.html, both downloaded 27 April 2007.
12. James Shotwell, *War as an instrument of national policy and its renunciation in the pact of Paris* (London, 1929), p. xii.
13. Ibid., p. 33.
14. Hoffman Nickerson, *Can we limit war?* (Bristol, 1933), p. 13.
15. Ibid., p. 215; for a development of some of these points, see Hew Strachan, 'War and society in the 1920s and 1930s', in Roger Chickering and Stig Förster (eds.), *The shadows of total war: Europe, east Asia, and the United States, 1919–1939* (Cambridge, 2003).
16. Christopher Bassford, *Clausewitz in English: the reception of Clausewitz in Britain and America 1815–1945* (New York, 1994), p. l.
17. Brian Bond, *Liddell Hart: a study of his military thought* (London, 1977), pp. 170–1.
18. Liddell Hart on limited war, 21 February 1953, Liddell Hart papers 1/219/18, King's College London.

19. B. H. Liddell Hart, *Defence of the west: some riddles of war and peace* (London, 1950), pp. 376–7, 379.
20. Bruno Colson and Hervé Coutau-Bégarie (eds.), *Pensée stratégique et humanisme de la tactique des anciens à l'éthique de la stratégie* (Paris, 2000), p. viii.
21. Robert E. Osgood, *Limited war revisited* (Boulder, CO, 1979), p. 27.
22. Ibid., pp. 48–9.

6 European armies and limited war

1. J. F. C. Fuller, *The reformation of war* (London, 1923), p. 103.
2. B. H. Liddell Hart, *The remaking of modern armies* (London, 1927), p. 17.
3. Jean-Jacques Becker, 'Vers l'armée de demain?', in Vincent Duclert (ed.), *Le colonel Mayer de l'affaire Dreyfus à de Gaulle: un visionnaire en République* (Paris, 2007), pp. 285–94. For further development of these points, see Hew Strachan, 'War and society in the 1920s and 1930s', in Roger Chickering and Stig Förster (eds.), *The shadows of total war: Europe, east Asia and the United States, 1919–1939* (Cambridge, 2003), pp. 35–45.
4. *The Times*, 30 November 1990.
5. *Monocle*, 6, no. 56 (September 2012), p. 34.
6. See Michael P. M. Finch, 'The Galliéni–Lyautey method and pacification campaigning in Tonkin and Madagascar, 1885–1900', DPhil. thesis, Oxford University, 2010; revised and published as *A progressive occupation? The Galliéni–Lyautey method and colonial pacification in Tonkin and Madagascar, 1885–1900* (Oxford, 2013).
7. *Die Zeit*, 27 January 2011.
8. *VG*, 27 September 2010.
9. Janne Haaland Matlary, *European Union security dynamics: in the new national interest* (Basingstoke, 2009).
10. Carl von Clausewitz, *On war*, ed. and trans. Michael Howard and Peter Paret (Princeton, 1976), p. 69.
11. B. H. Liddell Hart, *The ghost of Napoleon* (London, 1933), pp. 118–29.
12. Michael Howard, *The continental commitment: the dilemma of British defence policy in the era of two world wars* (Harmondsworth, 1974), p. 149; Peter Struck referred to the Hindu Kush when German defence minister in 2002.
13. See Carl von Clausewitz, *Schriften-Aufsätze-Studien-Briefe*, ed. Werner Hahlweg (2 vols. in 3 parts, Göttingen, 1966–90) vol. I, pp. 682–750.
14. Robert E. Osgood, *Limited war revisited* (Boulder, CO, 1979), pp. 2, 10.
15. Excerpts from Begin speech at National Defense College, *The New York Times*, 21 August 1982.
16. Lawrence Freedman, 'On war and choice', *The National Interest*, May–June 2010.
17. Richard N. Hass, *War of necessity, war of choice: a memoir of two Iraq wars* (New York, revised paperback edn 2010), pp. xvii–xxv.

18. See Joseph Lelyveld, 'Obama abroad: the report card', *New York Review of Books*, 16 August 2012.

19. Dominic Tierney, *How we fight: crusades, quagmires, and the American way of war* (New York, 2010), pp. 250–2.

7 The limitations of strategic culture: the case of the British way in warfare

1. Jack Snyder, *Soviet strategic culture: implications for limited nuclear operations*, RAND R-2154-AF (Santa Monica, 1977), p. v.

2. Jack Snyder, 'The concept of strategic culture: caveat emptor', in C. G. Jacobsen (ed.), *Strategic power: USA/USSR* (New York, 1990); Colin Gray, 'Strategic culture as context: the first generation of theory strikes back', *Review of International Studies*, 25 (1999), pp. 49–69; for a discussion of the debate, see Lawrence Sondhaus, *Strategic culture and ways of war* (London, 2006).

3. Russell Weigley, *The American way of war: a history of United States military strategy and policy* (New York, 1973), p. 477.

4. Weigley, *American way of war*, p. xvii.

5. Hew Strachan, 'German strategy in the First World War', in Wolfgang Elz and Sönke Neitzel (eds.), *Internationale Beziehungen im 19 und 20 Jahrhundert* (Paderborn, 2003), pp. 127–44; on Weigley's confused logic, see Brian Linn, 'The American way of war revisited', *Journal of Military History*, 66 (2002), pp. 501–33, and more extensively Linn, *The echo of battle: the army's way of war* (Cambridge, MA, 2007).

6. Max Boot, 'The new American way of war', *Foreign Affairs*, 82, no. 4 (July–August 2003), pp. 41; see also Boot, *The savage wars of peace: small wars and the rise of American power* (New York, 2002).

7. Antulio Echevarria, jr., *Toward an American way of war*, Strategic Studies Institute, US Army War College (Carlisle, PA, 2004), p. vi. This is a criticism reflected in the approach adopted by Dominic Tierney, *How we fight: crusades, quagmires, and the American way of war* (New York, 2010), see esp. pp. 10–12, 248–9.

8. Robert M. Citino, *The German way of war: from the Thirty Years' War to the Third Reich* (Lawrence, KS, 2005), p. xiv.

9. See Richard D. Hooker, jr., *Maneuver warfare: an anthology* (Novato, CA, 1993) for a heavy representation of German influences on the USA.

10. Boot, 'The new American way of war', p. 44.

11. Brian Bond, *Liddell Hart: a study of his military thought* (London, 1977), pp. 46–7.

12. Basil Liddell Hart, 'The historic strategy of Britain', in *When Britain goes to war: adaptability and mobility* (London, 1935; revised edn of *The British way in warfare*, 1932), p. 41.

13. Michael Howard, 'The British way in warfare: a reappraisal', reprinted in his book, *The causes of war and other essays* (London, 1984), is the classic revision

of the Liddell Hart argument; Hew Strachan, 'The British way in warfare', in David Chandler and Ian Beckett (eds.), *The Oxford illustrated history of the British army* (Oxford, 1994), puts the case for the incorporation of colonial campaigning, and Hew Strachan, 'The British way in warfare revisited', *Historical Journal*, 26 (1983), pp. 447–61 is a historiographical review.

14. Basil Liddell Hart, *Decisive wars of history: a study in strategy* (London, 1929), pp. 147, 149.

15. Azar Gat, 'The hidden sources of Liddell Hart's strategic ideas', *War in History*, 3 (1996), pp. 293–308; see also Gat, *Fascist and liberal visions of war: Fuller, Liddell Hart, Douhet and other modernists* (Oxford, 1998), esp. pp. 157–62.

16. On Corbett, see Donald M. Schurman, *Julian S. Corbett, 1854–1922: historian of British maritime policy from Drake to Jellicoe* (London, 1981); Schurman, 'Civilian historian: Sir Julian Corbett', in *The education of a navy: the development of British naval thought, 1867–1914* (Chicago, 1965); Andrew Lambert, 'The Naval War Course, *Some principles of maritime strategy* and the origins of "the British way in warfare"', in Keith Neilson and Greg Kennedy (eds.), *The British way in warfare: power and the international system 1856–1956: essays in honour of David French* (Farnham, 2010). Azar Gat, *The development of military thought: the nineteenth century* (Oxford, 1992), pp. 212–25 puts Corbett in the context of British naval thought. In the mid-1980s, I suggested in conversation with the naval historian Brian McL. Ranft that Corbett, not Liddell Hart, was the true author of the British way in warfare, a proposal he strongly rebutted, but it is a connection made by Brian Bond, in *Liddell Hart: a study of his military thought* (London, 1977), pp. 69, 71, 75.

17. Julian Corbett, *Some principles of maritime strategy* (London, 1911; reprinted Annapolis, 1998, with an introduction by Eric Grove), p. 294.

18. Schurman, *Corbett*, p. 89.

19. Corbett, *Some principles*, p. 15.

20. B. H. Liddell Hart, *The real war 1914–1918* (London, 1930), pp. 504–5; see also Liddell Hart, *The decisive wars of history*, p. 231.

21. Carl von Clausewitz, *On war*, ed. and trans. Michael Howard and Peter Paret (Princeton, 1976), p. 69.

22. Corbett, *Some principles*, p. 57.

23. Ibid., p. 60.

24. Ibid., p. 66.

25. 'Strategy at sea', copy in Wilkinson papers 13/54, microfilm in Codrington Library, All Souls College, Oxford.

26. Corbett, 'The green pamphlet', in *Some principles*, p. 308.

27. J. F. C. Fuller, *The reformation of war* (London, 1923), particularly chapter 11 on 'the meaning of grand strategy'. Liddell Hart, *Decisive wars of history*, pp. 147–51, briefly addressed the issue; *Strategy: the indirect approach* (4th edn, London, 1967), devoted a chapter to grand strategy.

28. House of Commons Public Administration Select Committee session 2010–11, 1st report, *Who does UK national strategy?*, HC 435 (London, 18 October 2010).

29. The older treatments of this issue are John Coogan, *The end of neutrality: the United States, Britain and maritime rights, 1899–1915* (Ithaca, NY, 1981); Avner Offer, 'Morality and Admiralty: "Jacky" Fisher, economic warfare and the laws of war', *Journal of Contemporary History*, 23 (1988), pp. 99–119. They have now been overtaken by Nicholas Lambert, *Planning Armageddon: British economic warfare and the First World War* (Cambridge, MA, 2012), which appeared too late for proper incorporation in this chapter. On these points I have benefited from conversations with my doctoral pupil, Gabriela Frei.

30. Members of the Oxford Faculty of Modern History, *Why we are at war: Great Britain's case* (Oxford, 1914), p. 115.

31. J. A. Hall, *The law of naval warfare* (London, 1921), p. vi; the official history by A. C. Bell, *A history of the blockade of Germany and the countries associated with her in the Great War: Austria-Hungary, Bulgaria, and Turkey* (London, 1961) bears abundant testimony to Britain's determination to secure international consent for what it was doing. I have also benefited from the comments of Isabel Hull, whose history of international law in the First World War is forthcoming and promises to transform our understanding of the subject.

32. Corbett, *Some principles*, p. 97.

33. Liddell Hart, *The decisive wars of history*, p. 231.

34. Corbett, *Some principles*, p. 16.

35. See Hew Strachan, 'War and society in the 1920s and 30s', in Roger Chickering, Stig Förster and Daniel Mattern (eds.), *The shadows of total war: Europe, east Asia and the United States, 1919–1939* (Cambridge, 2003), pp. 47–52.

36. Stefan Schmidt, *Frankreichs Aussenpolitik in der Julikrise 1914. Ein Beitrag zur Geschichte des Ausbruchs des Ersten Weltkrieges* (Munich, 2009), pp. 100–1.

37. Basil Liddell Hart, *Paris, or the future of war* (London, 1925); see also below, pp. 00–00.

38. Rupert Smith, *The utility of force: the art of war in the modern world* (London, 2005), part 3.

39. Questions after Cameron's speech at the NATO summit, 20 November 2010; www.number10.gov.uk/news/press-conference-at-the-nato-summit/.

8 Maritime strategy and national policy

1. For a discussion of these issues, albeit one which sees the roots of naval strategy in naval tactics, see Michel Depeyre, *Tactiques et stratégies navales de la France et du Royaume-Uni de 1690 à 1815* (Paris, 1998), pp. 21–7; also N. A. M. Rodger, 'The idea of naval strategy in Britain in the eighteenth and nineteenth centuries', in

Geoffrey Till (ed.), *The development of British naval thinking: essays in memory of Bryan Ranft* (Abingdon, 2006), pp. 19–33, and also Till's introduction.

2. Bernard Semmel, *Liberalism and naval strategy: ideology, interest and sea power during the Pax Britannica* (Boston, 1986), pp. 13–14.

3. John B. Hattendorf, 'The struggle with France, 1689–1815', in J. R. Hill (ed.), *The Oxford illustrated history of the Royal Navy* (Oxford, 1995), p. 119.

4. Alfred Thayer Mahan, *Naval strategy compared and contrasted with the principles and practices of military operations on land* (London, 1911), p. 2.

5. Alfred Thayer Mahan, *The influence of seapower upon history* (New York, 1957; first published 1890), p. 8.

6. Ibid., p. 19.

7. Julian Corbett, *Some principles of maritime strategy*, ed. Eric Grove (Annapolis, 1988; first published 1911), p. 15.

8. Quoted in Geoffrey Till, *Seapower: a guide for the twenty-first century* (London, 2004), p. 49.

9. *A strong Britain in an age of uncertainty: the National Security Strategy*, CM 7953 (London, 2010), p. 21.

10. Ibid., p. 9.

11. Department of Defense, *Sustaining US global leadership: priorities for 21st century defense* (January 2012), p. 3; see also Congressional Research Service, *Pivot to the Pacific? The Obama administration's 'rebalancing' toward Asia*, 7–5700, www.crs.gov, R42448, 28 March 2012.

9 Technology and strategy

1. Richard North, *Ministry of defeat: the British war in Iraq 2003–2009* (London, 2009), deals with this debate.

2. For a brief survey, see 'IEDs: the home-made bombs that changed modern war', *Strategic Comments*, International Institute for Strategic Studies, vol. 18, comment 24, August 2012.

3. Nik Gowing, *'Skyful of lies' and black swans*, Reuters Institute for the Study of Journalism (Oxford, 2009).

4. Carl von Clausewitz, *On war*, ed. and trans. Michael Howard and Peter Paret (Princeton, 1976), book VIII, chapter 3, pp. 592–3; chapter 6, pp. 609–10.

5. *Moltke on the art of war: selected writings*, ed. Daniel J. Hughes (Novato, CA, 1993), pp. 108, 109, 111.

6. Ibid., pp. 47, 257.

7. Max Schwarte (ed.), *Technik des Kriegswesens* (Leipzig, 1913), p. v.

8. On the pre-First World War arms race, see David Stevenson, *Armaments and the coming of war: Europe 1904–1914* (Oxford, 1996).

9. An English translation of the article can be found in *Alfred von Schlieffen's military writings*, trans and ed Robert T. Foley (London, 2003), pp. 194–205.

10. Sven Lange, *Hans Delbrück und der 'Strategiestreit'. Kriegführung und Kriegsgeschichte in der Kontroverse 1879–1914* (Freiburg im Breisgau, 1995); on Schlieffen's influence on this debate, see pp. 53, 73, 77.

11. *Schlieffen's military writings*, ed. Foley, p. 227.

12. Friedrich von Bernhardi, *On war of to-day* (2 vols., London 1912), vol. II, pp. 170–1, 174–5, 178, 180–1.

13. E. A. Altham, *The principles of war historically illustrated* (2 vols., London, 1914), vol. I, p. 35.

14. Bernard Brodie, *A layman's guide to naval strategy* (Princeton, 1942), p. 9.

15. James Phinney Baxter III, *The introduction of the ironclad warship* (Cambridge, MA, 1933), p. 3.

16. C. I. Hamilton, *Anglo-French naval rivalry 1840–1870* (Oxford, 1993), p. 20.

17. Michael Stephen Partridge, *Military planning for the defense of the United Kingdom, 1814–1870* (Westport, CT, 1989); Hew Strachan, *Wellington's legacy: the reform of the British army, 1830–54* (Manchester, 1984), pp. 196–211; John Gooch, *Plans of war: the general staff and British military strategy c. 1900–1916* (London, 1974), pp. 166, 284–6, 279, 293–5; Nicholas d'Ombrain, *War machinery and high policy: defence administration in peacetime Britain 1902–1914* (Oxford, 1973), pp. 219–24, 108–10.

18. Erskine Childers caught the popular anxiety in his novel *The riddle of the sands*, first published in 1903; for a selection of fictionalised accounts of the invasion of Britain, see I. F. Clarke (ed.), *The tale of the next great war, 1871–1914* (Liverpool, 1995), and Clarke (ed.), *The great war with Germany, 1890–1914* (Liverpool, 1997).

19. Martin Motte, *Une éducation géostratégique: la pensée navale française de la Jeune École à 1914* (Paris, 2004).

20. See Patrick J. Kelly, *Tirpitz and the imperial German navy* (Bloomington, 2011), pp. 445–9, for a critique of Tirpitz's strategy; Michael Epkenhans, *Die wilhelminische Flottenrüstung 1908–1914. Weltmachtstreben, industrieller Fortschritt, soziale Integration* (Munich, 1991), deals with the construction policy.

21. Jon Tetsuro Sumida, *In defence of naval supremacy: finance, technology and British naval policy* (Boston, MA, 1989), especially on the battle cruiser; Nicholas Lambert, *Sir John Fisher's naval revolution* (Columbia, SC, 1999) on the submarine.

22. Clark G. Reynolds, *Command of the sea: the history and strategy of maritime empires* (New York, 1974), p. 402.

23. Ibid., p. 402.

24. D. M. Schurman, *The education of a navy: the development of British naval strategic thought 1867–1914* (Chicago, 1965), pp. 87–8; see also Andrew Lambert, *The foundations of naval history: John Knox Laughton, the Royal Navy and the historical profession* (London, 1998).

25. John B. Hattendorf, 'Alfred Thayer Mahan and his strategic thought', in Hattendorf and Robert S. Jordan (eds.), *Maritime strategy and the balance of power: Britain and America in the twentieth century* (Basingstoke, 1989), p. 84; see also the essays in that volume by Donald Schurman on 'Mahan revisited' and by Barry D. Hunt, 'The strategic thought of Sir Julian Corbett'.

26. Ivo Nikolai Lambi, *The navy and German power politics 1862–1914* (Boston, 1984), discusses plans; see also H. H. Herwig and David Trask, 'Naval operations plans between Germany and the USA, 1898–1913: a study of strategic planning in the age of imperialism', in Paul Kennedy (ed.), *The war plans of the great powers* (Boston, 1985).

27. Matthew S. Seligmann, *The Royal Navy and the German threat 1901–1914: Admiralty plans to protect British trade in a war against Germany* (Oxford, 2012), pp. 103–4, 155–7; Shawn T. Grimes, *Strategy and war planning in the British navy, 1887–1918* (Woodbridge, 2012), pp. 5, 225–6, 232; both Seligmann and Grimes see the outcomes as more positive than is suggested here, particularly in relation to a war on German trade.

28. Hew Strachan, 'Operational art and Britain, 1909–2009', in John Olsen and Martin van Creveld (eds.), *The evolution of operational art from Napoleon to the present* (Oxford, 2011), pp. 111–12.

29. This discussion of Douhet's background and the development of his thinking before 1921 owes an enormous amount to Thomas Hippler, *Bombing the people: Giulio Douhet and the foundations of air power strategy, 1884–1939* (Cambridge, 2013). What follows relies on Hippler, 'Democracy and war in the strategic thought of Giulio Douhet', in Hew Strachan and Sibylle Scheipers (eds.), *The changing character of war* (Oxford, 2011); see also Philip Meilinger, 'Giulio Douhet and the origins of airpower theory', in Meilinger (ed.), *The paths of heaven: the evolution of airpower theory* (Montgomery, AL, 1997); for his influence, see Jonathan Haslam, 'Giulio Douhet and the politics of airpower', *International History Review*, 34 (2012), pp. 753–73, and specifically in Britain, see John Peaty, 'The place of Douhet: a reassessment', paper given at the British Military History Commission summer conference 2010, available at www.bcmh.org.uk/archive/conferences/2011NoiseDouhetPeaty.pdf.

30. Cited by Hippler, 'Democracy and war', p. 173.

31. Giulio Douhet, *The command of the air*, trans. Dino Ferrari (London, 1943), pp. 11, 27.

32. Ibid., p. 30.

33. Ibid., p. 11.

34. Ibid., p. 78.

35. Ibid., pp. 21–2.

36. Ibid., p. 24.

37. Ibid., p. 52.

38. William Mitchell, *Skyways: a book on modern aeronautics* (Philadelphia, 1930), p. 278; see also Mark A. Clodfelter, 'Molding airpower convictions: development and legacy of William Mitchell's strategic thought', in Meilinger, *Paths of heaven*, esp. pp. 95–101; William Mitchell, 'The development of air power', in Eugene M. Emme (ed.), *The impact of air power* (New York, 1959); Alfred F. Hurley, *Billy Mitchell: crusader for air power* (Bloomington, 1975).

39. Mitchell, 'Development of air power', p. 173.

40. Basil Liddell Hart, *Paris, or the future of war* (London, 1925), p. 46.

41. Mitchell, 'Development of air power', p. 173.

42. For contrasting views, see John Mearsheimer, *Liddell Hart and the weight of history* (Ithaca, NY, 1988), and Azar Gat, *Fascist and liberal visions of war: Fuller, Liddell Hart, Douhet, and other modernists* (Oxford, 1998), and more specifically Gat, 'British influence and the evolution of the Panzer arm: myth or reality', *War in History*, 4 (1997), pp. 150–73, 316–38.

43. Gil-li Vardi, 'The change from within', in Strachan and Scheipers, *The changing character of war*, p. 83.

44. J. F. C. Fuller, *British light infantry in the eighteenth century* (London, 1925), p. 242.

45. Brian Holden Reid, *J. F. C. Fuller: military thinker* (Basingstoke, 1987), p. 57.

46. B. H. Liddell Hart, *The revolution in warfare* (London, 1946), pp. 83, 85; compare the slightly revised edition published by Yale University Press in 1947.

47. J. F. C. Fuller, *Armament and history: a study of the influence of armament on history from the dawn of classical warfare to the Second World War* (London, 1946), pp. 188–9, 208–9.

48. Bernard Brodie, *Sea power in the machine age* (first published 1941; Westport, CT, 1969), pp. 78, 91, 445.

49. Barry Scott Zellen, *State of doom: Bernard Brodie, the bomb, and the birth of the bipolar world* (New York, 2012), pp. 24, 27–30.

50. Ibid., p. 30.

51. Bernard Brodie, 'The absolute weapon', reprinted in Thomas G. Mahnken and Joseph A. Maiolo (eds.), *Strategic studies: a reader* (London, 2008), pp. 189, 205, 207, 213.

52. Zellen, *State of doom*, p. 14.

53. Hervé Coutau-Bégarie, *Traité de stratégie* (6th edn, Paris, 2008), p. 512.

54. Brodie, 'The absolute weapon', p. 186.

55. Bernard Brodie, *Strategy in the missile age* (Princeton, 1959), pp. 22, 98, 106.

56. Thomas Schelling, *Arms and influence* (New Haven, 1966), p. 23; for a discussion of Schelling's disciplinary approach to strategy, see Robert Ayson, *Thomas Schelling and the nuclear age: strategy as social science* (Abingdon, 2004).

57. Herman Kahn, *On thermonuclear war: three lectures and several suggestions* (Princeton, 2nd edn, 1961; first published 1960), pp. 521–2.

58. Robert H. Scales, *Certain victory: the US army in the Gulf War* (Washington, DC, 1993); for a survey of developments, see Thomas G. Mahnken, *Technology and the American way of war since 1945* (New York, 2008).

59. Richard Hallion, preface to the paperback edition of *Storm over Iraq: air power and the Gulf War* (Washington, DC, 1997; first published 1992), p. x; italics in the original.

60. Williamson Murray and Robert H. Scales jr., *The Iraq War: a military history* (Cambridge, MA, 2003), pp. 239–40.

61. Mark Benitz, *Six months without Sundays: the Scots Guards in Afghanistan* (Edinburgh, 2012; first published 2011), pp. 267–8; on problems with rifles, see pp. 150, 244.

62. Ewen MacAskill, 'Insurgents intercepted video feeds from US drones', *The Guardian*, 18 December 2009; Julian Borger, 'Experts question Iranian military's claim to have captured US surveillance drone', *The Guardian*, 9 December 2011.

63. Brodie, 'The absolute weapon', p. 183.

10 War is war: imperial legacies and current conflicts

1. Denis McLean, *Howard Kippenberger: dauntless spirit* (Auckland, 2008), p. 186.

2. Ian McGibbon, *The path to Gallipoli: defending New Zealand 1840–1915* (Wellington, 1991), pp. 43–9.

3. Ibid., p. 185.

4. Haig papers, National Library of Scotland Acc, 3155/81.

5. Jay Luvaas, *The education of an army: British military thought 1815–1940* (London, 1965), p. 244.

6. Patrick Macdougall, *Modern warfare as influenced by modern artillery* (London, 1864), p. 396.

7. Royal New Zealand Returned and Services' Association, *Defending New Zealand* (Wellington, April 2005), p. iii.

8. General Staff, War Office, *Field service regulations, part I: operations* (London, 1909), chapter 10, para 141.1, p. 196.

9. Report on a conference of general staff officers at the Staff College, 7th to 10th January 1908, held under the direction of the Chief of the General Staff, Haig papers, National Library of Scotland Acc 3155/81, pp. 3, 27, 46, 48; see also John Gooch, *Plans of war: the general staff and British military strategy c. 1900–1916* (London, 1974), pp. 113–15.

10. G. F. R. Henderson, *The science of war: a collection of essays and lectures 1891–1903* (London, 1919; first published 1906), p. 42.

11. Reginald Clare Hart, *Reflections on the art of war* (London, 1897), p. ix.

12. Liddell Hart Centre for Military Archives, King's College London, Robertson papers 1/2/12.

13. Howard Kippenberger, *Infantry brigadier* (London, 1949), p. 81.
14. Emmet McElhatton, *The strategic thinking of Major General Sir Howard Kippenberger*, Discussion Paper 06/08, Centre for Strategic Studies: New Zealand, Victoria University Wellington, 2008.
15. David Richards, 'European armies: the challenge', in Tim Huxley and Alexander Nicoll (eds.), *Perspectives on international security*, IISS Adelphi paper 400–401 (London, December 2008), pp. 53–62.
16. Johannes Leithäuser, 'Armee in Einsatz', *Frankfurter Allgemeine Zeitung*, 23 March 2013.
17. Vincent Desportes, *La guerre probable: penser autrement* (Paris, 2007). This book is now available in English as *Tomorrow's war: thinking otherwise* (Paris, 2009); here p. 115.
18. Rupert Smith, *The utility of force: the art of war in the modern world* (London, 2005), pp. 259, 306.
19. McLean, *Howard Kippenberger*, p. 337.

11 Strategy and the operational level of war

1. Quoted in Mehdi Hasan, 'Rise of the four-star deities', *New Statesman*, 5 July 2010.
2. 'Obama fires chief of Afghan effort', *International Herald Tribune*, 24 June 2010.
3. For example, *The Economist*, 26 June 2010, p. 33.
4. Carl von Clausewitz, *On war* (Princeton, 1976), ed. and trans. Michael Howard and Peter Paret, p. 177; see also pp. 202, 509.
5. Interview with Nathalie Guibert, *Le Monde*, 2 July 2010.
6. Richard M. Swain, 'AirLand battle', in George F. Hofmann and Donn A. Starry (eds.), *Camp Colt to Desert Storm: the history of US armored forces* (Lexington, KY, 1999), pp. 360–402; Frederick Kagan, *Finding the target: the transformation of American military policy* (New York, 2006), pp. 3–73.
7. European Security Study, *Strengthening conventional deterrence in Europe: proposals for the 1980s* (London, 1983) was the clearest response to this pressure.
8. Robert M. Citino, *Quest for decisive victory: from stalemate to Blitzkrieg in Europe, 1899–1940* (Lawrence, KS, 2002); Citino, *Blitzkrieg to Desert Storm: the evolution of operational warfare* (Lawrence, KS, 2004); Christopher Bellamy, *The evolution of modern land warfare: theory and practice* (London, 1990).
9. Richard Simpkin, *Deep battle: the brainchild of Marshal M. N. Tukhachevskii* (London, 1987); Simpkin, *Race to the swift: thoughts on twenty-first century warfare* (London, 1985); Shimon Naveh, *In pursuit of military excellence: the evolution of operational theory* (London, 1997).

10. Richard Hooker (ed.), *Maneuver warfare: an anthology* (Novato, CA, 1993) embodies this approach.

11. Claus Telp, *The evolution of operational art, 1740–1813: from Frederick the Great to Napoleon* (Abingdon, 2005); Hew Strachan, 'Clausewitz en anglais: la césure de 1976', in Laure Bardiès and Martin Motte (eds.), *De la guerre? Clausewitz et la pensée stratégique contemporaine* (Paris, 2008), pp. 112–14.

12. Kagan, *Finding the target*, provides a summary.

13. Michael R. Gordon and Bernard E. Trainor, *The generals' war: the inside story of the conflict in the Gulf* (Boston, 1995), p. 443; see also pp. 413–16, 476–7.

14. Williamson Murray and Robert H. Scales, jr., *The Iraq War: a military history* (Cambridge, MA, 2003), pp. 7, 12–13.

15. Colin L. Powell, 'US forces: challenges ahead', *Foreign Affairs*, Winter 1992/3, pp. 32–45; Colin Powell with Joseph Persico, *My American journey* (New York, 1995), p. 576.

16. A. S. H. Irwin, 'The levels of war: operational art and campaign planning', *The Occasional*, no. 5 (Strategic and Combat Studies Institute, 1993).

17. Samuel P. Huntington, *The soldier and the state: the theory and politics of civil–military relations* (Cambridge, MA, 1957); for criticisms of Huntington, see Peter D. Feaver, *Armed servants: agency, oversight and civil–military relations* (Cambridge, MA, 2003); Eliot Cohen, *Supreme command: soldiers, statesmen and leadership in wartime* (New York, 2002), pp. 224–51; also see above pp. 64–97.

18. Clausewitz, 'Strategische Kritik des Feldzugs von 1814 in Frankreich', in *Sämtliche hinterlassen Werke über Krieg und Kriegführung*, ed. Wolfgang von Seidlitz (3 vols. n.p., 1999), vol. III, p. 235; see the discussion of this point in Hew Strachan, *Clausewitz's 'On war': a biography* (London, 2007), pp. 169–71.

19. Bob Woodward, *Obama's wars* (New York, 2010), p. 129.

20. Wesley Clark, *Waging modern war: Bosnia, Kosovo and the future of combat* (Oxford, 2001), p. 427.

21. Tommy Franks, *American soldier* (New York, 2004), p. 440; emphasis in the original.

22. Stanley McChrystal, 'COMISAF's initial assessment', 30 August 2009, Annex E-2; see also Andrew Mackay and Steve Tatham, 'Behavioural conflict from general to strategic corporal: complexity, adaptation and influence', *The Shrivenham Papers*, no. 9 (Defence Academy of the United Kingdom, December 2009).

23. US Army and Marine Corps, *Counter-insurgency field manual: US Army field manual no. 3–24; Marine Corps warfighting publication no. 3–33.5* (Chicago, 2007; first issued 15 December 2006).

24. Quoted in Max Benitz, *Six months without Sundays: the Scots Guards in Afghanistan* (2nd edn, Edinburgh, 2011), p. 154; emphasis added.

25. McChrystal, 'COMISAF's initial assessment', Annex D-6.
26. Steven Metz, *Iraq and the evolution of American strategy* (Washington, DC, 2008), pp. 181–5; Andrew Bacevich, 'Surge to nowhere', *Washington Post*, 20 January 2008; Bacevich, 'The Petraeus doctrine', *Atlantic Monthly*, October 2008; Woodward, *Obama's wars*, p. 168.
27. Woodward, *Obama's wars*, pp. 332, 338.
28. Gian P. Gentile, 'A strategy of tactics: population-centric COIN and the army', *Parameters*, 39, no. 3 (Autumn 2009), p. 6.
29. Woodward, *Obama's wars*, pp. 332–5; see also pp. 190, 263, 268, 275.
30. Hew Strachan, 'One warfare but joint warfare', *Journal of the Royal United Services Institution*, 154, no. 4 (August 2009), pp. 20–4, and see Chapter 10.
31. Sarah Sands, 'Sir Richard Dannatt: a very honest general', *Daily Mail*, 12 October 2006.
32. Jack Fairweather, *A war of choice: the British in Iraq 2003–9* (London, 2011), pp. 261–83.
33. Woodward, *Obama's wars*, pp. 165, 169, 375–6.
34. Ibid., pp. 34, 72.
35. Fred Kaplan, *The insurgents: David Petraeus and the plot to change the American way of war* (New York, 2012), p. 303.
36. Woodward, *Obama's wars*, pp. 85–6, 123–4, 190–7.
37. McChrsytal, 'COMISAF's initial assessment', 2–1.
38. Ibid., 1–2.
39. Ibid., 1–3.
40. Ibid., 2–5 and 2–11.
41. Gentile, 'A strategy of tactics', p. 15.
42. McChrystal, 'COMISAF's initial assessment', 2–3.
43. Ibid., 2–2.
44. Woodward, *Obama's wars*, pp. 172–3, 193–4.
45. Ibid., pp. 124, 137–8, 140–5, 158–9, 194, 197, 322.
46. Ibid., p. 314; see also pp. 148–50, 297–9, 302, 329.
47. Ibid., pp. 301–2.
48. Ibid., pp. 278, 321–2, 325.
49. Kaplan, *Insurgents*, pp. 351–2.
50. Woodward, *Obama's wars*, p. 319.
51. Landon lecture, Kansas State University, 3 March 2010; for a British insider's perspective on what happened in the USA in 2009, see Matt Cavanagh, 'Inside the Anglo-Saxon war machine', *Prospect*, December 2010, pp. 69–71.
52. Mark O'Neill, *Confronting the hydra: big problems with small war*, Lowy Institute Paper 28 (Sydney, 2009); emphasis added.
53. Brigadier Justin Kelly and Dr Michael James Brennan, *Alien: how operational art devoured strategy* (Carlisle, PA: Strategic Studies Institute, US Army War College, September 2009), p. 97.

54. Landon lecture, Kansas State University, 3 March 2010.
55. Christopher D. Kolenda, *The counterinsurgency challenge: a parable of leadership and decision making in modern conflict* (Mechanicsburg, PA, 2012), p. xiv.
56. Frederick W. Kagan and Kimberly Kagan, 'The Patton of counterinsurgency: with a sequence of brilliant offensives, Raymond Odierno adapted the Petraeus doctrine to a successful operational art', *The Weekly Standard*, 13, no. 25, 10 March 2008.
57. *International Herald Tribune*, 24 March 2010.
58. Kelly and Brennan, *Alien*, p. 98.
59. For a British military perspective on these points, inspired by the work of DCDC and by the concern expressed by the Chief of the Defence Staff at the lack of strategic thinking in the UK, see Paul Newton, Paul Colley and Andrew Sharpe, 'Reclaiming the art of British strategic thinking', *Journal of the Royal United Services Institution*, 155, no. 1 (February/March 2010), pp. 44–50.
60. Woodward, *Obama's wars*, pp. 157–9, 268, 322, 361–2.
61. 'Top Pentagon leaders do damage control', *International Herald Tribune*, 25 June 2010.
62. Montgomery C. Meigs, 'Operational art in the new century', *Parameters*, 31 (Spring 2001), p. 13.
63. Leslie Gelb, quoted in *The New Yorker*, 5 July 2010, p. 19.
64. Andrew J. Bacevich, 'Obama is in hock to the hawks', *The Spectator*, 3 July 2010.
65. Henry A. Kissinger, 'In Afghanistan, America needs a strategy, not an alibi', *International Herald Tribune*, 25 June 2010.

12 Strategy and contingency

1. Nicolas Sarkozy (preface), *Défense et sécurité nationale: le livre blanc* (Paris, 2008), p. 313; an English language summary is available at www.ambafrance-ca.org/IMGpdf/Livre_blanc_Press_kit_english_version.pdf, Présidence de la République, *The French white paper: on defence and national security*, p. 2.
2. Australian Government, Department of Defence, *Defending Australia in the Asia Pacific century: Force 2030* (Canberra, 2009).
3. United States Joint Force Command, *The joint operating environment (JOE)*, approved for public release 18 February 2010 (Suffolk, VA), pp. 2, 4, 10.
4. New Zealand Government, Ministry of Defence, *Defence white paper 2010* (Wellington, New Zealand, November 2010), p. 4.
5. Ministry of Defence, *Strategic trends programme: global strategic trends out to 2040* (Development, Concepts and Doctrine Centre, Shrivenham, 2010), p. 1.
6. House of Commons Defence Committee Session 2010–11, HC 600-I, *Appointment of the Chief of the Defence Staff*, minutes of evidence, 17 November 2010, published 27 January 2011.

7. Paul Kennedy (ed.), *Grand strategies in war and peace* (New Haven, 1991), p. 5.

8. A point reflected in the comments made by Professor Wang Jisi, the Dean of the School of International Studies at Beijing University, at the Australian Strategic Policy Institute Conference on 'Global Forces 2011', on 11 August 2011, at which this chapter also received its first airing; see also Wang Jisi, 'China's search for a grand strategy: a rising great power finds its way', *Foreign Affairs*, 90, no. 2 (March/April 2011), p. 68.

9. I am thinking here of the contributions to public debate of such thinkers and pundits as the Colomb brothers, Charles Dilke, Spenser Wilkinson, Halford Mackinder, Julian Corbett *et al.*

10. J. F. C. Fuller, *The reformation of war* (London, 1923), chapter 11, 'The meaning of grand strategy'; Basil Liddell Hart, *When Britain goes to war* (London, 1935), esp. pp. 81–6, and *Thoughts on war* (London, 1944), chapter 7, 'Grand strategy'.

11. Thomas P. M. Barnett, 'Globalogization', http://thomaspmbarnett.com/glossary, accessed 16 August 2011.

12. *Joint operating environment* (2010), preface.

13. *Defending Australia in the Asia Pacific century*, p. 26.

14. Robert Gates's farewell speech to NATO, 10 June 2011.

15. Williamson Murray, 'Thoughts on grand strategy', in Williamson Murray, Richard Hart Sinnreich and James Lacey (eds.), *The shaping of grand strategy: policy, diplomacy, and war* (Cambridge, 2011), p. 1. Kennedy was of a similar view, saying that only 'great' powers make grand strategy: Kennedy, *Grand strategies*, p. 6, and p. 186 fn 18.

16. House of Commons Public Administration Select Committee, *Who does UK national strategy?*, 1st report of session 2010–11, HC 435 (London: The Stationery Office, 18 October 2010), p. 8.

17. I am grateful to Brigadier Richard Iron for this extension of the point about the relationship between good strategy and limited resources, derived from Edward Luttwak, as well as for other comments and insights.

18. *Joint operating environment* (2010), p. 5.

19. *Defending Australia in the Asia Pacific century*, p 15.

20. Rupert Smith, *The utility of force: the art of war in the modern world* (London, 2005), pp. 269, 306.

21. Richard North, *Ministry of defeat: the British war in Iraq 2003–2009* (London, 2009).

22. United States Army/United States Marine Corps Field Manual, *Counterinsurgency* (Chicago, 2007).

23. Carl von Clausewitz, *On war*, ed. and trans. by Michael Howard and Peter Paret (Princeton, 1976), book III, chapter 1, p. 177. See also the definition of strategy given by Clausewitz in 1812, 'the combination of individual engagements to

attain the goal of the campaign or war': Carl von Clausewitz, *Principles of war*, ed. and trans. Hans Gatzke (London, 1943), p. 38.

24. Clausewitz, *On war*, book IV, chapter 3, p. 228.

25. See Alanbrooke's diary entry for 23 January 1943, Field Marshal Lord Alanbrooke, *War diaries 1939–1945*, ed. Alex Danchev and Daniel Todman (London, 2001), p. 367; Alanbrooke defined strategy most often when addressing what he perceived to be the Americans' inadequacies in that regard, ibid., 7 August 1943, p. 440. Grand strategy was defined by J. F. C Fuller before the war, and his idea was taken up and promoted by Basil Liddell Hart; so it had entered British currency before 1939.

26. Peter Paret has argued that only book I of *On war* can be taken as a final statement by Clausewitz, principally because he dates an undated prefatory note to 1830, rather than 1827; I disagree: see Hew Strachan, *Clausewitz's 'On war': a biography* (London, 2007), pp. 70–3.

27. Carl von Clausewitz, *Two letters on strategy*, ed. and trans. Peter Paret and Daniel Moran (Carlisle, PA: US Army War College, November 1984), p. 10.

28. Général d'Urbal, 'L'armée qu'il nous faut', *Revue militaire générale*, 11, no. 4 (April 1922), pp. 241–7; I am grateful to Michael Finch for this reference.

29. Terence Holmes, 'Planning versus chaos in Clausewitz's 'On war', *Journal of Strategic Studies*, 30 (2007), pp. 129–51.

30. Barry Watts, *Clausewitzian friction and future war*, McNair Paper 52 (National Defense University, Washington, DC, 1996); Alan Beyerchen, 'Clausewitz, nonlinearity and the unpredictability of war', *International Security*, 17, no. 3 (Winter 1992–3), pp. 59–90; Beyerchen, 'Clausewitz and the non-linear nature of war: systems of organized complexity', in Hew Strachan and Andreas Herberg-Rothe (eds.), *Clausewitz in the twenty-first century* (Oxford, 2007).

31. Bruno Colson, *La culture stratégique americaine: l'influence de Jomini* (Paris, 1993), esp. p. 293 for the first of these reasons.

32. This is the central argument of Jean-Jacques Langendorf, *Faire la guerre: Antoine-Henri Jomini* (2 vols., Geneva, 2001–4), vol. II, pp. 289–91, 328–9.

33. Ami-Jacques Rapin, *Jomini et la stratégie: une approche historique de l'oeuvre* (Lausanne, 2002), pp. 23–4, 33–5, 73–4, 91, 98, 102, 215–38.

34. Ibid., p. 102.

35. The best English version is Baron de Jomini, *The art of war* (Philadelphia, 1862), trans. G. H. Mendell and W. P. Craighill, even if it does omit Jomini's preface, which addresses his differences with Clausewitz.

36. Peter G. Tsouras (ed.), *The Greenhill dictionary of military quotations* (London, 2000), pp. 363–4 gives several references, but see also Daniel Hughes, *Moltke on the art of war: selected writings* (Novato, CA, 1995).

37. Terence Zuber, *The Moltke myth: Prussian war planning 1857–1871* (Lanham, MD, 2008); Arden Bucholz, *Moltke, Schlieffen and Prussian war planning* (Providence, RI, 1991).

38. See Colin Gray, *National security dilemmas: challenges and opportunities* (Washington, DC, 2009), pp. 57, 64, 277; for an early flavour of the SIOPs, Aaron Friedberg, 'A history of the US strategic "doctrine" 1945 to 1980', in Amos Perlmutter and John Gooch (eds.), *Strategy and the social sciences* (London, 1981); Peter Pringle and William Arkin, *SIOP: the secret US plan for nuclear war* (New York, 1983); David Alan Rosenberg, 'The origins of overkill: nuclear weapons and American security, 1945–1960', *International Security*, 7, no. 4 (1983), pp. 3–71.

39. Samuel P. Huntington, *The soldier and the state: the theory and politics of civil–military relations* (Cambridge, MA, 1957), pp. 31, 55–8, 68, 73, 307, 372, 388.

40. Robert Osgood, *Limited war: the challenge to American strategy* (Chicago, 1957), pp. 20–1, 53–5, 123, 176; Osgood, *Limited war revisited* (Boulder, CO, 1977), p. 2. See also Sven Lange, *Hans Delbrück und der 'Strategiestreit'. Kriegführung und Kriegsgeschichte in der Kontroverse 1879–1914* (Freiburg im Breisgau, 1995).

41. Rapin, *Jomini*, p. 92.

42. Barry R. Posen, *The sources of military doctrine: France, Britain, and Germany between the world wars* (Ithaca, NY, 1984), pp. 13, 33.

43. Jack Snyder, *The ideology of the offensive: military decision making and the disasters of 1914* (Ithaca, NY, 1984), p. 10.

44. Elizabeth Kier, *Imagining war: French and British military doctrine between the wars* (Princeton, 1997), pp. 3, 5.

45. Harry Yarger, *Strategic theory for the 21st century: the little book for big strategy* (Carlisle, PA: Strategic Studies Institute, US Army War College, February 2006), pp. 4, 54.

46. Steven Jermy, *Strategy for action: using force wisely in the 21st century* (London, 2011), pp. 118–19.

47. Jim Molan, *Running the war in Iraq: an Australian general, 300,000 troops, the bloodiest conflict of our time* (Sydney, 2008; paperback edn 2009), pp. 136, 170.

48. Clausewitz, *On war*, book I, chapter 3, p. 102.

49. Arndt Niebisch, 'Military intelligence: on Carl von Clausewitz's hermeneutics of disturbance and probability', in Elisabeth Krimmer and Patricia Anne Simpson (eds.), *Enlightened war: German theories and cultures of warfare from Frederick the Great to Clausewitz* (Rochester, NY, 2011), pp. 266–7.

50. Quoted in Michael I. Handel, *Masters of war: classical strategic thought* (3rd edn, London, 2001), p. 246.

51. Quoted by Jean-Paul Charnay, *Critique de la stratégie* (Paris, 1990), p. 235.

52. Gary Hart, *The fourth power: grand strategy for the United States in the 21st century* (Oxford, 2004), p. 33.

53. Yarger, *Strategic theory for the 21st century*, p. 5.

54. Torgeir Sævaraas, 'Effects-based operations: origins, implementation in US military doctrine, and practical usage', in Karl Erik Haug and Ole Jørgen Maaø, *Conceptualising modern war* (London, 2011), pp. 185–204.

13 Strategy: change and continuity

1. See, for example, David Parrott, 'Had a distinct template for a "western way of war" been established before 1800?', and Michael Broers, 'Changes in war: the French Revolutionary and Napoleonic Wars', in Hew Strachan and Sibylle Scheipers (eds.), *The changing character of war* (Oxford, 2011).

2. Marc Bloch, *Strange defeat: a statement of evidence written in 1940*, trans. Gerard Hopkins (New York, 1999), pp. 117–18.

3. Lawrence Sondhaus, *Strategic culture and ways of war* (London, 2006), p. vi. It is noticeable that the first edition of the textbook *Strategy in the contemporary world: an introduction to strategic studies*, edited by John Baylis, James Wirtz, Eliot Cohen and Colin Gray (Oxford, 2002), contained no chapter on strategic culture; that was only added in 2007, to the second edition.

4. Jack Snyder, *The Soviet strategic culture: implications for limited nuclear operations*, RAND R-2154-AF (Santa Monica, CA, 1977), pp. 8–9; see also above, p. 136.

5. See the comparative definitions given by Sondhaus, especially under the heading of 'durability/changability', *Strategic culture*, pp. 124–5; for the development of Snyder's own thinking, see ibid., pp. 3–6.

6. Laurence Martin, 'Security in an insecure age', *Naval War College Review*, 35, 5 (1982), p. 1. For an earlier attack on deterrence theory and its problems with identifying change by the present author, see Hew Strachan, 'Deterrence theory: the problems of continuity', *Journal of Strategic Studies*, 7 (1984), pp. 394–404.

7. Sondhaus, *Strategic culture*, p. 126; see Colin Gray, *Strategy and history: essays on theory and practice* (Abingdon, 2006), pp. 151–69.

8. Colin Gray, *Modern Strategy* (Oxford, 1999), p. 1.

9. Napoléon, *De la guerre*, introduction and annotated by Bruno Colson (Paris, 2011), pp. 104–6, 148.

10. For his most recent statement of his position (after an exchange with the present author), see his conclusion to John Andreas Olsen and Colin S. Gray (eds.), *The practice of strategy: from Alexander the Great to the present* (Oxford, 2011).

11. For example, the index to Louis Rawlings, *The ancient Greeks at war* (Manchester, 2007), has many references to strategy but the text does not address what the word means, except by implication (and that meaning is not today's).

12. *Maurice's Strategikon*, trans. George T. Dennis (Philadelphia, 1984); here pp. 64–78.

13. Edward Luttwak, *The grand strategy of the Byzantine empire* (Cambridge, MA, 2009), pp. 11, 409; see also *Strategy: the logic of war and peace* (1987), pp. 62–5, 138; contrast pp. 239–40; Luttwak, *The grand strategy of the Roman empire from the first century AD to the third* (Baltimore, 1979). For a recent assertion of similar points, see Beatrice Heuser, 'Strategy before the word: ancient wisdom for the modern world', *Journal of the Royal United Services Institute*, 155, 1 (February/March 2010), pp. 36–43.

14. Donald Kagan, 'Athenian strategy in the Peloponnesian War', in Williamson Murray, Macgregor Knox and Alvin Bernstein (eds.), *The making of strategy: rulers, states, and war* (Cambridge, 1994); for a text which illustrates what can follow, see Athanassios G. Platias and Constantinos Koliopoulos, *Thucydides on strategy: Athenian and Spartan grand strategies in the Pelopponesian War and their relevance today* (Athens, 2006). I am grateful to Simon Hornblower for discussing these issues with me.

15. Hugh Bicheno, *Razor's edge: the unofficial history of the Falklands War* (London, 2006), p. 157. Bicheno himself gives the 'grand strategic' context to support the political pressure for the attack, and see Lawrence Freedman and Virginia Gamba-Stonehouse, *Signals of war: the Falklands conflict of 1982* (London, 1991), pp. 367–8.

16. Carl von Clausewitz, *On war*, trans. O. J. Matthijs Jolles (Washington, 1950), book VIII, chapter 2, p. 570.

17. Colin Gray, *After Iraq: the search for a sustainable national security strategy* (Carlisle, PA: Strategic Studies Institute, US Army War College, January 2009), p. 38.

18. Lawrence Freedman, *The official history of the Falklands campaign* (2 vols., Abingdon, 2005), vol. I, pp. 208–11; however, some argue – not least in the light of a reduced Conservative vote at the next election in 1983, that the turn around in Thatcher's personal position preceded the campaign.

19. Bob Woodward, *Bush at war* (New York, 2002), pp. 24, 44, 61, 99, 128–9, 174–5; Seymour Hersh, *Chain of command* (London, 2005), p. 176; Frederick W. Kagan, *Finding the target: the transformation of American military policy* (New York, 2006), pp. 289–300, 326–8; Michael Gordon and Bernard Trainor, *Cobra II: the inside story of the invasion and occupation of Iraq* (London, 2006), pp. 38–47; Steven Metz, *Iraq and the evolution of American strategy* (Washington, DC, 2008), pp. 120–1; Thomas E. Ricks, *Fiasco: the American military adventure in Iraq* (London, 2006), pp. 37, 40–1, 66–7, 89–90.

20. James Fallows, 'Blind into Baghdad', *Atlantic Monthly*, January/February 2004, pp. 53–74; Anthony H. Cordesman, *The Iraq War: strategy, tactics and military lessons* (Washington, DC, 2003), pp. 153–71, 496–509; Kagan, *Finding the*

target, pp. 333–45; Metz, *Iraq and the evolution of American strategy*, pp. 130–44; Ricks, *Fiasco*, pp. 78–81.

21. *A secure Europe in a better world: European Security Strategy*, 12 December 2003; see also Anne Deighton, 'The European Union, multilateralism and the use of force', in Strachan and Scheipers, *The changing character of war*.

22. Andrew Clark, 'Climate change threatens security, UK tells UN', *The Guardian*, 18 April 2007.

23. *The Economist*, 12 February 2009.

24. Janne Haaland Matlary, 'Much ado about little: the EU and human security', *International Affairs*, 84, 1 (2008), pp. 131–43; see also Mary Kaldor, 'Human security: a new strategic narrative for Europe', *International Affairs*, 83, 2 (2007), pp. 273–88.

25. Cabinet Office, *The National Security Strategy of the United Kingdom: security in an interdependent world*, Cm 7291 (March 2008), pp. 4, 10 (para. 2:1), 11 (para. 2.9), 28 (para. 4.15).

26. *The Guardian*, 15 January 2009.

27. Oliver Burkeman, 'War on terror is over, overseas contingency operations begin', *The Guardian*, 26 March 2009.

28. See Audrey Kurth Cronin, 'What is really changing? Change and continuity in global terrorism', in Strachan and Scheipers, *The changing character of war*.

29. Vaughan Lowe, Adam Roberts, Jennifer Welsh and Dominik Zaum (eds.), *The United Nations Security Council and war: the evolution of thought and practice since 1945* (Oxford, 2008), pp. 44–58.

30. Ibid., p. 47, albeit followed by less optimistic comments on p. 49; Jean-Pierre Derriennic, *Les guerres civiles* (Paris, 2001), pp. 261–70 is cautiously positive; but see especially Stathis Kalyvas, 'The changing character of civil wars 1800–2009', in Strachan and Scheipers, *The changing character of war*.

31. Adam Tooze, *The wage of destruction: the making and breaking of the Nazi economy* (London, 2006) is the most recent and sophisticated treatment of the issues; see also T. W. Mason, 'Some origins of the Second World War', in Esmonde M. Robertson (ed.), *The origins of the Second World War* (London, 1971).

32. Damian Carrington, 'Climate changes double risk of civil war, scientists warn', *The Guardian*, 25 August 2011.

33. Paul Collier, *The bottom billion: why the poorest countries are failing and what can be done about it* (Oxford, 2008), pp. 1, 17–21.

34. Georges-Henri Soutou, *L'or et le sang; les buts de guerre économiques de la première guerre mondiale* (Paris, 1989) is the most convincing exposition of these points, and an answer to Fritz Fischer, *Germany's aims in the First World War* (London, 1967).

35. Tom Parfitt, 'Russia plans military force to patrol Arctic as "cold rush" intensifies', *The Guardian*, 28 March 2009; 'Russia won't bully Canada in

Arctic', *Globe and Mail* (Toronto), 27 March 2009; Terry Macalister, 'Cold rush or cold war? States square up to claim share of Arctic bonanza', *The Guardian*, 7 July 2011; see also Jeffrey Mazo, *Climate conflict: how global warming threatens security and what to do about it*, Adelphi 409 (London: International Institute for Strategic Studies, March 2010).

36. Robert Kaplan has popularised its arguments, most obviously in *The revenge of geography: what the map tells us about coming conflicts and the battle against fate* (New York, 2012).

37. Sarah Percy, *Mercenaries: the history of a norm in international relations* (Oxford, 2007); Percy, 'The changing character of private force', in Strachan and Scheipers, *The changing character of war*; Herfried Münkler, 'Clausewitz and the privatization of war', in Hew Strachan and Andreas Herberg-Rothe (eds.), *Clausewitz in the twenty-first century* (Oxford, 2007), pp. 222–4.

38. John Mueller, *Retreat from doomsday: the obsolescence of major war* (New York, 1989); Mueller, *The remnants of war* (Ithaca, NY, 2004).

39. Hew Strachan, 'On total war and modern war', *International History Review*, 22 (2000), pp. 341–70; on the issue of total war, see also the series of volumes edited by Roger Chickering and Stig Förster, *Great war, total war: combat and mobilization on the western front, 1914–1918* (Cambridge, 2000); *The shadows of total war: Europe, east Asia, and the United States, 1919–1939* (Cambridge, 2003); (with Bernd Greiner), *A world at total war: global conflict and the politics of destruction, 1937–1945* (Cambridge, 2005). I find the arguments of David Bell, *The first total war: Napoleon's Europe and the birth of modern warfare* (London, 2007) unpersuasive.

40. Odd Arne Westad, *The global cold war: third world interventions in the making of our times* (Cambridge, 2005), pp. 2–6, 158, 332, 396–401.

41. Ibid., pp. 405–6.

42. Philip Bobbitt, *Terror and consent: the wars for the twenty-first century* (London, 2008); self-evidently, this chapter profoundly disagrees with Bobbitt's use of history, and his attempt to build a structure on what seem to be false foundations. For a critical (and in this writer's opinion well-founded) review, see Adam Roberts, 'Limits of a new-age worldview', *Survival*, 51 (April–May 2009), pp. 183–90.

43. David Kilcullen, 'Counterinsurgency redux', *Journal of Strategic Studies*, 28 (2005), pp. 597–617; Kilcullen, *The accidental guerrilla* (London, 2009), pp. 12–16; see also John Mackinlay, *The insurgent archipelago from Mao to bin Laden* (London, 2009); for a critique of 'global insurgency', see David Martin Jones and M. L. R. Smith, 'Whose hearts and whose minds? The curious case of global counter-insurgency', and a riposte by John Nagl and Brian M. Burton, 'Thinking globally and acting locally: counter-insurgency lessons from modern wars – a reply to Jones and Smith', *Journal of Strategic Studies*, 33, 1 (February 2010), pp. 81–121, 123–38.

44. Joseph Stiglitz and Linda J. Bilmes, *The three trillion dollar war: the true cost of the Iraq conflict* (London, 2008) shows how the true costs of the war had been obscured.

45. Bob Woodward, *Obama's wars* (New York, 2010), pp. 20–2; on the financial question, see Stiglitz and Bilmes, *The three trillion dollar war*.

46. Gordon Brown, 'We are about to take the war against terror to a new level,' *Observer*, 22 March 2009; Richard Norton-Taylor, 'Hutton tells allies to "step up to the plate" over Afghanistan', *The Guardian*, 16 January 2009.

47. Samuel P. Huntington, *The soldier and the state: the theory and practice of civil–military relations* (Cambridge, MA, 1957), pp. 80–5.

48. See also Pascal Vennesson, 'War without the people', in Strachan and Scheipers, *The changing character of war*.

49. *The US Army * Marine Corps Counterinsurgency Field Manual: US Army Field Manual No. 3–24: Marine Corps Warfighting Publication No. 3–33.5* (Chicago, 2007; first issued 15 December 2006), *passim*, but for example 5–4, 5–60 to 5–80, 7–8.

50. 'Behind TV analysts: Pentagon's hidden hand', *The New York Times*, 20 April 2008.

51. Rupert Smith, *The utility of force: the art of war in the modern world* (London, 2005), pp. 284–5.

52. Colin McInnes, *Spectator sport war: the west and contemporary conflict* (Boulder, CO, 2002).

53. Nik Gowing, *'Skyful of lies' and black swans: the new tyranny of shifting information power in crises*, RISJ Challenges, Reuters Institute for the Study of Journalism, University of Oxford, 2009.

54. Extract from Campbell's diary, 16 April 1999, published in *The Guardian*, 15 January 2011; see also Wesley Clark, *Waging modern war: Bosnia, Kosovo and the future of combat* (Oxford, 2001), pp. 273–5.

55. Jim Molam, *Running the war in Iraq: an Australian general, 300,000 troops, and the bloodiest conflict of our time* (Sydney, 2009), pp. 226–8.

INDEX